262.13   7611
Pop

Pope John Paul II:
"Building Up the Body of
Christ"

Pope John Paul II

"Building up the Body of Christ"

POPE JOHN PAUL II

"Building up the Body of Christ"

Pastoral Visit to
the United States

Edited and Illustrated by the National Catholic News Service

7611

Ignatius Press • San Francisco

National Catholic News Service • Washington, D.C.

General Editor: Richard W. Daw, Director and Editor-in-Chief, National Catholic News Service
Editor, Part One: The Visit: Jerry Filteau
Editor, Part Two: The Message: Mary Esslinger
Photo Editor: Robert A. Strawn
With the collaboration of Julie L. Asher, Katharine Bird, Agostino A. Bono, Mary Bozzonetti, Bessie J. Briscoe, Diana Buckley, Linda Christensen, Mary Charlene DeLong, Susan Dolibois, Regina Edwards, Greg Erlandson, Barb Fraze, David Gibson, Randolph Hall, Laurie Hansen, Charles Isenhart, Elizabeth A. Jones, James Lackey, Joseph Larson, Cindy Liebhart, Thomas N. Lorsung, Dana L. Lott, Margaret M. Maher, Gloria T. Moore, Nancy Frazier O'Brien, Stephenie Overman, Robert Plocheck, Bill Pritchard, Charles Rehwaldt, Pamela Reid, Elizabeth Schevtchuk, Michele Grandison Smith, John Thavis, Sister Mary Ann Walsh, R.S.M., and Marie A. Williams.

Cover photograph by National Catholic News Service
Cover design by Marcia Ryan

ISBN 0-89870-178-3 (HB)
Library of Congress catalogue number 87-82683
Printed in the United States of America

CONTENTS

PART ONE: THE VISIT

PART TWO: THE MESSAGE

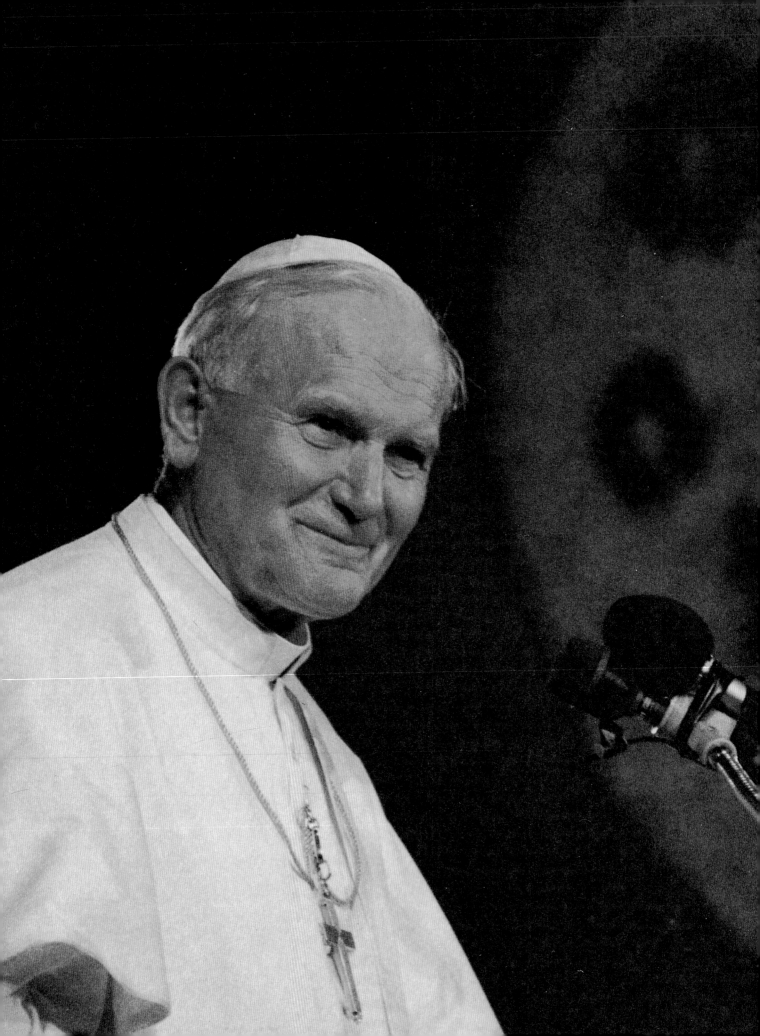

PART ONE

THE VISIT

MIAMI
September 10-11

Within moments of his arrival at Miami International Airport, Pope John Paul II set forth in clear terms the purpose of his second pastoral visit to the United States, a 10-day tour that would take him across a vast expanse of diversity into nine dioceses. "I come to proclaim the Gospel of Jesus Christ to all those who freely choose to listen to me; to tell again the story of God's love in the world; to spell out once more the message of human dignity, with its inalienable human rights and its inevitable human duties," he said in an arrival speech which was nationally televised. "I come here as a pastor.... I come as a friend." He called himself "a pilgrim in the cause of justice and peace and human solidarity — striving to build up the one human family."

Under blue skies studded with light clouds, and with President Reagan beside him, John Paul praised the U.S. system of government, noting the bicentennial of the Constitution which would be formally observed only a few days later. He thanked God for "the providential way in which the Constitution has served the people of this nation for two centuries: for the union it has formed, the justice it has established, the tranquility and peace it has ensured, the general welfare it has promoted and the blessings of liberty it has secured."

He struck an immediate note of interfaith cooperation, calling himself "a friend of America and of all Americans: Catholics, Orthodox, Protestants and Jews, people of every religion, and all men and women of good will."

And he made clear his concern for all: "I come as a friend of the poor and the sick and the dying; those who are struggling with the problems of each day; those who are rising and falling and stumbling on the journey of life; those who are seeking and discovering, and those not yet finding, the deep meaning of life, liberty and the pursuit of happiness."

But he also started off with a challenge, praying that God would "inspire you — as Americans who have received so much in freedom and prosperity and human enrichment — to continue to share all this with so many brothers and sisters throughout the other countries of the world who are still waiting and hoping to live according to the standards worthy of the children of God." In the days ahead he would spell out that challenge in detail.

During his flight from Rome aboard a chartered Alitalia Airlines Boeing 747 dubbed Shepherd I, the pope had told reporters accompanying him, in response to their questions, that dissent from Church teachings in the United States "is a serious problem," but that "the other question is if that is the dissent of many, many faithful people or ... the dissent of some very pronounced theologians or publishers, writers, and perhaps journalists." He said Catholics who believe they can violate Church teachings and still be good Catholics are mistaken because "it is necessary to follow the teaching of our Lord expressed through the Church."

9

During his U.S. visit, he said, he planned on "speaking to the great silent majority that is faithful and also speaking to those who are dissenting."

When one of the reporters asked him about the possibility of a schism in the U.S. church, he responded simply and straightforwardly: "Don't exaggerate," adding, "I am convinced that the American church is a good church, a very good church" with "so many wonderful aspects."

Ronald and Nancy Reagan were the first ones to greet the pope as he stepped onto U.S. soil. All three major U.S. television networks were broadcasting the arrival live, and some of their commentators expressed surprise that the pope did not kiss the ground as he had been seen to do so often on his many travels; they were unaware that it is John Paul's practice to make that symbolic sign of reverence and love only when he is visiting a country for the first time.

Reagan told the pope that "all America applauds your return.... In Poland you experienced Nazism and Communism. As pope you suffered a terrorist attack that nearly claimed your life. Still you proclaim that the central message of our time — that the central message of all time — is not hatred but love.... You have done so much to help a troubled world."

Seated in the front row before the dark blue podium were Mrs. Reagan, U.S. ambassador to the Holy See Frank Shakespeare, Vatican secretary of state Cardinal Agostino Casaroli and papal pronuncio to the United States Archbishop Pio Laghi. Archbishop Edward A. McCarthy of Miami, host bishop for the pope's Miami stay, was there, along with numerous other U.S. bishops. Standing out because of their bright red caps and sashes were American Cardinals Joseph L. Bernardin of Chicago, John J. O'Connor of New York, Bernard F. Law of Boston and William W. Baum, former archbishop of Washington who since 1981 had worked in the Vatican as head of its Congregation for Catholic Education. Dutch Cardinal Johannes Willebrands, head of the Vatican's Secretariat for Promoting Christian Unity and elder statesman of Catholic ecumenism, was also there.

John Paul's first stop was St. Mary's Cathedral, where he spoke with 1,000 priests, Religious and laity of the archdiocese. In a city that has become a haven for hundreds of thousands of Cubans fleeing communist rule and tens of thousands of Haitians who fled the economic and political oppression of former Duvalier dictatorships, he urged Catholics to pray not only for those who suffer but for those who inflict suffering. "We must never underestimate the power of prayer to further the Church's redemptive mission and to bring good where there is evil," he said.

In Spanish, the pope thanked Miami Catholics for prayers on his behalf. Perhaps thinking of some of the difficult meetings that lay ahead of him over the coming days and some of the messages he planned to deliver, he asked them — as St. Paul had asked the Ephesians — "to pray 'also for me, that speech may be given me to open my mouth, to make known with boldness the mystery of the Gospel ... so that I may have the courage to speak as I must.'"

From the cathedral he went to St. Martha's Church for a meeting with 750 representatives of the nation's approximately 53,000 priests. It was the first of a series of structured dialogues during which representatives of whatever group the pope was meeting with would speak first, telling him of the group's views, activities, hopes, concerns, and then the pope would respond. Advance texts had been sent to the Vatican by the speakers so that the pope, in preparing his response, would know ahead of time what was going to be said.

Speaking for the nation's priests was Father Frank J. McNulty, pastor of Blessed Sacrament Parish in Roseland, N.J., and a former seminary theology professor and Newark archdiocesan vicar for priests. McNulty was selected by the Committee for Priestly Life and Ministry of the National Conference of Catholic Bishops.

"These recent years have not been easy for priests," McNulty told the pontiff in his half-hour talk. "But where there are valleys, there are also mountains;

and if priests could open up their hearts and tell you of their priesthood, you would hear of 'top-of-the-mountain' moments ... moments of joy, peace and satisfaction. They would speak of ministry, and if you looked into their eyes you would see a spark, a rejoicing in the Lord as their shepherd, a rejoicing in their love of ministry.

"Ministry is the center of our lives," he continued. Through ordination, "we became co-workers with the bishop, collaborators in his mission and yours to continue the work of Jesus Christ. Thus our loyalty has a solid base and so does our desire for unity with you, our bishops and with each other.... There is communion. We treasure it; we yearn for more. Priests value diversity too. Ours is a pluralistic society, and we have learned how to hold fast to our Catholic value system while respecting the convictions of other people."

McNulty said priests rejoice that "the renewed Church in this country is alive and well" and that priests are committed to social justice and feel close bonds with their people. At ordination priests were charged "not to be served but to serve," he said. "Because priests take that charge so seriously, there are some serious concerns about our ministry.... We sometimes find ourselves in tension."

The Church is "committed to a bold proclamation of truth," yet it is "also a forgiving Church," he said. "It troubles us that people often do not perceive the Church as proclaiming integral truth and divine mercy, but rather as sounding harsh, demanding."

He also spoke of the "worries" of priests. "There is a real and dramatic shortage of priests.... Age and ministerial fatigue are harsh realities. Morale suffers when we see so few young men follow in our footsteps. Morale suffers when we see our parishes without priests and prayer services taking the place of Sunday Mass. We worry that we might become only a church of the word and lose our sacramental tradition."

As he neared the end of his remarks, McNulty raised two controversial issues, priestly celibacy and the role of women in the Church, but he carefully avoided any tone of confrontation or demand for change. "Even as we promote vocations," he said, "the celibacy question — as you so well know — continues to surface. Its value has eroded and continues to erode in the minds of many. This ... has serious implications for the Church." He said priests are grateful for the pope's "unequivocal" support for their celibate commitment "because it is not easy to strive to be warm, loving and affective men and yet remain faithful to that commitment. We can only ask you to continue along paths of support and exploration. Support for those who want to persevere; exploration of the gift of celibacy, which has such a long tradition; exploration of how the discipline of celibacy can be most effectively implemented today; exploration of how priests can help each other make it a transparent sign of pastoral charity and the coming of the kingdom in the pattern of Jesus Christ, our high priest."

McNulty made a similar appeal for attention to women's roles in Church ministry, saying that "the bonds of close collaboration between priests and women in ministry" prompted him to address the issue. "We would also be greatly encouraged if the Holy See, together with the local churches, would continue to explore the range of service that women might appropriately offer the Church," he said. "Their collaboration with priests has been generous and effective. Our ministry tells us that they are gifted, willing and needed. The movement of women toward practical equality is a major dynamic of our time. Because of the complexity and urgency of this movement, especially as it relates to the Church, there is need for study, reflection and above all, more dialogue with women."

Fourteen times during his talk McNulty was interrupted by applause from the gathered priests. As he finished he went up to John Paul and the pope stood and embraced him. "I had a sense he was not just embracing me, he was embracing every priest in the country," McNulty said later. The next evening ABC News anchorman Peter Jennings paid tribute to McNulty as ABC's "person of the week" because, in Jennings' words, "his eloquence on behalf of his brother priests struck us as a lesson in gentle persuasion. We thought it a very refreshing change from most people who think the only way to accomplish their goal is by making a lot of noise in public."

In his response, John Paul made no reference to women in ministry and referred explicitly to priestly celibacy only once, strongly reaffirming it with the declaration, "Our love for Christ, rekindled frequently in prayer — especially prayer before the Blessed Sacrament — is at the foundation of our commitment to celibacy. This love also makes it possible for us, as servants of God's kingdom, to love our people freely and chastely and deeply." The pope emphasized "the importance of personal prayer" in the priesthood, saying it "is neither a luxury nor an option to be taken up or put aside as seems convenient. Prayer is essential to the pastoral life."

Along with prayer at the heart of John Paul's message to American priests were faith, truth, spiritual asceticism, fidelity to Church teaching and unity with the whole Church. "I have come to you because I want all distances to be bridged, so that together we may grow and become ever more truly a communion of faith, hope and love," he said. He warned priests not to reduce their expectations of the priesthood to psychological or emotional satisfaction. "We know that proclaiming the Gospel and living out our ministry very definitely entail hardship," he said. "It would be wrong to reduce priestly life to this one dimension of suffering, but it would also be wrong not to recognize this dimension or to resent it when we encounter it.... It is important that we find satisfaction in our ministry and that we be clear about the nature of the satisfaction which we can expect. The physical and emotional health of priests is an important factor.... Yet the fulfillment that comes from our ministry does not, in the final analysis, consist in physical or psychological well-being; nor can it ever consist in material comfort and security. Our fulfillment depends on our relationship with Christ and on the service that we offer to his body, the Church."

While praising efforts of priests "to be merciful and gentle and forgiving like the Good Shepherd," he added: "Sometimes, however, what is asked of you in the name of compassion may not be in accord with the full truth of God." If "what is claimed to be a gesture of mercy" is in fact contrary to God's demands, "it can never be truly compassionate or beneficial," John Paul said. His words anticipated, in a low-key style, a much stronger message against dissent or toleration of dissent that he would deliver to the bishops of the nation nearly a week later. In his talk to the priests the pope urged them to conduct their ministry in accord with the magisterium, the Church's official teaching authority. The magisterium is a gift to the Church from the Holy Spirit "through which he guides the whole community to the fullness of truth," the pope said. "By its nature, therefore, this teaching of the Church is normative for the life of the Church and for all pastoral service."

He called on priests to preach "with dynamic fidelity" to Scripture, tradition and "the living pastoral authority of the Church." Preachers of the Gospel must also live it and teach by the example of their own "total conversion," he said. "This is particularly true in our own use of the sacrament of penance, through which we are repeatedly converted to the Lord.... People expect us to be men of faith and prayer. People look to us for Christ's truth and the teaching of the Church. They ask to see Christ's love incarnate in our lives."

On "the need for new vocations to the priesthood," John Paul counseled faith in "the power of Christ's paschal mystery." Followers of Christ, he said, are called "to proclaim that he is able, in virtue of his death and resurrection, to draw young people to himself, in this generation as in the past; to declare that he is strong enough to attract young men even today to a life of self-sacrifice, pure love and total dedication to the priesthood."

From the meeting with priests the pope went to Vizcaya Museum and

Gardens, an estate on Biscayne Bay, for a private meeting with Reagan. They were together for about an hour, with no aides or interpreters present.

The next morning John Paul met with U.S. Jewish leaders and told them the Church will join in educating future generations about the Holocaust "so that never again will such a horror be possible. Never again!"

Controversy had arisen over plans for the meeting when some Jewish leaders threatened to boycott it because the pope met with Austrian President Kurt Waldheim, who for more than 40 years kept secret his World War II connection with a Nazi military unit that was involved in war crimes. An unprecedented series of meetings in Italy, only a few weeks before the beginning of the pope's trip, had improved the atmosphere dramatically, but in the Jewish community there was still a significant undercurrent of ambivalence. Speaking to reporters on the plane from Rome to Miami, John Paul for the first time publicly defended his decision to meet with Waldheim. "He came as a president, democratically elected, of a people. It's necessary to show the same appreciation, the same esteem for every people," the pontiff said.

Symbolizing the difficulty that the pope's stance caused Jews was the absence from the Miami meeting of Rabbi Gilbert Klaperman, president of the Synagogue Council of America, an umbrella organization of major Jewish groups. He was to have addressed the pope, but the Rabbinical Council of America, representing Orthodox rabbis, boycotted the meeting, contending that the pope had not been sufficiently forthcoming on major Jewish concerns. That group asked Klaperman, who is Orthodox, not to attend. His prepared speech was delivered instead by Rabbi Mordecai Waxman, the synagogue council's honorary president. Waxman told the pope that Vatican establishment of full, formal diplomatic ties with Israel would reflect a "constructive contribution by the Vatican" to peace in the Middle East.

John Paul affirmed the right of Jews to a homeland and the importance of the modern state of Israel in terms of the biblically based "religious attachment to the land" of Jewish tradition. He added, however, that "the right to a homeland also applies to the Palestinian people." He also made a strong public plea for recognition of "how hard and effectively" Pope Pius XII worked to assist Jews during World War II. He spoke of "strong, unequivocal efforts" by both Pius XII and his predecessor, Pius XI, "against anti-Semitism and Nazism," and declared that "history will reveal ever more clearly how deeply Pius XII felt the tragedy of the Jewish people." Disputes over how much Pius XII did or did not do to help the Jews, and whether he could have done more, have been a major point of controversy for the past two decades.

Responding to Jewish complaints that the Holocaust's special significance for Jews has been minimized in Catholic circles, John Paul repeated the promise he made during the pre-trip meetings that a new in-depth study and "Catholic document on the Shoah and anti-Semitism will be forthcoming." Shoah is the Hebrew word for the Holocaust. Waxman, while praising recent Church condemnations of anti-Semitism, said that "Christian teachings bear a heavy responsibility" for the centuries of European anti-Semitism which resulted in the Shoah. The pope supported examining the anti-Semitic roots of the Holocaust, which he called "that ruthless and inhuman attempt to exterminate the Jewish people in Europe," but he did not link that history to Christian teachings or practices.

Both John Paul and Waxman noted projects for eliminating anti-Semitism in Catholic educational programs. The pope asked every Catholic diocese to implement Vatican guidelines "regarding the correct way to preach and teach about Jews and Judaism."

As the pope and Jewish leaders met, tens of thousands of people streamed into Tamiami Park to join John Paul in a mid-morning Mass. It was the first Mass of the visit and his final event in Miami before flying to Columbia, S.C., to meet with non-Catholic Christian leaders. The bright morning sun quickly brought temperatures into the 90s. Several people at the Mass site were treated

Miami

September 10-11

13

for heat prostration before the pope arrived. On his arrival John Paul toured in his popemobile among the estimated 150,000 to 250,000 Mass-goers, smiling and waving while the choir sang "Alleluia!"

A heavy cloud cover rolled in just as the Mass was about to begin. An announcer concerned about storm warnings and the dangers of lightning asked people near several tall broadcast towers to move to a different area. "We would not want to send any of you home to the Lord today," he said. The first raindrops actually cheered up many in the crowd, giving them some relief from the heat. But as the liturgy progressed the rain pelted harder and lightning crackled through the air. As the pope began his homily, reading from his prepared text with an aide holding an umbrella over his head, he made a reference to Florida as "this beautiful land of the sun." As if on cue, a sharp crack of thunder punctuated his words. Looking up and smiling, the pope ad-libbed that in this case "the sun" must also mean "rain."

The storm worsened as the pope continued his homily. Lightning blew out two broadcast communications towers. Local authorities and Secret Service officials decided it was unsafe to continue. Archbishop McCarthy, informed of the decision, interrupted the pope to tell the crowd that the Mass was being halted and they should leave for their safety. Many people called out "No!" in response to McCarthy's words. The archbishop said later that the shouts brought tears to the pope's eyes. It was the first time in 36 trips abroad that he had been forced to cancel a scheduled Mass. Vatican press corps veterans recalled that in 1981, in Nagasaki, Japan, he had even celebrated Mass outdoors during a raging snowstorm.

John Paul finished the Mass in a trailer with about 30 bishops, priests and cardinals. When he completed the celebration, he returned to the altar and greeted several thousand people who had remained in the park. "I was sad to interrupt the celebration because of the atmospheric circumstances," he said. "I want to express to all of you my admiration for your persistence and perseverance." He then blessed the crowd and left.

In his rain-shortened homily the pope addressed the theme of his trip, "Unity in the Work of Service," by talking about the "mystery of unity in diversity" found in America and exemplified in the ethnic and racial diversity of Florida. "Christ gives the Church a rich variety of charisms for the purpose of deepening our communion as his body," he said.

In the portion of his text which he was unable to deliver because of the rain, John Paul intended to condemn many of the social and personal sins found in American society and plead for a return to sound moral values. "Basic human and Christian values are challenged by crime, violence and terrorism," the prepared text said. "Honesty and justice in business and public life are often violated. Throughout the world great sums are spent on armaments while millions of poor people struggle for the basic necessities of life. Alcohol and drug abuse take a heavy toll on individuals and on society. The commercial exploitation of sex through pornography offends human dignity and endangers the future of young people. Family life is subjected to powerful pressures as fornication, adultery, divorce and contraception are wrongly regarded as acceptable by many. The unborn are cruelly killed and the lives of the elderly are in serious danger from a mentality that would open the door wide to euthanasia."

Had he been able to finish the homily, the pope would have said that despite those evils, "faithful Christians must not be discouraged nor can they conform to the spirit of the world. Instead, they are called upon to acknowledge the supremacy of God and his law, to raise their voices and join their efforts on behalf of moral values, to offer society the example of their own upright conduct and to help those in need."

14

1 Pope John Paul II greets the crowd upon arrival in Miami.

2 President Reagan welcomes the pope to the United States.

3 A cheering, flag-waving crowd sights the pope.

4 A gust of wind lifts the cowl on the pope's robe and the president offers a hand.

5 Children welcome the pope to Miami.

6 Pope John Paul II prays in a chapel after arriving at St. Mary's Cathedral.

7 The pope embraces Father Frank McNulty, who spoke for the American priests.

8 The pope listens as Rabbi Mordecai Waxman speaks during the meeting with Jewish leaders.

9 The two leaders have their discussion surrounded by the renaissance setting of the Vizcaya mansion.

10 President Reagan and the pope walk in the Vizcaya garden.

11 The pope is greeted again by President and Mrs. Reagan as he arrives at Vizcaya.

12 An enthusiastic crowd sights the pope.

13 Pope John Paul II and Archbishop McCarthy arrive in a popemobile for the Mass.

14 Prior to the Mass at the Dade County Youth Fairgrounds, priests hear confessions.

15 The pope began the Mass, but driving rain and lightning forced it to be interrupted, and the pope finished the Mass in a small trailer.

16 The rains came during the Mass and the faithful covered themselves any way they could.

17 Despite the rain Ileana Espinosa manages a smile after the Mass.

18 The pope gives a blessing before leaving Miami.

3

4a

4b

5

6

7

8

"We thank you, Your Holiness, for the courage and sanctity, the kindness and wisdom, with which you have done so much to help our troubled world. On behalf of all Americans, Your Holiness, welcome back."

* * *

"On my part I come to you—America—with sentiments of friendship, reverence and esteem. I come as one who already knows you and loves you, as one who wishes you to fulfill completely your noble destiny of service to the world.... I come to proclaim the Gospel of Jesus Christ.... I come as a pilgrim...."

11

12

13

14

COLUMBIA
September 11

Newspapers, television and radio told people that if they wanted to see the pope in Columbia, South Carolina's capital, they had better get there early. So Marie and Jimmy McKnight and their daughter, Debbie Smith, packed their patio table and chairs and arrived at 10:30 a.m. at the South Carolina State Fairgrounds. In the shade of their patio umbrella, they set their table and chairs in the back of their pickup truck and had a picnic. The three, members of St. Peter's Parish in Columbia, were like thousands of others who gathered at the fairgrounds. Only at 2 p.m. would they be permitted to enter Williams-Brice Stadium, across the street, for a 5:30 p.m. "Service of Christian Witness" with John Paul and leaders of other Christian faiths. Well before the pope's midafternoon arrival at the airport, temperatures had climbed to 92 degrees.

Small groups of fundamentalist Christians prepared in a different way for the first-ever papal visit to South Carolina, deep in Bible-belt territory where the entire state is a single diocese and Catholics make up about 2 percent of the population. In Greenville, Bob Jones University published a leaflet questioning whether the pope's visit to the United States was a violation of the separation of church and state. The Rev. Bob Jones insisted that Catholicism "is not Christian in the bibilical sense by any means" and called South Carolina Protestants "traitors against almighty God" for "fawning over" the pope. Members of the Faith Free Presbyterian Church in Greenville bought a full-page advertisement in a local newspaper asking "Bible believers" to "expose and oppose the deception" of the pope's visit. Thousands of anti-Catholic leaflets were stuck under the windshield wipers of cars parked by those who had come to see John Paul.

The South Carolina Christian Action Council, a statewide organization with 18 member denominations, condemned the anti-Catholic activities. "We call on all who confess the name of Christ to disassociate themselves from these acts of intolerance, incompatible with both our Christian faith and our American heritage," the council said in a statement two days before the pope arrived.

Arriving from Miami at 3:30 p.m., the pope went first to St. Peter's Church, where he was welcomed by Charleston's Bishop Ernest L. Unterkoefler. During the 45-minute service the pope urged 550 representatives of Catholic parishes and organizations to continue the "long tradition" of Catholic ecumenical efforts in South Carolina. "From Christ, we must learn the way to overcome those sad divisions which still exist today among Christians. At the same time you must never cease to strive for personal holiness and conversion of heart," he said. Hailed by Unterkoefler as a missionary, John Paul said the congregation made him and his fellow visitors, "especially Cardinal Bernardin," feel at home.

The Chicago cardinal, a former priest of the diocese, was born in Columbia and baptized in St. Peter's.

From St. Peter's the pope was whisked off to the president's house of the University of South Carolina for the chief event of his visit, a meeting with 26 leaders of Christian faiths that are in formal dialogue with the Catholic Church. After an exchange of formal statements, the meeting included a short period of informal discussions as well — a departure from the usual style of the pope's ecumenical meetings during his foreign travels. Bishop Philip R. Cousin, secretary of the Council of Bishops of the African Methodist Episcopal Church and president of the National Council of Churches, read a statement to the pope on behalf of the Christian leaders. Their statement emphasized the pluralism of churches in the United States and asked how they could work with the Catholic Church.

"The variety of (U.S.) church life almost exceeds imagination," they said. "American Christians have been shaped by this pluralism, which includes freedom of religious expression, and have helped in turn to influence the nature of this pluralism." Among ecumenical issues the leaders expressed interest in was the Catholic response to the World Council of Churches' 1982 document "Baptism, Eucharist and Ministry." The document, also known as the Lima document because it was drafted in Lima, Peru, is an effort by an international team of theologians to express common traditions which they hope all churches could agree on or accept regarding baptism, the Eucharist and ministry.

In his reply the pope disclosed that the Holy See had sent a 40-page, not-yet-public comment on the document to the WCC's Commission on Faith and Order. Speaking on the grounds for Christian unity, John Paul said that when the churches address one another, "we must do so from the foot of the cross of Jesus Christ." Unity grows through "self-denial and unstinted love," he said. He praised ecumenical progress, saying that despite lack of full agreement "it is no small achievement of the ecumenical movement that after centuries of mistrust, we humbly and sincerely recognize in each other's communities the presence and fruitfulness of Christ's gifts at work."

Orthodox, Episcopal, Lutheran, Methodist and Baptist leaders attended the meeting, as well as representatives of Polish National Catholic, Disciples of Christ and (Dutch) Reformed churches. The Presbyterian, Armenian Apostolic and African Methodist Zion churches also were represented.

Several of the leaders who met with the pope said afterwards that the visit had been significant, but church unity would not be reached in the near future. Bishop Arthur A. Vogel, head of the Episcopal Diocese of West Missouri, called the event "a strong reaffirmation" of the churches' commitment to unity but added that in a meeting of that type "nobody would expect a specific problem to be resolved." Bishop James R. Crumley Jr., bishop of the Lutheran Church in America, called the meeting "another most important" step in the long path to Christian unity. The Rev. John O. Humbert, president of the Christian Church (Disciples of Christ), said the encounter would probably give an added "impetus to the official dialogues" among churches. "It is obvious that we are not going to have union pretty soon, but it is a pilgrimage that we are committed to," he added.

About 10,000 University of South Carolina students, faculty, staff and others turned out on the Horseshoe, the historic grassy common at the center of the campus, to cheer John Paul as he arrived for the ecumenical meeting. Greeted by rebel yells from students and chants of "John Paul II, we love you," he answered, "The pope loves you, too." Students in residence halls next to the Horseshoe had been turned out of their rooms at 7:30 that morning so the U.S. Secret Service could search and secure the area. The students had the day off from classes because of the papal visit and could have slept late, but they didn't seem to mind having been dislocated. They had been notified in the spring that they would have to vacate their rooms that day. Some commemorated the occasion with T-shirts that proclaimed, "I was moved by the pope."

After the ecumenical meeting, the pope traveled in his Mercedes-Benz popemobile down a parade route to Williams-Brice Stadium. Crowd estimates along the route ranged from 10,000 to 25,000, far fewer than predictions of 250,000 people. Many said they thought advance warnings of crowds and traffic made people decide to stay home and watch the pope on television.

The ecumenical "Service of Christian Witness" at the stadium had begun with a program of readings and hymns while the pope and Christian leaders were meeting. He and the other leaders arrived at the stadium shortly before 7 p.m. and ascended the stage to join in the service. The pope personally read the Gospel reading — another departure from tradition in papal ceremonies — then told the 60,000 people present that Americans must defend traditional family values. He also urged Americans not to lose sight of the "true meaning" of freedom. "America," he declared, "you cannot insist on the right to choose without also insisting on the duty to choose well, the duty to choose in the truth. Our Christian conscience should be deeply concerned about the way in which sins against love and against life are often presented as examples of 'progress' and emancipation. Most often, are they not but the age-old forms of selfishness dressed up in a new language and presented in a new cultural framework?"

Temperatures cooled into the 80s by the time the pope returned to the airport for a brief evening encounter with former President Jimmy Carter before leaving Columbia. Carter, who welcomed John Paul to the White House in 1979, had requested the Columbia meeting. He almost cancelled it when he was called to Atlanta to the bedside of his brother Billy, who was hospitalized with inoperable cancer of the pancreas. Carter decided at the last minute to make the trip to Columbia anyway. The former president and Mrs. Carter talked with the pope at the foot of the stairs of Shepherd I, and Carter said afterwards they discussed human rights.

As John Paul flew off from the land of Bible-belt Protestantism to the Mardi Gras Catholicism of New Orleans, he left behind his chief ecumenical aide, Cardinal Willebrands, for further discussions with about 200 church leaders and ecumenists the next day. Willebrands told the group that "serious dialogue" with Anglicans is needed to resolve the issue of women priests, because Roman Catholics consider the male priesthood part of the "truly apostolic tradition." Resolution of that issue could "radically change" Catholic-Anglican relations, he said.

In reviewing the status of interfaith dialogues, Willebrands said that "all of the dialogues are important ... but the Lutheran-Catholic dialogue is important especially for Western Christianity because at the heart of the Reformation in the 16th century was the conflict between Martin Luther and the authorities in Rome. Reconciliation between Lutherans and Catholics would therefore be highly symbolic as well as significant."

Bishop Crumley, Lutheran co-chairman of the International Lutheran-Roman Catholic Dialogue, gave the official response to the cardinal's address. He said the "urgency" for unity was felt prominently in the United States, which has many interfaith marriages. Churches insist that they are concerned about family stability but do not let families "come to the altar together," Crumley said. He added that he was convinced "the walls built around those altars are human."

Willebrands, who was given a birthday cake by his non-Catholic colleagues to mark the 78th birthday he had celebrated a week earlier, urged his fellow ecumenists to engage in "the dialogue of love" along with theological dialogue and other ecumenical endeavors. Ecumenism needs "some spontaneous acts" of good will, he said. "You should not leave everything to theological dialogue and theologians."

19

19 *At the home of the university president, the pope greets Orthodox Primate Theodosius and Protestant leaders.*

20 *The pope prays with the congregation at St. Peter's Church.*

21 *The pope kisses the Bible during the ecumenical service with other Christian leaders at Williams-Brice Stadium.*

22 *The pope prays with Christian leaders during the service.*

23 *A child gets a kiss from the pope as he blesses 25 children at the end of the service.*

20

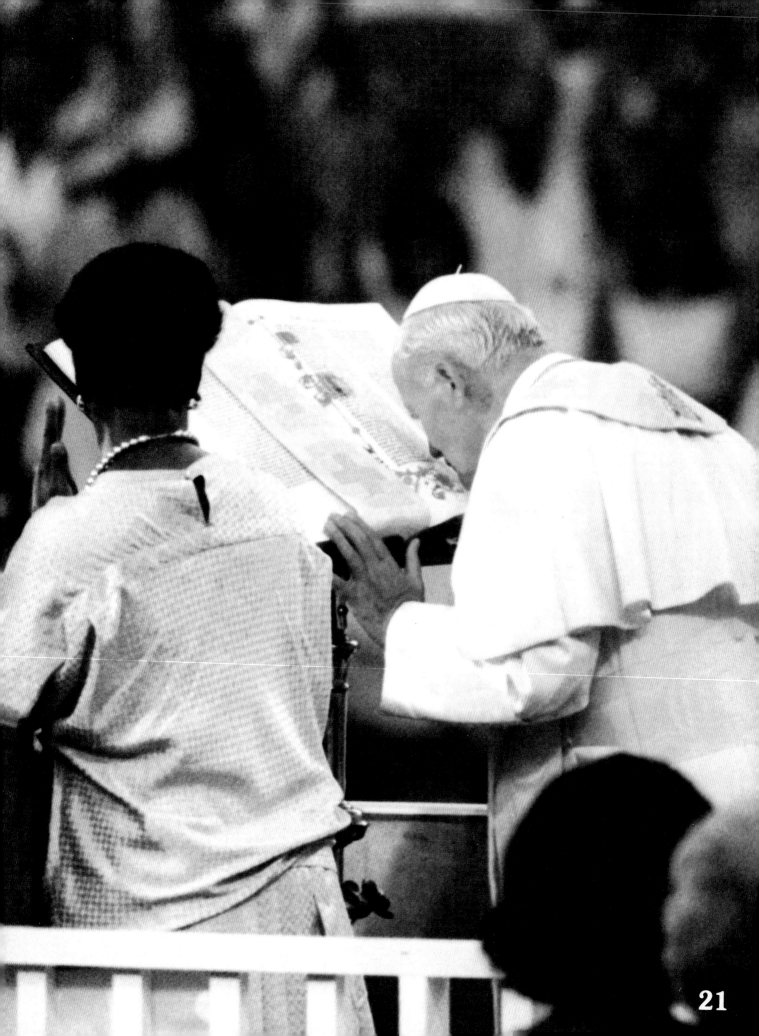

NEW
ORLEANS
September 12

I n New Orleans, an island of Catholicism in the Protestant South, John Paul
caught some glimpses of Mardi Gras and jazz and delivered serious messages
on premarital sex, marital love and forgiveness, Catholic education and racial
justice for blacks.

He started his day early after having spent the night at the residence of New
Orleans Archbishop Philip M. Hannan on arrival from a full day in Miami and
Columbia. Speaking to 1,100 priests and Religious in historic St. Louis
Cathedral, in the French Quarter, he told them: "Always remember that the
supernatural effectiveness of your service within the Church is linked to the
witness of your life lived in union with Christ. The precise goal of all apostolic
service is to lead all people to communion with the most Holy Trinity." In the
enthusiastic congregation was a group of Discalced Carmelite nuns from Mobile,
Ala., who in order to see the pope had obtained permission to leave their
monastery for the first time since it was established in 1943.

From the cathedral a motorcade took the pope to the New Orleans Superdome for successive meetings in large conference rooms with black Catholics
and with Catholic educators, followed by a midday youth rally in the stadium
itself. The motorcade moved quickly to make up time the pope lost by linger-
ing among the priests and nuns in the cathedral.

In a meeting with 11 black bishops and 1,800 other black Catholics, John
Paul urged: "Keep alive and active your rich cultural gifts" because "your black
heritage enriches the Church. You are part of the Church and the Church is
part of you." He criticized the continuing discrimination against blacks in society and asked U.S. Catholic leaders to fight to overcome it. "The black community suffers a disproportionate share of economic deprivation. Far too many
of your young people receive less than an equal opportunity for a quality education and for gainful employment," he said.

He also praised black Americans for their use of non-violence as a means
of overcoming discrimination, and he noted the religious motivations behind
that stance. "The response of non-violence stands, in the memory of this nation, as a monument of honor to the black community," he said. "As we recall
those who with Christian vision opted for non-violence as the only truly effective approach for ensuring and safeguarding human dignity, we cannot but think
of the Rev. Dr. Martin Luther King Jr." It was not the first time John Paul had

praised King. In 1986, when King's birthday was first celebrated as a national holiday, he sent a message urging Americans to recall the "worthy ideals" of the slain Baptist preacher and civil rights worker.

Greeting the pope for black Catholics was Bishop Joseph L. Howze of Biloxi, Miss., one of the nation's first black bishops and the only one so far to be named head of a diocese. "Racism is a major hindrance to full development of black leadership within the Church," Howze told the pope.

When told by Archbishop Hannan that he should feel at home among black Catholics in the United States, John Paul motioned to his personal secretary, Msgr. Emery Kabongo, a black from Zaire, and said, "I am at home with black Catholics in America, and even in the Vatican."

The Superdome room for the meeting was festooned with red, white, burgundy and yellow banners bearing drawings of the tree cited in the Old Testament as that used to build the Ark of the Covenant, the acacia. A deep-rooted tree known for its ability to survive drought, the acacia is a symbol of Africa. As the white Polish pope hugged America's 11 black bishops at the start of the meeting, the rest of the crowd clapped hands in unison and sang Gospel music composed by Afro-Americans. The scene showed the growing importance and impact of black culture on the U.S. Catholic Church, which now counts 1.3 million blacks among its members. Four months before the papal visit, 1,500 black Catholics from across the country gathered at the Catholic University of America for a national congress at which they developed a pastoral plan for black Catholics with a strong emphasis on evangelization. Some 34,000 blacks participated in months of local consultations that preceded the congress. "It used to be considered an anomaly to be black and Catholic," said Auxiliary Bishop Emerson J. Moore of New York after the Superdome meeting. "The pope buried that myth."

In the pope's speech black bishops saw support for their calls to end racism within the Church as well as in society. Racism is as "American as apple pie," said Moore. He called the pope's talk a "ringing encouragement" to solve concrete racial problems within the Church. Moore added, however, that the problems within the Church are not as grave as those in general U.S. society. "In the Church we can always point to the teachings. This isn't always possible in society."

Moving directly to another meeting, this one with Catholic elementary and high school teachers and parish religious educators, John Paul heard descriptions of U.S. Catholic education efforts from several presenters. In his response he warmly endorsed Catholic education, but he probably endeared himself most to the group at the end of his talk, when he ad-libbed, "I have come here first as a student. So as a student I thank you for all you have taught me this morning." He said like any student, he was worried about his grade. "I am anxious about what kind of notes (marks) I shall receive," he said. If applause counted for grades, his were high.

In his address John Paul stressed the importance of Catholic education, praised the reputation of U.S. Catholic schools for academic excellence and community service, and challenged the U.S. system of not providing the kind of public funding for Catholic schools that would give parents true freedom to select the school of their choice. He also alluded briefly to employer-employee disputes and other problems in Catholic education. "I am aware," he said, "that not all the questions relating to the organization, financing and administration of Catholic schools in an increasingly complex society have been resolved to the satisfaction of all. We hope that such matters will be settled with justice and fairness for all." He added, however, that Catholic teachers should see themselves as sharing in the mission of the Church, so that the Church is more than just "an employer."

The pope especially praised U.S. Catholic education's reputation for service to poor and minority students. "We cannot doubt that such is part of God's call to the Church in the United States. It is a responsibility that is deeply inscribed in the history of Catholic education in this country," he said. In speaking of parental rights in education, he made a brief allusion to U.S. Catholic complaints that the denial of public funding or tax breaks for Catholic education places an unfair double burden on parents who choose Catholic schools for their children. "Nor should parents in any way be penalized for choosing for their children an education according to their beliefs," the pope said.

Salvation in Jesus Christ is the ultimate goal of all Catholic education, John Paul said. Its challenge is to transmit "the full truth concerning the human person, created in God's image and called to life in Christ through the Holy Spirit." Catholic educators must "foster in your students a social consciousness," he said, but "the world needs more than just social reformers. It needs saints. Holiness is not the privilege of a few; it is a gift offered to all. The call to holiness is addressed also to you and to your students."

Kimberly Ball, an 18-year-old freshman from New Orleans' Loyola University, began crying when John Paul arrived by popemobile in another area of the Superdome for a youth rally. "I was just overwhelmed," she said. "Maybe it was seeing a symbol of so much holiness. The pope looked so angelic." She was far from alone in her reaction. The exuberant rally lasted nearly two hours. Sandwiched between two talks by the pope were a Mardi Gras-style parade, a ceremonial presentation of gifts from the youth, and entertainment by Dana, an Irish singer. About 60,000 young people gave the pope a rousing welcome and cheered and applauded often during his talks. John Paul, warmed by their enthusiasm, was clearly enjoying himself as well. He stood and clapped throughout the three-float mini-parade and smiled as he tried to put on a Mardi Gras mask given to him by the young people.

Amid the festivities, against the backdrop of a massive mural celebrating New Orleans, the Mississippi River and the bayou country of southern Louisiana, the pope delivered a serious message to America's youth. He spoke about international solidarity, justice, unselfishness, love, the sacredness of marriage and the importance of living the Gospel in a world that often rejects it. Jesus teaches "meekness, mercy and humility. Other voices in the world will immediately shout out: 'Weakness!' " the pope said. "Jesus emphasizes the value of honesty, uprightness, justice and fairness. But when you practice these virtues, you are liable to be accused of being 'naive.'

"Jesus and his Church," the pope continued, "hold up to you God's plan for human love, telling you that sex is a great gift of God that is reserved for marriage. At this point the voices of the world will try to deceive you with powerful slogans, claiming that you are 'unrealistic,' 'out of it'.... But the message of Jesus is clear. Purity means true love and it is the total opposite of selfishness and escape." John Paul's comments were greeted with thunderous applause.

He also called for young people to say no to drug use and said it was time for youth to join together and help change the world. "What is needed today is a solidarity between all of the young people of the world, solidarity especially with the poor and all those in need," he said.

During the parade after his first address, youths sitting in the end-zone seats spelled out the word "sharing" with colored cards. The float themes were "dreaming," "sharing" and "celebrating." Following the parade, Dana led the crowd in singing "Totus Tuus." The hymn's title comes from the pope's motto, which means "all yours" and expresses John Paul's devotion to Mary. When the pope was given the plumed-and-spangled purple, green and gold Mardi Gras mask, he tried to put it on but failed despite an assist from Archbishop Hannan. He was also given a drawing of youths working together and a wood carving. "What is my gift for you today?" the pope asked as he ad-libbed a shortened version of his prepared closing address. "It was a message of Jesus Christ.... The pope will still find a home with the young people. And the young people will still find themselves at home with the pope."

From the youth rally the pope went back to Hannan's residence for a luncheon with bishops of the region. It featured lump crabmeat remoulade, roast beef, creamed spinach, brabant potatoes, cherries jubilee, wine and coffee. The meal was prepared and served by Antoine's restaurant on commemorative china, emblazoned with the papal coat-of-arms, which the Lenox company made especially for the occasion and donated. Bishop Warren L. Boudreaux of Baton Rouge said later that the pope "ate lightly" but "seemed to enjoy the food." During the luncheon gathering the pope's ambassador to the United States, Archbishop Laghi, mentioned that Boudreaux was a good singer. Hannan and other bishops chimed in to urge Boudreaux to sing his favorite song, "The Impossible Dream." "It does not take much to get this Cajun bishop to get up and sing," Boudreaux recounted later. "When I had concluded, the Holy Father smiled at me and said, 'Instead of giving homilies, you ought to sing to your people.' To which I responded, 'I do, Holy Father. Believe me, I do it all the time.'"

By midafternoon John Paul was out in public again, traveling by helicopter to the Lakefront Arena of the University of New Orleans to celebrate the second Mass of his U.S. visit. Heavy afternoon rains made it look like New Orleans might experience a repeat of the storm-interrupted Miami Mass the previous day. But just after the 4:15 starting time the clouds moved away, leaving a patch of blue over the Mass site. Hannan told the pope the rain had given a chance to the 200,000 people there to "defy the weather to show you that you are our father."

In his homily, John Paul again spoke about marriage. He cited the just-read Gospel parable — about the servant who would not forgive another man's debt after his master had forgiven him — as an illustration of the need for love and forgiveness in marriage. "No relationship as intense and close as marriage and the family can survive without forgiveness 'seventy times seven times,'" the pope declared. If marriage partners approach their relationship strictly in terms of justice, he said, worrying about real or perceived injustices can lead to estrangement and divorce. "The plight of the children alone should make us realize that the refusal to forgive is not in keeping with the true nature of marriage as God established it and as he wants it to be lived."

Defending Church teaching on the indissolubility of marriage, John Paul said some people claim that such teaching lacks compassion, but "what must be seen is the ineffectiveness of divorce, and its ready availability in modern society, to bring mercy and forgiveness and healing to so many couples and their children, in whose troubled lives there remain a brokenness and a suffering that will not go away."

In a section of his prepared text which he deleted due to lack of time, John Paul also said resolution of the international debt crisis calls for forgiveness. "'Blind' justice alone cannot solve this problem in an ethical way that promotes the human good of all parties. Merciful loves calls for mutual understanding and a recognition of human priorities and needs, above and beyond the 'blind' justice of financial mechanisms. We must arrive at solutions that truly reflect both complete justice and mercy." The pontiff said the Church's concern about these matters is reflected in the U.S. bishops' 1986 pastoral letter on the economy. He quoted in his homily from a portion of the letter in which the bishops said their purpose was "to lift up the human and ethical dimensions of economic life" and that Christians are called not only to "do justice" but also to "love."

The pope suggested that a failure to forgive others is closely linked to a practical atheism and loss of a sense of sin: "Modern man easily forgets that he has received a great gift. As man loses this awareness, he also forgets the debt and the fact that he is a debtor. He loses his consciousness of sin. Many people today, especially those caught up in a civilization of affluence and pleasure, live as though sin did not exist and as if God did not exist."

In the final event of his long day in New Orleans, John Paul visited Xavier University, the only predominantly black Catholic university in the United States. There, in an evening outdoor ceremony slightly dampened by a light rain, he met with Xavier students and faculty and representatives of Catholic colleges and universities across the country. He said the "greatest challenge" of Catholic colleges and universities is "that of strengthening and preserving (their) Catholic character." The "religious and moral education of students and their pastoral care" is a "matter of supreme importance" in Catholic institutions of higher learning, he said.

The pope also noted the "special role" of theology in the institutions, "which are privileged settings for the encounter between faith and culture." But he also stressed "the intimate relationship between the Catholic university and the teaching office of the Church" and said that the work of theologians "must ultimately be tested and validated by the magisterium." Theology, he said, "is much more than an academic discipline.... Theology is at the service of the whole ecclesial community." When theologians assist the pope and bishops in "authentically teaching the message of Christ," he added, they "perform an inestimable service to the Church."

In his talk John Paul walked a careful line on controversial points in proposed Vatican guidelines now under study which would give local bishops more direct juridical authority to remove theology professors who hold views at odds with the accepted understanding of Church teachings. The Association of Catholic Colleges and Universities, which sponsored the papal meeting at Xavier, prepared a synthesis in 1986 in which 110 presidents of Catholic colleges said that the norms, as proposed, would violate U.S. standards of academic freedom and would result in the loss of accreditation of Catholic colleges.

The pope made no reference to the proposed norms themselves and did not try to define directly how bishops should relate juridically to Catholic institutions of higher learning in their dioceses. He addressed the issue on the level of principles, however, saying that "there is an intimate relationship between the Catholic university and the teaching office of the Church. The bishops ... should be seen not as external agents but as participants in the life of the Catholic university." At the same time he acknowledged that the "Catholic identity" of such institutions "is a complex and vitally important matter" which must be lived out "amid changing circumstances."

In welcoming the pope, Francis J. Kerins, ACCU chairman and president of Carroll College, Helena, Mont., said Catholic colleges "play an essential role in a society that has always found a special strength in its pluralism." He added that of all higher education in the country "the best utilization of the talents of women in positions of leadership has been in Catholic colleges sponsored by congregations of religious women." Catholic people recognize the unique worth of higher education and support it, often at great sacrifice, Kerins said.

John Paul would leave New Orleans early the next morning, but behind him there would be a lasting memorial of the first pope ever to visit the nation's second-oldest diocese. In a brief ceremony when the pope emerged from St. Louis Cathedral after his meeting with priests and nuns, New Orleans Mayor Sidney Barthelemy renamed Chartres Street in front of the cathedral. Following the tradition of French street names in that area of the city, it is now officially called Place Jean Paul II.

29

30

31

SAN ANTONIO
September 13

D uring his day in San Antonio John Paul celebrated Mass and led the Angelus before more than a quarter-million people gathered under a blazing Texas sun. He met with U.S. Catholic Charities workers, candidates for the priesthood and religious life, members of a west side Hispanic parish, and Polish-Americans from America's oldest Polish community. He also passed the historic Alamo in his popemobile and was cheered by hundreds of thousands as he traveled through the city by motorcade. He delivered messages urging social justice, stronger prayer life, preservation of cultural traditions and a return to the sacrament of penance.

The pontiff left New Orleans about 8:45 a.m., arriving in San Antonio a few minutes after 10. He was almost immediately whisked off to Westover Hills, a large natural amphitheater half a mile wide, where worshippers had been gathering since early morning for the 11 a.m. Mass.

Two days earlier, just after the pope concluded his meeting with President Reagan in Miami, a fierce gust of wind in San Antonio had toppled the twin 12-story steel-girder towers flanking the altar built for the Mass. The towers collapsed in less than 10 seconds, bringing down a large, radiating golden cross that workers had just finished hanging between them and the banners and bold floral paintings covering the girders. As the pope traveled from Miami to Columbia to New Orleans, construction crews in San Antonio worked frantically to clean up the debris and erect a new backdrop. Two large cranes were brought in, and large banners were strung between them, showing bright pink flowers below the golden tiara and crossed keys that symbolize the papacy. Father David Garcia, chairman of the site preparation committee, was philosophical about the accident, in which no one was hurt. "Buildings are not the Church. People are. They will be the ones who will really make the event significant," he said.

An estimated 300,000 people were present when John Paul, flanked by San Antonio Archbishop Patrick F. Flores and 50 other bishops, began Mass. Temperatures were already in the high 80s and climbed to 92 degrees before the Mass was over. Officials had originally planned to shade the altar platform with a huge helium-filled cloud, built in Baltimore and shipped to San Antonio for the occasion. After the towers collapsed, however, the organizers decided not to put up the cloud. At least 500 Mass-goers were treated for heat-related illness, and about 70 were hospitalized.

In a bilingual Spanish-English homily the pope called for greater compassion toward immigrants. He praised "people of great courage and generosity" who have been helping Central Americans seeking shelter in the United States. Some reporters interpreted that remark as a papal endorsement of efforts by the sanctuary movement to aid illegal aliens, particularly from Guatemala and El Salvador. But Vatican spokesman Joaquin Navarro-Valls told reporters at a news briefing the next day that the pope was not specifically referring to the sanctuary movement. In his comments on the problems of immigrants, John Paul called the Southwest United States "a meeting of cultures, indigenous and immigrant, sometimes marked by tensions and conflicts ... a kind of laboratory testing America's commitment to her founding moral principles and human values."

He had words of praise for the Hispanic community and said it faces great challenges. Hispanics — "so numerous, so long present in this land, so well equipped to respond" — must make efforts to address their own needs, he said.

But John Paul devoted the major portion of his homily to what he called "the great neglect of the sacrament of penance." He said the idea that Catholics should seek forgiveness through the sacrament "has always remained firm and unchanged in the consciousness of the Church." He linked the decline in confession over the past quarter-century, well documented in surveys, to "an obscuring of the religious and moral conscience, a loss of the sense of sin, or a lack of adequate instruction on the importance of this sacrament in the life of Christ's Church."

The pope said the Second Vatican Council "never intended" to discourage use of confession, and he asked bishops and priests to do "everything possible to make the administration of this sacrament a primary aspect" of their job. "Come back to this source of grace; do not be afraid," he told Catholics. "Christ himself is waiting for you."

After an afternoon lunch with the Texas bishops at Flores' residence on the grounds of Assumption Seminary, John Paul left for San Antonio's Municipal Auditorium and a meeting with U.S. social justice and Catholic Charities leaders gathered for a national conference of Catholic Charities USA. He mounted his popemobile for the first of three motorcades through San Antonio which officials estimated drew a combined crowd of 675,000 — the largest reception to be given the pope in any city throughout his visit.

The all-white popemobiles seen so often in papal trips abroad are two identical, specially equipped autos donated to the Vatican after the 1981 assassination attempt against the pope in St. Peter's Square. Built on a Mercedes-Benz station wagon chassis, they have a transparent, bullet-proof enclosure behind the driver's cab, high enough so that the pope can stand and wave to the crowds as he moves along. The cars have retractable side and rear running boards that security officers can ride on and a wide seat behind the pope, where the bishop of the diocese he is visiting usually rides. The enclosure, which can be lit up for night motorcades, is completely removable or can be opened on the back or either side. During John Paul's U.S. visit the two popemobiles were leap-frogged by cargo plane so that one would always be waiting for him in the next city when he landed.

At Municipal Auditorium Catholic Charities workers and their guests were entertained by the Circle C Western band and singers Billy Davis Jr. and Marilyn McCoo while awaiting the pope's arrival. A highlight of John Paul's message was his stirring warning against "a very special and pitiable form of poverty: the poverty of selfishness, the poverty of those who have and will not share, of those who could be rich by giving but choose to be poor by keeping everything they have." He added: "Where the pursuit of wealth is treated as the supreme good, human beings become imprisoned in the hardening of their hearts and in the closing of their minds."

He praised the U.S. church for its strong tradition of "works of mercy, justice and compassion" carried out through "countless institutions and structures" to aid the sick, the poor, the needy, immigrants, orphans and others. "The Church

45

has always proclaimed a love of preference for the poor," the pope said.
"Perhaps the language is new, but the reality is not. Nor has the Church taken
a narrow view of poverty and the poor. Poverty, certainly, is often a matter
of material deprivation. But it is also a matter of spiritual impoverishment, the
lack of human liberties and the result of any violation of human rights and human
dignity."

In urging efforts to change unjust social structures, John Paul quoted ap-
provingly from the 1986 economy pastoral of the U.S. bishops, which said that
ultimately social change depends on personal conversion. "In the final analysis,"
the pope said, "we must realize that social injustice and unjust social structures
exist only because individuals and groups of individuals deliberately maintain
or tolerate them. It is these personal choices, operating through structures, that
breed and propagate situations of poverty, oppression and misery. For this
reason, overcoming 'social' sin and reforming the social order itself must begin
with the conversion of our hearts."

The pope particularly urged a life of "worship and prayer" as an essential
part of "generous service." "It is in prayer that the Church develops and evaluates
her social consciousness and unceasingly discovers anew her vocation to serve
the needy of the world, as Jesus did," he said.

Traveling again by popemobile with Flores beside him, on his way from
Municipal Auditorium to San Fernando Cathedral the pope passed the Alamo,
San Antonio's most famous landmark. Excited crowds lined the streets, up to
15 deep at some spots, to catch a glimpse of the pope and cheer him as he
went by.

At the cathedral the pope told seminarians that each of them is called to "embrace freely a celibate life for the sake of Jesus and his Kingdom.... If modeled
on the generous divine and human love of Jesus for his Father and for every
man, woman and child, your celibacy will mean an enhancement of your life,
a greater closeness to God's people, an eagerness to give yourself without
reserve." Celibacy is difficult because of human weakness, and "without prayer
it is impossible," he said. He told them that "the Eucharist is the principal reason
for the ordained priesthood" and "preaching the Gospel is of supreme importance." To minister effectively as priests, he said, seminarians must cultivate
"a deep love for the Eucharist" and "a deep understanding of the word of God
as it is lived and proclaimed by the Church.... Nourish in your own mind and
heart a real internal adherence to the magisterium of the Church."

Turning to candidates for religious life, he said that in their religious consecration they are called to "accept ever more generously the radical demands of
the Gospel and bear public witness to them." For this, he said, they need "the
habit and discipline of prayer," a strong "liturgical life," and regular use of the
sacrament of penance. After his discourse, when Hispanic seminarians and
religious candidates began to chant: "Juan Pablo Segundo, te quiere todo el
mundo" (John Paul II, everyone loves you), John Paul answered with a smile
that there are exceptions. When the applause and cries of "Viva el Papa" seemed
unending, the pope said with emotion, "I find myself in the United States, but
I could easily think I am in Mexico."

From the cathedral the pope went by popemobile to Our Lady of Guadalupe
Plaza, in front of the church of that name in a heavily Hispanic neighborhood
where crime and violence are commonplace. Delivering the only all-Spanish
talk of his U.S. visit, John Paul focused on the parish as a "family of families"
which depends upon its members for its life. He urged the members of parishes
to develop a strong catechetical, community, sacramental and prayer life. Noting
that Spanish was the language of the first evangelizers of the continent, he said
Hispanics today "must be no less zealous" in evangelization and Christian service than their predecessors. He appealed to Hispanic families to encourage
their young people to become priests, nuns and brothers. Behind the pope as
he spoke was a larger-than-life mural depicting Our Lady of Guadalupe, the

pope greeting San Antonians and churches of the city's west side. The mural was a project completed by inmates at the Bexar County Detention Center in San Antonio. John Paul concluded his talk with a wish that Our Lady of Guadalupe, patroness of the Americas, would "love and protect the Hispanic people of the land." "Viva la Virgen de Guadalupe," said the pope. "Viva! Viva el Papa!" the people shouted back.

Returning to Assumption Seminary, before retiring for the night the pope met on the seminary grounds with some 1,000 members of the Polish community of Texas. Among the group were residents of Panna Maria, about 65 miles south of San Antonio. Founded in 1854, Panna Maria is the oldest permanent Polish settlement in the United States. "Whenever we meet with Poles our thoughts go back to the old country — our hearts and minds go back to the old country," the Polish-born pontiff said. He led the group in singing a traditional Polish hymn to Our Lady of Czestochowa, the title by which Mary is known as patroness of Poland.

More than 16,000 journalists were accredited to cover the papal trip, and all wanted the same thing: closeup views of the pope as a person, inside information about his daily life. One of them — Richard C. Dujardin of the Journal-Bulletin, Providence, R.I. — was allowed to observe the pope at close range during the day he was in San Antonio and pass his observations along to the others. Here is some of what Dujardin learned:

—During airline flights, the flight attendants are so concerned about the pope's welfare that if they notice his eyes are closed at a time that they need to make an announcement over the speaker system, they won't make the announcement; instead they will go from seat to seat whispering the announcement to each passenger, such as "Please fasten your seat belt."

—The pope recites the breviary right after breakfast. It takes him about 40 minutes.

—He shaves the old-fashioned way: brush, cream and razor. No electric gadget for him.

—He is a light eater. His biggest meal of the day is likely to be breakfast, when he will have some fresh fruit and juice and perhaps a croissant or pastry. He will have some meats and greens at lunch. Dinner is apt to be simply a small bowl of consomme and a bit of cheese. When on one flight he was served lobster tail and filet mignon and on another, strip sirloin, he left most of the food on his plate.

—He is an avid reader. On a trip such as the current one, he will read as many as five books during flights and at night.

—Before Mass, he prefers to be alone rather than with those who will be concelebrating with him so that his total concentration can be on the liturgy he is about to celebrate.

At the conclusion of the Westover Hills Mass, Dujardin reported, aides tried to get John Paul into the air-conditioned popemobile for a ride to the rear of the altar. He resisted, walking instead and blessing the crowd. The reporter wrote: "The lines on his face are wet with perspiration. He looks into our eyes with the look of a runner determined to finish a marathon.... (Later) I ask the pope if he is tired. 'I don't know,' he says. 'I don't know.'" Vatican spokesman Navarro-Valls tells Dujardin the pope no doubt meant exactly what he said. "He is a man with a very strong sense of duty.... Extraordinary people who do extraordinary things do not know if they are tired because they are not looking at themselves."

36

36 *Yellow and white umbrellas help the bishops ward off the hot sun.*

37 *Singers Marilyn McCoo and Billy Davis Jr. meet the pope after entertaining the Catholic Charities meeting.*

38 *From the popemobile, Archbishop Patrick Flores points out a San Antonio attraction.*

39 *Pope John Paul II arrives for Mass at Westover Hills in San Antonio.*

40 *The pope is greeted by well-wishers at the San Fernando Cathedral.*

41 *The popemobile rolls past the historic Alamo.*

42 *The pope listens as he is introduced to the Hispanic audience.*

43 *At the cathedral the pope speaks to seminarians and others preparing for religious life.*

44 *Gathered at Our Lady of Guadalupe Plaza, the crowd welcomes the pope.*

45 *At Assumption Seminary, the pope speaks to about 1,000.*

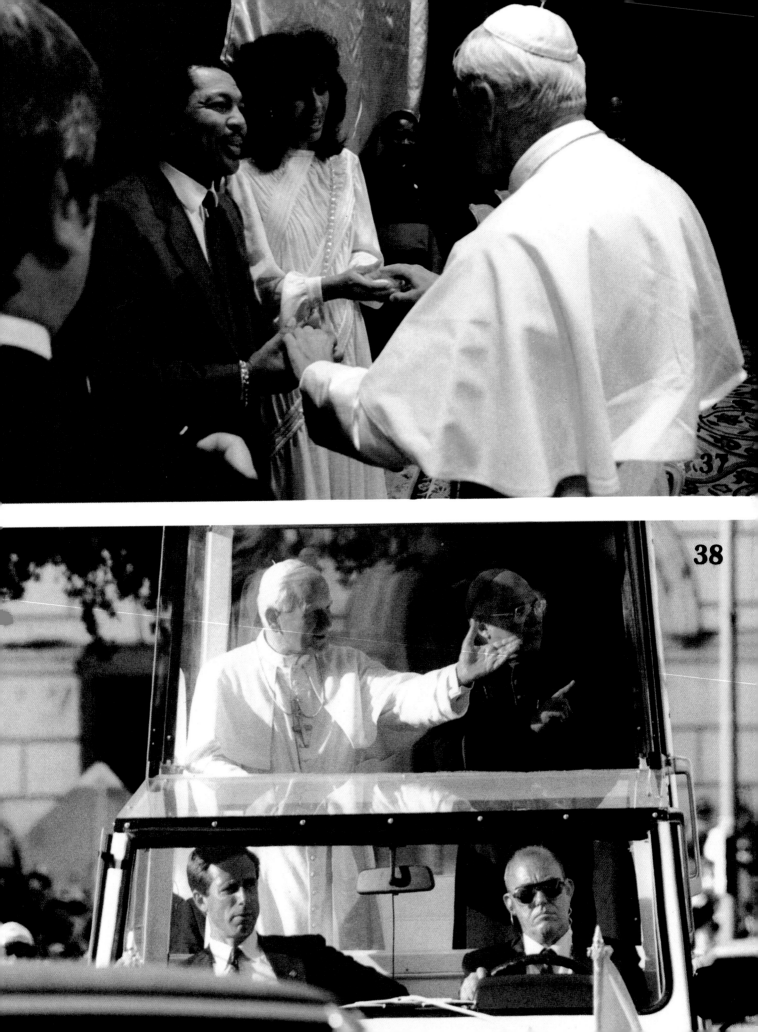

38

PHOENIX
September 14

O n his morning flight from San Antonio to Phoenix, John Paul spoke to the people of New Mexico as he flew over their state. Through a plane-to-ground transmission that was broadcast live on radio, he noted that "the Catholic faith has greatly influenced the history and culture of New Mexico." He cited the place names, many of them given by Spanish missionaries, such as Santa Fe (holy faith), the state's capital, and San Andreas and San Mateo mountains. He especially greeted the native Americans of the state, saying, "The ancient Indian dwellings which still remain today speak eloquently of the richness of your unique heritage. May you always preserve and draw strength from the worthy traditions which have been handed down to you from the past." The issue of inculturation, or bringing the Gospel to life within different cultural situations, was one that he would address in more detail later in the day.

The pope visited Phoenix to meet with native Americans, visit the sick, address Catholic health care workers, and celebrate Mass. No specific address to Phoenix's large Hispanic population was included in his stay. But the pope interspersed remarks in Spanish throughout his talks, and the Hispanic cultural influence was felt all day in song, dance and costume. In the Valley of the Sun, whose climate has made it a mecca for retirees and people with chronic illnesses, John Paul anointed the sick during Mass and preached on the importance of bearing sufferings with courage and faith. Despite earlier forecasts of temperatures up to 110 degrees, he met the mildest weather of his trip so far. Under cloudless skies the temperatures went into the low 90s, but without the humidity that had made the heat oppressive in Florida, South Carolina, Louisiana and Texas.

Arriving at Phoenix's Sky Harbor Airport at 8:36 a.m. after a two-hour flight, the pope went directly to Phoenix's only Catholic hospital, St. Joseph's, run by the Sisters of Mercy of Burlingame, Calif. There he held in his arms Brooke Johnson, a critically ill two-and-a-half-month-old baby who was born three months prematurely. He also visited Johnny Adrian, a 15-year-old boy with an inoperable brain tumor, whose mother Hope burst into tears as the pope blessed her child. And he visited with Issis "Lottie" Velasquez, a 6-year-old girl paralyzed from the neck down. He visited other children in the hospital's pediatrics ward, including 10 who were gathered in the playroom to meet him. He spent a few minutes chatting with Boguslawa Hyziak, a resident doctor who had been confirmed by the pope when she was a youth in Krakow and he was an auxiliary bishop there.

In his only impromptu remarks of the day, directed to hospital employees, he praised their work, saying that it is "an evangelical mission to heal the suffering and the sick and to assist them."

A 2.5-mile motorcade, which drew only a small percentage of the 400,000 spectators expected, took the pope to St. Mary's Basilica. John Paul prayed privately in the basilica with Phoenix Bishop Thomas J. O'Brien and St. Mary's pastor Father Warren Rouse. Then from the balcony between the basilica's twin Spanish-mission-style towers, the pope addressed the crowd gathered in the streets around the church. True human development, he told them, is for the good of the whole person, not merely for economic or material gain.

Echoing what has become a familiar theme for him, he said those better off must help the poor, locally, nationally and globally. He noted Arizona's "remarkable progress and development" in recent decades. "This brings with it increased obligations and responsibilities," he said. "By its very nature, true human advancement is necessarily outgoing; it cannot be concentrated on itself.... Any progress which would secure the betterment of a select few at the expense of the greater human family would be an erroneous and distorted progress. It would be an outrage against the demands of justice and an affront to the dignity of every human being." He quoted the words of Pope Paul VI, "Both for nations and for individuals, avarice is the most evident form of moral underdevelopment." John Paul's strong language in Phoenix was reminiscent of his Yankee Stadium speech in New York in 1979, when he called on Americans to give until it hurts to help the poor of the world.

John Paul gave a special greeting in Spanish to Hispanics and praised their "great strength, vitality and generosity." Before and after he spoke, the street in front of St. Mary's came alive with Spanish singing and dancing.

In a meeting with 2,200 representatives of the Catholic Health Association in the Phoenix Civic Plaza, John Paul decried the "great evil of abortion and euthanasia" and urged quality care for AIDS victims and the poor. He said Catholic health care ministry must defend "the inalienable dignity of every human being" and "reflect the mission of the Church as the teacher of moral truth." Part of that truth, he said, is the need to defend human life "from the moment of conception to the moment of natural death." He cited the Vatican's recent instruction on procreation issues as an example of the Church encouraging "genuine advances in knowledge" while insisting that such knowledge serve "the integral well-being of human persons" through responsible moral use. The instruction said the use of procreative technology is morally acceptable only if it does not involve techniques that separate procreation from the conjugal act, and if it respects the dignity of each new human being from conception.

The CHA address marked the first time that John Paul in a prepared speech had mentioned AIDS — acquired immune deficiency syndrome, a fatal disease often contracted through homosexual activity or heterosexual promiscuity. "Today you are faced with new challenges, new needs," he said. "One of these is the present crisis of immense proportions which is that of AIDS and AIDS-related complex. Besides your professional contribution and your human sensitivities toward all affected by this disease, you are called to show the love and compassion of Christ and his Church. As you courageously affirm and implement your moral obligation and social responsibility to help those who suffer, you are individually and collectively living out the parable of the good Samaritan."

Four days earlier, in response to questions from journalists during the flight aboard Shepherd I from Rome, the pope had addressed the linkage of AIDS with homosexuality. He said that homosexuals, especially AIDS victims, are not "outcasts" and their place is "in the heart of the Church." It is impossible to say if AIDS is God's punishment for homosexuals, he told the reporters. "It's not easy to know the intentions of God. He is justice. He is mercy. He is love."

Before the pope's speech, John E. Curley Jr., CHA president, told the pontiff of changes in health care that challenge Catholic institutions in the United States. He spoke of the challenges from advances in biomedical technology in an increasingly secular society. He also described the transition to more lay leadership in hospitals once run almost exclusively by religious orders, the problems of meeting the health-care needs of the elderly and the poor with limited resources, and the challenge that the movement toward national care systems poses as personnel try to keep a personal touch amid the "management maze."

From Civic Plaza John Paul went to Sts. Simon and Jude Cathedral to meet with priests, nuns and lay leaders of the Phoenix Diocese. He took the occasion to deliver a short but stirring appeal for missionaries to preach the Gospel. "The work of evangelization is not over. On earth, it will never be over," he said. "Indeed, so much remains to be done…. Missionary activity is a supremely great and sacred task of the Church. The duty of carrying forward this work rests on the whole Church and on every member." The pope praised the work of two early missionaries to Arizona, Jesuit Father Eusebio Kino and Franciscan Father Francisco Garces, saying the Church today "has need of many more missionaries" like them.

Although it was early afternoon, the two biggest events of the pope's stay in Phoenix were still to come. After lunch and a rest at O'Brien's residence, he had a 4:30 meeting with native Americans, where he would acknowledge the Church's "mistakes of the past" in suppressing native cultures, and a 6:30 Mass in Tempe, where he would anoint the sick and preach on the meaning of the cross.

His meeting with more than 10,000 native Americans representing some 200 tribes started nearly half an hour behind schedule because he arrived at Veterans Memorial Coliseum 20 minutes late and spent 10 minutes circling the center stage to shake hands with adults and kiss babies. The stage, which was built to rotate slowly as the pope spoke, featured an orange and turquoise altar and a massive carved and inlaid wooden chair, both made by Indian craftsmen. Emmett White, a Pima medicine man from the Gila River Reservation south of Phoenix, began the meeting by placing a charcoal fire in front of the pope, ceremonially blessing an eagle feather in the smoke, and presenting the feather to John Paul.

Coadjutor Bishop Donald E. Pelotte of Gallup, N.M., the country's only native American bishop, welcomed John Paul and urged the canonization of Blessed Kateri Tekakwitha, the 17th-century Mohawk convert who lived a vow of virginity despite tribal pressures to marry. She was declared venerable in 1953, and John Paul presided at her beatification in 1980. Tekakwitha has become a symbol of intertribal unity among U.S. Catholic Indians, who number about 285,000, or nearly a fifth of all native Americans. The tribal gathering in Phoenix to see the pope was an annual assembly of the Tekakwitha Conference.

After Pelotte came Alfretta M. Antone, a Pima Indian and vice president of the Salt River Pima-Maricopa Indian Community. She told the pope of the "abuse of our land" suffered by native Americans under waves of European immigration and the history of treaties broken by the U.S. government. She asked that the government give Indians the opportunity to determine their own political destiny and to "share in the social benefits of the Americas."

In his talk John Paul walked a narrow line. On the one hand he admitted the Church's "difficulties, and occasionally its blunders" in missionary efforts among native Americans. On the other hand he emphasized that during the "harsh and painful" period of white colonization there were "many missionaries who strenuously defended the rights of the original inhabitants of this land." He particularly praised Franciscan Father Junipero Serra, founder of the first missions in California, for his "frequent clashes with civil authorities over the treatment of Indians." Serra is a candidate for sainthood in the Church, but some critics accuse him of cruelty toward the Indians, saying he beat those who tried to leave his missions. The pope would defend Serra again, three days later, upon visiting his grave in Carmel, Calif.

John Paul used strong terms to condemn injustice and prejudice toward native Americans. "The cultural oppression, the injustices, the disruption of your life and of your traditional societies must be acknowledged," he said. "It is clear that stereotyping, prejudice, bigotry and racism demean the human dignity which comes from the hand of the Creator." But he asked his audience not to confuse those evils with the Gospel or the Church. "Your encounter with the Gospel has not only enriched you; it has enriched the Church," the pope said. In 1537, he recalled, when Europeans were first exploring the New World, "Pope Paul III proclaimed the dignity and rights of the native peoples of the Americas by insisting that they not be deprived of their freedom or the possession of their property."

The papal meeting with the native Americans ended with a brief Indian dance and the singing of the Our Father by Miles Brandon, an Innuit (Eskimo) who is a member of the Washington Opera Society. As Brandon sang, representatives of different tribes stationed around the stage said the prayer in sign language.

The Sun Devil had to go into hiding for the pope's final public event in Arizona, an evening Mass in Tempe, at Arizona State University's Sun Devil Stadium. Preparations for the liturgy included covering up images around the stadium of the horned, trident-carrying football mascot, because organizers thought his devilish visage an inappropriate backdrop to a Mass.

Another preparation for the Mass highlighted the tight security that accompanied the pope across the country. Between 2 p.m. and 4 p.m. the line of people trying to get into the stadium steadily grew, to an estimated two miles long, as metal detectors set up at the North Gate failed and security agents resorted to hand searches of all bags. As the line got longer, tempers grew shorter. When someone broke through a barricade, thousands followed suit and police had to move in quickly to restore control. The Secret Service finally resolved the problem by opening the stadium's South Gate as well and only checking the entrants visually.

Dominating the Mass site were a 70-foot cross of copper and steel and an 84-foot-wide cloth backdrop to the altar featuring a phoenix rising up from the mountains of Arizona. A legendary bird that rose again from its own ashes after it died, the phoenix has been adopted in Christian art as a symbol of Christ's resurrection. As the crowd of about 75,000 filled the stadium, dancers, singers and a mariachi band performed.

Celebrating the feast of the Triumph of the Cross, John Paul preached on "the mystery of the victory of the cross," contrasting the human and divine views of history's most significant public execution. "To be crucified, humanly speaking, is to be disgraced and humiliated," he said. "But from God's point of view it means being lifted up.... Christ is the Lord, and he becomes Lord of everything and everyone in this elevation by means of the cross." He said the anointing of the sick that would be celebrated immediately after the homily reflects the mystery of the cross "in a particular way and with a special power."

"This holy anointing does not prevent physical death nor does it promise a miraculous healing of the human body," he said. "But it does bring special grace and consolation to those who are dying, preparing them to meet our loving Savior with lively faith and love, and with firm hope for eternal life. It also brings comfort and strength to those who are not dying but who are suffering from serious illness or advanced age.... Every time the Church celebrates this sacrament, she is proclaiming her belief in the victory of the cross." The 25 people he anointed ranged from a 9-year-old Phoenix boy with cerebral palsy, to a 48-year-old police chief from Mesa paralyzed from the chest down by a car accident, to an 83-year-old Flagstaff woman with heart problems. Many of those being anointed or accompanying them wept as the pope went from person to person, laying his hands on their heads and making the sign of the cross on their foreheads and palms with the oil of the sick.

46

46 *To the delight of St. Joseph's Hospital workers, Pope John Paul II kisses 16-month-old Angelina Tsukas-Spiera.*

47 *Escorted by Bishop Thomas O'Brien, the pope blesses Brooke Johnson, who weighed only one pound at birth.*

48 *Pope John Paul II meets with representatives of the health care profession.*

49 *The pope pauses in the choir loft of St. Mary's Basilica.*

50 *At the Civic Plaza, the pope speaks to Catholic health care leaders.*

51 *Three generations of native Americans come to meet the Holy Father.*

52 *Bobby Guocaddle, a Kiowa from Shiprock, N.M., takes part in the celebration.*

53 *The pope acknowledges the crowd at the meeting with native Americans.*

54 *At the meeting with native Americans, the pope walks on traditional hand-crafted rugs.*

55 *Emmett White, a Pima Indian, presents the pope an eagle feather, a symbol of honor for many native American tribes.*

56 *The pope reads his message to the native Americans.*

57 *Two dancers wearing native costumes greet the pope.*

58 *This group of native Americans came all the way from Idaho to see the Holy Father.*

59 *The phoenix provides a dramatic backdrop for the Mass at Sun Devil Stadium.*

60 *The pope greets the faithful gathered for the Mass.*

61 *The pope incenses the altar.*

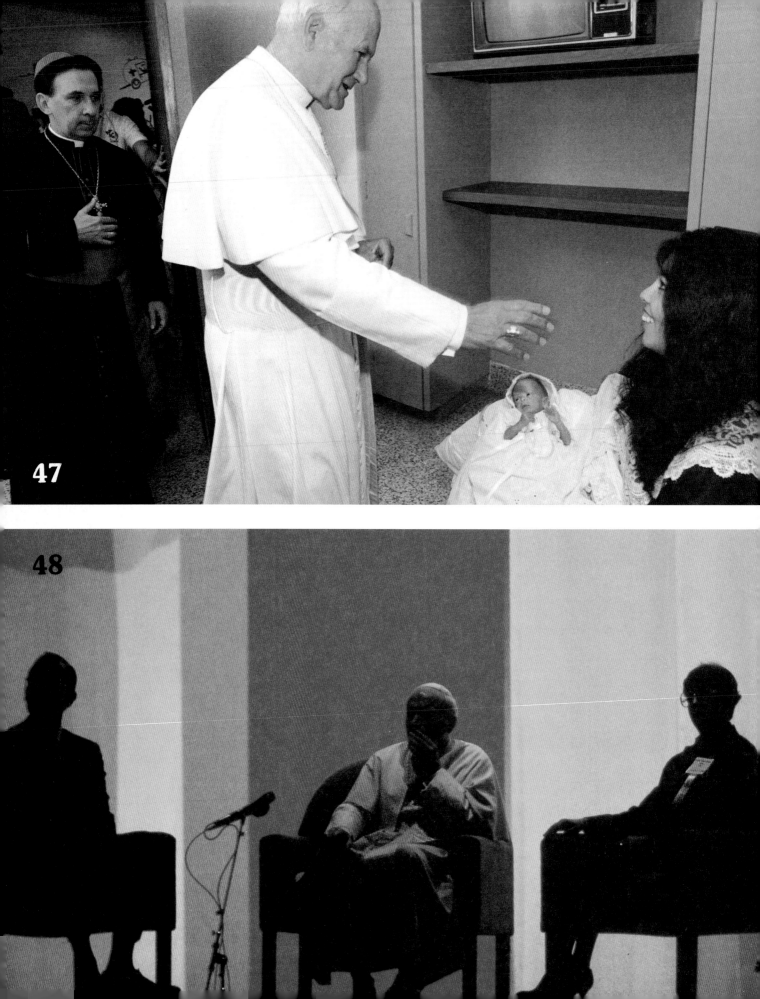

47

48

GIFT OF ...AS ...EILLY AND ...AMILY.

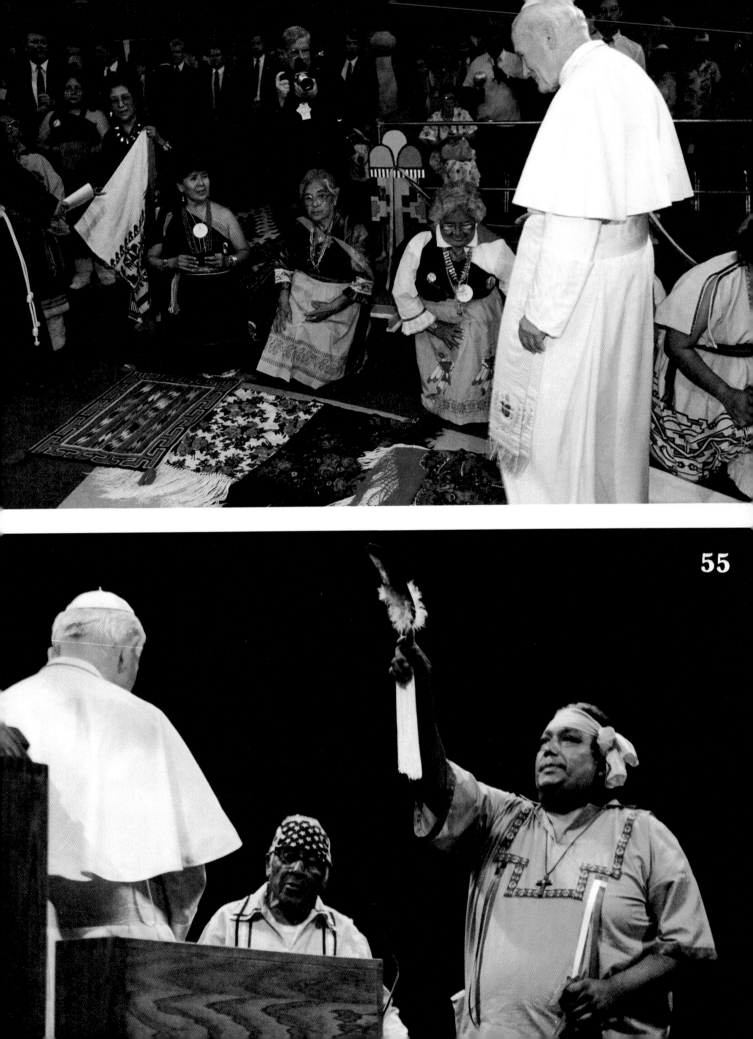

57

COEUR D'ALENE TRIBE
SACRED HEART MISSION
OF IDAHO
SINCE

ST. ANNE'S

58

59

60

LOS ANGELES
September 15-16

Los Angeles is a sprawling mega-city built around a network of clogged freeways. Its place names alone evoke a myriad of images: Beverly Hills, symbol of making it in America. Watts, the ghetto that exploded in 1965 in one of the worst race riots in U.S. history. Hollywood, world capital of mass entertainment and popular culture. Santa Monica, San Gabriel and San Fernando, memorializing the area's Spanish missionary history and perhaps reminding one of the tens of thousands of Hispanics, many undocumented, who call Los Angeles their home.

John Paul's 47-hour stay in the City of the Angels was almost as varied as the city. It was the longest (12 hours more than second-place New Orleans) and by far the most thematically diverse of any stop on his 10-day U.S. tour. He celebrated the city's racial and ethnic richness. He tenderly embraced a 25-year-old armless guitarist who played and sang for him. He visited with representatives of major non-Christian religions. He conducted a four-city teleconference with young people. And spoke to Hollywood stars and everyday journalists about the power of the communications media. And sat in a classroom with Nancy Reagan fielding questions from grade school students. And consecrated the United States to the Blessed Virgin Mary. And — in the most important event of his visit — dialogued, prayed and ate with the nation's bishops for more than five hours.

To get from Los Angeles International Airport to his first stop, St. Vibiana's Cathedral, a distance of nearly 22 miles through the city, the pope traveled first by limousine to the Western Avenue Fire Station. There he transferred to the by-now-familiar popemobile, with Los Angeles Archbishop Roger M. Mahony at his side, to ride the last seven miles in a motorcade. As in other cities, the crowds along the parade route fell far short of predictions. City officials had prepared for up to 2 million people. Actual crowd estimates, initially given as 500,000, were soon scaled down to 300,000. Those who did come enjoyed the balmy California weather as they waited.

At St. Vibiana's, John Paul's first message to Los Angelenos was on the countercultural nature of Catholic faith. To follow the Gospel in a secularized world often makes one "out of step with majority opinion" and sometimes an object of "opposition and even ridicule," he said in his late-morning meeting with archdiocesan priests, nuns and lay leaders. U.S. Catholics must give thanks for the religious liberty they enjoy, he said, but "freedom to follow your Catholic faith does not automatically mean that it will be easy to 'speak and act' in the name of the Lord Jesus with a conscience formed by the word of God authentically interpreted by the Church's teaching." He said his countercultural message was meant particularly for "young people who are trying to live a responsible moral life in the face of a tide of popular culture and peer pressure that is indifferent, if not hostile, to Christian morality."

After he blessed the group, someone in the congregation called out a blessing on him. "I thank you for this blessing," he answered with a smile. "It is true that all popes and bishops need special blessings from the people of God."

After lunch at Mahony's residence, the pope traveled by helicopter to Universal Amphitheater for a 75-minute encounter with young people of four cities. It was the first of seven helicopter rides he would take in Los Angeles, where officials feared that blocking off roads for extended surface trips could cause almost citywide gridlock.

One of John Paul's most noted talents is his ability to interact with groups of young people, and the youth teleconference in Los Angeles — billed as "'I Call You Friend' — Papal Spacebridge '87," — lived up to expectations. Besides the 6,000 youths gathered at Universal Amphitheater, there were another 2,000 at the Regency Hotel in Denver who greeted his televised appearance with deafening screams; 1,900 who applauded and waved banners at the TV image in St. Louis Cathedral, St. Louis; and an equally enthusiastic 3,000 gathered at the Civic Auditorium in Portland, Ore. In all four cities they cheered as he answered their questions, joked with them, praised acts of generosity, listened to their songs, and told them, "The future of the world shines in your eyes." The pope talked about teen suicide, about hope and about his own childhood. He said he always makes it a point on his trips to meet with young people. He fielded questions from both the Los Angeles audience and the three electronically linked sites.

In Denver, where youths waved signs at the pope with messages like "Come ski with us," Bobby and Vonnie Stransky, both 22 and married 15 months earlier, asked the pope about the vocations of married couples in the service of the Church. The pope told the couple that their most fundamental ministry was to be a "Christian new family." "It was the next best thing to talking to God," the young husband said afterward. "What he said gave us plenty to chew on. Our vocation in life is through our family. Having a family is where it starts."

In St. Louis mimes and dancers entertained the audience until the pope appeared. Chris Johnson, a high school student asked what motivated the pope to come to the United States now. "Ahh," John Paul responded. "Perhaps it means that I should not come?" After the chorus of "No" died away, he explained that Christ "wasn't always invited, but he went — he went."

In Portland, high school students prepared for the teleconference by working in soup lines, delivering food to shut-ins and painting a new St. Vincent de Paul building the previous Saturday. Their gift to the pope was a videotape of their volunteer work.

The high-energy meeting reached its emotional climax at the end, however, when Tony Melendez, an armless 25-year-old musician from Chino, Calif., played the guitar with his toes and sang "Never Be the Same," a wedding ballad composed by Ron Griffin.

After Melendez strummed the last soft chords, John Paul rose, leaped lightly off the 30-inch-high platform he was seated on, and walked over to Melendez' ministage a few feet away. He reached up, touched Melendez's legs, and motioned to the young, bearded musician to bend down. The pope pulled Melendez toward him and kissed him on the cheek.

"Awesome!" was Melendez' description of the moment afterwards. "I can't believe it. It was the highlight of my life." The music director of Our Lady of Guadalupe Parish in Chino, Melendez was born in Nicaragua without hands or arms and with a clubfoot. He was a victim of thalidomide, a drug commonly used as a sedative for pregnant women before its link to severe birth deformities was discovered in the 1960s. Melendez told reporters that no words were spoken during his encounter with the pope, but the din of the crowd would have drowned out any words anyway. "I really felt honored. Very, very honored," he said.

At the Registry Hotel half a mile from his meeting with young people, John Paul told an audience sprinkled with big-name entertainers that those who work in the performing arts, broadcasting, film or the printed word have the power to "build or destroy, uplift or cast down." If they "promote what is debased in people," they face the judgment of God and history, he said. He criticized programming which presents "dehumanized sex through pornography or through a casual attitude toward sex and human life; greed through materialism and consumerism or irresponsible individualism; anger and vengefulness through violence or self-righteousness." News organizations must "avoid any manipulation of truth," which occurs "when certain issues are deliberately passed over in silence, in order that others may be unduly emphasized," he said. "It also occurs when information is altered or withheld so that society will be less able to resist the imposition of a given ideology."

It was the first time the pope had addressed a major gathering of leaders in the U.S. communications industry, which he called "one of the most important American influences on the world today." Most of the 1,500 participants were in the entertainment business.

In the U.S. Constitution, John Paul said, "the same amendment that guarantees freedom of speech and freedom of the press also guarantees freedom of religious practice…. The Church recognizes the need for freedom of speech and freedom of the press, just as does your Constitution. But she goes further. Rights imply corresponding duties. The proper exercise of the right to information demands that the content of what is communicated be true and — within the limits set by justice and charity — complete." In a system protecting free expression, "your accountability to the community is not easily rendered juridically" so society must "rely on your good will," he said.

John Paul closed his first day on the West Coast with an evening Mass in Los Angeles Coliseum, where he warned that technology increases options for either good or evil, "but it is we who must choose."

The Mass's theme of suffering and the sorrow Mary felt at the foot of the cross seemed in sharp contrast to the lighthearted joy expressed by the 100,000 gathered in the stadium when they saw the pope. Faces in the congregation reflected the ethnic diversity of the Los Angeles Archdiocese, largest in the nation with an estimated 3 million Catholics. The rapidly growing Hispanic population forms at least half the Catholic population. Blacks, Vietnamese, Chinese and Japanese are only a few of the other substantial minorities in the archdiocese. As the pope entered the stadium, Mass-goers threw handkerchiefs into the air, waved flags and filled the air with cries of "Viva el Papa." Mahony acknowledged the large Hispanic presence as he welcomed the pope with the words, "Your Holiness, bienvenido a California." Although the pope spoke in English throughout the liturgy, some prayers and readings were in Spanish.

In his homily John Paul again stressed California's leading role in forming popular culture. "Today the people of California play a major role in shaping the culture of the United States, which has such a profound influence on the rest of the world," he said. "Your state also leads in research and technology designed to improve the quality of human life and to transcend the limitations which impede human freedom and progress." The Gospel is no enemy of progress, he added, "but neither does the paschal mystery allow us to run away from human sorrow and suffering."

Despite the beauty and prosperity surrounding them, the pope said, Californians could relate to Mary's sorrow and suffering. "All of us, in some way, experience sorrow and suffering in our lives." He asked Catholics to learn compassion by imitating Mary. "We must be the compassionate 'neighbor' of those in need, not only when it is emotionally rewarding or convenient, but also when it is demanding and inconvenient," he said. Compassion, he said, is needed in a world when many suffer poverty, hunger and disease and "oppression, deprivation and underdevelopment." In the United States, he added, compassion is also needed for those who enjoy material prosperity but suffer "spiritual emptiness and aimlessness."

The next day the pope spent all morning and part of the afternoon in a meeting with the U.S. bishops, but he filled the rest of the afternoon and the evening with a visit to a Los Angeles Catholic grade school, a meeting with non-Christian religious leaders, and a Mass in Dodger Stadium.

At Immaculate Conception school in downtown Los Angeles, Mrs. Reagan joined him in front of 20 sixth, seventh and eighth-grade students. John Paul talked about prayer and studies and fielded questions about himself. Mrs. Reagan warned them against drug abuse, with the pope seconding her remarks. "Drugs destroy everything the Holy Father loves and cherishes," she said.

"I have no speech prepared for you," the pope said. Instead, he asked them to ask him questions, as he had done with a group of Australian children when he visited there in 1986. He raised his hands in mock horror as almost all the children immediately raised their hands, clamoring for a chance to ask a question.

One student asked if he had ever thought he would become pope. John Paul said the thought never entered his mind when he entered the priesthood. "I did not aspire to this election" to the papacy, he said. He told students to pay attention in school because it is the stepping stone to being good Christians and good citizens. "You must collaborate with your teacher." He pointed to a smiling teacher behind the students. "It seems like your teacher is very satisfied with what I say." He paused when he noticed the anxiety of some students waiting to ask a question. "I speak too much?" he asked. After about 20 minutes, the pope rose from his seat and individually handed a rosary to each of the students. He then went to each of them again and kissed them.

After leaving the classroom John Paul spoke to the 300-member student body and the teachers and administrators on the importance of Catholic education. In a Catholic school students will learn "to know the difference between good and bad influences, and how important it is to avoid those things — such as use of drugs — which hurt yourselves and others and which give offense to God," he told the student body. "One of the most important things you can learn here is to pray: to speak to God, to express what is in your heart, to show your dependence on him."

From the school John Paul went to the Japanese Cultural Center, a little over two miles away, to meet with representatives of major non-Christian religions. Speaking of shared religious values, he encouraged interfaith dialogue and urged greater efforts for world peace by the world's religions. Spiritual values lead to "a common concern for man's earthly welfare, especially world peace," the pope said. "We have not always been peacemakers." World religions need to challenge "old divisions and social evils" in the world and take up "constant initiatives on behalf of the rights of individuals," he said.

In October 1986, John Paul had invited representatives of the world's religions to gather with him in Assisi, Italy, to pray for world peace. He and others who spoke recalled that event as a symbol of advances already made in interreligious cooperation and a reference point for future relations.

With Los Angeles representatives of Buddhism, Hinduism, Islam and Judaism before him, the pope said, "The Catholic Church remains firmly committed to the proclamation of the Gospel and to dialogue with people of other religions." Such dialogue, he added — quoting from his address at the Assisi meeting — "does not imply any intention of seeking a religious consensus among ourselves or of negotiating our faith convictions.... Nor is it a concession to relativism in religious beliefs, because every human being must sincerely follow his or her upright conscience with the intention of seeking and obeying the truth."

73

John Paul also praised the individual religions represented. He commended the "compassion and loving kindness" and the "yearning for peace, prosperity and harmony for all beings" that followers of Buddha profess. To Moslems he said: "I share your belief that mankind owes its existence to the one, compassionate God who created heaven and earth." He singled out the Hindu religion's "concern for inner peace and for the peace of the world, based ... on self-purification, unselfishness, love and sympathy for all."

To Jews he recalled the belief Christians share with them in God's revelation in the Old Testament. Reiterating a theme he struck at his meeting with Jewish leaders in Miami five days earlier, he said, "I oppose every form of anti-Semitism. May we work for the day when all peoples and nations may enjoy security, harmony and peace."

John Paul closed his talk by reciting the prayer of St. Francis of Assisi, "universally recognized as a man of peace." He said St. Francis' prayer to be a man of peace, love, pardon, faith, hope, light and joy "expresses my sentiments in meeting with all of you."

In introductory remarks, Buddhist leader Dr. Havanpola Ratanasara praised the pope's world moral leadership. "Your Holiness has visited a number of trouble spots at the risk of your own life, with the hope of bringing back sanity among warring parties. This gesture of Your Holiness is appreciated by the Buddhist community," he said. "Let us urge for peace with a more vigorous voice, with more vigorous actions and with more vigorous speed," he added, calling for religious people to "be the active, unresting conscience of the world." Ratanasara said the Vatican II document on Church relations with other religions "influenced the attitude of the various religious communities," fostering interfaith cooperation not only with the Catholic Church but among themselves.

The Moslem spokesman, Dr. Maher Hathout, called the participants in the interreligious gathering "glimpses of hope" in an era of unprecedented dangers and suffering "when half the world denies God and most of the other half disobeys him."

Swami Swahananda, representing the Hindu community, said many groups work for peace for reasons of "expediency and self-interest and survival of man," but religion adds "a more basic appeal, for it speaks of self-sacrifice and love." John Paul's efforts to engage religious leaders of all faiths in promoting peace "have endeared him to all," Swahananda said.

Rabbi Alfred Wolf repeated pleas of fellow Jews earlier in Miami, asking for help in the struggle against anti-Semitism and world acceptance of the state of Israel. He told the pope that at the Assisi gathering "you taught the world that we need not set aside our particular beliefs and traditions to unite for a universal task." Wolf asked John Paul to treat Assisi as a beginning and "continue to lead us toward a time when the world's religions will not only pray for peace between the nations but will live in peace with each other, a 'United Religions,' a guide and model for a real and effective United Nations."

For the third day in a row John Paul concluded his public day with a Mass in a sports stadium — this time Dodger Stadium, where more than 300 bishops from around the country joined him at the altar before a congregation of 57,000 people.

Croatian, Japanese and Polish folk dancers, a Vietnamese choir and black gospel singers were among those who took to the stage in native costume during a colorful 90 minutes of pageantry prior to the Mass. In recognition that it was Mexican Independence Day, the crowds cheered vigorously as Aztec dancers and Mexican mariachis entertained before the pontiff's arrival. Both English and Spanish were used in the Mass.

In his homily John Paul commended the bishops "for your active collaboration in helping several million undocumented immigrants to become legal residents. This pastoral care of the immigrant in our own day reflects the love of Christ in the Gospels and the legitimate work of the Church in carrying on the challenge of the Lord: 'I was a stranger and you welcomed me.'" U.S. Catholic dioceses, with Los Angeles in the lead, were in the midst of a massive, nationwide effort to help legalize illegal aliens during the one-year amnesty established by the 1986 immigration reform law. John Paul called California a "haven for immigrants" and Los Angeles "the new major point of entry for the latest waves of immigrants." It is a place, he said, where people from every continent have come together to "fashion a society of the most varied ethnic diversity."

"Today in the church in Los Angeles, Christ is Anglo and Hispanic, Christ is Chinese and black, Christ is Vietnamese and Irish, Christ is Korean and Italian, Christ is Japanese and Filipino, Christ is native American, Croatian, Samoan, and many other ethnic groups," he declared, his words punctuated by cheers from the ethnic groups he mentioned. With all its diverse membership, he said, the Church remains the "one body of Christ, professing the same faith, united in hope and in love." That is what makes the Church "truly catholic in the fullest sense," he added. "This unity does not at all erase diversity. On the contrary, it develops it."

While the Church welcomes all cultures and promotes what is good in them, he said, "at the same time, there must be no betrayal of the essential truth" of the Gospel and Church teachings. "The Church faces a particularly difficult task in her efforts to preach the word of God in all cultures in which the faithful are constantly challenged by consumerism and a pleasure-seeking mentality, where utility, productivity and hedonism are exalted while God and his law are forgotten. In these situations ... the Church's witness must be unpopular. She must take a clear stand on the word of God."

At the end of the Mass, John Paul entrusted the entire U.S. church to the Virgin Mary. He has made such acts of consecration in many of the countries he has visited. In this case the dedication came during the Marian year which the pope opened in June and planned to conclude on Aug. 15, 1988.

In his prayer the pope entrusted "all the faithful of this land" to Mary, but he singled out for special mention some, such as families, women, youths, the elderly and the poor and needy. "In particular I entrust to you the families of America, in their quest for holiness, in their struggle against sin, in their vocation to be vital cells in the body of Christ," he said.

He also entrusted to Mary "all the women in the Church and the cause of their true human advancement in the world and their ever fuller participation in the life of the Church, according to the authentic plan of God." He asked that women discover in Mary the "secret of living totally their femininity in fulfillment, progress and love."

The role of women, one of the most controversial issues in the U.S. Catholic Church in the 1980s, had also occupied the pope's thoughts that morning, when he told the country's bishops that the Church promotes the advancement of women and their full equal dignity with men, but this does not change their exclusion from ordained priesthood. He returned to the theme of women in the Church two days later in San Francisco where, speaking on Catholic laity, he said that "the special gifts of women are needed in an ever-increasing measure" in the Church's life. On the plane from Rome to Miami, when a reporter asked if the Church should allow women priests, he said supporters of women's ordination should read what Vatican II said about Mary in its Constitution on the Church. The document's final chapter is devoted to Mary. It makes no reference to the ordination issue, which emerged as a major controversy only after the council. It describes Mary as "a wholly unique member of the Church," the Church's "outstanding model in faith and charity," and the pre-eminent "exemplar both of virgin and mother."

62 Well-wishers greet the pope after he arrives at Los Angeles International Airport.

63 Armless guitar player Tony Melendez of Chino, Calif., plays a song with his feet at the pope's teleconference with youth.

64 The pope receives an enthusiastic greeting from the youth assembled at the Universal Amphitheater.

65 It is a moving moment for all when the pope gives Tony Melendez a kiss for his gift of a song.

66 The pope speaks with a youth during the teleconference linking three U.S. cities with Los Angeles.

67 Accompanied by Lou Wasserman, the pope meets actors Patty Duke, Bob Hope and Charlton Heston at the meeting with communications leaders.

68 A crowd of more than 100,000 fills the Coliseum for the Mass.

69 Children in costumes from countries of their ancestry add to the colorful celebration.

70 The pope arrives for the Mass.

71 The pope elevates the chalice during the consecration.

72 In a classroom, the pope and Mrs. Reagan listen to questions from students.

73 Outside the school, the pope talks with young children.

74 The pope listens to one of the four speakers at his meeting with non-Christian religious leaders.

75 John Carlos Lothian passes out flowers to the participants.

76 The pope delivers his message to those gathered for the meeting.

77 Showing the ethnic diversity at the Mass, a dancer waits to perform.

78 Jennifer Webber and youths from Claremont, Calif., entertain with hoops prior to the Mass at Dodger Stadium.

79 Bishops process to the altar at the beginning of the Mass.

80 A tired Ruth McNamara gets a lofty view of the pope from the shoulders of her father, Dominic, of Maynooth, Ireland.

81 One woman shows her enthusiasm as the pope appears.

82 A baby brings a smile to the pope.

83 Dressed in red, the pope sits during a quiet moment of the Mass.

63

68

THE
BISHOPS
September 16

John Paul's meeting with the bishops of the United States took place behind closed doors, but it gave Americans an unprecedented chance to compare the pope's views with those of the bishops because the texts of the formal presentations were made public. The pope forthrightly condemned dissent from Church teachings — both in theory and in practice — and reiterated oft-stated stands against ordination of women as priests and the use of contraception. There was also a notable omission in the pope's talk. He said nothing about two major projects of the U.S. bishops in the 1980s — their pastoral letters on peace and on the U.S. economy — despite references to the pastorals or the teaching role of the bishops' conference by three of the four bishops who spoke to him.

In the three-hour formal exchange that formed the heart of the meeting, the pope addressed a wide range of issues. He urged the bishops to continue their work against abortion and to maintain the Catholic character of the nation's Catholic colleges and universities. He asked them to uphold Church teaching on divorce and remarriage, on homosexuality, and on parents' rights in sex education. He called for enforcement of Church discipline restricting the use of general absolution. He praised efforts to promote natural family planning as an alternative to contraception, and urged direct episcopal support for such programs in all dioceses. He called for more prayer and work for vocations to the priesthood and religious life. He strongly supported the bishops' efforts to promote respect for the dignity of human life at every stage and in every situation. He encouraged the advancement of women in Church and society, while stipulating that this cannot include ordination. And he questioned how effectively U.S. Catholics are using their high educational achievements to advance Christian principles in U.S. social and cultural values.

At least 320 of the nearly 400 bishops in the United States traveled to Los Angeles to meet with John Paul. They started their meeting at 9 o'clock with morning prayer at Mission San Fernando, the beautifully reconstructed church marking one of the original missions along the California coast that were founded by Junipero Serra and other California missionaries. In a brief homily during the prayer service the pope said he and the bishops needed "to be for our people a living sign of Jesus Christ." This, he said, meant that bishops must be prayerful, compassionate, loving with "a love which is stronger than sin and death," servants like the Good Shepherd, and faithful to God "and therefore like Christ a sign of contradiction."

From Mission San Fernando the pope and bishops moved next door to Our Lady Queen of the Angels High School Seminary to meet in the students' dining room. For 45 minutes John Paul moved among the bishops, shaking hands with them and chatting informally in a cordial, friendly atmosphere. Archbishop May, as president of the bishops' conference, opened the formal meeting with a brief address welcoming the pope and presenting the four bishops who would speak to him on behalf of the conference. May thanked John Paul for the "pastoral zeal" he shows with his "worldwide pastoral visits" and for "the generous period of time you are giving to this visit with us."

Cardinal Bernardin led off for the bishops, speaking on relations between local churches and the universal Church. The three other speakers were Archbishops John R. Quinn of San Francisco, speaking on moral teaching; Rembert G. Weakland of Milwaukee, on U.S. laity; and Daniel E. Pilarczyk of Cincinnati, on vocations to the priesthood and religious life. The four bishops and their topics had been chosen by their fellow bishops earlier in the year. In June they had submitted their prepared presentations to the Vatican, so that the pope and his aides would have time to study them and prepare the pope's response. John Paul broke his speech into four parts which he delivered separately, one in response to each bishop's presentation.

Bernardin emphasized that U.S. Catholics "live in an open society where everyone prizes the freedom to speak his or her own mind." Because of America's tradition of freedom, many Americans "almost instinctively react negatively when they are told that they must do something, even though in their hearts they may know they should do it," he said. "As a result, the impression is sometimes given that there is a certain rebelliousness in many American Catholics, that they want to 'go it alone.' " One result is that when the Vatican reaffirms traditional Church teaching "it is sometimes accused of retrogression." On the other hand, when a U.S. Catholic "questions how a truth might be better articulated or lived today, he or she is sometimes accused of rejecting the truth itself or portrayed as being in conflict with the Church's teaching authority," the Chicago prelate added. "As a result, both sides are sometimes locked into what seem to be adversarial positions. Genuine dialogue becomes almost impossible."

"The practical question that must be addressed today," Bernardin said, is how to maintain both unity and diversity, "how to discern a proper balance between freedom and order." He said that "there are bound to be misunderstandings and tensions at times," but that "tension in itself need not be debilitating or destructive." The nation's bishops, he added, are particularly pained "when we are cast in an adversarial position with the Holy See or with certain groups within our own dioceses." He called for "much greater trust" in the presence of the Holy Spirit throughout the Church. He asked for an atmosphere in which dialogue among the bishops themselves and between the bishops and the Holy See could take place "in complete candor, without fear.... In such a mutual exchange — conducted with objectivity, honesty and openness — we can discern what will truly enhance the Church's unity and what will weaken or destroy it."

Bernardin also praised the pope's "extraordinarily generous and effective" efforts to support and strengthen Catholics and their bishops around the world "in their understanding and acceptance of the legacy given to us by the Lord himself," even though "at times you are misunderstood; some allege that you do not understand the actual situation in which the Church finds herself in the different parts of the world today." He said the majority of U.S. Catholics "have a deep faith and accept the Church as described in the conciliar documents." Fuller and more open sharing would benefit both U.S. Catholics and the whole Church, he suggested. "The church in the United States has much to contribute to the universal Church. I am thinking, for example, of our role in the development of the documents on religious freedom and ecumenism of the Second Vatican Council. But how much we have to learn from the universal Church, whose experience touches *every corner of the world and reaches back for 20 centuries!"*

As he drew to a close, Bernardin made a plea for recognition of the role of the National Conference of Catholic Bishops in the life of the church in the United States. It is a role that has been criticized by Cardinal Joseph Ratzinger, head of the Congregation for the Doctrine of the Faith. Ratzinger takes the position, as he put it in a 1984 interview, that national conferences "have no theological basis, they do not belong to the structure of the Church, as willed by Christ, that cannot be eliminated; they have only a practical, concrete function....It happens that with some bishops there is a certain lack of a sense of individual responsibility, and the delegation of his inalienable powers as shepherd and teacher to the structures of the local conference leads to letting what should remain very personal lapse into anonymity."

Bernardin made no direct mention of Ratzinger's views on the role of bishops' conferences or on his equally strong views against dissent. But Bernardin candidly commented that it "is ... painful" for bishops to be "cast in an adversarial position with the Holy See" over handling dissent. His emphasis was different from Ratzinger's, however, when he told the pope that "we must affirm and continue to grow in our appreciation of the conciliar vision of collegiality as both a principle and a style of leadership in the Church. Here in the United States our national conference has been a visible expression of that collegiality. It has served to enhance the pastoral role of each bishop precisely because it provides a framework and a forum for us to share ideas, to teach and elucidate sound Catholic doctrine, set pastoral directions and develop policy positions on contemporary social issues. I believe that we are learning how to balance this dimension of collegiality with the collegiality of the bishops of the universal Church in union with you as head of the episcopal college."

In his response to Bernardin, John Paul gave strong emphasis to the "vertical dimension" of the Church's one faith and union with Rome, warning against an overemphasis on its "horizontal dimension." He stressed the "'global' service" of the successor of Peter "as belonging already to the essence of each particular church from 'within.'" In comments on collegiality interspersed through his response, he spoke only of the collegiality of the worldwide body of bishops in union with Rome. He made no reference to the bishops' conference as an expression of collegiality or to its practical role, as described by Bernardin, in assisting individual bishops in their pastoral, doctrinal and public policy leadership.

In warning against too "horizontal" a view of the Church, John Paul said, "The 'vertical dimension' of ecclesial communion is of profound significance in understanding the relationship of the particular churches to the universal Church." Where Bernardin said that "secular models" are certainly inadequate for understanding local-universal Church relations but nevertheless helpful, John Paul only stressed their inadequacy. "It is important to avoid a merely sociological view of this relationship," he said, adding that "this universal Church cannot be conceived as the sum of the particular churches, or as a federation of particular churches." The term "particular church" in Catholic theology refers to the faithful of a diocese gathered around their local bishop in union with Rome.

On the role of bishops as moral teachers, Quinn told John Paul that in a changing and questioning society the U.S. bishops "cannot fulfill our task simply by an uncritical application of solutions designed in past ages for problems which have qualitatively changed or which did not exist in the past." There are "critical new realities" confronting the church in the U.S. which bishops and moral theologians are trying to deal with, Quinn said. Among these he cited the U.S. position as "a major military power in the world," the "pervasive divorce and family instability," the permissive climate brought about by "the sexual revolution," and the "immensely high standard of living" of Americans. He also spoke of the moral challenges raised by "the development of new medical technologies" and by the acceptance of medicine as "a destroyer of human life through widespread abortion."

Church reflection on human nature and morality is also challenged by the advance of "psychological and sociological" insights into "the nature of human sexuality and of the human emotional life" and by "the dramatically altered and changing social status of women with its concomitant impact on personal meaning and social identity," Quinn said. The church in the United States must also deal with "the increased, widespread high level of education among American Catholics and its impact on their understanding of and expectations about their role in the Church," he said.

"Our constant effort as pastors to focus the moral tradition of the Church faithfully on these complex and rapidly changing issues is a source of tremendous difficulties," said the San Francisco archbishop. "We accept the great transcendent moral imperatives of the Gospel and the Church's perennial teaching. We recognize our grave obligation to teach courageously and bear witness to the whole, and not just part, of the Gospel, even in the face of ridicule and opposition. At the same time ... moral theology must respond to these new human realities in a manner which at once reflects what newness there is in these issues, the legitimate development of the human sciences, the enduring nature of the human person, the tradition of moral wisdom in the Church and the absolute claims of the Gospel."

He said the Church needs "to lay new foundations for a critical mediation of the moral tradition in a transformed cultural and social context." That effort, he added, has to involve careful consultation with educated Catholics and dialogue with moral theologians in order to fulfill the Church's teaching office. "Dialogue and discussion, of course, are never a substitute for the decisions of the magisterium" but they are an "indispensable" part of formulating it, he said.

Among "remarkable" examples of the Church's efforts to deal effectively with moral issues raised in new ways, Quinn cited the U.S. bishops' national pastoral letters on war and peace in 1983 and on the U.S. economy in 1986 as well as several Vatican documents on moral issues in recent years.

It was in response to Quinn's talk that John Paul denounced widespread dissent in practice from Church moral teachings. He noted reports "that a large number of Catholics today do not adhere to" or "are selective in their adherence to" Church teachings on "sexual and conjugal morality, divorce and remarriage ... (and) abortion." "It is sometimes claimed," the pope said, "that dissent from the magisterium is totally compatible with being a 'good Catholic' and poses no obstacle to the reception of the sacraments. This is a grave error that challenges the teaching office of the bishops of the United States and elsewhere."

Addressing the issue of dissent on the theoretical or intellectual level, John Paul urged the U.S. bishops to dialogue with theologians "to show the inacceptability of dissent and confrontation as a policy and method in the area of Church teaching." The Church, he said, "is a community of faith. To accept faith is to give assent to the word of God as transmitted by the Church's authentic magisterium." For Catholics, "theological discussion takes place within the framework of faith," he added, and theological dissent "may not be proposed or received on an equal footing with the Church's authentic teaching" or "proposed as a basis for pastoral practice."

Noting that Quinn had referred to the need for conversion of both mind and heart in the faith life of people, John Paul said that "throughout the length and breadth of the Church there is need today for a new effort of evangelization and catechesis directed to the mind," especially in forming young people to be Catholic "in terms of doctrine and thought.... Here the Catholic press can make a magnificent contribution to raising the general level of Catholic thought and culture." Evangelization of culture, he said, also requires sound intellectual formation in seminaries, in "continuing education programs for priests,

Religious and laity," and in the country's Catholic colleges and universities. "Much is already being done, and I take the opportunity to encourage you to seek ways of intensifying these apostolates."

The pope's blunt rejection of dissent as a way of thinking or acting in the Church was the main topic of questions at a news conference following the meeting. Pilarczyk, as vice president of the NCCB, fielded questions. As conference president, May was scheduled to appear before the news media as well, but the meeting between the pope and the bishops ran late and May was seated alongside the pope for lunch, making it impossible for him to leave in time for the news conference.

The pope "is not saying that those who do not accept all the teaching are out of the Church," Pilarczyk said. He interpreted the pope's words to mean that there is what he called a "problem" for a person "who realizes the full import of a Church teaching ... and chooses freely and knowingly to disregard that." "The Holy Father, I think, wants to be very careful to underline the fact that Catholic teaching is not a kind of grocery store where Catholics are free to take what they want and not take what they want," he said. Several reporters asked what were the implications for people like married couples practicing artificial birth control, in violation of Church teaching, when the pope said that dissent from moral teachings can pose an "obstacle to reception of the sacraments." Pilarczyk repeatedly stressed that the issue was a pastoral one and could not be answered in the abstract. He therefore didn't answer the question directly. He limited himself to describing various states of conscience — erroneous, malformed, etc. — and to saying that such a matter would have to be considered in each case individually, dealing with the state of conscience of the persons involved and solved in a confessional or counseling situation. "The status of Church teaching is the same this afternoon as it was this morning (before the pope spoke)," he said.

He said the pope spoke in a "straightforward, unambiguous way" to the bishops but was not telling bishops "to go home and raise general Cain" with Catholics who disobey or disagree with some Church teachings. He also denied suggestions from some reporters that the pope was showing displeasure with American Catholics or the U.S. bishops with his remarks. "I don't think the tone of that interpretation is correct. I don't think he is displeased with our country." There is "a gap" between the church in the U.S. and Rome in the sense that "in every country, the Church has a different flavor, its own culture, its own mindset," Pilarczyk added. "That's what being a Church incarnate means. But we are not dealing with a big face-off here."

The Cincinnati archbishop described the meeting as "very cordial, very warm" and "a very moving experience" for himself and the other bishops. Asked if he was not concerned about Catholics leaving the Church over some of its teachings, he said, "Of course I am concerned — but the fact that I am concerned does not mean that I will change Church teaching to keep them coming." Translating the theological language of the issue into more earthy metaphors, he said if people need meat and potatoes in their diet, he would not give them oatmeal instead. "I'm going to give them meat and potatoes, even if it gives some of them indigestion." The pope's message on dissent, he said, was that "you cannot in good conscience pick and choose and then sit back and say everything is the same as before."

Summarizing in broadest terms the pope's comments on whether one can dissent and be a good Catholic, the archbishop said, "Is it OK to dissent from non-infallible Church teaching? No, it's not OK. If I dissent, am I therefore out of the Church? I don't think the pope said that." To a suggestion that the pope was calling for a "more conservative, more controlling" approach from the bishops, Pilarczyk said, "I don't think so." The pope said that unpopular Church teachings must still be taught, he said, but "the Church has always taught unpopular truths."

Weakland, third bishop to address the pope, spoke about Catholic laity in the United States, with special reference to women. He told John Paul that there are more well-educated Catholics in the United States than in any other country in the world. With their higher social, educational and professional achievements, he said, U.S. Catholics today often have scientific or other professional expertise in fields that Church teaching touches on. "The faithful are more inclined to look at the intrinsic worth of an argument proposed by the teachers in the Church than to accept it on the basis of the authority itself," he said. "This demands a new kind of collaboration and a wider range of consultation on the part of the teaching office of the Church.... An authoritarian style is counterproductive." He also stressed the desire of U.S. Catholics "to contribute their skills and knowledge to the life and growth of the Church."

Women in particular are eager to contribute more, Weakland said. "There are no words to explain so much pain on the part of so many competent women today who feel they are second-class citizens in a Church they love.... They seek a Church where the gifts of women are equally accepted and appreciated." He told the pope that "even if women are not called" to ordained priesthood, "you rightly point out the role of Mary herself as an exemplar (for women in the Church today). Women today want to reclaim that scriptural sense of co-discipleship."

The Milwaukee archbishop briefly noted significant problems in U.S. Catholicism, such as widespread divorce, consumerism and waste, and a tendency toward fundamentalism. But he said that U.S. Catholics also show a renewed sense of Scripture in their lives and are involved in a variety of social concerns and spiritual renewal movements. He called the challenge of moral leadership in an affluent and internationally powerful society a major concern that the U.S. bishops tried to address in their economy and peace pastorals.

The pope responded that the "major achievement" of high-level U.S. Catholic education, which he attributed to decades of effort by Catholic schools, "offers great promise and potential." But he asked whether American Catholics are using their talents and skills to build a culture "influenced by the Gospel." In that area he particularly encouraged the bishops' work to promote family values. He quoted extensively from Paul VI praising the efforts by American bishops to build a comprehensive ethic of human life and human dignity, "to oppose whatever wounds, weakens or dishonors human life" and "to proclaim in practice that all aspects of human life are sacred."

In discussing "the advancement of women" at the conclusion of his response, John Paul said that "the aim of all the Church's efforts on behalf of women" is "to promote their human dignity." He said that "the personal dignity of women as women — a dignity equal to that of men's dignity" — must be affirmed "even before consideration is given to any of the special and exalted roles fulfilled by women as wives, mothers or consecrated women." All Church consideration of women must be based on "two firm principles: the equal human dignity of women and their true feminine humanity," the pope said.

He reaffirmed the Catholic Church's position that "women are not called to the priesthood," adding: "Although the teaching of the Church on this point is quite clear, it in no way alters the fact that women are indeed an essential part of the Gospel plan to spread the good news of the kingdom. And the Church is irrevocably committed to this truth."

Pilarczyk was the last bishop to address the pope. Speaking on vocations, he framed his speech in the classic format of Scholastic theology: "Quaeritur ... Et videtur quod sit ... Sed contra ... Respondeo ..." (The question is raised ... And so it would seem ... But on the other hand ... My answer is ...)

The question he asked was "Whether the ministry of the Church in the United States is in a state of turmoil and crisis." After weighing the evidence on both sides of the argument, he concluded, "Affirmative, but it is not the turmoil and crisis of death and decay, but of development and of life."

Favoring the "turmoil and crisis" argument, Pilarczyk noted the statistics showing a decline in religious vocations and a drop in the ratio of priests to Catholics over the past quarter century. As further evidence he cited several other factors, such as an "increasingly secular" society and widespread questioning of the Church's discipline of priestly celibacy and its teaching on ordination of women. "Certain aspects of our present situation are a source of great anxiety for us bishops," he said.

But there are many hopeful signs in the country as well, such as expanded lay ministries, "a broadening of the concept of Church vocation and ministry," the growth of the permanent diaconate, new appreciation of religious life, growing awareness of the need for evangelization and the growth of spiritual renewal programs throughout the Church, Pilarczyk said. "I believe that the Holy Spirit is hard at work among the dioceses and parishes of our country ..., that Catholic people in our country have available to them a depth and variety of ministry in the Church far greater than ever before," he said.

John Paul called it "indeed encouraging to note how lay people in ever-increasing numbers have become involved in the life of the Church." He said he hoped the world Synod of Bishops coming up in Rome in October, which was devoted to the topic of the laity, would "give fresh impetus to this participation and solid direction for its continued growth and consolidation." The pope stressed that priestly and lay ministry "are not at all opposed to one another. On the contrary, the one complements the other. Just as the priestly ministry is not an end in and of itself, but serves to awaken and unify the various charisms within the Church, so too the involvement of the laity does not replace the priesthood, but supports it, promotes it and offers it space for its own specific service."

As he had six days earlier in talking with priests in Miami, the pope stressed the need to pray for priestly and religious vocations and actively recruit them. He made no explicit mention of sentiment among some U.S. Catholics for resolving the clergy shortage through relaxed rules on priestly celibacy or women priests or by returning married priests to active ministry. That seemed the evident point of reference, however, when he said that on the one hand the Church must use "prudence and pastoral realism" in assessing the situation, but "at the same time we know that today, as always, there are 'prophets of doom.' We must resist them in their pessimism, and continue in our efforts to promote vocations." "The basis of our hope" in looking at the prospect of future vocations, he said, "is the power of Christ's paschal mystery.... He is strong enough to attract young men even today" to the priesthood.

Near the end of his final response John Paul broke from the structure of responding to the themes of the four papers and briefly took up issues of general absolution, sex education and pastoral care of homosexual persons. He asked the bishops to maintain Church discipline restricting the use of general absolution as a substitute for individual confession. He called on them to uphold the church's "unpopular" teaching on homosexual activity "in the pastoral care that you give to homosexual persons." On sex education, he urged that any Church-sponsored programs respect the primary "right and duty of parents" to oversee the education of their children.

In another comment on miscellaneous topics at the end of his talk, John Paul singled out for praise a passage from a joint pastoral issued the previous April by the bishops of California, in which the bishops said, "The recovery of the virtue of chastity may be one of the most urgent needs of contemporary society." The pastoral, titled "A Call to Compassion," was mainly a plea for sensitive, non-judgmental spiritual and physical care for those who suffer from AIDS. The following evening in San Francisco, the pope would be meeting with a group of people with AIDS.

84

84 *American bishops join in prayer with the pope at San Fernando Mission.*

85 *Flanked by Archbishop John May and Cardinal Agostino Casaroli, the pope prays with the bishops.*

86 *Bishops applaud as the pope walks among them in the mission.*

85

MONTEREY
September 17

J ohn Paul's seven-hour visit to Monterey and Carmel-by-the-Sea was as
short as his visit to Columbia had been six days earlier, but it was among
the most expensive stops on his itinerary. The cost of the whole papal
trip — estimated at $22 million for the Church and possibly more than that
for the security and other arrangements provided by local, state and federal
governments — was a source of controversy in many places, but particularly
in Monterey and Carmel, where the Monterey Diocese estimated its own costs
at $2 million. The diocese, which has only 45 parishes and is not wealthy, tried
months before the visit to recoup some of the $500,000 it was putting out for
communications facilities by seeking bids from local TV stations for live coverage
rights of the papal Mass at Laguna Seca Raceway. The diocese quickly drop-
ped the plan when stations objected to paying for rights to cover a news event.
In allocating Mass tickets, diocesan officials assessed local parishes $15 per ticket,
with a suggestion that parishioners receiving them be asked to make a dona-
tion to offset the costs of the Mass. That plan provoked further controversy
as some news reports erroneously indicated that people were being charged
for the tickets. Church law forbids levying admission fees for any Mass. Neighboring dioceses in California helped Monterey cover some of the papal visit costs.
There and elsewhere Church officials defended the costs, saying the amounts
were small for the magnitude of the event and the publicity that the pope and
his message would receive.

On the lighter side, cartoonists and pundits had a field day with the prospect
of the pope being welcomed to Carmel-by-the-Sea by Mayor Clint Eastwood,
the movie actor who became a cult hero with his hard-as-nails roles as a gun-
fighter in 1960s spaghetti Westerns and as a vigilante cop in 1970s movies like
"Dirty Harry" and "Magnum Force." Souvenir T-shirts on sale in the Monterey-
Carmel area showed Eastwood welcoming the pope with the words, "Thou
hast made my day" or "Make my eternity" — variations on Dirty Harry's face-
off threat, as a tough criminal contemplated making a move for his gun, "Go
ahead, make my day."

Arriving in Monterey shortly before 10 a.m., John Paul was welcomed at
the airport by Monterey's Bishop Thaddeus A. Shubsda, Eastwood, and other
local dignitaries. He went almost immediately to Laguna Seca Raceway to
celebrate Mass and preach on agriculture and migrant workers. Later he would
visit Junipero Serra's tomb in Carmel and preach on evangelization, defending
Serra's life and work.

The Mass at the raceway drew about 75,000 people, a receptive crowd but
smaller than the 100,000 expected. Organizers said many buses chartered for
the Mass suddenly became unavailable, being pressed into service instead by
local officials to transport firefighters to forest fires in northern California and

Oregon. The bus shortage was so acute that by 10 p.m. — hours after the Mass was over — thousands of people were still stranded at the raceway. Many Mass-goers had begun to arrive as early as 2 a.m. and sat wrapped in blankets to ward off the nightime chill. As morning broke a thick fog rolled in but dissipated shortly before the pope arrived. The expansive motor raceway took on a liturgical air with a 100- by 300-foot altar built on a lake in the infield. Two 40-ton pontoon bridges connected the altar to the main area. At least 110,000 pots of deep-red petunias in a 40-foot-wide strip ran from the altar and up a hill to the base of a 100-foot cross of fabric stretched across steel rods.

In his homily John Paul said landowners and growers must recognize the rights of farmworkers to organize in order to make social, cultural and economic gains. He also recognized that the farm crisis has pushed many U.S. farmers into "poverty and indebtedness." The agricultural theme was fitting in one of the country's most fertile regions. Just inland from Monterey Bay and within the boundaries of the diocese is the Salinas Valley, known for its vast fields of artichokes and other produce. The pope called California "a land among the richest and most fruitful of the earth" but said even the most fertile land would produce nothing without human labor.

"Work is good for us" as individuals, but also stabilizes the family and society at large, the pope said, adding that agricultural work "exemplifies" all three dimensions. He said all involved in the food process — growers, workers, packers, shippers, retailers and consumers — are equal "in the eyes of God." "I appeal to landowners, growers and others in positions of power to respect the just claims of their brothers and sisters who work the land," he said. Their claims, he added, include the right to share in decisions affecting their work and the right to "free associations" to improve their situation, an oblique reference to unionization.

The pontiff recognized the tough economic times farmers face and said that the agricultural industry is "highly complex," but he urged those in the industry to focus on the dignity, rights and well-being of people and solve problems in "solidarity." He also urged sharing the harvest with poor nations and protecting it with "faithful stewardship" of the land.

Noting that the U.S. immigration law reform allows certain illegal aliens to become citizens, he urged Americans to accept them as people with a dream for improving life, much like their ancestors. He added that an ongoing requirement for a country celebrating the 200th anniversary of its Constitution is a "renewed commitment" to policies that ensure "equity and justice will be preserved and fostered."

The Mass-goers included about 3,000 migrant workers from nearby camps. Because the pope delivered his homily in English, his words were lost on many of them because they spoke only Spanish. One employer gave his workers the day off without pay and provided two tickets each and set up buses to take them to the raceway. But thousands of others could not afford to attend because loss of a day's pay was too much for their tight family budgets.

From Laguna Seca the pope went to the basilica of Mission San Carlos Borromeo del Rio Carmelo, a historic landmark and still-active parish better known simply as Carmel Mission. Originally founded in Monterey in 1770 by Serra, the mission was later moved to its present site near the Carmel River, at the edge of the town of Carmel. It was reportedly Serra's favorite mission. He made it his headquarters as president of the network of California missions, and he was buried there at his request.

After praying at Serra's grave, John Paul gave a talk on evangelization in which he praised Serra as a defender of native American rights and expanded on the defense of the Spanish missionary he had given three days earlier in Phoenix. "He not only brought the Gospel to the native Americans, but as one who lived the Gospel he also became their defender and champion," the pope said. "At the age of 60 he journeyed from Carmel to Mexico City to intervene with the viceroy on their behalf — a journey which twice brought him close to death — and presented his now famous 'Representacion' with its 'bill of rights,' which had as their aim the betterment of every phase of missionary activity in California, particularly the spiritual and physical well-being of its native Americans."

The pope suggested that the methods of missionary work in the "age of discovery and exploration" more than 200 years ago should be judged in terms of their motivation and within their own historical context. "The missions are the result of a conscious moral decision made by people of faith in a situation that presented many human possibilities, both good and bad, with respect to the future of this land and its native peoples," he said. "It was a decision rooted in a love of God and neighbor. It was a decision to proclaim the Gospel of Jesus Christ at the dawn of a new age, which was extremely important for both the European settlers and the native Americans." Despite differences in the era when Serra worked, the pope said, the way he carried out his work of preaching the Gospel "corresponds faithfully to the Church's vision today of what evangelization means."

Before the pope arrived, Secret Service agents moved from the area a group of native Americans who were trying to hold a protest prayer vigil at the mission. Some native Americans have accused Serra of being a participant in genocide because he was part of the Spanish colonization effort that brought with it cruelties, killings and new deadly diseases which decimated previously unexposed Indian tribes. The Diocese of Monterey, which is promoting Serra's beatification, issued a special "Serra Report" almost a year before the pope's visit in response to the criticisms. The report included a synopsis of Serra's sainthood cause and interviews with a panel of eight historians who disputed the claims. Many had hoped that the pope, who declared Serra "venerable" in 1985, would beatify the man known as the apostle of California during his visit to Monterey. In the Church's lengthy procedures leading up to the declaration of sainthood, the two key preliminary steps are proclaiming the person "venerable" and "blessed." Shortly before the pope's U.S. trip, Vatican officials said there would be no beatification in Monterey because the process of studying Serra's cause had not yet reached that stage.

In his remarks at Carmel, the pope not only defended Serra's record of fighting for Indian rights, but stressed the missionary's personal "holiness of life" as well. He called Serra a historic figure "larger than life ... who in the providence of God was destined to be the apostle of California and to have a permanent influence over the spiritual patrimony of this land and its people."

John Paul called on Catholics today "to be evangelizers, to share actively in the Church's mission of making disciples of all people" with the same "passionate" zeal that Serra and his fellow missionaries showed. "This singlemindedness is not reserved for great missionaries in exotic places," he said, but must be shared by priests in their pastoral ministry, Religious in their Gospel witness, and lay people in their work and married and family life. "The covenant of love between two people in marriage and the successful sharing of faith with children require the effort of a lifetime," he said. "If couples cease believing in their marriage as a sacrament before God or treat religion as anything less than a matter of salvation, then the Christian witness they might have given to the world is lost."

87 *Actor Clint Eastwood, who is mayor of Carmel, meets the pope at the Monterey Airport.*

88 *During the Mass, the pope recites prayers.*

89 *Gifts from farmworkers are carried to the altar.*

90 *The pope arrives at Laguna Seca raceway for Mass.*

91 *The pope incenses the altar at the start of the Mass.*

92 *In the Carmel Mission Basilica, the pope prays before the Blessed Sacrament.*

93 *The faithful crowd into the mission to be with the pope.*

94 *The pope prays at the grave of Father Junipero Serra, who founded the mission.*

89

93

94

SAN
FRANCISCO
September 18

From Monterey John Paul took a short afternoon flight to San Francisco, where the first item on his agenda gave him a rare opportunity to play tourist. He went directly from the airport to an overlook by the Golden Gate Bridge where, flanked by top Vatican officials and San Francisco's Archbishop Quinn, he stood and admired the graceful, bright orange arcs of the world's second-longest suspension bridge. Then he headed downtown. A popemobile motorcade along Geary Boulevard brought sparse crowds, variously estimated by police at 50,000 to 125,000 — far short of the 1.3 million some planners had projected. "I think we scared people off" with warnings of large crowds and traffic jams, said Father Miles O'Brien Riley, San Francisco archdiocesan spokesman. "We just shot ourselves in the foot."

At the end of the motorcade was Mission Dolores Basilica, where the largest anti-papal demonstration of the trip awaited the pope. Kept a block away from the basilica by police and barricades, the crowd of about 2,000 chanted slogans like "Pope, go home!" and "Shame, shame, shame." The protest was organized mainly by San Francisco gay and lesbian groups. Other demonstrators at the basilica and elsewhere in San Francisco had other causes. Scattered signs could be seen promoting atheism, feminism and abortion as a matter of choice. In front of St. Mary's Cathedral, which the pope was to visit the following morning, several hundred Jews protested his June meeting with Kurt Waldheim.

Inside Mission Dolores, John Paul spoke to a gathering of elderly and sick people which included more than 50 who suffered from AIDS. Two of them were priests. In a poignant moment he held 4-year-old Brendan O'Rourke, who contracted AIDS through a blood transfusion, and Brendan tugged playfully at the pope's ears. "God loves you all, without distinction," the pope told the group. "He loves those of you who are sick, those who are suffering from AIDS and from AIDS-related complex. He loves the relatives and friends of the sick and those who care for them. He loves us all with an unconditional and everlasting love."

"God's love has many aspects," he said. "God's love for us as our Father is a strong and faithful love, a love which is full of mercy.... It is also true that God loves us as a mother ... tender and merciful, patient and full of understanding."

During his visit the pope also went next door to pray in the much smaller former mission church, an adobe structure that is the oldest intact building in San Francisco.

107

At an evening meeting with Religious in St. Mary's Cathedral, John Paul was interrupted by applause 15 times during a talk in which he told 3,000 nuns, brothers and priests not to stray from official Church teaching when they try to reconcile the Church with American culture. "Adherence to the magisterium is an indispensable condition for a correct reading of 'the signs of the times,' " he said. He strongly praised the renewal efforts of U.S. Religious in the years since Vatican II and urged them to have "courage and trust" in the face of problems many religious orders now face.

Following the structured dialogue approach established for the meeting, John Paul first heard from representatives of women and men Religious: Sister Helen M. Garvey, president of the Leadership Conference of Women Religious, and Father Stephen Tutas, president of the Conference of Major Superiors of Men. Both described the religious orders in the United States as renewed, committed communities trying to live out the Gospel and witness it to others. Both called for greater recognition of women in the Church and for more dialogue and collaboration in carrying out the Church's mission.

In his response John Paul described members of religious orders as having "an important role in the Church's dialogue" with U.S. culture, a role that requires "a true understanding of the values involved in America's historical experience." But he stressed that discernment of Christ's will "is the work of the whole Church. No person or group of people can claim to possess sufficient insights so as to monopolize it.... The first law of this dialogue is fidelity to Christ and to his Church.... The faithful have the right to receive the true teaching of the Church in its purity and integrity, with all its demands and power."

Seconding remarks by the two Religious, John Paul praised the three-year study of U.S. Religious which he ordered in 1983. Following the study, led by Quinn, "there now exists a fresh cooperative spirit between your religious institutes and the local churches," he said.

He praised U.S. Religious for "your deep love of the Church and your generous service to God's people." Citing the contributions of contemplative orders to the Church's spiritual life and those of apostolic orders to education, health care and social services, he added: "The spiritual vigor of so many Catholic people testifies to the efforts of generations of Religious in this land. The history of the church in this country is in large measure your history at the service of God's people."

At the same time the pope lauded Religious for their postconciliar renewal efforts, saying the "good fruits of this response are evident in the Church: We see a Gospel-inspired spirituality ... a clearer sense of the Church as a communion of faith and love ... a new appreciation of the legacy of your founders and foundresses ... a heightened awareness of the urgent needs of the modern world.... Many of these insights, conceived in the experience of prayer and penance and authenticated by the teaching charism of the Church, have contributed greatly to ecclesial life."

Even in speaking of "certain weaknesses affecting the structure of your institutes," John Paul struck a positive and encouraging note. He cited two key problems, "the decline in vocations and the aging of your membership," which affect both men and women Religious in the United States, but especially nuns. These problems "are serious challenges for each one of your institutes and the corporate reality of religious life," the pontiff said, "and yet these are not new phenomena in the long experience of the Church. History teaches that in ways generally unpredictable the radical 'newness' of the Gospel message is always able to inspire successive generations to do what you have done.... You are called at this hour to fresh courage and trust."

The next morning the pope heard further calls for a more dialogical and collaborative spirit in the Church as he returned to St. Mary's Cathedral to meet at 8:15 with representatives of the U.S. Catholic laity. The presenters who addressed him were Donna Hanson, director of social ministries of the Diocese of Spokane, Wash., and chairwoman of the U.S. bishops' National Advisory Council, and Patrick S. Hughes, director of pastoral ministry of the San Francisco Archdiocese.

"Unity, not division, is our goal; service, not power, is our mission," Hanson said of U.S. Catholic laity. She described extensive pastoral needs and concerns in the U.S. church. She told the pope she would like to walk with him and understand his burdens "as you seek to preserve orthodox teachings and challenge the world with Gospel values." In turn, she asked him to be "also willing to walk with me" and understand the perspective she brings to the Church as an American Catholic. "I know that we in the United States are not representative of the majority of people in the world. At the same time, I know that our concerns are universal: family, spirituality, collaboration.... Accustomed as I am to dialogue, consultation and collaboration, I do not always feel that I am heard. In my cultural experience, questioning is neither rebellion nor dissent. Rather, it is a desire to participate and is a sign of both love and maturity."

In counterpoint to Hanson's panoramic overview of U.S. Catholic culture, Hughes spoke of some of the specific areas that concern lay professionals working in the Church. Their numbers have grown rapidly, and "their ministry contributes tremendous time, energy and talent to the Church," he said.

While John Paul expressed joy at the "great flowering of gifts" of lay people involved in service and ministry in the Church, he also stressed the distinction between clergy and laity and warned the group to see to it "both in theory and in practice that these positive developments are always rooted in the sound Catholic ecclesiology taught by the council. Otherwise we run the risk of 'clericalizing' the laity or 'laicizing' the clergy."

He also emphasized that the primary role of the laity is to live Christian lives "within the everyday world.... You are called to live in the world, to engage in secular professions and occupations, to live in those ordinary circumstances of family life and life in society from which is woven the very web of your existence."

The temporal order that Vatican II described as the laity's sphere of work "is vast," the pope said. "It encompasses the social, cultural, intellectual, political and economic life in which all of you rightly participate.... As Catholic lay people you have an important moral and cultural contribution of service to make to the life of your country."

John Paul leveled some frank criticisms at U.S. society, saying Catholic lay people must be a "sign of contradiction" challenging widespread secularism, relativism, consumerism and hedonism. "You are in the forefront of the struggle to protect authentic Christian values from the onslaught of secularization," he said. "We face a growing secularism that tries to exclude God and religious truth from human affairs. We face an insidious relativism that undermines the absolute truth of Christ and the truths of faith, and tempts believers to think of them as merely one set of beliefs or opinions among others.

"We face a materialistic consumerism that offers superficially attractive but empty promises conferring material comfort at the price of inner emptiness," he continued. "We face an alluring hedonism that offers a whole series of pleasures that will never satisfy the human heart." Those who lose their Christian faith through "these and other deceptions" often commit themselves "to passing fads, or to bizarre beliefs that are either shallow or fanatical," he said.

The pope made no direct response to Hanson's plea for more acceptance of dialogue and questioning in the Church or to Hughes' list of concerns aimed at improving and expanding the opportunities for professional lay service in the Church. He expanded on Hanson's references to diverse pastoral needs in the Church, however, urging that loving pastoral service be given within the framework of firm adherence to Church teaching.

He praised "those separated and divorced Catholics who, despite their loneliness and pain, are striving to preserve their fidelity," adding: "The Church assures them not only of her prayers and spiritual nourishment, but also of her love, pastoral concern and practical help." For divorced persons who have remarried outside the Church, the pope affirmed Church teaching that they are not allowed to receive Communion. But he said the Church still has a "deep love" for them and urges them to attend Mass and "undertake a way of life that is no longer in contradiction to the indissolubility of marriage."

Calling married love "the first way that couples exercise their mission" as lay Christians, the pope reaffirmed Church teaching against contraception. Procreation of children is a "service of life" in cooperation with God, he said, and the conjugal act "must always be open to bringing forth new life."

He expressed gratitude "for all the contributions made by women over the centuries to the life of the Church and of society" and said that any "true advancement" of women demands clear recognition of "the value of their maternal and family role." At the same time, he said, "the special gifts of women are needed in an ever-increasing measure" in the life of the Church. Because they are fully equal in dignity to men — "revealed as such in the account of creation contained in the word of God" — the access of women "to public functions" must be assured, the pope said.

Candlestick Park, filled with 70,000 worshippers, was the scene of John Paul's final stop in San Francisco. Although the Mass was not scheduled to start until 10:45, people began arriving at dawn. As they waited they were entertained by music and a program of Irish, African, Japanese, Korean and other national dances.

A 12-foot-high altar platform had been hastily erected overnight in right field and carpeted and adorned with flowers after a major league baseball game. Thunderous cheers greeted the pope as he entered the ball park, and the scoreboard flashed "John Paul II!" in large lighted letters as the popemobile circled the field.

The entrance music for the Mass was composed especially for the occasion by jazz musician-composer Dave Brubeck, a native of the San Francisco area and a convert to Catholicism who turned his talents to religious themes in the 1970s after decades as one of the nation's leading figures in contemporary jazz. The altar, lectern and other furnishings were locally crafted, all made of black walnut.

In his homily John Paul continued his message to American Catholics that they must be a sign of contradiction and face "criticism, ridicule or rejection" if they want to follow Christ. "Christ remains today a sign of contradiction — a sign of contradiction in his body, the Church," he said. He built his homily around two themes: What it means to be a Christian and the importance of catechesis, or religious education and formation, in deepening one's understanding of the faith and commitment to it.

"What does it mean to be a Christian?" the pope asked. "It means accepting the testimony of the apostles concerning the crucified and risen Christ. Indeed, it means accepting Christ himself.... To be a Christian means to go up to the mountain to which Christ leads us ... learning from Christ the ways of the Lord so as to be able 'to walk in his paths.'"

Turning to his second theme, John Paul said: "Here in San Francisco and in every city and place it is necessary for the followers of Jesus to deepen their communion with him so that they are not just Christians in name. The primary means the Church has always employed for this task is a systematic catechesis." He said Jesus did not tell his disciples merely to baptize, but "to baptize and to teach. Baptism alone is not sufficient.... There is no substitute for a systematic presentation of all the essentials of our faith, a presentation which can provide the basis for sound judgments about the problems of life and society, and which can prepare people to stand up for what they believe with both humility and courage."

The Church, he said, must "call people to conversion of mind and heart, just as Jesus did," trying to lead them to follow Christ ever more closely. "For this reason," he said, "the Church never ceases to proclaim the whole Gospel message, whether it is popular or unpopular, convenient or inconvenient."

95 *The pope talks with Archbishop John Quinn near the Golden Gate Bridge.*

96 *At Mission Dolores, the oldest building in San Francisco, the pope prays before the Blessed Sacrament.*

97 *Brendan O'Rourke, a 4-year-old AIDS patient, is hugged by the pope.*

98 *"Filia Ecclesiae Sum" (I am a daughter of the Church). Carmelite sisters greet the Holy Father at the meeting with Religious.*

99 *The Holy Father encourages priests and Religious at St. Mary's Cathedral.*

100 *The pope's name is up in lights at Candlestick Park.*

101 *Prior to Mass, the Candlestick crowd watches the proceedings of the pope's meeting with the laity on the big screen.*

102 *A friendly crowd awaits the arrival of the Holy Father for Mass at Candlestick Park.*

103 *The pope listens to the readings.*

104 *Close to 70,000 gather for Mass at Candlestick Park.*

105 *Scores of priests stand before the altar during the consecration.*

106 *Colorful banners provide a backdrop for the pope as he elevates the chalice.*

107 *Concelebrants extend their hands at the moment of consecration.*

108 *The pope offers Communion to a young person in a wheelchair.*

109 *As the popemobile leaves Candlestick Park, the Holy Father is saluted in Chinese.*

98

99

100

107

08

DETROIT
September 19

Although John Paul left San Francisco early in the afternoon of Sept. 18, it was 9 p.m. when he arrived in Detroit, so the main activities of his visit were scheduled for the following day.

Before retiring for the night, however, the pope visited the Cathedral of the Most Blessed Sacrament, where Archbishop Edmund C. Szoka of Detroit introduced him to archdiocesan priests, Religious and lay workers. Also present was Cardinal John R. Dearden, approaching his 80th birthday, who was a significant figure at Vatican II and a leading voice in U.S. Catholicism in the 1960s and '70s. Parishioners of the predominantly black cathedral parish were seated on bleachers in front of the church and got the first glimpse of the pope on his arrival. They had been waiting more than two hours, passing the time with meditations, music and listening to readings from the pope's writings.

As he had done in visiting other churches throughout his trip, the pope went slowly up the aisle. He patted children on the head, grasped outstretched hands, and occasionally stopped for a word or two with someone Szoka wanted to introduce.

In brief remarks, the pope referred to the Church as a "mystery of communion … Christ's body, his bride and our mother." This means, he said, that "the Church is more than just a community, or tradition with shared beliefs and practices, more than an organization with moral influence." It is "an instrument of redemption." He urged Detroiters "amid the social, cultural, political and economic forces that shape the life of the great metropolis of Detroit" to help build the body of Christ "by personal conversion and holiness and by your daily witness to the Gospel."

As John Paul slept at Szoka's residence next door to the cathedral, excited residents of Hamtramck, a city of 22,000 of mostly Polish descent, were up throughout the night celebrating and preparing for his visit first thing the next morning. By 8 a.m. about 150,000 people, mostly Poles, had crowded into Hamtramck along the motorcade route and in the open square where the pope was to speak against the backdrop of a huge portrait of Our Lady of Czestochowa, patroness of Poland. The glass-enclosed popemobile took the pontiff along Joseph Campau Avenue, Hamtramck's main street, which is lined with Polish bakeries, sausage-filled meat markets, and other shops that reflect the Polish and Slavic origins of most of the people. Windows were decked out in red and white banners, the Polish national colors, and signs saying "Witamy," Polish for "Welcome."

The Polish-born pope delivered his speech almost entirely in his native tongue. He urged Polish-Americans to maintain their faith, family values and strong cultural heritage as they contribute to the common good of the United States. He called the family "perhaps the most threatened institution in today's world."

He recapitulated the history of Poles in America, recalling the successive waves of immigration that go back to 1608 when the first Poles arrived in Jamestown, Va. "Our strength comes from faith, from God himself and from our millenary heritage," he said. "The more you are aware of your identity, your spirituality, your history and Christian culture ... the more you will be able to serve your country."

John Paul was no stranger in Hamtramck. A 10-foot bronze statue of him in a park at the center of town commemorates an earlier visit when he was still Cardinal Karol Wojtyla of Krakow.

The popemobile was used again for the pope's six-mile trip to his next stop, a meeting with some 2,800 permanent deacons and wives at Ford Auditorium. During a videotape presentation of deacons engaged in various ministries, many wept as they spontaneously joined in singing its theme song, "Here I Am, Lord." U.S. permanent deacons, numbering nearly 8,000, make up 60 percent of those in the Church around the world. Revival of the permanent diaconate as an ordained ministry on its own merits was mandated by Vatican II and carried out by Paul VI in 1967.

Samuel Taub, executive director of U.S. bishops' Secretariat for the Permanent Diaconate and one of the earliest permanent deacons in the country, described to the pope America's developing experience of the diaconate in its 20-year history. "We are keenly aware that the focal point of the deacon's mission and ministry is the human person," he said. "We are coming to appreciate increasingly how the diaconate can be and is a means of strengthening the presence of the Church in the marketplace. We continue to remind ourselves that, as we are a recognized sacramental sign of service, it is expected that we be a catalyst for an expanding notion of Church and ministry and that we see the empowerment of the laity as one of our prime responsibilities."

John Paul affirmed permanent deacons as "a great and visible sign of the working of the Holy Spirit" after Vatican II and as "living signs of the servanthood of the Church." The "specific dimension" of the diaconate in the Church, he said, is that "the service of the deacon is the Church's service sacramentalized. Yours is not just one ministry among others, but it is truly meant to be, as Paul VI described it, a 'driving force' for the Church's 'diakonia' (service). By your ordination you are configured to Christ in his servant role." He praised the U.S. church for its response to the renewal of the permanent diaconate, and he called it "a great source of satisfaction to learn that so many permanent deacons in the United States are involved in direct service to the needy."

It was in speaking of the deacons' "ministry of charity" that the pope articulated, in language stronger than in any previous papal or Vatican statement, the difference between priests and deacons in their relation to the "temporal order," the concerns of society and public life. "The 'temporal order' includes marriage and the family, the world of culture, economic and social life, the trades and professions, political institutions, the solidarity of peoples and issues of justice and peace," John Paul said. "The sacramental grace of his (the deacon's) ordination is meant to strengthen him and to make his efforts fruitful, even as his secular occupation gives him entry into the temporal sphere in a way that is normally not appropriate for other members of the clergy."

Taub said afterwards that popes have not spoken or written a great deal about the permanent diaconate during its 20-year history, and John Paul's remarks on the deacon's role in work and society were the clearest statement from the Holy See on that issue.

John Paul also linked the role of the married deacon's wife to the ministry of the deacon more closely and integrally than any previous Vatican statements in that area. He said the service of married deacons depends not only on the "love and support" of their wives, but on their "collaboration." He also spoke of the joint conjugal witness of husband and wife in "the contribution that a married deacon makes to the transformation of family life." A deacon and his wife, the pope said, "having entered into a communion of life, are called to help and serve each other. So intimate is their partnership and unity in the sacrament of marriage that the Church fittingly requires the wife's consent before her husband can be ordained…. The nurturing and deepening of mutual sacrificial love between husband and wife constitute perhaps the most significant involvement of a deacon's wife in her husband's public ministry in the Church."

Taub said the visit of a top Vatican official to study the permanent diaconate in the United States the previous spring appeared to have had a significant impact on the pope's Detroit speech. Archbishop Lajos Kada, secretary of the Vatican Congregation for the Sacraments, went to Denver to attend the four-day 1987 convention of the National Association of Permanent Diaconate Directors and to conduct an in-depth study of the diaconate program in the Denver Archdiocese. Key elements in the papal speech confirmed conclusions that Kada reached in his report back to the Holy See, Taub said.

Moving out of Ford Auditorium to adjacent Hart Plaza, John Paul told an outdoor audience in the city which gave birth to the modern assembly line that industrial technology can breed "new hardships and injustices." He cited "the introduction of robotics, the rapid development of communications, the necessary adaption of industrial plants, the need to introduce new skills in management" as challenges which, taken uncritically, may "produce undue hardship for many." Other problems challenging U.S. society include protecting the unborn, reducing unemployment and ending discrimination against "newly arrived immigrants," he said.

The pope also told Americans to develop a "new global solidarity" because many of today's problems "transcend the boundaries of countries." He cited disarmament, human rights, ecology and an increasingly interdependent world economy. "America is a very powerful country," he said. "You may choose to close in on yourselves to enjoy the fruits of your own form of progress and to try to forget about the rest of the world, or you may choose to live up to the responsibilities that your own history and accomplishments place on your shoulders." He asked his audience for "your personal involvement in that never-ending quest for justice and peace."

John Paul praised the United Nations for working toward "the establishment and maintenance of a just and lasting peace." U.N. disarmament efforts are "recognized and appreciated as being an incentive and support for the bilateral negotiations by the superpowers for arms reduction," he said. "I pray that despite its shortcomings it (the U.N.) will be able to fulfill ever more effectively its unique role of service to the world."

Catholics should be guided in their social action by Church teachings and their faith, he said: "As Christians you find in your faith a deep motivation for your social responsibility and involvement. Do not let this hour pass without renewing your commitment to action for social justice and peace. Turn to the Gospel of Jesus Christ to strengthen your resolve."

For the final Mass of his visit the pope went to the Pontiac Silverdome, where a crowd of 90,000 made it the largest indoor Mass he had ever celebrated. A 1,200-member choir and a 45-piece orchestra, stationed near the 50-yard-line, made the stadium's roof and walls reverberate with their music. The Mass-goers, who had begun to gather several hours before the 5 p.m. starting time, viewed the pope's arrival by helicopter on a large-screen television. Applause broke out several times as the waiting congregation watched him emerge from the helicopter and board the popemobile to circle the stadium before Mass.

John Paul, delivering the last major talk of his visit, preached a homily that drew from the central theme of his 1981 social encyclical, "Laborem Exercens" (On Human Work): People take primacy over things, and work is for man, not man for work. It is the Church's task, he said, to focus attention on the dignity and rights of workers and condemn any violence against those principles. "Conduct yourselves in a way worthy of the Gospel," the pope told his listeners.

"The only gift we can offer God that is truly worthy of him is the gift of ourselves."

"The person is both the subject and purpose of all work and cannot be reduced to a mere instrument of production," he said. Men and women have a place in the "earthly vineyard" of the workplace because it is "where you and I must earn our daily bread." Humanity requires work in order "to be maintained and developed," he added.

But there is also the "vineyard of the Lord," for which man gives the gift of self, "the greatest gift of all," he said. He urged people of faith to measure the world by the standard of God's kingdom and "not the other way around."

Applause interrupted the pope's homily several times but reached its height at the end of Mass, when he broke from the prepared text to thank Detroit and the United States for the hospitality shown him. He also expressed a fervent wish that his second pastoral visit would bring deep unity to the church in the United States and that his visit would be "spiritually fruitful."

As he left the Silverdome, people were on their feet cheering, shouting and clapping. They had been asked to remain in their places until the pope left by helicopter for the airport, but thousands streamed out and lined pathways to get a glimpse of the papal helicopter.

Although John Paul's last major appearance in the United States was over, he would not be returning to Rome immediately. In 1984, when he visited Canada, dense fog had prevented him from making a planned stop at Fort Simpson in the Northwest Territories to meet with native Americans. To make up the missed appointment, the pope would fly from Detroit to Edmonton, stay overnight there, and then take a smaller plane up to Fort Simpson to deliver a message of justice and encouragement to the original inhabitants of northern Canada.

As dusk fell over Detroit, John Paul's green-and-white helicopter, dubbed Ascension I, lifted off from the Silverdome grounds and took him to the Detroit airport. Szoka accompanied him and Vice President George Bush greeted him at the airport. The pope and vice president met privately in the terminal for about 15 minutes. Bush was preparing for a trip to Poland, and he said afterward that that was the main topic of discussion. Archbishop May and Cardinals Bernardin, O'Connor and Dearden were also among those present for the departure.

"Our land is built on freedom," Bush said in a farewell speech. "But as you have taught, 'Freedom develops best if it keeps to the rules of morality.'"

John Paul used his farewell to make a final plea to Americans to respect every human person, "especially the weakest and most defenseless ones — those yet unborn." He praised the nation's ideals and ecumenical spirit and noted that the United States is still a land that immigrants look to with hope. "America the Beautiful!" he proclaimed. "Yes, America, you are beautiful indeed and blessed in so many ways.... For this reason, America, your deepest identity and truest character as a nation is revealed in the position you take toward the human person," he said.

"The best traditions of your land presume respect for those who cannot defend themselves," he added. "If you want equal justice for all, and true freedom and lasting peace, then, America, defend life!"

A few moments later John Paul was at the stairs leading into Shepherd I, the TWA Boeing 747 that would take him to Canada. He waved to the crowd, kissed Szoka on both cheeks, and disappeared into the plane.

110 With Archbishop Edmund Szoka the pope follows the parade route to Hamtramck.

111 The pope says a prayer at Blessed Sacrament Cathedral after arriving in Detroit.

112 Angela Jakubowski of Bridgeport, Conn., holds a papal pennant.

113 Before a mural of Our Lady of Czestochowa, the pope speaks to the Polish community of Hamtramck.

114 The pope stops to greet some of the Hamtramck audience.

115 Hands reach out for the pope at the meeting with permanent deacons at Ford Auditorium.

116 An elevator lifts the pope to the Hart Plaza platform where he addresses the audience on social justice.

117 Dominic Valeri, on the shoulders of his mother Linda, smiles as he sees the pope arrive at Hart Plaza.

118 Women strain to get a good photo of the pope.

119 Aretha Franklin sings with the St. James gospel choir as they perform at Hart Plaza.

120 About 90,000 people fill the football stadium for the Mass.

121 With Cardinal John Dearden at his side, the pope elevates the host.

122 The pope blesses the faithful before leaving the stadium.

123 A native American woman sits in the rain at Fort Simpson awaiting the pope's arrival.

124 Beneath a large teepee the pope addresses the Fort Simpson audience.

125 During the Mass the pope sits on a chair made of moose antlers.

111

112

United States Papal Visit
of His Holiness
POPE JOHN PAUL II
September 1987

114

115

117

118

119

121

124

125

EPILOGUE
September 23

John Paul's trip was over. He had spent 10 days in the United States, visiting nine dioceses and traveling 5,331 miles within the country. He celebrated nine Masses and delivered more than 40 homilies and addresses. Counting his flight from Rome and his return via Edmonton and Fort Simpson, he had been gone from the Vatican for just over 11 days and traveled a total of 18,888 miles. Most American Catholics who followed his travels on television and radio and in newspapers and magazines had probably already formed their opinions of the trip. But how did the pope view it? What were his impressions of the United States and the Catholic Church in America after such an extended and often intense visit?

Archbishop May, who as NCCB president accompanied the pope to all cities, described some of the impressions John Paul related to him in the course of the trip. In an interview in his archdiocesan newspaper, the St. Louis Review, May said John Paul left with a positive impression of the church in the U.S. According to him, the pope was impressed by liturgical reform, ecumenism, lay leadership, the vitality of Hispanic Catholics and the tolerance of U.S. society.

John Paul "couldn't believe the response" in Columbia, where the overwhelmingly non-Catholic student body at the University of South Carolina "stayed until the pope's visit with religious leaders was finished to say goodbye to him," May said. Also in Columbia, the strength of the ecumenical movement was a "great revelation" to the pope, the archbishop said. "He said you don't find that anywhere else in the world."

The pontiff also learned how strongly lay leadership had contributed to the work of the church in the U.S. in education, health care, and social service, May added. He said the "beautiful liturgies" around the country impressed the pope with the state of the "liturgical revival" in the United States.

Both the pope and his secretary of state, Cardinal Casaroli, remarked on the tolerance shown toward the scattered protesters along papal motorcade routes, May said. "They said in many parts of the world people who come out with a sign against the majority would be attacked or hauled off by the police and not allowed to speak."

John Paul made his own impressions public a few days after he returned to Rome. Following a custom he has developed for each of the 36 trips abroad he has taken during nine years as pope, he spoke at length about the trip during his Wednesday general audience in St. Peter's Square.

He said the bonds between the universal Church and the church in the United States "remain strong and vibrant," and he praised the "sincere communion" of U.S. Catholics with the papacy.

"One of the salient features of the church in America is its rich pluralism, shown quite vividly in the ethnic background of the faithful," the pope said.

He cited his meetings with Hispanics, blacks, Indians and Poles. The French heritage in Louisiana and the presence of Asians in the Church along the West Coast were also notable, he said. Behind the ethnic pluralism, he added, "for generations, confessional or religious pluralism has developed." He said that "ecumenical dialogue and collaboration are very lively.... Also lively are the contacts with non-Christian religions."

He singled out his meeting with Jews, calling it "one of the most important moments of my visit" and "an important step on the path of dialogue between the Church and Judaism."

John Paul particularly praised the "working" meetings he had with the U.S. bishops and with the representatives of priests, Religious, laity, Catholic education and Catholic charitable and social services. He said his meeting with the bishops provided an opportunity "to touch on the neuralgic problems, both doctrinal and pastoral, of the life of the Church in that great and diverse society that forms the United States."

"The Church in the rest of the world looks with hope and expectation to her American brothers and sisters, conscious of their great potential for good," the pope said. He also asked U.S. Catholics to develop a "fruitful evangelization, adequate to the needs of today's society." That society, he said, is filled with scientific and technological advances and "high achievements in the field of material culture." Spreading the Gospel effectively in such a context "demands an ever more mature inculturation," he said.

There was not time at the general audience for John Paul to repeat all the challenges and teachings he had delivered to American Catholics during his pastoral visit to them: To priests and Religious to develop a strong prayer life and Eucharist-centered spirituality; to bishops to uphold Church teachings as they engaged in their many pastoral tasks; to young people to avoid drugs and premarital sex as they study and grow in the faith in preparation for becoming the next generation of leaders in the Church and the world; to women to model themselves after Mary as they seek their rightful place in Church and society; to married couples to develop a strong family life and fight the widespread mentality of abortion, contraception and divorce; to all lay people to be leaven to the world and to use their education to bring Gospel values into U.S. culture. There was his emphasis throughout his trip on the importance of prayer life and the sacraments, especially penance and the Eucharist, and on the need of all Catholics for conversion, accompanied by both intellectual and spiritual formation.

In his comments, however, John Paul singled out once again a challenge he had frequently raised to all Americans, Catholic or not: to share their wealth more and close the rich-poor gap.

"It is not possible," he said, "to forget the Gospel parable that sets before our eyes the figure of the rich man and Lazarus. The Church and Christianity in America must have a deep awareness of the challenge that today's world poses concerning the division between the rich North, the fully developed countries, and an underdeveloped South, the so-called Third World.

"In the name of the Gospel, the Church and Christianity must constantly repeat this challenge."

PART TWO

THE MESSAGE

Arrival Ceremony
Miami Airport, Sept. 10

President Reagan:

Your Holiness, after an audience with you five years ago in Vatican City, I met a group of American priests and seminarians studying in Rome. And when I happened to mention my hope that one day you would return to the United States and that perhaps this time your visit would extend to the South and West, when I mentioned this, those priests and seminarians broke into applause. Today, Your Holiness, you begin just such a return visit, and today all America applauds.

In a document of the Second Vatican Council that you helped to draft, it is written: "In language intelligible to every generation, (the Church) should be able to answer the ever-recurring questions which men ask about the meaning of this present life and of the life to come."

"In language intelligible to every generation" — certainly no one can speak with greater force to our own generation than you yourself. In Poland you experienced Nazism and communism. As pope, you suffered a terrorist attack that nearly claimed your life. Still you proclaim that the central message of our own time, that the central message of all time, is not hatred, but love.

During your papacy you have taken this message to some 68 countries. You have celebrated Mass in the ancient capitals of Europe. You have spoken words of truth and comfort on the African savannah. You have visited new churches on the islands of the Pacific. You have addressed vast gatherings throughout South America and the Far East. Now you have come back to the United States, the nation of citizens from all nations.

If I might just interject something, Your Holiness, I know that in your travels you've made it a point to speak to people in their own language. Well, here in Miami I have a suspicion that you will find many in your audience eager to hear you speak the beautiful language of Spain.

But in this, the very month of your visit, we in the United States will be celebrating the 200th anniversary of our own Constitution. That document says a great deal about the fundamental values in which we Americans believe. In the words of the distinguished Catholic philosopher Jacques Maritain: "The founding fathers were neither metaphysicians nor theologians, but their philosophy of life, and their political philosophy, their notion of natural law and of human rights, were permeated with concepts worked out by Christian reason and backed up by an unshakable religious feeling."

From the first, then, our nation embraced the belief that the individual is sacred and that as God himself respects human liberty, so too must the state. In freedom we Americans have in these 200 years built a great country, a country of goodness and abundance. Indeed, Your Holiness, it is precisely because we believe in freedom, because we respect the liberty of the individual in the economic as well as the political sphere, that we have achieved such prosperity.

We are justly proud of the Marshall Plan, whose 40th anniversary was celebrated in Europe earlier this year. In Europe and elsewhere, we continue to place our might on the side of human dignity. In Latin America and Asia, we are supporting the expansion of human freedom, in particular, the powerful movement toward democracy. And yet we Americans admit freely to our shortcomings. As you exhort us, we will listen. For with all our hearts, we yearn to make this good land better still.

In Florida and South Carolina, in Louisiana and Texas, in Arizona, California and Michigan, tens of thousands of America's more than 50 million Catholics will greet you. They do great works, America's Catholics, in the name of their church.

Here in the United States, American Catholics put their faith into action in countless ways: maintaining parochial schools that give underprivileged children in our inner cities the chance to receive a good education; supporting the AIDS hospices established by Mother Teresa's Missionaries of Charity; perhaps simply helping to put on a fund-raising dinner for the local parish. Abroad, American Catholics likewise seek to translate their faith into deeds, whether supporting missionaries in distant lands or helping America's Knights of Columbus restore the façade of St. Peter's in Rome.

But it will not be Catholics alone who greet you. Protestants of every denomination, Jews, Moslems, even many with no defined faith at all — Americans of every kind and degree of belief will wish you well, Your Holiness, responding to your moral leadership. Today's Florida sunshine is no warmer than the affection you will meet.

I began a moment ago by quoting from one document of the Second Vatican Council. Permit me to close by quoting from a second: "By the hidden and kindly mystery of God's will, a supernatural solidarity reigns among men. A consequence of this is that ... one person's holiness helps others."

Today Americans feel this solidarity. And we thank you, Your Holiness, for the courage and sanctity, the kindness and wisdom, with which you have done so much to help our troubled world. On behalf of all Americans, Your Holiness, welcome back.

Pope John Paul II:

Mr. President, dear friends, dear people of America,

1. It is a great joy for me once again to be in your country, and I thank you for your warm welcome. I am deeply grateful to you all.

I express my special thanks to the President of the United States, who honors me by his presence here today. I thank the bishops' conference and all the individual bishops who have invited me to their dioceses and who have done so much to prepare for my visit.

My cordial greetings and good wishes go to all the people of this land. I thank you for opening your hearts to me and for supporting me by your prayers. I assure you of my own prayers.

2. To everyone I repeat on this occasion what I said on that memorable day in 1979 when I arrived in Boston:

"On my part I come to you — America — with sentiments of friendship, reverence and esteem. I come as one who already knows you and loves you, as one who wishes you to fulfill completely your noble destiny of service to the world" (Oct. 1, 1979).

Today, like then, I come to proclaim the Gospel of Jesus Christ to all those who freely choose to listen to me; to tell again the story of God's love in the world; to spell out once more the message of human dignity, with its inalienable human rights and its inevitable human duties.

3. Like so many before me coming to America and to this very city of Miami, I come as a pilgrim: a pilgrim in the cause

of justice and peace and human solidarity — striving to build up the one human family.

I come here as a pastor — the pastor of the Catholic Church, to speak and pray with the Catholic people. The theme of my visit, "Unity in the Work of Service," affords me the welcome opportunity to enter into ever deeper communion with them in our common service to the Lord. It also enables me to experience ever more keenly with them their hopes and joys, their anxieties and griefs.

I come as a friend — a friend of America and of all Americans: Catholics, Orthodox, Protestants and Jews, people of every religion, and all men and women of good will. I come as a friend of the poor and the sick and the dying; those who are struggling with the problems of each day; those who are rising and falling and stumbling on the journey of life; those who are seeking and discovering, and those not yet finding, the deep meaning of "life, liberty and the pursuit of happiness."

4. And finally I come to join you as you celebrate the bicentennial of that great document, the Constitution of the United States of America. I willingly join you in your prayer of thanksgiving to God for the providential way in which the Constitution has served the people of this nation for two centuries: for the union it has formed, the justice it has established, the tranquillity and peace it has ensured, the general welfare it has promoted and the blessings of liberty it has secured.

I join you also in asking God to inspire you — as Americans who have received so much in freedom and prosperity and human enrichment — to continue to share all this with so many brothers and sisters throughout the other countries of the world who are still waiting and hoping to live according to standards worthy of the children of God.

With great enthusiasm I look forward to being with you in the days ahead. Meanwhile, my prayer for all of you, dear people of America, is this:

"The Lord bless you and keep you! The Lord let his face shine upon you, and be gracious to you! The Lord look upon you kindly and give you peace" (Nm 6:24-26).

God bless America!

Meeting with Priests
St. Martha's, Miami, Sept. 10

Father Frank J. McNulty:

Your Holiness ... Welcome! Those of us here this afternoon represent a group of men far too large for this church, the priests of the United States. We come from every diocese in our country, and we bring the love, affection, esteem and loyalty of all our brothers at home. We come with enthusiasm and with happy hearts because we have been chosen to spend this time with you. Your Holiness, the priests of this country are glad you have returned to us once again ... a warm, joyful welcome from all of us.

I have titled my presentation "If Priests Could Open up Their Hearts" and begin with a story.

After a large dinner at one of England's stately mansions, a famous actor entertained the guests with stunning Shakespearean readings. Then, as an encore, he offered to accept a request. A shy, gray-haired priest asked if he knew Psalm 23. The actor said, "Yes, I do and I will give it on one condition: that when I am finished you recite the very same psalm."

The priest was a little embarrassed, but consented. The actor did a beautiful rendition: "My shepherd is the Lord, there is nothing I shall want," and on and on. The guests applauded loudly when the actor was done, and then it was the priest's turn. The man got up and said the same words, but this time there was no applause, just a hushed silence and the beginning of a tear in some eyes.

The actor savored the silence for a few moments and then stood up. He said, "Ladies and Gentlemen, I hope you realize what happened here tonight. I knew the psalm, but this man knows the Shepherd."

All of us gathered here are dedicated to knowing the Shepherd. The men here tonight and their brothers back home have gotten to know him even better by walking the valleys of darkness with him. These recent years have not been easy for priests. But where there are valleys, there are also mountains; and if priests could open up their hearts and tell you of their priesthood, you would hear of "top-of-the-mountain" moments ... moments of joy, peace and satisfaction. They would speak of ministry, and if you looked into their eyes you would see a spark, a rejoicing in the Lord as their shepherd, a rejoicing in their love of ministry.

Ministry is the center of our lives. Baptism and confirmation called us to that ministry, but ordination added a special dimension. On that day we became co-workers with the bishop, collaborators in his mission and yours to continue the work of Jesus Christ. Thus our loyalty has a solid base and so does our desire for unity with you, our bishops and with each other. Bonding among priests and bishops has increased in our country through support groups, presbyteral councils, retreats, continuing education, convocations and the like. There is communion. We treasure it; we yearn for more.

Priests value diversity too. Ours is a pluralistic society, and we have learned how to hold fast to our Catholic value system while respecting the convictions of other people. Our backgrounds are diverse and we minister to multicultural, multiracial groups. Here in Miami, the priests serve at least 28 nationalities. In your letter to our bishops before their last meeting you spoke of "Petrine service," which among other things guarantees the church her Catholic unity and protects our legitimate variety. We welcome all your efforts to do that. We share a dream with you and each other, to proclaim Jesus and his Gospel, even if at times there are differences among us on just how to make that dream a reality. Because of this dream the current emphasis on evangelization has captured our imagination.

If priests could open up their hearts and tell you of their priesthood, they would speak of joy and consolations. At times the responsibility to minister in the name of Jesus is awesome, but what a source of happiness. The longer we are priests, the more convinced we are that our lives make a difference. Through our ministry of word and sacrament we are the instruments Jesus uses to nourish his people spiritually and to build them up as a community of faith and love.

This awesome responsibility is not without concerns. Today's world does not always appreciate the values which give our lives meaning. In such a climate we must struggle to model our lives after that of Jesus, as we promised we would do when we were ordained. Those of us who give retreats to priests are edified to find in them such a deep longing, thirst and hunger for a life of prayer. But we ask how we can develop that inner life when daily pressures and demands claim so much of our time and energy. Priests identify easily with the scene in Mark when the Lord goes off by himself to pray and his disciples find him to say, "Everyone is looking for you." We also ask how we can maintain our identity and spirituality precisely as priests, while walking the journey with our people and sharing life's challenges with them.

If priests could open their hearts and tell you of their priesthood, they would speak of Vatican II. Bishops and theologians may have been the architects of that council, but your priests are the ones who struggle to enflesh it every day in varied ministerial settings. Priests continue to bring the council documents to life, especially the vision of Church in "Lumen Gentium" and "Gaudium et Spes." They try hard to make their service collaborative and collegial; they try hard to make their decisions consultative and their responsibilities shared. They keep getting better at it. As they orchestrate the scene, they call the laity to their rightful roles and walk the journey with them as fellow pilgrims. The renewed Church in this country is alive and well.

If priests could open up their hearts and tell you of their priesthood, they would speak of social justice. As we try to take courageous and prophetic stands, it helps us to know how close these questions are to your own heart and to hear your strong words. In a climate where we must at times be countercultural, we are heartened and strengthened by the episcopal conference of this country. Our bishops have not backed away from the complex and controversial issues of social justice.

If priests could open up their hearts and tell you of their priesthood, they would speak of God's people. We are eyewitnesses to wonderful things which do not get officially recorded: their enthusiasm, their spirit, their remarkable generosity and especially their genuine love for priests. They understand our humanness, they forgive our failings and they are a constant source of joy. And, with all this, they constantly challenge us to be holy.

On our part, we identify readily with the words of Ambrose to another bishop that "the most important thing is the people entrusted to our care." We recall our ordination day when we were urged to "always remember the example of the Good Shepherd, who came not to be served but to serve and to seek out and rescue those who were lost." Because priests take that charge so seriously, there are some serious concerns about our ministry.

As we proclaim the moral message and help our people live out our value system, we sometimes find ourselves in tension. Our God is a God who calls us to be the best we can be, and a God rich in mercy, tenderness and forgiveness. Our Church and we, as a part of it, are committed to a bold proclamation of the truth even when it weighs heavy or is countercultural. Yet we are also a forgiving Church, ready to reflect the merciful Lord whose ambassadors we are. It troubles us that people often do not perceive the Church as proclaiming integral truth and divine mercy, but rather as sounding harsh, demanding. Sometimes it may be a question of style, for example, the technical approach of some of our ecclesial documents. Or it may be an altogether false perception, with no foundation in fact. But whatever the reason, as we meet the brokenhearted, wipe away tears and seek out the lost sheep, we want them to hear the full truth and the full-hearted mercy of the Gospel.

When Pope John XXIII opened the Vatican Council he said, "Nowadays, the spouse of Christ prefers to make use of the medicine of mercy rather than that of severity. She con-

siders that she meets the needs of the present day by demonstrating the validity of her teaching rather than by condemnation."

As we go about trying to heal the wounded, it saddens us that many have a different image of the Church we love and serve. It saddens us that the Church is not as credible to those within it and to those outside it as we would like it to be.

If priests could open up their hearts and tell you of their priesthood, they would speak of worries. There is a real and dramatic shortage of priests, a situation critical enough to make us worry about the future. In some areas, each passing day finds the priest less able to meet needs and fulfill expectations. Age and ministerial fatigue are harsh realities. Morale suffers when we see so few young men follow in our footsteps. Morale suffers when we see parishes without priests and prayer services taking the place of Sunday Mass. We worry that we might become only a Church of the word and lose our sacramental tradition. The suffering intensifies when we realize that in 10 years we could have half the present number of priests.

Yes, we must surely work and pray for vocations. Despite the many possibilities which compete for their attention, there are many generous young men who are willing to give their lives in service of the Lord as priests. We must personally invite them. Perhaps the greatest motivation of all for them is the joy we project in our own lives and ministry.

But even as we promote vocations, the celibacy question — as you so well know — continues to surface. Its value has eroded and continues to erode in the minds of many. This is of great concern to us because it has serious implications for the Church. We know, Holy Father, that you have been unequivocal in your support for the celibate commitment which thousands of priests in the United States have made and intend to keep. For your support we are grateful, because it is not easy to strive to be warm, loving and affective men and yet remain faithful to that commitment. We can only ask you to continue along paths of support and exploration. Support for those who want to persevere; exploration of the gift of celibacy, which has such a long tradition; exploration of how the discipline of celibacy can be most effectively implemented today; exploration of how priests can help each other make it a transparent sign of pastoral charity and the coming of the kingdom in the pattern of Jesus Christ, our high priest.

If priests could open up their hearts and tell you of their priesthood, they would speak of hopes. They hope that all charisms will be fully recognized, celebrated and utilized in the Church. The charisms mentioned by St. Paul in his letters provide a striking theme for your visit. Priests see the charism of pope and bishops as integral, necessary and irrevocable. You are the authoritative teachers. As pastors, we share in this teaching function.

Theologians have a charism too, and we are grateful for their gift. They draw the traditions of faith into a fruitful encounter with contemporary realities and concerns. Our hope for them is for a free sense of inquiry and a loving fidelity to the wider mission of the Church. When they function with freedom and fidelity, we priests are supported in our pastoral efforts.

Those of us in pastoral work have a charism too. There is a collective wisdom that should be heard by the rest of the Church. Priests help people live and die, they baptize and bury, they celebrate sacraments, they lead the worship. They listen in every season and in every setting to the tearing complexities and the wrenching ambiguities that the love and pain of human life create. Vatican II encourages people to speak their minds humbly and courageously about those matters in which they enjoy competence.

Priests enjoy competence in pastoral practices, the serving of that human life. We hope that real, effective and felt participation from those engaged in pastoral work will always be the prelude to definitive decisions relating to pastoral practices. The point is not democratic consensus. Rather, priests hope that their collective wisdom will be heard as part of a process. This is why priests applaud the selection of a bishop who shares their competence. This is why they hope to continue to have a consultative voice in the selection of their bishops.

Although I am speaking today for the priests of the country and not for women in ministry, still the bonds of close collaboration between priests and women in ministry prompt me to offer some words about them. Priests are encouraged by Your Holiness' words of support to women whose service — as you have amply indicated — is essential for the life of the Church. We would also be greatly encouraged if the Holy See, together with the local churches, would continue to explore the range of service that women might appropriately offer the Church. Their collaboration with priests has been generous and effective. Our ministry tells us that they are gifted, willing and needed. The movement of women toward practical equality is a major dynamic of our time. Because of the complexity and urgency of this movement, especially as it relates to the Church, there is need for study, reflection and, above all, more dialogue with women.

If priests could open up their hearts and tell you of their priesthood, they could not do so without some controversial questions surfacing. In our country there is an attitude toward questions; it comes from our heritage, those historical events which help make us the way we are. We treasure freedom — freedom of conscience, freedom of religion, freedom of expression. Questions brought our nation into being. In such settings people do not run from questions about what they believe and how they live out those beliefs. Priests know well that there are no easy answers, but want to face the questions with honesty.

Last year, the priests of one diocese asked me to speak at their convocation about the state of the priesthood and gave simple instructions. "Be honest," they said, "but also be encouraging." I have tried this afternoon to be both. To be dishonest would be a terrible disservice to you and my brother priests.

And we do need encouragement — from you, from your Roman congregations, from our bishops, from each other. It has been encouraging for all of us to look into the hearts of priests. How wonderful it is that priests care enough to have concerns, worries, fears, hopes and questions about the Church and how she prospers. What an encouraging sign that they care so deeply about their people, particularly the alienated.

It has been encouraging to look into the hearts of priests, but not easy to articulate what is found there. A poet once said it this way:

> Sometimes it happens in conversation:
> we stand facing truth and lack the words,
> have no gesture, no sign;
> and yet — we feel — no word,
> no gesture or sign would convey
> the whole image...

This is part of a poem called "Thought's Resistance to Words," by Karol Wojtyla. And this too is an encouraging note: that we have a pope who is also a poet, because poets know the human heart.

But most encouraging of all, Your Holiness, is this moment, this event. We and our priest brothers throughout our country are touched that you care enough to ask us how it has been for us. You have listened; we will do the same. Tell us what we can do to help build up the body of Christ.

Your Holiness, our prayer is that today's words will be the deepening of an honest, ongoing, heart-to-heart dialogue.

Pope John Paul II:

Dear brother priests,

1. Coming here today, I wish to open my heart to you and to celebrate with you the priesthood that we all share. I am convinced that there is no better way to start than to direct our thoughts to that shepherd whom we all know — the Good Shepherd, the one High Priest, our Lord and Savior Jesus Christ.

My heart is full of gratitude and praise as I express my love for the priesthood, the vocation in which we participate not because we are worthy, but because Christ loves us and has entrusted to us this particular ministry of service. And I thank God for you, my brother priests. In the words of St. Paul: "I thank God ... whenever I remember you in my prayers — as indeed I do constantly, night and day" (2 Tm 1:3).

I am also grateful to you, my brother priests, for your welcome of fraternal love, expressed personally and through Father McNulty as your representative. I address my words to all of you present here and to all the priests in the United States. To all of you I express my gratitude for your ministry, for your perseverance, for your faith and love, for the fact that you are striving to live the priesthood, close to the people, in truth — the truth of being ministers of Christ, the Good Shepherd.

As priests, we all hold a "treasure in earthen vessels" (2 Cor 4:7). Through no merit of our own and with all our human weaknesses, we have been called to proclaim God's word, to celebrate the sacred mysteries, especially the Eucharist, to care for the people of God and to continue the Lord's ministry of reconciliation. In this way, we are servants both of the Lord and of his people, being ourselves constantly called to conversion, constantly invited to "walk in newness of life" (Rom 6:4).

I have come to the United States, my brother priests, in order to confirm you in your faith, according to the will of Christ (cf. Lk 22:32). I have come to you because I want all distances to be bridged, so that together we may grow and become ever more truly a communion of faith, hope and love. I affirm you in the good gifts you have received and in the generous response you have made to the Lord and his people, and I encourage you to become more and more like Jesus Christ, the eternal high priest, the good shepherd.

St. Paul reminds us, as he reminded Timothy, to be fearless in serving Christ: "The spirit God has given us is no cowardly spirit, but rather one that makes us strong, loving and wise. Therefore, never be ashamed of your testimony to our Lord ... but with the strength which comes from God bear your share of the hardship which the Gospel entails" (2 Tm 1:7-8). We know that proclaiming the Gospel and living out our ministry very definitely entail hardship. It would be wrong to reduce priestly life to this one dimension of suffering, but it would also be wrong not to recognize this dimension or to resent it when we encounter it. We are not exempt from the human condition nor can we ever escape that emptying of self, after the example of Jesus, who "was himself tested through what he suffered" (Heb 2:18).

2. It is important that we find satisfaction in our ministry and that we be clear about the nature of the satisfaction which we can expect. The physical and emotional health of priests is an important factor in their overall human and priestly well-being, and it is necessary to provide for these. I commend your bishops and you yourselves for giving particular attention to these matters in recent years. Yet the fulfillment that comes from our ministry does not, in the final analysis, consist in physical or psychological well-being; nor can it ever consist in material comfort and security. Our fulfillment depends on our relationship with Christ and on the service that we offer to his body, the Church. Each of us is most truly himself when he is "for others."

3. And just here, of course, arises a problem for us in our ministry. So much is asked of us by so many different people, and so often it seems that our response is inadequate to their needs. Sometimes this is due to our own human limitations. We can then be tempted to indulge in excessive self-criticism, forgetting that God can use our weakness as easily as our strength in order to accomplish his will.

It is a great credit to you, my brothers, that you are striving to be merciful and gentle and forgiving like the Good Shepherd, whom you know and imitate and love, and to whom you have pledged your fidelity. No other path is possible. Sometimes, however, what is asked of you in the name of compassion may not be in accord with the full truth of God, whose eternal law of love can never contradict the fact that he is always "rich in mercy" (Eph 2:4). True mercy takes into account God's plan for humanity, and this plan — marked by the sign of the cross — was revealed by a merciful High Priest, who is able "to sympathize with our weakness, ... one who was tempted in every way that we are, yet never sinned" (Heb 4:15). If, on the other hand, what is claimed to be a gesture of mercy goes contrary to the demands of God's word, it can never be truly compassionate or beneficial to our brothers and sisters in need. Jesus, who was himself the perfect expression of the Father's mercy, was also conscious of being "a sign of contradiction" (Lk 2:34). The apostle John tells us that at a certain point in the Lord's ministry, "many of his disciples broke away and would not remain in his company any longer" (Jn 6:66).

And today there are indeed many sensitive issues which priests must deal with in their daily ministry. I know from listening to many priests and many bishops that there are different approaches to such issues. What is seen in one way by some of our brothers is evaluated differently by others. Yes, we all have questions that arise from the exercise of our priesthood, questions which require us to seek continually the light and wisdom that come only from the Holy Spirit.

In this regard, however, it is important for us to realize that the same Holy Spirit from whom come all the different and wonderful charisms and who dwells in the hearts of all the faithful has placed in the Church the specific charism of the magisterium, through which he guides the whole community to the fullness of truth. Through the action of the Holy Spirit the promise of Christ is constantly being fulfilled: "Know that I am with you always, until the end of the world" (Mt 28:20). We know that through the Second Vatican Council the Church has clearly and collegially expressed her teaching on many of the sensitive issues and that much of this teaching has subsequently been reiterated in the different sessions of the Synod of Bishops. By its nature, therefore, this teaching of the Church is normative for the life of the Church and for all pastoral service. The forthcoming synod, after extensive consultation and fervent prayer, will consider at length and take a pastoral position on other important issues in the life of the Church.

I am very much aware that your fidelity to Christ's will for his Church and your pastoral sensitivity demand great sacrifice and generosity of spirit. As I told the bishops of the United States, just a few weeks after I was elected pope:

"Like yourselves, I learned as a bishop to understand firsthand the ministry of priests, the problems affecting their lives, the splendid efforts they are making, the sacrifices that are an integral part of their service to God's people. Like yourselves, I am fully aware of how much Christ depends on his priests in order to fulfill in time his mission of redemption" (Nov. 9, 1978).

4. In expressing the conviction that Christ needs his priests and wills to associate them with himself in his mission of salvation, we must also emphasize the consequence of this: the need for new vocations to the priesthood. It is truly necessary for the whole Church to work and pray for this intention. As Father McNulty stated so well, we priests must personally invite generous young men to give their lives in the service of the Lord; they must truly be attracted by the joy that we project in our own lives and ministry.

There is still one more factor to be considered in evaluating the future of vocations, and it is the power of Christ's paschal mystery. As the Church of Christ, we are all called to profess his power before the world; to proclaim that he is able, in virtue of his death and resurrection, to draw young people to himself in this generation as in the past; to declare that he is strong enough to attract young men even today to a life of self-sacrifice, pure love and total dedication to the priesthood. As we profess this truth, as we proclaim with faith the power of the Lord of the harvest, we have a right to expect that he will grant the prayer that he himself has commanded to be offered. The present hour calls for great trust in him who has overcome the world.

5. The authentic renewal of the Church initiated by the Second Vatican Council has been a great gift of God to his people. Through the action of the Holy Spirit an immense amount of good has been done. We must continue to pray and work that the Holy Spirit will bring his design to fulfillment in us. In this regard priests have an indispensable role to play in the renewed life of the Church.

Each day the Church is being renewed by grace as she seeks a deeper and more penetrating understanding of the word of God as she strives to worship more authentically in spirit and in truth, and as she recognizes and develops the gifts of all her members. These dimensions of renewal require those enduring tasks of priests which give their ministry its unique character: namely, the ministry of word and sacrament, the tending of the flock of Christ.

True renewal presupposes the clear, faithful and effective proclamation of the word of God. The Second Vatican Council indicated that this is the priest's first task ("Presbyterorum Ordinis," 4). Those who preach must do so with dynamic fidelity. This means being ever faithful to what has been handed on in tradition and Scripture, as taught by the living pastoral authority of the Church, and making every effort to present the Gospel as effectively as possible in its application to new circumstances of life. As often as the word is truly proclaimed, Christ's work of redemption continues. But what is proclaimed must first be lived.

Renewal in Christ greatly depends on the development of

the Church's life of worship. Because we priests preside at the liturgy, we must come to know and appreciate the rites of the Church through study and prayer. We are called to lead celebrations which are both faithful to the Church's discipline and legitimately adapted, according to her norms for the good of our people.

Genuine renewal also depends upon the way in which priests exercise their task of tending the flock of Christ, especially as they encourage the faithful to use their gifts in the apostolate and in various special forms of service. The Church's commitment to evangelization, to proclaiming the word of God, to calling people to holiness of life, cannot be sustained without the tireless efforts and selfless support of priests. In the matter of inviting people, as Jesus did, to conversion — the total conversion of the Gospel — the example of priests is extremely important for the authenticity of the Church's life.

This is particularly true in our own use of the sacrament of penance, through which we are repeatedly converted to the Lord. On this condition rests the full supernatural effectiveness of our "ministry of reconciliation" (2 Cor 5:18) and of our whole priestly lives. The experience of the Church teaches us that "the priest's celebration of the Eucharist and administration of the other sacraments, his pastoral zeal, his relationship with the faithful, his communion with his brother priests, his collaboration with his bishop, his life of prayer — in a word, the whole of his priestly existence, suffers an inexorable decline if by negligence or for some other reason he fails to receive the sacrament of penance at regular intervals and in a spirit of genuine faith and devotion. If a priest were no longer to go to confession or properly confess his sins, his priestly being and his priestly action would feel its effects very soon, and this would also be noticed by the community of which he was the pastor" ("Reconciliatio et Paenitentia," 31).

People expect us to be men of faith and prayer. People look to us for Christ's truth and the teaching of his Church. They ask to see Christ's love incarnate in our lives. All this reminds us of a very basic truth, that the priest is "another Christ." In a sense, we priests are Christ to all those to whom we minister. This is true of all aspects of our priestly work. But it is particularly true in the eucharistic sacrifice — from which our priestly identity flows and in which it is expressed most clearly and effectively. This truth has special relevance also for our service as ministers of the sacrament of reconciliation, through which we render a unique service to the cause of conversion and peace, and to the advancement of God's kingdom on earth. At this point I would like to repeat those words which I have already addressed to the priests of the Church: "Praise then to this silent army of our brothers who have served well and serve each day the cause of reconciliation through the ministry of sacramental penance" (ibid., 29).

In her mission to the world, the Church is renewed as she calls humanity to respond to God's commandment of love, and as she upholds and promotes the values of the Gospel as they affect public life. In doing this she becomes a prophetic voice on matters of truth and justice, mercy and peace. In these tasks involving the world, the leadership of priestly ministry has been and continues to be decisive. Priests who encourage and support the laity help them to exercise their own mission to bring the values of the Gospel into public life. Thus, priests and lay people working together can challenge society itself to defend life and all human rights, to protect family life, to work for greater social justice, to promote peace.

6. One of the notable experiences of priests in the United States in the years since the council has been a renewal of their spiritual lives. Many priests have sought this renewal in groups of fraternal support, through spiritual direction, retreats and other commendable endeavors. These priests have found their ministry revitalized by a rediscovery of the importance of personal prayer. As you continue to discover Christ both in your prayer and in your ministry, you will experience more deeply that he — the Good Shepherd — is the very center of your life, the very meaning of your priesthood.

My brothers: In speaking to you about prayer I am not telling you what you do not know or urging you to do something that you do not practice. Prayer has been part of your daily lives since your seminary years and even earlier. But perseverance in prayer, as you know, is difficult. Dryness of spirit, external distractions, the tempting rationalization that we could be spending our time more usefully — these things are familiar to anyone who is trying to pray. Inevitably, at one time or another, these elements assail the prayer life of a priest.

For us priests, prayer is neither a luxury nor an option to be taken up or put aside as seems convenient. Prayer is essential to the pastoral life. Through prayer we grow in sensitivity to the Spirit of God at work in the Church and in ourselves. And we are made more aware of others, becoming more "attentive to their needs, to their lives and destiny" (Holy Thursday Letter to Priests, 1987, No. 11). Indeed, through prayer we come to love deeply those whom Jesus has entrusted to our ministry. Of special importance for our lives and our ministry is the great prayer of praise — the Liturgy of the Hours — which the Church enjoins on us and which we pray in her name and in the name of our Lord Jesus Christ.

7. In recent years, priests have often told me of the need they feel for support in their ministry. The challenges of priestly service today are indeed great, and the demands on our time and energy seem to increase every day. In such circumstances how easily we can give in to temptations to discouragement! But, dear brothers, at these times it is more important than ever that we heed the advice of the Letter to the Hebrews: "Let us keep our eyes fixed on Jesus, who inspires and perfects our faith. For the sake of the joy which lay before him he endured the cross, heedless of its shame.... Remember how he endured the opposition of sinners; hence do not grow despondent or abandon the struggle" (12:2-4).

The encouragement and support that we find in one another is a great gift of God's love — a characteristic of Christ's priesthood. The increase of mutual support among brother priests through prayer and sharing is a most encouraging sign. The same can be said, on a different level, for the development of presbyteral councils committed to the solidarity of priests with one another and with their bishop in the mission of the universal Church.

As priests we also need examples of priestly ministry, "artists" of pastoral work who both inspire us and intercede for us — priests like Philip Neri, Vincent de Paul, John Vianney, John Bosco and Maximilian Kolbe. And we can also reflect upon the priestly lives of men whom we have known personally, exemplary priests who inspire us — because they have lived the one priestly ministry of Jesus Christ with deep generosity and love.

To persevere in our pastoral ministry we need above all that "one thing only" which Jesus tells us is "required" (cf. Lk 10:42). We need to know the Shepherd very well. We need a deep personal relationship with Christ — the source and supreme model of our priesthood — a relationship that requires union in prayer. Our love for Christ, rekindled frequently in prayer — especially prayer before the Blessed Sacrament —

is at the foundation of our commitment to celibacy. This love also makes it possible for us, as servants of God's kingdom, to love our people freely and chastely and deeply.

8. My brothers: Sharing in the one priesthood of Christ, we share the same joys and sorrows. What a joy it is for me to be with you today. I thank you again for the gift of yourselves to Christ and his Church, and I want you to know that I am close to you in your efforts to serve the Lord and his people. You have my gratitude, my prayers, my support and my love. And as I conclude, I express the hope that each of us will always experience the joy of which the psalmist speaks: "Behold, how good it is, and how pleasant, where brethren dwell at one!" (Ps 133:1).

Dear brother priests: Catholic unity is our vocation. As priests in America you are called to live this Catholic unity in the particular churches — the dioceses — to which you belong. But all these particular churches are never more completely themselves, never more faithful to their identity, than when they are living to the full the communion of faith and love of the universal Church. At the summit of your priestly ministry is this mystery of ecclesial unity, and you are called to live it in sacrifice and love, in union with Mary, the mother of Jesus.

The protection and tender human love of our Blessed Mother is a great support to all of us priests. Her prayers assist us, her example challenges us, her closeness consoles us. In her presence we experience the joy and hope that we need so much. Is this not the day and the hour, dear brother priests, to turn to her, as we must have done on our ordination day, and to entrust to her anew ourselves, our people and our sacred ministry? Why? For the glory of the Father, and of the Son and of the Holy Spirit.

Dear priests of America, dear brothers: "My love to all of you in Christ Jesus" (1 Cor 16:24).

Meeting with Jews Miami, Sept. 11

Rabbi Mordecai Waxman:

It is our honor and pleasure to welcome you to the United States. We do so on behalf of the Jewish organizations who are represented here today; organizations that have been in fruitful conversations with the Roman Catholic Church through the years.

They include representatives of the American Jewish Committee, the American Jewish Congress, the Anti-Defamation League of B'nai B'rith and the Synagogue Council of America, which is here representing the Union of American Hebrew Congregations, United Synagogue of America, Central Conference of American Rabbis and Rabbinical Assembly. Also present with us this morning are the leaders of other major organizations in American Jewish life, as well as members of the Greater Miami Jewish community.

The men and women assembled here reflect the rich diversity of American Jewish life; we constitute a variety of religious and communal affiliations; American-born and immigrant; some are survivors of the Shoah, the Nazi Holocaust, while others have never experienced the dark shadow of anti-Semitism in their own lives. We come from all sections of the United States, and we come as full participants in the pluralistic and democratic society that has encouraged us to be proudly American and fully Jewish at the same time.

Your visit to this country happily coincides with the 200th anniversary of the U.S. Constitution, a document that guarantees religious liberty for all American citizens which has enabled all faith communities to flourish in an atmosphere of religious pluralism. This has made possible a free and flourishing religious life for all.

It has been 22 years since the conclusion of the Second Vatican Council and the promulgation of "Nostra Aetate." The broad teachings that emerged in 1965 have been further enriched and strengthened by a series of formal Catholic documents and pronouncements, some of them your own. These statements have transformed Catholic-Jewish relationships throughout the world, and this positive change is especially evident here in the United States.

As the largest Jewish community in the world, we have developed close and respectful ties with many Roman Catholics, both lay and clergy, and we value these warm relationships and treasure these friendships. We particularly cherish our relationship with the National Conference of Catholic Bishops and its Secretariat for Catholic-Jewish Relations. In almost every place where Catholics and Jews live in the United States, we relate to each other in some organized fashion. We constantly exchange views and opinions, and as Jews and Catholics we often share our positions, sometimes agreeing, sometimes disagreeing, but always striving for a spirit of mutual respect and understanding.

Throughout the United States, American Jews and Catholics work in concert with one another on a wide range of social justice issues and fight for global human rights and against all forms of racism and bigotry. Our common agenda has always embraced, and our future agenda will continue to embrace, the many crucial problems of the human family as a whole.

One of the major achievements of our joint encounters is the shared recognition that each community must be understood in its own terms, as it understands itself. It is particularly gratifying that our Catholic-Jewish meetings are conducted in a spirit of candor and mutual respect.

Such meetings took place last week at the Vatican and at Castel Gandolfo. These conversations, although quickly arranged, were highly significant. You and high Church leaders listened to the deeply felt concerns of the Jewish community that were raised following last June's state visit to the Vatican by Austrian President Kurt Waldheim, who has never expressed regrets for his Nazi past.

Obviously, the differences expressed at last week's meeting have not been resolved. However, this opportunity for us to express the pain and anger of the Jewish community in face-to-face meetings and for you and leaders of your Church to listen with respect and openness represents an important confirmation of the progress our communities have made in recent decades. One of the results of those meetings will be an instrumentality to develop closer communication and contact between our communities.

A basic belief of our Jewish faith is the need "to mend the world under the sovereignty of God" ("L'takken olam b'malkhut Shaddai"). To mend the world means to do God's work in the world. It is in this spirit that Catholics and Jews should continue to address the social, moral, economic and political problems of the world. Your presence here in the United States affords us the opportunity to reaffirm our commitment to the sacred imperative of "tikkun olam" ("the mending of the world").

But before we can mend the world, we must first mend ourselves. A meeting such as this is part of the healing process that is now visibly under way between our two communities. It is clear that the teachings proclaimed in "Nostra Aetate" are becoming major concerns of the Catholic Church and under your leadership are being implemented in the teachings of the Church and in the life of Catholics everywhere.

Catholics and Jews have begun the long overdue process of reconciliation. We still have some way to go because Catholic-Jewish relations are often filled with ambivalences, ambiguities and a painful history which must be confronted. Yet in a world of increasing interreligious, interracial and interethnic strife, the progress in Catholic-Jewish relations is one of this century's most positive developments.

We remain concerned with the persistence of anti-Semitism — the hatred of Jews and Judaism, which is on the rise in some parts of the world. We are encouraged by your vigorous leadership in denouncing all forms of anti-Semitism and by the Church's recent teachings. The Church's repudiation of anti-Semitism is of critical importance in the struggle to eradicate this virulent plague from the entire human family. Anti-Semitism may affect the body of the Jew, but history has tragically shown that it assaults the soul of the Christian world and all others who succumb to this ancient, but persistent pathology.

We hope that your strong condemnations of anti-Semitism will continue to be implemented in the schools, the parishes, teaching materials and the liturgy, and reflected in the attitudes and behavior of Catholics throughout the world. Greater attention needs to be paid to the Christian roots of anti-Semitism. The "teaching of contempt" for the Jews and Judaism must be ended once and for all.

The "teaching of contempt" reaped a demonic harvest during the Shoah, in which one-third of the Jewish people were murdered as a central component of a nation's policy. The Nazi Holocaust-Shoah brought together two very different forms of evil: On the one hand, it represented the triumph of an ideology of nationalism and racism, the suppression of human conscience and the deification of the state — concepts that are profoundly anti-Christian as well as anti-Jewish. On the other hand, the Shoah was the culmination of centuries of anti-Semitism in European culture for which Christian teachings bear a heavy responsibility.

While your sensitive concerns and your noteworthy pronouncements about the Shoah have been heartening, we have observed recent tendencies to obscure the fact that Jews were the major target of Nazi genocidal policies. It is possible to visit Nazi death camps today and not be informed that the majority of its victims were Jews. Your letter about Shoah, sent last month to Archbishop John May, the president of the NCCB, represented a deep level of understanding of that terrible period.

We look forward to the forthcoming Vatican document on the Shoah, the historical background of anti-Semitism and its contemporary manifestations.

Many Catholic schools in the United States are already teaching about the Holocaust and efforts are under way to develop a specific curriculum about the Shoah for Catholic students. This material is being jointly developed by Catholic and Jewish educators.

Even though many of the great centers of Jewish learning were destroyed during the Shoah, there has been a remarkable renewal of Jewish religious life throughout the world. This renaissance of the spirit is taking place not only in the United States, in the State of Israel and in other lands of freedom, but in the Soviet Union as well. Many Soviet Jews are discovering that the covenant between God and the people of Israel is indeed "irrevocable" as you declared last year at the Grand Synagogue in Rome. The struggle of Soviet Jews to achieve freedom is a major concern of the Jewish community, and we appreciate the support American Catholics have given to this cause.

The return to Zion and the re-establishment of Jewish sovereignty in the land of Israel play a paramount role in Jewish self-understanding today. Because of the importance that the State of Israel occupies in the mind, spirit and heart of Jews, whenever Christians and Jews meet in serious conversation Israel is at the center of that encounter. The re-emergence of an independent Jewish state onto the world stage in 1948 has compelled Christians and Jews to examine themselves and each other in a new light.

We must express our concern at the absence of full diplomatic relations between the Holy See and the State of Israel. We welcome the recent statements from Vatican leaders declaring that no theological reasons exist in Catholic doctrine to inhibit such relations. We strongly urge once again that full and formal diplomatic relations be established soon between the Vatican and the State of Israel. Such a step would be a positive and constructive contribution by the Vatican to the peace process, and it would send a strong signal to the international community that the Holy See recognizes Israel as a permanent and legitimate member of the family of nations.

One of the most welcome results of the recent Catholic-Jewish encounter has been the recognition by Catholics that Judaism has continued and deepened its unique spiritual development after the separation of the Christian Church from the Jewish people some 1,900 years ago.

A meeting such as today's is a vivid reminder that we live in a historic moment. Clearly, as two great communities of faith, repositories of moral and spiritual values, Catholics and Jews need to move together in this new movement. The last quarter-century has irreversibly changed the way we perceive and act toward each other.

In an age of great challenges and great possibilities there is a compelling need for a "vision for the times" "Chazon L'moed" (Hb 2:3). Our vision for Catholics and Jews is a prayer of the synagogue.

At the end of the Torah reading, the scroll is held high so the entire congregation may see the words of God, and together the congregation prays, "Hazak, Hazak, v'nithazek" ("Be strong, be very strong, and let us strengthen one another").

Pope John Paul II:

Dear friends — representatives of so many Jewish organizations assembled here from across the United States, my dear Jewish brothers and sisters,

1. I am grateful to you for your kind words of greeting. I am indeed pleased to be with you, especially at this time when the U.S. tour of the Vatican Judaica Collection begins. The wonderful material, including illuminated Bibles and prayerbooks, demonstrates but a small part of the immense spiritual resources of Jewish tradition across the centuries and up to

the present time — spiritual resources often used in fruitful cooperation with Christian artists.

It is fitting at the beginning of our meeting to emphasize our faith in the one God, who chose Abraham, Isaac and Jacob, and made with them a covenant of eternal love which was never revoked (cf. Gn 27:13; Rom 11:29). It was rather confirmed by the gift of the Torah to Moses, opened by the prophets to the hope of eternal redemption and to the universal commitment for justice and peace. The Jewish people, the Church and all believers in the merciful God — who is invoked in the Jewish prayers as " 'Av Ha-Rakhamim" — can find in this fundamental covenant with the patriarchs a very substantial starting point for our dialogue and our common witness in the world.

It is also fitting to recall God's promise to Abraham and the spiritual fraternity which it established: "In your descendants all the nations shall find blessing — all this because you obeyed my command" (Gn 22:18). This spiritual fraternity, linked to obedience to God, requires a great mutual respect in humility and confidence. An objective consideration of our relations during the centuries must take into account this great need.

2. It is indeed worthy of note that the United States was founded by people who came to these shores, often as religious refugees. They aspired to being treated justly and to being accorded hospitality according to the word of God, as we read in Leviticus: "You shall treat the alien who resides with you no differently than the natives born among you; have the same love for him as for yourself; for you too were once aliens in the land of Egypt. I, the Lord, am your God" (19:34). Among these millions of immigrants there was a large number of Catholics and Jews. The same basic religious principles of freedom and justice, of equality and moral solidarity, affirmed in the Torah as well as in the Gospel, were in fact reflected in the high human ideals and in the protection of universal rights found in the United States. These in turn exercised a strong positive influence on the history of Europe and other parts of the world. But the paths of the immigrants in their new land were not always easy. Sadly enough, prejudice and discrimination were also known in the New World as well as in the Old. Nevertheless, together Jews and Catholics have contributed to the success of the American experiment in religious freedom and in this unique context have given to the world a vigorous form of interreligious dialogue between our two ancient traditions. For those engaged in this dialogue, so important to the Church and to the Jewish people, I pray: May God bless you and make you strong for his service!

3. At the same time, our common heritage, task and hope do not eliminate our distinctive identities. Because of her specific Christian witness, "the Church must preach Jesus Christ to the world" (1974 Guidelines and Suggestions for Implementing "Nostra Aetate," I). In so doing we proclaim that "Christ is our peace" (Eph 2:14). As the apostle Paul said: "All this is from God, who through Christ reconciled us to himself and gave us the ministry of reconciliation" (2 Cor 5:18). At the same time, we recognize and appreciate the spiritual treasures of the Jewish people and their religious witness to God. A fraternal theological dialogue will try to understand, in the light of the mystery of redemption, how differences in faith should not cause enmity but open up the way of "reconciliation," so that in the end "God may be all in all" (1 Cor 15:28).

In this regard I am pleased that the National Conference of Catholic Bishops and the Synagogue Council of America are initiating a consultation between Jewish leaders and bishops which should carry forward a dialogue on issues of the greatest interest to the two faith communities.

4. Considering history in the light of the principles of faith in God, we must also reflect on the catastrophic event of the Shoah, that ruthless and inhuman attempt to exterminate the Jewish people in Europe, an attempt that resulted in millions of victims — including women and children, the elderly and the sick — exterminated only because they were Jews.

Considering this mystery of the suffering of Israel's children, their witness of hope, of faith and of humanity under dehumanizing outrages, the Church experiences ever more deeply her common bond with the Jewish people and with their treasure of spiritual riches in the past and in the present.

It is also fitting to recall the strong, unequivocal efforts of the popes against anti-Semitism and Nazism at the height of the persecution against the Jews. Back in 1938, Pius XI declared that "anti-Semitism cannot be admitted" (Sept. 6, 1938), and he declared the total opposition between Christianity and Nazism by stating that the Nazi cross is an "enemy of the cross of Christ" (Christmas Allocution, 1938). And I am convinced that history will reveal ever more clearly and convincingly how deeply Pius XII felt the tragedy of the Jewish people and how hard and effectively he worked to assist them during the Second World War.

Speaking in the name of humanity and Christian principles, the bishops' conference of the United States denounced the atrocities with a clear statement: "Since the murderous assault on Poland, utterly devoid of every semblance of humanity, there has been a premeditated and systematic extermination of the people of this nation. The same satanic technique is being applied to many other peoples. We feel a deep sense of revulsion against the cruel indignities heaped upon the Jews in conquered countries and upon defenseless peoples not of our faith" (Nov. 14, 1942).

We also remember many others who, at risk of their own lives, helped persecuted Jews and are honored by the Jews with the title of "Tzaddiqe 'ummot ha-'olam" (righteous of the nations).

5. The terrible tragedy of your people has led many Jewish thinkers to reflect on the human condition with acute insights. Their vision of man and the roots of this vision in the teachings of the Bible, which we share in our common heritage of the Hebrew Scriptures, offer Jewish and Catholic scholars much useful material for reflection and dialogue.

In order to understand even more deeply the meaning of the Shoah and the historical roots of anti-Semitism that are related to it, joint collaboration and studies by Catholics and Jews on the Shoah should be continued. Such studies have already taken place through many conferences in your country such as the national workshops on Christian-Jewish relations. The religious and historical implications of the Shoah for Christians and Jews will now be taken up formally by the International Catholic-Jewish Liaison Committee, meeting later this year in the United States for the first time. And as was affirmed in the important and very cordial meeting I had with Jewish leaders in Castel Gandolfo on Sept. 1, a Catholic document on the Shoah and anti-Semitism will be forthcoming, resulting from such serious studies.

Similarly, it is to be hoped that common educational programs on our historical and religious relations, which are well developed in your country, will truly promote mutual respect and teach future generations about the Holocaust so that never again will such a horror be possible. Never again!

147

When meeting the leaders of the Polish Jewish community in Warsaw in June of this year, I underscored the fact that through the terrible experience of the Shoah, your people have become "a loud warning voice for all of humanity, for all nations, for all the powers of this world, for every system and every individual … a saving warning" (Address of June 14, 1987).

6. It is also desirable that in every diocese Catholics should implement, under the direction of the bishops, the statement of the Second Vatican Council and the subsequent instructions issued by the Holy See regarding the correct way to preach and teach about Jews and Judaism. I know that a great many efforts in this direction have already been made by Catholics, and I wish to express my gratitude to all those who have worked so diligently for this aim.

7. Necessary for any sincere dialogue is the intention of each partner to allow others to define themselves "in the light of their own religious experience" (1974 Guidelines, Introduction). In fidelity to this affirmation, Catholics recognize among the elements of the Jewish experience that Jews have a religious attachment to the land, which finds its roots in biblical tradition.

After the tragic extermination of the Shoah, the Jewish people began a new period in their history. They have a right to a homeland, as does any civil nation, according to international law. "For the Jewish people who live in the State of Israel and who preserve in that land such precious testimonies to their history and their faith, we must ask for the desired security and the due tranquillity that is the prerogative of every nation and condition of life and of progress for every society" ("Redemptionis Anno," April 20, 1984).

What has been said about the right to a homeland also applies to the Palestinian people, so many of whom remain homeless and refugees. While all concerned must honestly reflect on the past — Moslems no less than Jews and Christians — it is time to forge those solutions which will lead to a just, complete and lasting peace in that area. For this peace I earnestly pray.

8. Finally, as I thank you once again for the warmth of your greeting to me, I give praise and thanks to the Lord for this fraternal meeting, for the gift of dialogue between our peoples and for the new and deeper understanding between us. As our long relationship moves toward its third millennium, it is our great privilege in this generation to be witnesses to this progress.

It is my sincere hope that, as partners in dialogue, as fellow believers in the God who revealed himself, as children of Abraham, we will strive to render a common service to humanity, which is so much needed in this our day. We are called to collaborate in service and to unite in a common cause wherever a brother or sister is unattended, forgotten, neglected or suffering in any way; wherever human rights are endangered or human dignity offended; wherever the rights of God are violated or ignored.

With the psalmist, I now repeat: "I will hear what God proclaims; the Lord — for he proclaims peace to his people, and to his faithful ones, and to those who put in him their hope" (Ps 85:9).

To all of you, dear friends, dear brothers and sisters; to all of you dear Jewish people of America: With great hope I wish you the peace of the Lord: Shalom! Shalom! God bless you on this sabbath and in this year: "Shabbath Shalom! Shanah Tovah we-Hatimah Tovah!"

Williams-Brice Stadium Columbia, S.C., Sept. 11

Pope John Paul II:

Praised be Jesus Christ!
Dear brothers and sisters,

1. I greet each one of you in our Lord and Savior Jesus Christ. It is indeed the "Lord of both the dead and the living" (Rom 14:9) who has brought us together in this holy assembly of Christian people, a joy-filled gathering of different ecclesial communions: Orthodox, Anglicans, Methodists, Baptists, Lutherans, Presbyterians, members of the United Church of Christ and of other Reformed churches, Disciples of Christ, members of the peace churches, Pentecostals, members of the Polish National Catholic Church and Catholics.

We stand side by side to confess Jesus Christ, "the one mediator between God and man" (1 Tm 2:5), for "at Jesus' name every knee must bend in the heavens, on the earth and under the earth, and every tongue proclaim to the glory of God the Father: Jesus Christ is Lord!" (Phil 2:10).

We have come here to pray, and in doing so we are following the example of all the saints from the beginning, especially the apostles, who in awaiting the Holy Spirit "devoted themselves to prayer, together with the women and Mary, the mother of Jesus, and with his brethren" (Acts 1:14). Together we are renewing our common faith in the eternal redemption which we have obtained through the cross of Jesus Christ (cf. Heb 9:12), and our hope that, just as Jesus rose from the dead, so too we shall rise to eternal life (cf. Phil 3:11). In fact, through our baptism in the name of the Father and of the Son and of the Holy Spirit, we have been buried with Christ "so that, just as Christ was raised from the dead by the glory of the Father, we too might live a new life" (Rom 6:4). Living a new life in the Spirit, we are a pilgrim people, pressing forward amid the persecutions of the world and the consolations of God, announcing the death of the Lord until he comes (cf. 1 Cor 11:26; "Lumen Gentium," 8).

Brothers and sisters: We are divided in many ways in our faith and discipleship. But we are here together today as sons and daughters of the one Father, calling upon the one Lord, Jesus Christ, in the love which the same Holy Spirit pours forth into our hearts. Let us give thanks to God and let us rejoice in this fellowship! And let us commit ourselves further to the great task which Jesus himself urges upon us: to go forward along the path of Christian reconciliation and unity "without obstructing the ways of divine providence and without prejudging the future inspiration of the Holy Spirit" ("Unitatis Redintegratio," 24).

2. In this service of Christian witness we have listened together to the word of God given to us in the Holy Scriptures. The Scriptures are dear to all of us. They are one of the greatest treasures we share. In the Sacred Scriptures and in the deeds of divine mercy which they narrate, God our Father, out of the abundance of his love, speaks to us as his children and lives among us. The Bible is holy because in its inspired and unalterable words the voice of the Holy Spirit lives and is heard among us, sounding again and again in the Church from age to age and from generation to generation (cf. "Dei Verbum," 21).

3. Today this stadium has resounded with passages from

Holy Scripture bearing on the reality of the family. We have heard the plea and promise made by the young widow Ruth: "Wherever you go I will go, wherever you lodge I will lodge, your people shall be my people, and your God my God. Wherever you die I will die and there be buried" (Ru 1:16-17). To hear these words is to be moved with a deep feeling for the strength of family ties: stronger than the fear of hardships to be faced; stronger than the fear of exile in an unfamiliar land; stronger than the fear of possible rejection. The bond that unites a family is not only a matter of natural kinship or of shared life and experience. It is essentially a holy and religious bond. Marriage and the family are sacred realities.

The sacredness of Christian marriage consists in the fact that in God's plan the marriage covenant between a man and a woman becomes the image and symbol of the covenant which unites God and his people (cf. Hos 2:21; Jer 3:6-13; Is 54:5-10). It is the sign of Christ's love for his Church (cf. Eph 5:32). Because God's love is faithful and irrevocable, so those who have been married "in Christ" are called to remain faithful to each other forever. Did not Jesus himself say to us: "What therefore God has joined together, let no man put asunder" (cf. Mt 19:6)?

Contemporary society has a special need of the witness of couples who persevere in their union as an eloquent, even if sometimes suffering, "sign" in our human condition of the steadfastness of God's love. Day after day Christian married couples are called to open their hearts ever more to the Holy Spirit, whose power never fails and who enables them to love each other as Christ has loved us. And, as St. Paul writes to the Galatians, "the fruit of the spirit is love, joy, peace, patient endurance, kindness, generosity, faith, mildness and chastity" (Gal 5:22-23). All of this constitutes the rule of life and the program of personal development of Christian couples. And each Christian community has a great responsibility to sustain couples in their love.

4. From such love Christian families are born. In them children are welcomed as a splendid gift of God's goodness, and they are educated in the essential values of human life, learning above all that "man is more precious for what he is than for what he has" (cf. "Gaudium et Spes," 35). The entire family endeavors to practice respect for the dignity of every individual and to offer disinterested service to those in need (cf. "Familiaris Consortio," 37).

Christian families exist to form a communion of persons in love. As such, the Church and the family are each in its own way living representations in human history of the eternal loving communion of the three persons of the Most Holy Trinity. In fact, the family is called the Church in miniature, "the domestic church," a particular expression of the Church through the human experience of love and common life (cf. ibid., 49). Like the Church, the family ought to be a place where the Gospel is transmitted and from which the Gospel radiates to other families and to the whole of society.

5. In America and throughout the world, the family is being shaken to its roots. The consequences for individuals and society in personal and collective instability and unhappiness are incalculable. Yet it is heartening to know that in the face of this extraordinary challenge many Christians are committing themselves to the defense and support of family life. In recent years the Catholic Church, especially on the occasion of the 1980 synod of the world's bishops, has been involved in an extensive reflection on the role of the Christian family in the modern world. This is a field in which there must be the maximum collaboration among all who confess Jesus Christ.

So often the pressures of modern living separate husbands and wives from one another, threatening their lifelong interdependence in love and fidelity. Can we also not be concerned about the impact of cultural pressures upon relations between the generations, upon parental authority and the transmission of sacred values? Our Christian conscience should be deeply concerned about the way in which sins against love and against life are often presented as examples of "progress" and emancipation. Most often, are they not but the age-old forms of selfishness dressed up in a new language and presented in a new cultural framework?

6. Many of these problems are the result of a false notion of individual freedom at work in our culture, as if one could be free only when rejecting every objective norm of conduct, refusing to assume responsibility or even refusing to put curbs on instincts and passions! Instead, true freedom implies that we are capable of choosing a good without constraint. This is the truly human way of proceeding in the choices — big and small — which life puts before us. The fact that we are also able to choose not to act as we see we should is a necessary condition of our moral freedom. But in that case we must account for the good that we fail to do and for the evil that we commit. This sense of moral accountability needs to be reawakened if society is to survive as a civilization of justice and solidarity.

It is true that our freedom is weakened and conditioned in many ways, not least as a consequence of the mysterious and dramatic history of mankind's original rebellion against the Creator's will, as indicated in the opening pages of the Book of Genesis. But we remain free and responsible beings who have been redeemed by Jesus Christ, and we must educate our freedom to recognize and choose what is right and good, and to reject what does not conform to the original truth concerning our nature and our destiny as God's creatures. Truth — beginning with the truth of our redemption through the cross and resurrection of Jesus Christ — is the root and rule of freedom, the foundation and measure of all liberating action (cf. Instruction on Christian Freedom and Liberation, 3).

7. It would be a great tragedy for the entire human family if the United States, which prides itself on its consecration to freedom, were to lose sight of the true meaning of that noble word. America: You cannot insist on the right to choose, without also insisting on the duty to choose well, the duty to choose the truth. Already there is much breakdown and pain in your own society because fundamental values essential to the well-being of individuals, families and the entire nation are being emptied of their real content.

And yet, at the same time, throughout this land there is a great stirring, an awareness of the urgent need to recapture the ultimate meaning of life and its fundamental values. Surely by now we must be convinced that only by recognizing the primacy of moral values can we use the immense possibilities offered by science and material progress to bring about the true advancement of the human person in truth, freedom and dignity. As Christians, our specific contribution is to bring the wisdom of God's word to bear on the problems of modern living in such a way that modern culture will be led to a more profoundly restored covenant with divine Wisdom itself (cf. "Familiaris Consortio," 8). As we heard proclaimed in the Gospel reading, Jesus indicates that the supreme norm of our behavior and our relationships, including our relationship with him, is always obedience to the will of the Creator: "Whoever does the will of my heavenly Father is brother and sister and mother to me" (Mt 12:50).

8. Brothers and sisters: To the extent that God grants us to grow in Christian unity let us work together to offer strength and support to families, on whom the well-being of society depends and on whom our churches and ecclesial communities depend. May the families of America live with grateful hearts, giving thanks to the Lord for his blessings, praying for one another, bearing one another's burdens, welcoming one another as Christ has welcomed them.

My prayer for all of you at the end of this second day of my visit echoes the words of Paul to the Thessalonians: "May the God of peace make you perfect in holiness.... May the grace of our Lord Jesus Christ be with you" (1 Thes 5:23, 28).

Meeting with Blacks New Orleans, Sept. 12

Bishop Joseph L. Howze:

Most Holy Father, bishop of Rome and vicar of Jesus Christ:
The representatives of black Catholics in the United States of America are highly honored to have the privilege of this audience with you during your second pastoral visit to the United States. In the name of all black Catholics in the United States of America, we heartily welcome you.

There are approximately 1,295,000 black Catholics in the United States of America. The black Catholic population is about 5 percent of the total black population, 30 million, and approximately 2 percent of the total Catholic population, 52 million, of the United States.

Historically, black Americans have not been affiliated with the Catholic Church as have other ethnic and national groups. Consequently, in the minds of some people being black and Catholic is not a spontaneous concept.

But when we speak of the Catholic Church we are speaking of that institution which Jesus Christ established to bring salvation to all peoples. The Catholic Church comprises peoples of all races, nations, colors, and many languages and customs. "To be Catholic is to be universal. To be universal is not to be uniform" ("What We Have Seen and Heard").

We hear the expression today: "being black and Catholic." This expression is not to denote separatism, but rather to identify those gifts and talents which integrate the faith and culture of black Americans into the common heritage of the Church which is shared by all.

The gifts of black people within the Church are our contribution to building up the whole Church. The witness of blacks, sharing our gifts within the Catholic Church, is a confirmation of the expression: "authentically black and truly Catholic."

Black Catholics desire to find salvation in Jesus Christ and his Church by offering our giftedness to the Church through our traditional art forms, spirituality and rich customs. Black Catholics want to express our faith, reflecting our unique identity and experiences. Yet, at the same time, we want our expression of faith to become ever more a part of the Christian Catholic tradition, already rich in diversity and redemptive in Jesus Christ, the center of unity.

A full participation of black Catholics in the life of the Church was most recently expressed in the pastoral plan developed during the National Black Catholic Congress at The Catholic University of America, Washington, D.C., on May 21-24, 1987.

Part of the pastoral plan dealt with leadership and pastoral ministry, and how best to evangelize in the black community. The pastoral plan proposes that the Church recognize shared responsibility for the development and empowerment of black Catholic leadership.

In the pastoral letter of the black Catholic bishops, "What We Have Seen and Heard," we acknowledged that racism is a major hindrance to full development of black leadership within the Church, but we also said that even though the strain of racism is a scandal to many, "for us it must be the opportunity to work for the Church's renewal as part of our task of evangelization."

"Our demand for recognition, our demand for leadership roles in the task of evangelization, is not a call for separatism but a pledge of our commitment to the Church and to share in her witnessing to the love of Christ. For the Christ we proclaim is he who prayed on the night before he died: '... that all may be one as you, Father, are in me, and I in you; I pray that they may be (one) in us, that the world may believe that you sent me.' (Jn 17:21)" ("What We Have Seen and Heard").

Many opportunities for evangelization exist within the black community. For some of these, the black community can and must take the initiative. For others, we need the cooperation and encouragement of the entire American Church. The black Catholic community must encourage young men and women to follow Christ in the priesthood and in the consecrated religious life. But the matter of vocations is so crucial to the cause of evangelization in the black community that we need the collaboration of the entire Church.

Black Catholics love the Church and want to become a more significant part of its mission to evangelize and sanctify the world. We wish to share our gifts with others who do not know Jesus and the Church as we do.

Most Holy Father, we beseech your words of wisdom, spiritual counsel and encouragement in your address to us.

We turn to Mary, the mother of God, asking her intercession that, on our journey of faith, she may obtain for us the grace of eternal salvation.

Pope John Paul II:

Dear brothers and sisters in Christ,
1. "Go into the whole world and proclaim the good news to all creation" (Mk 16:15). With these words, our Lord Jesus Christ directed the Church to speak his own message of life to the whole human family. The apostles first responded to the Savior's call and traveled throughout the known world, sharing with everyone who would listen what they had seen and heard (cf. 1 Jn 1:3), speaking about God's kingdom and about reconciliation in Christ.

Today, almost 2,000 years later, the Church still seeks to respond generously to Christ's command. The world we must serve today is much bigger, and the people who long to hear the word of life are numerous indeed. While the words of the Lord remain true, "the harvest is good but laborers are scarce" (Mt 9:37), still we rejoice that the Holy Spirit has enriched the Church with many hands for the harvest. There are worthy laborers in every corner of the earth, people of every culture, who are eager to live the Gospel and to proclaim it by word and example.

I am especially happy to meet with you who make up the black Catholic leadership in the United States. Your great concern, both as blacks and as Catholics, is — and must always be — that all your black brothers and sisters throughout America may hear and embrace the saving and uplifting Gospel of Jesus Christ. I willingly join my voice to those of the bishops of your country, who are encouraging you to give priority to the great task of evangelization, to be missionaries of Christ's love and truth within your own black community. To all the members of the black community throughout the United States, I send my greetings of respect and esteem.

2. My dear brother bishops, who share with me the burdens and joys of the episcopacy: I am pleased that the universality of the Gospel and the cultural diversity of your nation are increasingly mirrored in the composition of the American hierarchy. While your apostolic ministry draws you to serve all the faithful of your respective dioceses — and in collegial unity the whole body of Christ — it is fitting for many reasons that your own black brothers and sisters should have a special right to your pastoral love and service. United with the successor of Peter in the college of bishops, you are a sign of the unity and universality of the Church and of her mission. As bishops, we are entrusted with the task of preserving in its integrity the good news of salvation and of presenting it as effectively as possible to our people, so that they may all discover in Jesus Christ "the way, and the truth, and the life" (Jn 14:6).

Our brothers in the priesthood, ministering in the person of Christ and in union with us, transmit the teaching of the faith and celebrate the sacred mysteries of salvation. How fruitful it is for the mission of the Church in America when so many priests from different racial and ethnic groups proclaim together Christ's liberating Gospel and thus bear witness to the fact that it rightfully belongs to everyone.

The Church in the United States is distinguished by its large number of deacons, among whom are several hundred from the black Catholic community. As heralds of the Gospel and servant ministers of Christ, dear brothers, you complete the threefold ministry of the sacrament of orders. In the Church you are called to the service of the word, of the Eucharist and of charity. Your generous response is a clear indication of the growing maturity of the black Catholic community, a maturity emphasized by the black bishops of your country in their pastoral letter "What We Have Seen and Heard."

Even in those days — by the grace of God now long past — when your people struggled under the terrible burden of slavery, brave spirits within the community embraced the evangelical counsels and dedicated themselves to the religious life. Thus they bore eloquent witness to the power of the Holy Spirit, accomplishing the work of spiritual freedom even in the moment of physical oppression. Black religious today offer a comparable witness to the Church and society, proclaiming God's kingdom to a world shackled by consumerism, mindless pleasure seeking and irresponsible individualism — shackles of the spirit which are even more destructive than the chains of physical slavery.

I am close to the whole black community in the great mission and responsibility of encouraging more and more young Americans of their race to respond to the Lord's invitation to religious life and the priesthood. I urge you to be faithful to prayer and to do all you can to ensure that those who are called will find the support and the assistance which they need in order to pursue these vocations and to persevere in them.

3. The Church's work of evangelization finds entry into the human community in a special way through the lives of lay people. As my predecessor Paul VI pointed out, the laity's "own field of evangelizing activity is the vast and complicated world of politics, society and economics, but also the world of culture, of the sciences and the arts, of international life, of the mass media" ("Evangelii Nuntiandi," 70). By fulfilling worthily the broad range of their temporal involvement, lay men and women bear witness in a unique way to the universal call to holiness. The witness of their faithful lives speaks an uplifting message to the world.

I express my deep love and esteem for the black Catholic community in the United States. Its vitality is a sign of hope for society. Composed as you are of many lifelong Catholics and many who have more recently embraced the faith, together with a growing immigrant community you reflect the Church's ability to bring together a diversity of people united in faith, hope and love, sharing a communion with Christ in the Holy Spirit. I urge you to keep alive and active your rich cultural gifts. Always profess proudly before the whole Church and the whole world your love for God's word; it is a special blessing, which you must forever treasure as a part of your heritage. Help us all to remember that authentic freedom comes from accepting the truth and from living one's life in accordance with it — and the full truth is found only in Christ Jesus. Continue to inspire us by your desire to forgive — as Jesus forgave — and by your desire to be reconciled with all the people of this nation, even those who would unjustly deny you the full exercise of your human rights.

4. I am sure that you share with me a special concern for that most basic human community, the family. Your faithful Christian families are a source of comfort in the face of the extraordinary pressures affecting society. Today you must rediscover the spirit of family life, which refuses to be destroyed in the face of even the most oppressive forces. Surely that spirit can be found in exploring your spiritual and cultural heritage. The inspiration you draw from the great men and women of your past will then allow your young people to see the value of a strong family life. Know that the pope stands united with the black community as it rises to embrace its full dignity and lofty destiny.

The family is the first setting of evangelization, the place where the good news of Christ is first received and then, in simple yet profound ways, handed on from generation to generation. At the same time, families in our time vitally depend upon the Church to defend their rights and to teach the obligations and responsibilities which lead to the fullness of joy and life. Thus, I urge all of you, especially the clergy and religious, to work for the promotion of family values within the local community. And I remind those responsible for making and administering laws and public policies that social problems are never solved, but only worsened, by positions which weaken or destroy the family.

5. Even in this wealthy nation, committed by its founding fathers to the dignity and equality of all persons, the black community suffers a disproportionate share of economic deprivation. Far too many of your young people receive less than an equal opportunity for a quality education and for gainful employment. The Church must continue to join her efforts with the efforts of others who are working to correct all imbalances and disorders of a social nature. Indeed, the Church can never remain silent in the face of injustice wherever it is clearly present.

In the most difficult hours of your struggle for civil rights amid discrimination and oppression, God himself guided your steps along the way of peace. Before the witness of history the response of non-violence stands in the memory of this nation as a monument of honor to the black community of

151

the United States. Today as we recall those who with Christian vision opted for non-violence as the only truly effective approach for ensuring and safeguarding human dignity, we cannot but think of the Rev. Dr. Martin Luther King Jr. and of the providential role he played in contributing to the rightful human betterment of black Americans and therefore to the improvement of American society itself.

My dear brothers and sisters of the black community: It is the hour to give thanks to God for his liberating action in your history and in your lives. This liberating action is a sign and expression of Christ's paschal mystery, which in every age is effective in helping God's people to pass from bondage into their glorious vocation of full Christian freedom. And as you offer your prayer of thanksgiving, you must not fail to concern yourselves with the plight of your brothers and sisters in other places throughout the world. Black Americans must offer their own special solidarity of Christian love to all people who bear the heavy burden of oppression, whatever its physical or moral nature.

6. The Catholic Church has made a profound contribution to the lives of many members of the black community in this land through the gift of education received in Catholic schools. Because of the splendid commitment of dioceses and parishes, many of you here today have joined us at the table of unity and faith as a result of the evangelization carried out in these institutions. Catholic schools have a special place in the work of spreading the Gospel of Christ. They are a great gift from God. Keep your Catholic schools strong and active. Their uncompromising Catholic identity and Catholic witness at every level must continue to enrich the black communities of this nation.

7. In addition to the schools, other means of evangelization should also be given priority. Among these the means of social communication deserve special attention. The mass media are also a great gift of God's providence and should be fully utilized in the service of the Gospel of our Lord Jesus Christ. They can be of immense service to the millions of black people who long to hear the good news of salvation proclaimed in ways that speak to their own heritage and traditions.

While remaining faithful to her doctrine and discipline, the Church esteems and honors all cultures; she respects them in all her evangelizing efforts among the various peoples. At the first Pentecost, those present heard the apostles speaking in their own languages (cf. Acts 2:4f). With the guidance of the Holy Spirit, we try in every age to bring the Gospel convincingly and understandably to people of all races, languages and cultures. It is important to realize that there is no black church, no white church, no American church; but there is and must be in the one Church of Jesus Christ a home for blacks, whites, Americans, every culture and race. What I said on another occasion I willingly repeat: "The Church is catholic ... because she is able to present in every human context the revealed truth, preserved by her intact in its divine content, in such a way as to bring it into contact with the lofty thoughts and just expectations of every individual and every people" ("Slavorum Apostoli," 18).

Dear brothers and sisters: Your black cultural heritage enriches the Church and makes her witness of universality more complete. In a real way the Church needs you, just as you need the Church, for you are part of the Church and the Church is part of you. As you continue to place this heritage at the service of the whole Church for the spread of the Gospel, the Holy Spirit himself will continue through you his work of evangelization. With a joyful and a hopeful heart, I entrust you and the whole black community to the loving care of Mary, mother of our Savior. May she, who both listened to the word and believed in it, guide your lives and those of future generations of black Catholics within the one people of God, the one mystical body of Christ. Through her intercession may grace be to all of you "who love our Lord Jesus Christ with unfailing love" (Eph 6:23).

Meeting with Teachers New Orleans, Sept. 12

Dr. James Griesgraber:

Holy Father, we the leaders of Catholic education in the United States of America wish to teach you about the uniqueness of this system of education. Five characteristics identify it as unique, identify it as different from the educational systems of every other country in the world.

First, our education program rests on the principle of freedom of choice; attendance at a Catholic school or a parish religious education program is not required, yet students come by the hundreds of thousands, almost 8 million of them, because parents and children believe in the value of a Catholic education. Students in their daily lessons freely ask questions and even challenge their teachers. Catholic educators do not view this as a threat; rather, they recognize that it demonstrates the growth of critical thinking skills and the acquisition of new insights into the world in which they live.

The second unique aspect of American Catholic education is that it embraces all peoples. Black, Hispanic, Asian and native Americans compose over 20 percent of those in our schools. About 13 percent of our students are not Catholic; in some parishes this figure climbs as high as 60 percent. Our Catholic schools' emphasis on both racial integration and ecumenism reflects the importance they place on both social justice and service to children and youths of all faiths. Our special schools have been leaders in the education of handicapped children and young adults. Moreover, our regular elementary and high schools are making strides in serving these special students in their programs. This "mainstreaming" effort addresses the need for handicapped persons to be fully integrated into the Christian community and all facets of our Church's life.

The third unique aspect of American Catholic education is that this whole system depends on the voluntary financial support and service of thousands of people. No government funds are used directly to support Catholic schools. Nevertheless, these same parents also are required to pay taxes to support the public school system even though they do not send their children to it. And we must not forget the financial sacrifice made by many who choose to teach in Catholic schools, for they often do so for substantially lower salaries than they could command in the public school systems. In addition, hundreds of thousands of volunteer catechists serve in parish religious education programs with no financial return.

The fourth unique characteristic of American Catholic education is the degree to which parents are involved. On the day-to-day level, they can be found acting as teacher's aides and working with small groups; supervising play areas; recruiting new students; taking children on field trips; sharing their talents with students; and coaching sports. In addition to this, many have become active in the governance of schools and religious education programs. Many parents serve on these boards and, working with the pastor and the educational administrators, set policy, see that it is implemented, develop ways to finance programs, and thus continue to forge new partnerships in education.

The last characteristic of American Catholic education to which we direct your attention is its success. Year after year, students in Catholic schools score higher than the national average on government-sponsored and administered tests in reading, mathematics and composition. Each year over 80 percent of the students who graduate from Catholic secondary schools enter colleges to continue their education. Finally, a higher percentage of American Catholics more regularly practice their religion by attending Mass and receiving the sacraments than Catholics in other countries.

Travel though you may, you will not find a more vital program of Catholic education than in the United States. Its vitality springs from its uniquely American roots and in turn allows our Catholic education truly to be a gift to our nation.

Sister Patricia James Sweeney:

Teaching is not simply a gift given. It is a gift shared. Catholic education is a gift given and shared, a blessing to the whole church and to the nation. Teachers are the heart and soul of Catholic education.

What do teachers do? In words that will live, Christa McAuliffe, American teacher, religious educator and astronaut, said, "I touch the future. I teach."

As we Catholic teachers believe, we touch a future that stretches to eternity. Our students are God's own children. Each is infinitely valuable, infinitely lovable — even though this vision is sometimes blurred by the realities of the classroom, where the arrival of the peaceable kingdom is occasionally set back by the lions who aren't ready to lie down with the lambs.

So we as teachers are drawn daily into collaboration with parents, to teach as Jesus taught, to imitate the Word made Flesh as we pass along the words to the spirit made flesh each day, showing that the fullness and perfection of humanity is inseparable from divinity, that the two great commandments, love God and love your brothers and sisters, are ultimately one commandment.

Our sense of mission is not an addition, not a sum, not a congeries of tasks, but one task —
—To know is to love.
—To love is to serve.
—To serve is to build the kingdom.

It is clear that one of the most important things our teachers do is create and sustain an extraordinary sense of community in our schools and parish programs. From them flows the love that binds strangers into family.

This does not mean that things are perfect. Far from it. Salaries for teachers are low and, in real dollars, getting lower. We must find ways to share this financial burden, remove it from the shoulders of teachers. Members of the religious communities, in whose debt we all stand, are aging; collectively they face a $2.5 billion shortfall in what they need to care for those who for so long labored in the educational vineyards. We must also find ways to make up for this shortfall, secure the future dignity of all those who have served in this impor-

tant ministry. We must find these solutions and act to put an end to these problems that are pushing Catholic education out of reach of more and more who want it.

But we continue to learn … to learn more about ourselves, about the world around us and about how to help one another.

St. Paul tells us that the saints together make a unity in the work of service, building up the body of Christ. We continue to find new ways to become a family united by love.

We are deeply immersed in the Roman Catholic tradition, and we are changing. We are passing a major portion of the trust for Catholic education, both in schools and parish programs, to lay people. We continue to involve all our teachers in the spirituality of what they are called to do.

We are a different group from those who preceded us. We live in a different world and a different church. We sing different hymns and see different visions.

But as Catholic teachers, in this time and in this country, we not only reach out to touch the future, we are touched also by our own past, by the tradition that we inherited from those who taught us.

We are the future they reached out for.

Pope John Paul II:

Dear brothers and sisters,

1. I thank all of you for your warm welcome, and I praise our Lord and Savior Jesus Christ, who gives me this opportunity to meet with you, the representatives of Catholic elementary and secondary schools and leaders in religious education. My first word to you is one of esteem and encouragement: I wish to assure you that I fully appreciate the extraordinary importance of your commitment to Catholic education. I commend you for your concern for the vitality and Catholic identity of the educational centers in which you work throughout the length and breadth of the United States. I encourage you to continue to fulfill your special role within the Church and within society in a spirit of generous responsibility, intelligent creativity and the pursuit of excellence.

2. It is fitting that we should be meeting in this historic city, itself the meeting point of several rich cultures, where the Capuchin Fathers and the Ursuline Sisters founded schools at the very dawn of your emergence as a nation. You are preparing to observe the 200th anniversary of the signing of the Constitution of the United States. There is no doubt that the guarantee of religious freedom enshrined in the Bill of Rights has helped make possible the marvelous growth of Catholic education in this country.

Over the years much has been attempted and much has been achieved by Catholics in the United States to make available for their children the best education possible. Much has been done in the specific area of bringing the wealth of our Catholic faith to children and adults in the home, in schools and through religious education programs. The presence of the Church in the field of education is wonderfully manifested in the vast and dynamic network of schools and educational programs extending from the preschool through the adult years. The entire ecclesial community — bishops, priests, Religious, the laity — the Church in all her parts, is called to value ever more deeply the importance of this task and mission, and to continue to give it full and enthusiastic support.

3. In the beginning and for a long time afterward, women and men Religious bore the chief organizational and teaching

responsibilities in Catholic education in this country. As pioneers they met that challenge splendidly, and they continue to meet it today. The Church and — I am certain — the nation will forever feel a debt of gratitude toward them. The importance of the presence of committed Religious and of religious communities in the educational apostolate has not diminished with time. It is my heartfelt prayer that the Lord will continue to call many young people to the religious life and that their witness to the Gospel will remain a central element in Catholic education.

4. In recent years, thousands of lay people have come forward as administrators and teachers in the Church's schools and educational programs. By accepting and developing the legacy of Catholic thought and educational experience which they have inherited, they take their place as full partners in the Church's mission of educating the whole person and of transmitting the good news of salvation in Jesus Christ to successive generations of young Americans. Even if they do not "teach religion," their service in a Catholic school or educational program is part of the Church's unceasing endeavor to lead all to "profess the truth in love and grow to the full maturity of Christ the head" (Eph 4:15).

I am aware that not all questions relating to the organization, financing and administration of Catholic schools in an increasingly complex society have been resolved to the satisfaction of all. We hope that such matters will be settled with justice and fairness for all. In this regard it is important to proceed in a proper perspective. For a Catholic educator, the Church should not be looked upon merely as an employer. The Church is the body of Christ, carrying on the mission of the Redeemer throughout history. It is our privilege to share in that mission, to which we are called by the grace of God and in which we are engaged together.

5. Permit me, brothers and sisters, to mention briefly something that is of special concern to the Church. I refer to the rights and duties of parents in the education of their children. The Second Vatican Council clearly enunciated the Church's position: "Since parents have conferred life on their children, they have a most solemn obligation to educate their offspring. Hence, parents must be acknowledged as the first and foremost educators of their children" ("Gravissimum Educationis," 3). In comparison with the educational role of all others, their role is primary; it is also irreplaceable and inalienable. It would be wrong for anyone to attempt to usurp that unique responsibility (cf. "Familiaris Consortio," 36). Nor should parents in any way be penalized for choosing for their children an education according to their beliefs.

Parents need to ensure that their own homes are places where spiritual and moral values are lived. They are right to insist that their children's faith be respected and fostered. As educators you correctly see your role as cooperating with parents in their primary responsibility. Your efforts to involve them in the whole educational process are commendable. This is an area in which pastors and other priests can be especially supportive. To these I wish to say: Try to make every effort to ensure that religious education programs and, where possible, parish schools are an important part of your ministry; support and encourage teachers, administrators and parents in their work. Few efforts are more important for the present and future well-being of the Church and of the nation than efforts expended in the work of education.

6. Catholic schools in the United States have always enjoyed a reputation for academic excellence and community service. Very often they serve large numbers of poor children and young people and are attentive to the needs of minority groups. I heartily encourage you to continue to provide quality Catholic education for the poor of all races and national backgrounds, even at the cost of great sacrifice. We cannot doubt that such is part of God's call to the church in the United States. It is a responsibility that is deeply inscribed in the history of Catholic education in this country.

On another occasion, speaking to the bishops of the United States, I mentioned that the Catholic school "has contributed immensely to the spreading of God's word and has enabled the faithful 'to relate human affairs and activities with religious values in a single living synthesis' ("Sapientia Christiana," 1). In the community formed by the Catholic school, the power of the Gospel has been brought to bear on thought patterns, standards of judgment and norms of behavior. As an institution, the Catholic school has to be judged extremely favorably if we apply the sound criterion: 'You will know them by their deeds' (Mt 7:16), and again, 'You can tell a tree by its fruit' (Mt 7:20)" (Address of Oct. 28, 1983).

At this point I cannot fail to praise the financial sacrifices of American Catholics as well as the substantial contributions of individual benefactors, foundations, organizations and business to Catholic education in the United States. The heroic sacrifices of generations of Catholic parents in building up and supporting parochial and diocesan schools must never be forgotten. Rising costs may call for new approaches, new forms of partnership and sharing, new uses of financial resources. But I am sure that all concerned will face the challenge of Catholic schools with courage and dedication, and not doubt the value of the sacrifices to be made.

7. But there is another challenge facing all those who are concerned with Catholic education. It is the pressing challenge of clearly identifying the aims of Catholic education and applying proper methods in Catholic elementary and secondary education and religious education programs. It is the challenge of fully understanding the educational enterprise, of properly evaluating its content and of transmitting the full truth concerning the human person, created in God's image and called to life in Christ through the Holy Spirit.

The content of the individual courses in Catholic education is important both in religious teaching and in all the other subjects that go to make up the total instruction of human persons and to prepare them for their life's work and their eternal destiny. It is fitting that teachers should be constantly challenged by high professional standards in preparing and teaching their courses. In regard to the content of religion courses, the essential criterion is fidelity to the teaching of the Church.

Educators are likewise in a splendid position to inculcate into young people right ethical attitudes. These include attitudes toward material things and their proper use. The whole lifestyle of students will reflect the attitudes that they form during their years of formal education.

In these tasks you will find guidance in many documents of the Church. Your own bishops, applying the universal teaching of the Church, have helped point the way for you, notably in their pastoral letter "To Teach as Jesus Did," and in the National Catechetical Directory. I would also remind you of the Holy See's documents on "The Catholic School" and "Lay Catholics in Schools: Witnesses to Faith." There we are reminded that it is the school's task to cultivate in students the intellectual, creative and esthetic faculties of the individual; to develop in students the ability to make correct use of their judgment, will and affectivity; to promote in them a sense of values; to encourage just attitudes and prudent behavior; to introduce them to the cultural patrimony handed down from previous generations; to prepare them for their working lives and to encourage the friendly interchange among students of diverse cultures and backgrounds that will lead to mutual understanding and love.

8. The ultimate goal of all Catholic education is salvation in Jesus Christ. Catholic educators effectively work for the coming of Christ's kingdom; this work includes transmitting clearly and in full the message of salvation, which elicits the response of faith. In faith we know God and the hidden purpose of his will (cf. Eph 1:9). In faith we truly come to know ourselves. By sharing our faith we communicate a complete vision of the whole of reality and a commitment to truth and goodness. This vision and this commitment draw the strands of life into a purposeful pattern. By enriching your students' lives with the fullness of Christ's message and by inviting them to accept with all their hearts Christ's work, which is the Church, you promote most effectively their integral human development and you help them to build a community of faith, hope and love.

This Christian message is the more urgent for those young ones who come from broken homes and who, often with only one parent to encourage them, must draw support and direction from their teachers in school.

In your apostolate of helping to bring Christ's message into the lives of your students, the whole Church supports you and stands with you. The Synod of Bishops in particular has recognized the importance of your task and the difficulties you face. For these reasons it has called for concerted efforts to compose a universal catechism. This project will not eliminate the great challenge of a need for creativity in methodology nor will it minimize the continued need for the inculturation of the Gospel, but it will assist all the local churches in effectively presenting in its integrity the content of Catholic teaching. In the church in America an important part of the truly glorious chapter of Catholic education has been the transmitting of Christ's message through religious education programs designed for children and young people outside Catholic schools. For this too I give thanks to God, recalling all those who throughout the history of this nation have so generously collaborated in this "work of faith and labor of love" (1 Thes 1:3).

9. Community is at the heart of all Catholic education, not simply as a concept to be taught, but as a reality to be lived. In its deepest Christian sense, community is a sharing in the life of the Blessed Trinity. Your students will learn to understand and appreciate the value of community as they experience love, trust and loyalty in your schools and educational programs, and as they learn to treat all persons as brothers and sisters created by God and redeemed by Christ. Help them to grasp this sense of community by active participation in the life of the parish and the diocese and especially by receiving the sacraments of penance and the Eucharist. The Second Vatican Council explicitly includes learning to adore God in spirit and in truth among the aims of all Christian education (cf. "Gravissimum Educationis," 2).

A sense of community implies openness to the wider community. Often today Catholic education takes place in changing neighborhoods; it requires respect for cultural diversity, love for those of different ethnic backgrounds, service to those in need, without discrimination. Help your students to see themselves as members of the universal church and the world community. Help them to understand the implications of justice and mercy. Foster in your students a social consciousness which will move them to meet the needs of their neighbors and to discern and seek to remove the sources of injustice in society. No human anxiety or sorrow should leave the disciples of Jesus Christ indifferent.

10. The world needs more than just social reformers. It needs saints. Holiness is not the privilege of a few; it is a gift offered to all. The call to holiness is addressed also to you and to your students. To doubt this is to misjudge Christ's intentions: for "each of us has received God's favor in the measure in which Christ bestowed it" (Eph 4:7).

Brothers and sisters: Take Jesus Christ the teacher as the model of your service, as your guide and source of strength. He himself has told us: "You address me as 'teacher' and 'lord,' and fittingly enough; for that is what I am" (Jn 13:13-14). He taught in word and deed, and his teaching cannot be separated from his life and being. In the Apostolic Exhortation on Catechesis I stated: "The whole of Christ's life was a continual teaching: his silences, his miracles, his gestures, his prayer, his love for people, his special affection for the little and the poor, his acceptance of the total sacrifice on the cross for the redemption of the world and his resurrection.... Hence for Christians the crucifix is one of the most sublime and popular images of Christ the teacher" (No. 9).

11. Dear friends: Jesus shares with you his teaching ministry. Only in close communion with him can you respond adequately. This is my hope, this is my prayer: that you will be totally open to Christ. That he will give you an ever greater love for your students and an ever stronger commitment to your vocation as Catholic educators. If you continue to be faithful to this ministry today as you have been in the past, you will be doing much in shaping a peaceful, just and hope-filled world for the future. Yours is a great gift to the Church, a great gift to your nation.

Meeting with Youth
New Orleans, Sept. 12

Pope John Paul II:

Part I

Dear young people of New Orleans, dear young people of America,

1. Listening to what you are telling me by your presence and through your representatives, I know that you are very much conscious of having a special mission in this world, of being partners in the mission of the Church.

I also know that in fulfilling your mission you are willing to give, you are willing to share and you are willing to serve. And you are willing to do all this together, not alone! In this you are like Jesus: Jesus gave and he served and he was never alone! He tells us: "The one who sent me is with me. He has not left me alone" (Jn 8:29).

Yes, dear young people, I too want to speak about your mission, the reason for your life on earth, the truth of your lives. It is extremely vital for you to have a clear idea of your mission, to avoid being confused or deceived. In speaking to the Christians of his time, St. Paul explicitly urged them: "Let no one deceive you in any way (2 Thes 2:3). And today I say the same to you, young people of America: "Let no one deceive you in any way" — about your mission, about the truth, about where you are going. Let no one deceive you about the truth of your lives.

2. But what is the opposite of deception? Where can you

turn to find answers that satisfy, answers that will last? The opposite of deception is truth — the person who tells the truth, the person who is the truth. Yes, the opposite of deception is Jesus Christ, who tells us: "I am the way, and the truth, and the life" (Jn 14:6). Jesus Christ is the Son of God. He reveals the truth of God. But he is also man. He shares in our humanity and came into the world to teach us about ourselves, to help us discover ourselves.

You young people are proud to live in a free country, and you should be grateful to God for your freedom. But even though you can come and go as you like, and do what you want, you are not really free if you are living under the power of error or falsehood, or deceit or sin. Only Jesus Christ can make you fully free through his truth. And that is why he said: "You will know the truth, and the truth will set you free." And that is why he added: "If the Son frees you, you will really be free" (Jn 8:32, 36). Dear young people: The whole message of Jesus in the Gospels and through his Church helps you to discover who you really are, to discover all the dimensions of your lives.

3. Each of us is an individual, a person, a creature of God, one of his children, someone very special whom God loves and for whom Christ died. This identity of ours determines the way we must live, the way we must act, the way we must view our mission in the world. We come from God, we depend on God, God has a plan for us — a plan for our lives, for our bodies, for our souls, for our future. This plan for us is extremely important — so important that God became man to explain it to us.

In God's plan, we are individuals — yes — but we are also part of a community. The Second Vatican Council emphasized the fact that God did not call us to share his life merely as unrelated individuals. Rather he wanted to mold us into a people as his sons and daughters (cf. "Ad Gentes," 2). This aspect of our being a community, of our sharing God's life as a people is part of our identity — who we are, what we are, where we are going.

Right away we can see that as persons we have responsibilities and that these responsibilities are part of our freedom. The Vatican Council went so far as to say that "man is defined first of all by his responsibilities toward his brothers and sisters and toward history" ("Gaudium et Spes," 55).

To understand ourselves as members of a community, as individuals linked together to make up the people of God, as persons with responsibility for others is a great insight — an insight that is necessary for fulfilling our mission properly.

4. As Christians you have these insights, and Christ today wants to reinforce them in you. You speak about "being partners," of sharing and serving and working together. And all of this is linked to God's plan, according to which we are brothers and sisters in Christ — brothers and sisters who belong to the people of God and who are made to live in community, to think about others, to help others. Dear young people of America: In the Church there are many different gifts. There is room for many different cultures and ways of doing things. But there is no room in the Church for selfishness. There is no room in the world for selfishness. It destroys the meaning of life; it destroys the meaning of love; it reduces the human person to a subhuman level.

When we speak about the need of being open to others, of taking into account the community, of fulfilling our responsibilities to all our brothers and sisters, we are actually talking about the whole world. Your mission as young people today is to the whole world. In what sense? You can never forget the interdependence of human beings wherever they are.

When Jesus tells us to love our neighbor, he does not set a geographical limit. What is needed today is a solidarity between all the young people of the world — a solidarity especially with the poor and all those in need. You young people must change society by your lives of justice and fraternal love. It is not just a question of your own country, but of the whole world. This is certainly your mission, dear young people. You are partners with each other, partners with the whole Church, partners with Christ.

5. In order, however, to accomplish this great work, to be in a condition to change the world in the name of Jesus, you yourselves must actually be living according to your own identity — according to God's plan for your lives. Once again it is the word of Jesus that directs your lives and tells you what that plan is. You remember how much Jesus insisted on the commandment of love, how much he insisted on living according to certain norms called the Beatitudes: "Blessed are the meek.... Blessed are the merciful.... Blessed are the clean of heart.... Blessed are the peacemakers." All of this is part of the plan.

When St. Paul says, "Let no one deceive you," he is in effect saying: Do not believe anyone who contradicts Jesus or his message, which is transmitted to you by the Church. Jesus speaks to you young people and tells you the value of meekness, mercy and humility. Other voices in the world will immediately shout out: "Weakness!" In the Gospel Jesus emphasizes the value of honesty, uprightness, justice and fairness. But when you practice these virtues, you are liable to be accused of being "naive." Jesus and his Church hold up to you God's plan for human love, telling you that sex is a great gift of God that is reserved for marriage. At this point the voices of the world will try to deceive you with powerful slogans, claiming that you are "unrealistic," "out of it," "backward," even "reactionary." But the message of Jesus is clear: Purity means true love, and it is the total opposite of selfishness and escape.

6. Jesus' message applies to all the areas of life. He reveals to us the truth of our lives and all aspects of this truth. Jesus tells us that the purpose of our freedom is to say yes to God's plan for our lives. What makes our yes so important is that we say it freely; we are able to say no. Jesus teaches us that we are accountable to God, that we must follow our consciences, but that our consciences must be formed according to God's plan for our lives. In all our relationships to other people and to the world, Jesus teaches us what we must do, how we must live in order not to be deceived, in order to walk in truth. And today, dear young people, I proclaim to you again Jesus Christ: the way, and the truth and the life — your way, your truth and your life.

What is in accord with the truth of Jesus is fulfillment, joy and peace, even if it means effort and discipline. What is not in accord with his truth means disorder, and when done deliberately, it means sin. Deliberate or not, it eventually means unhappiness and frustration.

7. It is with the truth of Jesus, dear young people, that you must face the great questions in your lives as well as the practical problems. The world will try to deceive you about many things that matter: about your faith, about pleasure and material things, about the dangers of drugs. And at one stage or another the false voices of the world will try to exploit your human weakness by telling you that life has no meaning at all for you. The supreme theft in your lives would be if they succeeded in robbing you of hope. They will try, but not succeed if you hold fast to Jesus and his truth.

The truth of Jesus is capable of reinforcing all your energies. It will unify your lives and consolidate your sense of mission.

You may still be vulnerable to attack from the pressures of the world, from the forces of evil, from the power of the devil. But you will be invincible in hope: "in Christ Jesus our hope" (1 Tm 1:1).

Dear young people: The word of Jesus and his truth and his promises of fulfillment and life are the Church's response to the culture of death, to the onslaughts of doubt and to the cancer of despair.

Let me just add two practical thoughts from the Second Vatican Council. The council tells us that we must avoid thinking that we have at hand the solutions to all the particular problems of life (cf. "Gaudium et Spes," 33). But at the same time the Church knows that she possesses the light in which the solutions to the problems of humanity can be discovered (ibid., 12). What is this light? What can it be? Only the truth of Jesus Christ!

Naidja Taylor:

Good afternoon, Holy Father. My name is Naidja Taylor and it is indeed an honor and a pleasure to welcome you to New Orleans. We, as youth of today, can and should share our gifts not only with the Church but also with the world in which we live. Three such gifts are the gifts of love, understanding and wisdom. These gifts, I believe, are most worthy for me to give.

Love, a gift of oneself, comes from within; a person must experience love in order to know its true meaning. John 3:16 says, "For God so loved the world that he gave his only begotten Son...." It is the gift of love that helps us overcome our daily obstacles. The gift of love is truly a gift that we as youth can share not only with the Church but also with the world in which we live; for until we do, there will be no peace or unity among us. We should exercise love even toward our enemies. That is, we are to treat our enemies with proper respect.

Understanding, as a gift of the Holy Spirit, helps us to grasp the meaning of the truths of our holy religion. By faith we know them; by understanding we learn to appreciate and relish them. It enables us to penetrate the inner meaning of revealed truths and through them to quicken to newness of life. Our faith ceases to be sterile and inactive but inspires a mode of life. With the gift of understanding we need to see that we are all adequately fed, housed, educated and in good health. We need to work together regardless of the color of anyone's skin, the nature of anyone's religious or political beliefs, anyone's gender or the sound of anyone's name or language or the nation in which anyone was born or lives. We need to eliminate hunger, ignorance and oppression. We need to be engaged in making life better.

The gift of wisdom embodies all other gifts as charity embraces all other virtues. Of wisdom it is written, "All good things came to me with her innumerable riches through her hands." It is the gift of wisdom that strengthens our faith, fortifies hope, perfects charity and promotes the practice of virtue in the highest degree. Wisdom enlightens the mind to discern and relish things divine, in the appreciation of which earthly joys lose their savor while the cross of Christ yields a divine sweetness, according to the words of the Savior. When we realize the folly of our course, we will lift a voice of warning to save others from the bitter experience through which we ourselves have passed, hoping thereby to counteract as best we can the baleful influence of our own earlier example. As

youth, we can share these and other gifts with the Church and with the world in which we live. Thank you, Holy Father.

Alexander Ennis:

Praise be Jesus Christ!

Your Holiness, in the name of the young people assembled here and all those in the southern part of our country — we wish to thank you for visiting our city and welcome you to this youth gathering today. I hope to share with you those things what we, as America's young people, can give to the Church and to the world.

The poet Carl Sandburg once wrote, "A baby is God's opinion that the world should go on." As young people sharing in Christ's family through the Church, we have much to give and much to learn to merit God's opinion.

We can give of ourselves, our time and our energy to meet the needs of God's people for justice, peace and a better way of living.

Young people can give of their health so that others might live.

We can share our hope and optimism for the future. Our world presents itself to us and, especially for those who live in freedom, the potential seems unlimited — restricted only by our desire, our knowledge and our ability.

As young people, we can give our happiness and joy. For when we share our gifts — even a smile or a laugh — they multiply and come back to us as even greater gifts.

Our generation can contribute new ideas and new ways of doing things. We can create a safer and more secure world. Since we are the future, the building of God's kingdom of justice and love is up to us. We are important today as young people, but also tomorrow as we become leaders and followers.

Finally, we have to give of our love, our skills and our talents. Some of us are good in music, athletics, art or drama. We work. We play hard. We listen and we learn. Some of us can teach. Others are strong; some can make people laugh. We build and we fix things; we cook, hunt and fish. Our talents are many. We offer our prayers, our support and these symbolic gifts of a wood carving, a picture of youth working together and a Mardi Gras mask to you, Pope John Paul II, as you proclaim the Gospel to the world. We remember, as President Kennedy once said, "Here on earth God's work must truly be our own."

Pope John Paul II:

Part II

Dear young people,

8. I would like to add something else to what I have already said to you. I would like to speak to you briefly about prayer, about communion with God, a communion that is deeply personal between ourselves and God.

In prayer we express to God our feelings, our thoughts, our sentiments. We wish to love and be loved, to be understood and to understand. Only God loves us perfectly, with an everlasting love. In prayer, we open our hearts and our minds to this God of love. And it is prayer that makes us one with the Lord. Through prayer we come to share more deeply in God's life and in his love.

9. One of the most striking things about Jesus was his habit of prayer. In the midst of an active public ministry, we find him going away by himself to be alone in silence and communion with his Father in heaven. On the sabbath he made it a practice to go to the synagogue and pray with others in common. When he was together with his disciples or when he was by himself, he prayed to the Father, whom he dearly loved.

St. Mark's Gospel describes an evening in Capernaum when Jesus cured many who were sick and expelled many demons. After giving us this description of Christ's generous care for others, St. Mark adds: "Rising early the next morning, he went off to a lonely place in the desert; there he was absorbed in prayer" (Mk 1:35).

And St. Luke informs us that before Jesus selected the Twelve to be his apostles "he went out to the mountain to pray, spending the night in communion with God" (Lk 6:12). In fact, it seems that it was his example of prayer that prompted his disciples to want to pray: "One day he was praying in a certain place," Luke tells us, and "when he had finished, one of his disciples asked him, 'Lord, teach us to pray'" (Lk 11:1). That was the occasion when Jesus taught them the prayer that we call the Lord's Prayer or the Our Father.

10. If you really wish to follow Christ, if you want your love for him to grow and last, then you must be faithful to prayer. It is the key to the vitality of your life in Christ. Without prayer, your faith and love will die. If you are constant in daily prayer and in the Sunday celebration of Mass, your love for Jesus will increase. And your heart will know deep joy and peace, such as the world could never give.

But many young people tell me that they do not know how to pray or they wonder if they are praying in a way that is correct. Here again, you must look to the example of Christ. How did Jesus himself pray?

First of all, we know that his prayer is marked by a spirit of joy and praise. "Jesus rejoiced in the Holy Spirit and said: 'I offer you praise, O Father, Lord of heaven and earth'" (Lk 10:21). In addition, he entrusted to the Church at the Last Supper the celebration of the Eucharist, which remains for all ages the most perfect means of offering to the Father glory and thanksgiving and praise.

Yet there were also times of suffering when, in great pain and struggle, Jesus poured out his heart to God, seeking to find in his Father both comfort and support. For example, in the garden of Gethsemane, when the inner struggle became even more difficult, then, "in his anguish he prayed with all the greater intensity, and his sweat became like drops of blood falling to the ground" (Lk 22:44). "He prayed with all the greater intensity" — what an example for us when we find life difficult, when we face a painful decision or when we struggle with temptation. At times like these, Jesus prayed with all the greater intensity. We must do the same!

When it is difficult therefore to pray, the most important thing is not to stop praying, not to give up the effort. At these times, turn to the Bible and to the church's liturgy. Meditate on the life and teachings of Jesus as recorded in the Gospels. Ponder the wisdom and counsel of the apostles and the challenging messages of the prophets. Try to make your own the beautiful prayers of the psalms. You will find in the inspired word of God the spiritual food you need. Above all, your soul will be refreshed when you take part wholeheartedly with the community in the celebration of the Eucharist, the church's greatest prayer.

11. Do you recall the story of Jesus and his mother, Mary, at the wedding feast of Cana? At a certain point in the feast, when they have run out of wine, Mary tells those waiting on table, "Do whatever he tells you" (Jn 2:5). When the waiters follow Mary's advice, Jesus rewards their faith and changes water into wine, a wine that far surpasses the quality of what had been served before. And Mary's advice still holds true today. For the true success of our lives consists in knowing and doing the will of Jesus, in doing whatever Jesus tells us. When you pray, you must realize that prayer is not just asking God for something or seeking special help, even though prayers of petition are true ways of praying. But prayer should also be characterized by thanksgiving and praise, by adoration and attentive listening, by asking God's pardon and forgiveness. If you follow Jesus' advice and pray to God constantly, then you will learn to pray well. God himself will teach you.

Prayer can truly change your life. For it turns your attention away from yourself and directs your mind and your heart toward the Lord. If we look only at ourselves, with our own limitations and sins, we quickly give way to sadness and discouragement. But if we keep our eyes fixed on the Lord, then our hearts are filled with hope, our minds are washed in the light of truth and we come to know the fullness of the Gospel with all its promise and life.

12. Prayer also helps us to be open to the Holy Spirit, the Spirit of truth and love, the Spirit who was given to the church so that she could fulfill her mission in the world. It is the Holy Spirit who gives us the strength to resist evil and do good, to do our part in building up the kingdom of God.

It is significant that the symbol of the Holy Spirit on Pentecost was tongues of fire. In fact, fire is often the symbol that the Bible uses to speak of the action of God in our lives. For the Holy Spirit truly inflames our hearts, engendering in them enthusiasm for the works of God. And when we pray, the Holy Spirit stirs up within us love of God and love of our neighbor.

The Holy Spirit brings us joy and peace. The modern technological world can offer us many pleasures, many comforts of life. It can even offer us temporary escapes from life. But what the world can never offer is lasting joy and peace. These are the gifts which only the Holy Spirit can give. And these are the gifts that I ask for you so that you may be strong in hope and persevering in love. But the condition for all of this is prayer, which means contact with Christ, communion with God. Dear young people: My message to you is not new. I have given it before and, with God's grace, I will give it again. And so, as long as the memory of this visit lasts, may it be recorded that I, John Paul II, came to America to call you to Christ; to invite you to pray!

Lakefront Arena Mass New Orleans, Sept. 12

Pope John Paul II:

"My Lord be patient with me and I will pay you back in full" (Mt 18:26; cf. v. 29).

Dear brothers and sisters in Christ,

1. This plea is heard twice in the gospel parable. The first time it is made by the servant who owes his master 10,000 talents — an astonishingly high sum according to the value

of money in New Testament times. Shortly afterward the plea is repeated by another servant of the same master. He too is in debt, not to his master, but to his fellow servant. And his debt is only a tiny fraction of the debt that his fellow servant had been forgiven.

The point of the parable is the fact that the servant with the greater debt receives understanding from the master to whom he owes much money. The Gospel tells us that "the master let the official go and wrote off the debt" (Mt 18:27). Yet that same servant would not listen to the plea of his fellow servant who owed him money. He had no pity on him, but "had him put in jail until he paid back what he owed" (Mt 18:30).

Jesus often used parables like this one in his teaching; they are a special method of proclaiming the good news. They enable the listener to grasp more easily the "divine reality" which Jesus came to reveal. In today's parable, we sense almost immediately that it is a prelude to the words which Jesus commands us to use when we pray to our heavenly Father: "Forgive us our debts, as we forgive our debtors" (Mt 6:12).

These words from the Our Father also have something very important to teach us. If we want God to hear us when we plead like the servant — "Have patience with me" — then we must be equally willing to listen to our neighbor when he pleads: "Give me time and I will pay you back in full." Otherwise we cannot expect pardon from God, but punishment instead. In the parable the servant is punished because, though a debtor himself, he is intolerant as a creditor toward his fellow servant.

Christ is very clear: When we ourselves are without sympathy or mercy, when we are guided by "blind" justice alone, then we cannot count on the mercy of that "Great Creditor" who is God — God, before whom we are all debtors.

2. In the parable, we find two different standards or ways of measuring: God's standard and man's standard. The divine standard is one in which justice is totally permeated by merciful love. The human standard is inclined to stop at justice alone — justice which is without mercy and which in a sense is "blind" with regard to man.

Indeed, human justice is often governed by hatred and revenge, as the first reading from the Book of Sirach reminds us. It reads — and the words of the Old Testament are strong — "Should a man nourish anger against his fellows and expect healing from the Lord?... If he who is but flesh cherishes wrath, who will forgive his sins?... Remember your last days, set enmity aside.... Think of the commandments, hate not your neighbor.... Should a man refuse mercy to his fellows, yet seek pardon for his own sins?" (Sir 28:3, 5-7, 4).

The exhortations in the Book of Sirach and in the Gospel both move in the same direction. The human way of measuring — the measure of justice alone — which is often "blind" or "blinded" by hatred — must accept God's standard. Otherwise justice by itself easily becomes injustice, as we see expressed in the Latin saying: "Summum ius, summa iniuria." The rigorous application of the law can sometimes be the height of injustice.

As I said in my encyclical letter on the mercy of God: "In every sphere of interpersonal relationships justice must, so to speak, be 'corrected' to a considerable extent by that love which, as St. Paul proclaims, 'is patient and kind' or, in other words, possesses the characteristics of that merciful love which is so much of the essence of the Gospel and Christianity" ("Dives in Misericordia," 14).

3. Merciful love is also the basis of the Lord's answer to Peter's question: "When my brother wrongs me, how often must I forgive him? Seven times?" "No," Jesus replied, "not seven times; I say, seventy times seven times" (Mt 18:21-22). In the symbolic language of the Bible, this means that we must be able to forgive everyone every time. Surely this is one of the most difficult and radical commands of the Gospel. Yet how much suffering and anguish, how much futility, destruction and violence would be avoided, if only we put into practice in all our human relationships the Lord's answer to Peter.

Merciful love is absolutely necessary, in particular, for people who are close to one another: for husbands and wives, parents and children, and among friends (cf. "Dives in Misericordia," 14). At a time when family life is under such great stress, when a high number of divorces and broken homes are a sad fact of life, we must ask ourselves whether human relationships are being based, as they should be, on the merciful love and forgiveness revealed by God in Jesus Christ. We must examine our own heart and see how willing we are to forgive and to accept forgiveness in this world as well as in the next.

No relationship as intense and close as marriage and the family can survive without forgiveness "seventy times seven times." If couples cannot forgive with the tenderness and sensitivity that mercy brings, then they will inevitably begin to see their relationship only in terms of justice, of what is mine and what is yours — emotionally, spiritually and materially — and in terms of real or perceived injustices. This can lead to estrangement and divorce, and often develops into a bitter dispute about property and, more tragically, about children. The plight of the children alone should make us realize that the refusal to forgive is not in keeping with the true nature of marriage as God established it and as he wants it to be lived. No doubt some people will object that Christ's teaching about the indissolubility of marriage, as it is upheld by the Church, is lacking in compassion. But what must be seen is the ineffectiveness of divorce and its ready availability in modern society to bring mercy and forgiveness and healing to so many couples and their children, in whose troubled lives there remain a brokenness and a suffering that will not go away. The words of the merciful Christ, who fully understands the human heart, remain forever: "What therefore God has joined together, let no man put asunder" (Mt 19:6).

At the same time, merciful love and forgiveness are never meant to cancel out a person's right to justice, even in marriage. In the encyclical to which I referred a moment ago I said that "properly understood, justice constitutes ... the goal of forgiveness. In no passage of the gospel message does forgiveness or mercy ... mean indulgence toward evil, scandals, injury or insult.... Reparation for evil and scandal, compensation for injury and satisfaction for insult are conditions for forgiveness" ("Dives in Misericordia," 14). All forgiveness requires repentant love.

This also applies in the wider context of social, political, cultural and economic life within and among nations and peoples. May we not hope for what Pope Paul VI described as the "civilization of love" instead of "an eye for an eye and a tooth for a tooth," the attitude which ravages the face of the earth and scars the family of mankind? As I have said, this love, based on the forgiveness which Jesus described to Peter, does not mean that the objective demands of justice, which people legitimately seek, are thereby canceled out. Sometimes those demands, however, are very complex.

A case with special urgency today is the international debt question. As you know, many developing countries are heavily in debt to industrialized nations and for a variety of reasons are finding it harder and harder to repay their loans. "Blind" justice alone cannot solve this problem in an ethical way that promotes the human good of all parties. Merciful love calls for mutual understanding and a recognition of human priorities and needs, above and beyond the "blind" justice of financial mechanisms. We must arrive at solutions that truly reflect both complete justice and mercy (cf. Pontifical Justice and Peace Commission, "At the Service of the Human Community: An Ethical Approach to the International Debt Question," 1986).

The nature of the Church's concern in these matters is reflected in the pastoral message on the American economy issued by the bishops of the United States. They say: "We write ... as heirs of the biblical prophets who summon us 'to do justice, to love kindness and to walk humbly with our God' (Mi 6:8).... We speak as moral teachers, not economic technicians. We seek ... to lift up the human and ethical dimensions of economic life" (Nos. 4, 7). To do justice, yes — but also to love. This is at the heart of Christ's message. It is the only way to reach that "civilization of love" that ensures peace for ourselves and for the world.

4. "Forgive us ... as we forgive."

The Eucharist which we are celebrating and in which we are taking part is linked to the deepest truth of these words. Each time we participate in the Eucharist, we must translate, as it were, the parable of today's Gospel into the reality of that sacrament which is the "great mystery of faith." When we gather together, we must be aware of how much we are debtors to God the Creator, God the Redeemer. Debtors — first for our creation and then for our redemption. The psalmist exclaims: "Bless the Lord, O my soul; and all my being, bless his holy name. Bless ... and forget not all his benefits" (Ps 103:1-2).

This exhortation is directed to each one of us and at the same time to the whole community of believers. Forget not ... the gift of God. Forget not ... that you have received his bounty: in creation — that is to say, in your existence and in all that is in and around you; in redemption — in that grace of adoption as sons and daughters of God in Christ, at the price of his cross.

When we receive a gift we are a debtor. Indeed we are more than a debtor because it is not possible to repay a gift adequately. And yet we must try. We must give a gift in return for a gift. God's generous gift must be repaid by our gift. And our gift, reflecting as it does our great limitations, must aim at imitating the divine generosity, the divine standard of giving. In Christ our gift must be transformed so as to unite us with God. The Eucharist is the sacrament of such a transformation. Christ himself makes us "an everlasting gift to the Father." Truly this is the great mystery of faith and love.

5. "Forgive us our debts, as we forgive our debtors."

With these words from the prayer taught to us by the Son of God, I address all those gathered here in New Orleans in the spirit of the Gospel — all those who make up the eucharistic assemblies of the local churches of this region. I greet you as the proud heirs of a rich and diverse cultural history, as people who can therefore appreciate the need for merciful love among individuals and groups. Here we have represented the cultures of France and other European nations, of black people, Hispanics and more recently Vietnamese. Today this region continues to be the home of various races and cultures now united in one nation, the United States.

All of those races and cultures have enriched the life of your local church within the distinctively French heritage that men like Robert Cavelier Sieur de la Salle and Jean Baptiste Le Moyne Sieur de Bienville conferred upon this land centuries ago. You are also a people who have only to look about you to see the many wonderful gifts conferred by the mighty Mississippi River and its fertile delta, and by the riches of the sea. All this comes to you as a gift from God. By wise stewardship and the responsible use of these resources, you can find dignity in your work as you seek to provide for yourselves and your families. May you continue to work in harmony for the good of the society you belong to, always keeping in mind the words of Christ's prayer: "Forgive us our debts, as we forgive our debtors."

Modern man easily forgets the proportion, or rather, the lack of proportion between what he has received and what he is obliged to give. He has grown so much in his own eyes and is so sure that everything is the work of his own genius and of his own "industry," that he no longer sees the one who is the Alpha and the Omega, the Beginning and the End, the one who is the First Source of all that is as well as its Final End, the One in whom all that exists finds its proper meaning.

Modern man easily forgets that he has received a great gift. Yet at the base of all that he is and of all that the world is, there is the gift — the free gift of Love. As man loses this awareness, he also forgets the debt and the fact that he is a debtor. He loses his consciousness of sin. Many people today, especially those caught up in a civilization of affluence and pleasure, live as though sin did not exist and as if God did not exist.

For this reason we need to listen with special attention to the Letter to the Romans: "None of us lives as his own master and none of us dies as his own master. While we live we are responsible to the Lord, and when we die we die as his servants. Both in life and in death we are the Lord's. That is why Christ died and came to life again, that he might be Lord of both the dead and the living" (Rom 14:7-9). We must listen carefully to these words of St. Paul and remember them well.

"My Lord, be patient with me and I will pay you back in full."

"Love is patient; love is kind.... Love does not rejoice in what is wrong but rejoices with the truth.... Love never fails" (1 Cor 13:4, 6, 8). Yes, love is supreme! Amen.

Meeting with Universities New Orleans, Sept. 12

Dr. Francis J. Kerins:

Beloved Holy Father, Pope John Paul II:

1. It is my privilege to represent before you tonight the thousands of persons — lay women and men, priests and Religious — who are engaged in the ministry of Catholic higher education here in the United States. As chair of the Association of Catholic Colleges and Universities, I speak particularly on behalf of the 215 institutions of higher education that make up the membership of this association. But I am pleased also to represent the many dedicated Catholics who work in other institutions of higher education throughout the country, whether in a campus ministry program or as faculty and staff at those colleges and universities.

2. The institutions at which we work — Catholic, sponsored by other churches, publicly operated or without formal ties to church or state — are many and varied. My own institution, Carroll College of Helena, Mont., was originally called Mount Saint Charles College, for St. Charles Borromeo, the college's patron. Then, over 50 years ago, the board of trustees changed the name to honor John Patrick Carroll, who, at the beginning of this century, served as bishop of Helena, Mont., and founded the college. Today we have a student body of 1,500 and over 100 faculty members, most of whom are lay women and men.

Our college, like many of the other Catholic colleges and universities represented here, came into being because a wise and farsighted bishop, supported by the generous sacrifices of his people, recognized that Catholic higher education was part of the full life of the Church. In most instances, bishops encouraged religious congregations of men and women to found such institutions in the different communities of this vast and varied land. Today these institutions still enjoy the presence and reflect the distinctive traditions of the particular religious congregations which sponsored their birth and growth. In all of them, however, the overwhelming number of faculty and staff now are lay men and women, including significant numbers of persons of other faiths who find the Catholic environment of our institutions a congenial one for their own work of teaching and scholarship. These colleagues too are committed to the educational values of the Catholic tradition.

3. But whether we work at small regional colleges or at large research universities with national reputations, behind and within the diversity of our particular scholarly disciplines we share a common commitment, one that both encourages our differences and establishes our unity: the belief that our work in higher education — a work of teaching, scholarship and service — constitutes a sacred ministry in the church. We understand this to be a ministry of and for the truth: the continuing search for knowledge that will enlighten our understanding of ourselves, our history and the world in which we live, and then the communication of this understanding to others.

4. Our Catholic institutions of higher education are significant partners in the highly developed system of higher education in the United States, a system that takes pride in its diversity and seeks to make the choice of different kinds of educational experiences, whether in public state-supported institutions or in private independent colleges and universities, accessible to as many of our citizens as possible. Even as we share with all of these institutions a set of common concerns about the importance of higher education in the United States, we believe that our own Catholic colleges and universities, with their distinctive tradition, play an essential role in a society that has always found a special strength in its pluralism. As we celebrate the 200th anniversary of the Constitution of the United States, we recall with gratitude the religious freedom that has enabled us to build such an impressive system of Catholic higher education. We note with satisfaction also that in the history of all of higher education in this country the best utilization of the talents of women in positions of leadership has been in Catholic colleges sponsored by congregations of religious women.

5. The system of higher education in the United States, of which Catholic colleges and universities are an integral part, offers educational opportunities to its citizens to a degree which is unmatched anywhere else in the world. Our Catholic people recognize the unique worth of higher education offered within the ministry of the Church and continue to support our institutions, often at great sacrifice. Beyond this, the American society cherishes the value of Catholic colleges and universities. Government financial assistance to students attending our institutions and to their families is substantial and vital to our continued service. And we receive a great deal of help and support from our own trustees, donors, foundations and business firms not themselves Catholic but convinced of the importance of Catholic colleges and universities to our national well-being and to the good of our society.

6. We Catholics are proud to be part of the broad and rich array of American higher education even as we confidently affirm our own distinctive heritage as members of the universal Roman Catholic Church. We believe that through our research, teaching and service to society we are following the mandate held out by the Second Vatican Council: that we should by the witness of our work and our lives make the church a true sacrament of God's presence in the contemporary world and its culture.

7. This evening it is a great joy for all of us to be able to celebrate in your presence the achievement of the past, made possible by the sacrifices of so many for so many years and by God's providence. We ask your blessing as we renew our commitment to the promise of the future and to the sacred vocation we share in faith with one another.

Pope John Paul II:

Dear friends, dear leaders in Catholic higher education,

1. At the end of this day dedicated to the prayerful celebration of Catholic education in the United States, I greet you and all those whom you represent with esteem and with affection in our Lord Jesus Christ. I thank the Association of Catholic Colleges and Universities for having arranged this meeting. I express my gratitude to Dr. Norman Francis and to all at Xavier University for their hospitality at this institution, which in so many ways serves the cause of Catholic higher education.

"I will bless the Lord at all times; his praise shall be ever in my mouth. Glorify the Lord with me, let us together extol his name" (Ps 34:2, 4).

Yes, let us join in thanking God for the many good things that he, the Father of wisdom, has accomplished through Catholic colleges and universities. In doing so, let us be thankful for the special strengths of your schools — for their Catholic identity, for their service of truth and for their role in helping to make the church's presence felt in the world of culture and science. And let us be thankful above all for the men and women committed to this mission, those of the past and those of today, who have made and are making Catholic higher education the great reality that it is.

2. The United States is unique in its network of more than 235 colleges and universities which identify themselves as Catholic. The number and diversity of your institutions are in fact without parallel; they exercise an influence not only within the United States but also throughout the universal Church, and they bear a responsibility for her good.

Two years from now you will celebrate the 200th-anniversary of the founding by John Carroll of Georgetown University, the first Catholic university in the United States. After Georgetown, through the leadership of religious congregations and farseeing bishops and with the generous support of the Catholic people, other colleges and universities have been established in different parts of this vast country. For two centuries these institutions have contributed much to the emergence of a Catholic laity which today is intimately and extensively involved in industry, government, the professions, arts and all forms of public and private endeavor — all those activities that constitute the characteristic dynamism and vitality of this land.

161

Amid changing circumstances, Catholic universities and colleges are challenged to retain a lively sense of their Catholic identity and to fulfill their specific responsibilities to the Church and to society. It is precisely in doing so that they make their distinctive contribution to the wider field of higher education.

The Catholic identity of your institutions is a complex and vitally important matter. This identity depends upon the explicit profession of Catholicity on the part of the university as an institution and also upon the personal conviction and sense of mission on the part of its professors and administrators.

3. During my pastoral visit to this country in 1979, I spoke of various elements that contribute to the mission of Catholic higher education. It is useful once again to stress the importance of research into questions vital for the Church and society — a research carried out "with a just sense of history, together with the concern to show the full meaning of the human person regenerated in Christ"; to emphasize the need for educating men and women of outstanding knowledge who, "having made a personal synthesis between faith and culture, will be both capable and willing to assume tasks in the service of the community and of society in general, and to bear witness to their faith before the world"; and finally, to pursue the establishment of a living community of faith, "where sincere commitment to scientific research and study goes together with a deep commitment to authentic Christian living" (Address at Catholic University, Washington, D.C., Oct. 7, 1979, No. 3).

4. To appreciate fully the value of your heritage, we need to recall the origins of Catholic university life. The university as we know it began in close association with the Church. This was no accident. Faith and love of learning have a close relationship. For the fathers of the Church and the thinkers and academics of the Middle Ages, the search for truth was associated with the search for God. According to Catholic teaching — as expressed also in the First Vatican Council — the mind is capable not only of searching for the truth but also of grasping it, however imperfectly.

Religious faith itself calls for intellectual inquiry; and the confidence that there can be no contradiction between faith and reason is a distinctive feature of the Catholic humanistic tradition as it existed in the past and as it exists in our own day.

Catholic higher education is called to exercise, through the grace of God, an extraordinary "share in the work of truth" (3 Jn 8). The Catholic university is dedicated to the service of the truth, as is every university. In its research and teaching, however, it proceeds from the vision and perspective of faith and is thus enriched in a specific way.

From this point of view one sees that there is an intimate relationship between the Catholic university and the teaching office of the Church. The bishops of the Church, as "doctores et magistri fidei," should be seen not as external agents but as participants in the life of the Catholic university in its privileged role as protagonist in the encounter between faith and science and between revealed truth and culture.

Modern culture reflects many tensions and contradictions. We live in an age of great technological triumphs but also of great human anxieties. Too often today the individual's vision of reality is fragmented. At times experience is mediated by forces over which people have no control; sometimes there is not even an awareness of these forces. The temptation grows to relativize moral principles and to privilege process over truth. This has grave consequences for the moral life as well as for the intellectual life of individuals and of society. The Catholic university must address all these issues from the perspective of faith and out of its rich heritage.

5. Modern culture is marked by a pluralism of attitudes, points of view and insights. This situation rightly requires mutual understanding; it means that society and groups within society must respect those who have a different outlook from their own. But pluralism does not exist for its own sake; it is directed to the fullness of truth. In the academic context, the respect for persons which pluralism rightly envisions does not justify the view that ultimate questions about human life and destiny have no final answers or that all beliefs are of equal value, provided that none is asserted as absolutely true and normative. Truth is not served in this way.

It is true of course that the culture of every age contains certain ambiguities which reflect the inner tensions of the human heart, the struggle between good and evil. Hence the Gospel, in its continuing encounter with culture, must always challenge the accomplishments and assumptions of the age (cf. Rom 12:2). Since in our day the implications of this ambiguity are often so destructive to the community, so hostile to human dignity, it is crucial that the Gospel should purify culture, uplift it and orient it to the service of what is authentically human. Humanity's very survival may depend on it. And here, as leaders in Catholic education in the United States, you have an extremely important contribution to make.

Today there exists an increasingly evident need for philosophical reflection concerning the truth about the human person. A metaphysical approach is needed as an antidote to intellectual and moral relativism. But what is required even more is fidelity to the word of God, to ensure that human progress takes into account the entire revealed truth of the eternal act of love in which the universe and especially the human person acquire ultimate meaning. The more one seeks to unravel the mystery of the human person, the more open one becomes to the mystery of transcendence. The more deeply one penetrates the divine mystery, the more one discovers the true greatness and dignity of human beings.

6. In your institutions, which are privileged settings for the encounter between faith and culture, theological science has a special role and deserves a prominent place in the curriculum of studies and in the allocation of research resources. But theology, as the Church understands it, is much more than an academic discipline. Its data are the data of God's revelation entrusted to the Church. The deeper understanding of the mystery of Christ, the understanding which theological reflection seeks, is ultimately a gift of the Holy Spirit given for the common good of the whole church. Theology is truly a search to understand ever more clearly the heritage of faith preserved, transmitted and made explicit by the Church's teaching office. And theological instruction serves the community of faith by helping new generations to understand and to integrate into their lives the truth of God, which is so vital to the fundamental issues of the modern world.

7. Theology is at the service of the whole ecclesial community. The work of theology involves an interaction among the various members of the community of faith. The bishops, united with the pope, have the mission of authentically teaching the message of Christ; as pastors, they are called to sustain the unity in faith and Christian living of the entire people of God. In this they need the assistance of Catholic theologians, who perform an inestimable service to the Church. But theologians also need the charism entrusted by Christ to the bishops and, in the first place, to the bishop of Rome. The fruits of their work, in order to enrich the life stream of the ecclesial community, must ultimately be tested and validated by the magisterium. In effect, therefore, the ecclesial

context of Catholic theology gives it a special character and value even when theology exists in an academic setting.

Here the words of St. Paul concerning the spiritual gifts should be a source of light and harmony for us all: "There are different gifts but the same Spirit; there are different ministries but the same Lord; there are different works but the same God who accomplishes all of them in everyone. To each person the manifestation of the Spirit is given for the common good" (1 Cor 12:4-7). In the different offices and functions in the Church, it is not some power and dominion that is being divided up, but rather the same service of the body of Christ that is shared according to the vocation of each. It is a question of unity in the work of service. In this spirit I wish to express cordial support for the humble, generous and patient work of theological research and education being carried out in your universities and colleges in accordance with the church's mission to proclaim and teach the saving wisdom of God (cf. 1 Cor 1:21).

8. My own university experience impels me to mention another related matter of supreme importance in the Catholic college and university, namely, the religious and moral education of students and their pastoral care. I am confident that you too take this special service very seriously and that you count it among your most pressing and most satisfying responsibilities. One cannot meet with college and university students anywhere in the world without hearing their questions and sensing their anxieties. In their hearts your students have many questions about faith, religious practice and holiness of life. Each one arrives on your campuses with a family background, a personal history and an acquired culture. They all want to be accepted, loved and supported by a Christian educational community which shows friendship and authentic spiritual commitment.

It is your privilege to serve your students in faith and love; to help them deepen their friendship with Christ; to make available to them the opportunities for prayer and liturgical celebration, including the possibility to know the forgiveness and love of Jesus Christ in the sacraments of penance and the Eucharist. You are able, as Catholic educators, to introduce your students to a powerful experience of community and to a very serious involvement in social concerns that will enlarge their horizons, challenge their lifestyles and offer them authentic human fulfillment.

University students, for example, are in a splendid position to take to heart the gospel invitation to go out of themselves, to reject introversion and to concentrate on the needs of others. Students with the opportunities of higher education can readily grasp the relevance for today of Christ's parable of the rich man and Lazarus (cf. Lk 16:19ff), with all of its consequences for humanity. What is at stake is not only the rectitude of individual human hearts, but also the whole social order as it touches the spheres of economics, politics and human rights and relations.

Here in the Catholic university centers of this nation, vivified by the inspiration of the Gospel, must be drawn up the blueprints for the reform of attitudes and structures that will influence the whole dynamic of peace and justice in the world as it affects East and West, North and South. It is not enough to offer to the disadvantaged of the world crumbs of freedom, crumbs of truth and crumbs of bread. The Gospel calls for much more. The parable of the rich man and the poor man is directed to the conscience of humanity and, today in particular, to the conscience of America. But that conscience often passes through the halls of academe, through nights of study and hours of prayer, finally to reach and embrace the whole

prophetic message of the Gospel. "Keep your attention closely fixed on it," we are told in the Second Letter of Peter, "as you would on a lamp shining in a dark place until the first streaks of dawn appear and the morning star rises in your hearts" (2 Pt 1:19).

9. Dear brothers and sisters: As leaders in Catholic university and college education, you have inherited a tradition of service and academic excellence, the cumulative effort of so many who have worked so hard and sacrificed so much for Catholic education in this country. Now there lies before you the wide horizon of the third century of the nation's constitutional existence and the third century of Catholic institutions of higher learning serving the people of this land. The challenges that confront you are just as testing as those your forefathers faced in establishing the network of institutions over which you now preside. Undoubtedly, the greatest challenge is, and will remain, that of preserving and strengthening the Catholic character of your colleges and universities — that institutional commitment to the word of God as proclaimed by the Catholic Church. This commitment is both an expression of spiritual consistency and a specific contribution to the cultural dialogue proper to American life. As you strive to make the presence of the church in the world of modern culture more luminous, may you listen once again to Christ's prayer to his Father for his disciples: "Consecrate them by means of truth. Your word is truth" (Jn 17:17).

May the Holy Spirit, the Counselor and Spirit of Truth, who has enlivened and enlightened the church of Christ from the beginning, give you great confidence in the Father's word and sustain you in the service that you render to the truth through Catholic higher education in the United States of America.

Westover Hills Mass San Antonio, Sept. 13

Pope John Paul II:

"My soul, give thanks to the Lord; all my being, bless his holy name" (Ps 103:1).

Dear brothers and sisters, dear friends, citizens of San Antonio and of the state of Texas,

1. It gives me an immense joy to be with you on this Sunday morning and to invoke God's blessings upon this vast state and upon the whole church in this region.

Texas! The name immediately brings to mind the rich history and cultural development of this part of the United States. In this marvelous setting overlooking the city of San Antonio, I cannot but reverently evoke the memory of the Franciscan Father Massanet who, on the feast of St. Anthony of Padua, June 13, 1691, celebrated Mass along the banks of the San Antonio River for the members of an early Spanish expedition and a group of local Indian people.

Since then people of many different origins have come here, so that today yours is a multicultural society striving for the fullness of harmony and collaboration among all. I express my cordial gratitude to the representatives of the state of Texas and the city of San Antonio who have wished to be present at this moment of prayer. I also greet the members of the various Christian communions who join us in praising the name of our Lord Jesus Christ. A special word of thanks to

Archbishop Flores and to the bishops, priests, deacons, Religious and all the Catholic faithful of Texas. The peace of Christ be with you all!

2. Today is Sunday: the Lord's Day. Today is like the "seventh day" about which the Book of Genesis says that "God rested from all the work he had undertaken" (Gn 2:2). Having completed the work of creation, he "rested." God rejoiced in his work; he "looked at everything that he had made, and he found it very good" (Gn 1:31). "So God blessed the seventh day and made it holy" (Gn 2:3).

On this day we are called to reflect more deeply on the mystery of creation and therefore of our own lives. We are called to "rest" in God, the Creator of the universe. Our duty is to praise him: "My soul give thanks to the Lord.... Give thanks to the Lord and never forget all his blessings" (Ps 103:1-2). This is a task for each human being. Only the human person, created in the image and likeness of God, is capable of raising a hymn of praise and thanksgiving to the Creator. The Earth, with all its creatures, and the entire universe call on man to be their voice. Only the human person is capable of releasing from the depths of his or her being that hymn of praise proclaimed without words by all creation: "My soul, give thanks to the Lord; all my being, bless his holy name" (v. 1).

3. What is the message of today's liturgy? To us gathered here in San Antonio in the state of Texas and taking part in the eucharistic sacrifice of our Lord and Savior Jesus Christ, St. Paul addresses these words: "None of us lives as his own master, and none of us dies as his own master. While we live we are responsible to the Lord and when we die we die as his servants. Both in life and death we are the Lord's" (Rom 14:7-8).

These words are concise, but filled with a moving message. "We live" and "we die." We live in this material world that surrounds us, limited by the horizons of our earthly journey through time. We live in this world, with the inevitable prospect of death, right from the moment of conception and of birth. And yet we must look beyond the material aspect of our earthly existence. Certainly bodily death is a necessary passage for us all; but it is also true that what from its very beginning has borne in itself the image and likeness of God cannot be completely given back to the corruptible matter of the universe. This is a fundamental truth and attitude of our Christian faith. In St. Paul's terms: "While we live we are responsible to the Lord, and when we die we die as his servants." We live for the Lord, and our dying too is life in the Lord.

Today, on this Lord's Day, I wish to invite all those who are listening to my words not to forget our immortal destiny: life after death — the eternal happiness of heaven or the awful possibility of eternal punishment, eternal separation from God, in what the Christian tradition has called hell (cf. Mt 25:41; 22:13; 25:30). There can be no truly Christian living without an openness to this transcendent dimension of our lives. "Both in life and death we are the Lord's" (Rom 14:8).

4. The Eucharist that we celebrate constantly confirms our living and dying "in the Lord": "Dying you destroyed our death, rising you restored our life." In fact, St. Paul wrote: "We are the Lord's. That is why Christ died and came to life again, that he might be Lord of both the dead and the living" (Rom 14:8-9). Yes, Christ is the Lord!

The paschal mystery has transformed our human existence, so that it is no longer under the dominion of death. In Jesus Christ, our redeemer, "we live for the Lord" and "we die for the Lord." Through him and with him and in him, we belong to God in life and in death. We exist not only "for death" but "for God." For this reason, on this day "made by the Lord" (Ps 119:24), the Church all over the world speaks her blessing from the very depths of the paschal mystery of Christ: "My soul, give thanks to the Lord; all my being bless his holy name. Give thanks ... and never forget all his blessings" (Ps 103:1-2).

"Never forget"! Today's reading from the Gospel according to St. Matthew gives us an example of a man who has forgotten (cf. Mt 18:21-35). He has forgotten the favors given by his lord — and consequently he has shown himself to be cruel and heartless in regard to his fellow human being. In this way the liturgy introduces us to the experience of sin as it has developed from the beginning of the history of man alongside the experience of death.

We die in the physical body when all the energies of life are extinguished. We die through sin when love dies in us. Outside of love there is no life. If man opposes love and lives without love, death takes root in his soul and grows. For this reason Christ cries out: "I give you a new commandment: Love one another. Such as my love has been for you, so must your love be for each other" (Jn 13:34). The cry for love is the cry for life, for the victory of the soul over sin and death. The source of this victory is the cross of Jesus Christ: his death and his resurrection.

5. Again, in the Eucharist, our lives are touched by Christ's own radical victory over sin — sin which is the death of the soul and — ultimately — the reason for bodily death. "That is why Christ died and came to life again, that he might be Lord of the dead" (cf. Rom 14:9) — that he might give life again to those who are dead in sin or because of sin.

And so, the Eucharist begins with the penitential rite. We confess our sins in order to obtain forgiveness through the cross of Christ and so receive a part in his resurrection from the dead. But if our conscience reproaches us with mortal sin, our taking part in the Mass can be fully fruitful only if beforehand we receive absolution in the sacrament of penance.

The ministry of reconciliation is a fundamental part of the Church's life and mission. Without overlooking any of the many ways in which Christ's victory over sin becomes a reality in the life of the Church and of the world, it is important for me to emphasize that it is above all in the sacrament of forgiveness and reconciliation that the power of the redeeming blood of Christ is made effective in our personal lives.

6. In different parts of the world there is a great neglect of the sacrament of penance. This is sometimes linked to an obscuring of the religious and moral conscience, a loss of the sense of sin or a lack of adequate instruction on the importance of this sacrament in the life of Christ's Church. At times the neglect occurs because we fail to take seriously our lack of love and justice, and God's corresponding offer of reconciling mercy. Sometimes there is a hesitation or an unwillingness to accept maturely and responsibly the consequences of the objective truths of faith. For these reasons it is necessary to emphasize once again that "with regard to the substance of the sacrament there has always remained firm and unchanged in the consciousness of the Church the certainty that, by the will of Christ, forgiveness is offered to each individual by means of sacramental absolution given by the ministers of penance" ("Reconciliatio et Paenitentia," 30).

Again I ask all my brother bishops and priests to do everything possible to make the administration of this sacrament a primary aspect of their service to God's people. There can be no substitute for the means of grace which Christ himself has placed in our hands. The Second Vatican Council never intended that this sacrament of penance be less practiced; what the council expressly asked for was that the faithful might more easily understand the sacramental signs and more eagerly and frequently have recourse to the sacraments (cf. "Sacrosanctum Concilium," 59). And just as sin deeply touches the individual conscience, so we understand why the absolution of sins must be individual and not collective, except in extraordinary circumstances as approved by the Church.

I ask you, dear Catholic brothers and sisters, not to see confession as a mere attempt at psychological liberation — however legitimate this too might be — but as a sacrament, a liturgical act. Confession is an act of honesty and courage; an act of entrusting ourselves, beyond sin, to the mercy of a loving and forgiving God. It is an act of the prodigal son who returns to his Father and is welcomed by him with the kiss of peace. It is easy, therefore, to understand why "every confessional is a special and blessed place from which there is born new and uncontaminated a reconciled individual — a reconciled world!" ("Reconciliatio et Paenitentia," 31, V; cf. III).

The potential for an authentic and vibrant renewal of the whole Catholic Church through the more faithful use of the sacrament of penance is immeasurable. It flows directly from the loving heart of God himself! This is a certainty of faith which I offer to each one of you and to the entire Church in the United States.

To those who have been far away from the sacrament of reconciliation and forgiving love I make this appeal: Come back to this source of grace; do not be afraid! Christ himself is waiting for you. He will heal you, and you will be at peace with God!

To all the young people of the Church, I extend a special invitation to receive Christ's forgiveness and his strength in the sacrament of penance. It is a mark of greatness to be able to say: I have made a mistake; I have sinned, Father; I have offended you, my God; I am sorry; I ask for pardon; I will try again because I rely on your strength and I believe in your love. And I know that the power of your Son's paschal mystery — the death and resurrection of our Lord Jesus Christ — is greater than my weaknesses and all the sins of the world. I will come and confess my sins and be healed, and I will live in your love!

7. In Jesus Christ the world has truly known the mystery of forgiveness, mercy and reconciliation, which is proclaimed by God's word this day. At the same time, God's inexhaustible mercy to us obliges us to be reconciled among ourselves. This makes practical demands on the Church in Texas and the Southwest of the United States. It means bringing hope and love wherever there is division and alienation.

Your history registers a meeting of cultures, indigenous and immigrant, sometimes marked by tensions and conflicts, yet constantly moving toward reconciliation and harmony. People of different races and languages, colors and customs, have come to this land to make it their home. Together with the indigenous peoples of these territories, there are the descendants of those who came from almost every country in Europe: from Spain and France, from Germany and Belgium, from Italy, Hungary and Czechoslovakia, from Ireland, England and Scotland. And even from my own native Poland — for it was to Texas and Panna Maria that the first Polish immigrants came to the United States. There are descendants of those who came in chains from Africa; those from Lebanon, the Philippines and Vietnam, and from every Latin American country, especially from Mexico.

This land is a crossroads standing at the border of two great nations and experiencing both the enrichment and the complications which arise from this circumstance. You are thus a symbol and a kind of laboratory testing America's commitment to her founding moral principles and human values. These principles and values are now being reaffirmed by America as she celebrates the bicentennial of her Constitution and speaks once more about justice and freedom, and about the acceptance of diversity within a fundamental unity — a unity arising from a shared vision of the dignity of every human person and a shared responsibility for the welfare of all, especially of the needy and the persecuted.

8. Against this background one may speak of a current phenomenon here and elsewhere — the movement of people northward, not only from Mexico but from other southern neighbors of the United States. On this matter also there is work of reconciliation to be done. Among you there are people of great courage and generosity who have been doing much on behalf of suffering brothers and sisters arriving from the south. They have sought to show compassion in the face of complex human, social and political realities. Here human needs, both spiritual and material, continue to call out to the church with thousands of voices, and the whole Church must respond by the proclamation of God's word and by selfless deeds of service. Here too there is ample space for continuing and growing collaboration among members of the various Christian communions.

In all of this the Hispanic community itself faces the greatest challenge. Those of you of Hispanic descent — so numerous, so long present in this land, so well equipped to respond — are called to hear the word of Christ and take it to heart: "I give you a new commandment: Love one another. Such as my love has been for you, so must your love be for each other" (Jn 13:34). And Jesus specified that this love embraces the entire range of human needs from the least to the greatest: "I promise you that whoever gives a cup of cold water to one of these lowly ones ... will not want for his reward" (Mt 10:42). The Hispanic community also needs to respond to its own needs and to show generous and effective solidarity among its own members. I urge you to hold fast to your Christian faith and traditions, especially in defense of the family. And I pray that the Lord may provide many more vocations to the priesthood and to the religious life among your young people.

May you who have received so much from God hear the call to a renewal of your Christian life and to fidelity to the faith of your fathers. May you respond in the spirit of Mary, the Virgin Mother whom the Church sees "maternally present and sharing in the many complicated problems which today beset the lives of individuals, families and nations ... helping the Christian people in the constant struggle between good and evil, to ensure that it 'does not fall,' or if it has fallen, that it 'rises again' " ("Redemptoris Mater," 52).

9. Today's liturgy helps us to reflect deeply on life and death, on the victory of life over death. On this earth, in the visible world of creation, man exists "for death"; and yet, in Christ, he is called to communion with God, with the living God who "gives life." He is called to this communion precisely through the death of Christ — the death which "gives life."

Today all over the world countless people — people of many countries and continents, languages and races, are sharing sacramentally in the death of Christ. We here in Texas journey together with them toward the fulfillment of the paschal mystery in life. We journey, conscious of being sinners, conscious of being mortal. But we journey on in hope in union with the sacrifice of Christ through eucharistic communion with him and with love for each other. We live for the Lord! We die for the Lord! We belong to the Lord! Come, Lord Jesus! (cf. Rv 22:20). Amen.

Meeting with Charities
San Antonio, Sept. 13

Dr. Mary Ann Quaranta:

Holy Father, the film we have just seen touches on just a few of the many facets of our work in Catholic Charities. It is my privilege to share with you further elaboration on our mission, our structure and our activities.

Compassionate, direct service to those in need has been the hallmark of Catholic Charities throughout its 78-year history in the United States. Where there is human oppression, alienation or deprivation, all over this nation, in every diocese, Catholic Charities is there. Our concern extends to all hurting people: to the elderly, the handicapped, the unemployed, the homeless, the impoverished, the mentally ill, neglected, abandoned and abused children, the bereaved, struggling families and individuals.

Our extensive diocesan programs assisted over 7 million people last year. But we have found that the personal social service we provide so effectively is not enough. A critical part of our mission has always been to serve as the "attorneys of the poor," representing their needs in the public arena and working to solve societal problems at the root of human suffering.

It is the special structure and form of the Catholic Charities movement in this country which enables us to be successful in our twofold mission to serve those in need and work toward eliminating the causes of those needs. Local Catholic Charities can respond to local needs in a way that is immediate and effective. As part of the larger national network of Catholic Charities USA, local agencies join together to examine social issues, share successful strategies and plan for future needs. The national movement also enables Catholic Charities to join with other social service groups, many of which are represented here today, to present a unified approach to providing services and solving problems.

We are called to be deeply involved in social advocacy and action to ensure that the needs of the poor and disadvantaged are met today and to prepare for a better future for all people. We are fortunate that in this country pluralism and diversity are not only respected, but cherished. This philosophy of government has created a special partnership between the public and private sectors and offers a wide-open door for Catholic Charities to represent those in greatest need to those responsible for making and enforcing public policy.

Catholic Charities has always been on the inside of the sophisticated American process of legislation, presenting issues and proposing policies to benefit the poor, the alienated, the disenfranchised. Among the organization's more notable contributions to social policy include its participation in developing —:

—The Social Security Act of 1935.
—Public works programs for the unemployed.
—National housing legislation in 1949 and the 1960s.
—Title XX of the Social Security Act to provide funds to states for social services.
—The Office for Families in the U.S. Department of Health and Human Services.
—Federal funding for specialized care of children with severe disabilities; and
—Improved welfare legislation.
Our advocacy efforts enable Catholic Charities to reach

beyond those whom we serve directly to benefit the nearly 33 million Americans who now live in poverty.

We continue to call for welfare reform; for the establishment of job opportunities, training, education, counseling and job placement as primary tools in conquering poverty; and for the strong presence of our federal government in achieving a better quality of life for all Americans.

It is important to the fulfillment of our mission that we have the highest quality of professional services available. We are on the forefront of national developments which have professionalized social services. We have established a code of ethics and an accreditation process which encourage our agencies to evaluate their effectiveness and improve the quality of their services. We have encouraged Catholic universities to strengthen their schools of social work and establish graduate programs for dedicated Religious and lay persons who are committed to serving the poor and helpless. As dean of Fordham University's Graduate School of Social Services, I am proud to be part of this important educational effort.

Catholic Charities is also called to remind all members of the Catholic Church of the sharp relevance of the gospel message to the issues of our time. On the local level, we appeal to the strong American volunteer spirit and help parishes examine and serve the special needs of their communities and beyond. This program of parish social ministry reinforces the network of community-based voluntarism that is the backbone of social service delivery in this nation.

Holy Father, we share a special unity in the work of service as we work for mercy and justice, speaking out on behalf of the poor and joining together to root out the causes of poverty, oppression and alienation. We ask your blessing on these efforts and pray for continued strength and success. Thank you.

Father Thomas Harvey:

Your Holiness, I have the privilege of sharing with you a glimpse of the challenges we face in our nation and our hopes for the future.

Ours is a nation of unprecedented social, political and economic progress, but still a nation of great needs. The language of "Gaudium et Spes" is both a consolation and frightening mandate. "We must look at the signs of the times and understand the world in which we live; today the human race is going through a crisis of growth. Human experience is becoming increasingly polarized — with more knowledge, greater uncertainty; with wealth, hunger and poverty; with freedom, social and psychological slavery; with a search for a better world, little spiritual advancement." These very extremes involve us. We daily come in contact with the nation's wealthiest and poorest. We have great knowledge, and yet some of our greatest problems still beg for solutions.

We have the technical competence to extend the life of the majority of our citizens to 80, 90 or even 100 years. Yet we have not effectively mastered how to extend the social, religious or medical support systems to nurture adequately the frail elderly. We walk without the wisdom of history, since this is a new experience in the human family.

Just 50 years ago, the majority of our citizens were poor. Their very numbers forced the nation to hear their needs. Policies such as the Social Security Act and increasing levels of employment expanded opportunities for most. Now, however, the poor are not the majority, and the nation too often has other priorities. Thus, while we celebrate that we rank among the world's few nations which has so well reduced poverty, we in Catholic Charities lament the lack of commitment today to include ever more people in the opportunities of this nation. Millions of homeless persons live in our streets. Thirty-four million Americans live below the government-defined poverty line. One quarter of our children, one quarter of our nation's future, lives in poverty.

It is in the midst of these critical social pressures that Catholic Charities struggles to be a prophetic voice. Catholic Charities is the ministry of mediation, a mediation between the pain and suffering of our sisters and brothers and the hope of our Father's kingdom. Our ministry is to transform society into an environment worthy of the enhanced dignity Jesus conferred on all people when he taught us to say, "Our Father ...."

We call on our neighbors, our Church, our government to join us in this ministry.

To our bishops, the pastors of the local church community, who have spoken eloquently in their pastoral letters on peace and a just economy, we ask: Encourage and support the clergy and laity in your dioceses to live out their baptismal call to service especially to those in most need. Direct, with vigor, your resources toward the instruction and application of the social teachings of the Church. In your allocation of the financial resources of your dioceses give high priority to human services and advocacy for the poor.

To pastors in parishes, we ask: Be clear in your teaching of the faith. Inspire your parishioners to be compassionate and non-judgmental in reaching out to the needs of the hurting in your communities.

To our brothers and sisters in faith, we ask: Respond to the call which every Christian is given to serve as Jesus showed us. Bring good news to the poor; find ways to give hope to the 25 percent of the nation's children who live in poverty. Release the captives; fight discrimination, which denies opportunities for economic security to many of our citizens. Give sight to the blind; set free the oppressed. Embrace policies which give access to health care to the 35 million Americans without insurance.

To our friends and colleagues with whom we have labored on many issues — housing, tax structure, emergency services, Social Security, full employment — and to all people of good will: We entreat you to continue or join with us in our quest to build a fully humane and just society.

To our federal, state and local government officials: We pledge continued vigilance over your charge to promote, in justice, the general welfare and the common good. Do not be deceived by the perception that the only enemy which threatens this country is one which challenges the common defense. Poverty, unemployment and the erosion of family stability also attack our nation from within. We also pledge to act in partnership with you to channel services where needed.

From you, Holy Father, we ask continued and unrelenting commitment to a social doctrine which expands the horizons of human development. Where people are being exploited, we ask that you be unyielding in your cry for justice. Where people are suffering from such debilitating problems as divorce, diseases such as AIDS and the ambiguity of changing lifestyles, we ask patience of the Church's teachings so that we do not close the door to opportunities for better solutions to these pressures of our changing world than our present wisdom easily affords.

Holy Father, we pray that your visit to our nation will champion our cause and call all of us to new levels of generosity and commitment. We seek to create a society where all who seek work will obtain an adequate paying job; where the scandal of homeless families will no longer exist; where children who go to sleep hungry will have proper nourishment; where the elderly can live in dignity without the fear of medical impoverishment; where our youth will no longer snuff out their lives in the despair of a sex or drug culture, but will instead respond to their natural idealism and hope for the future.

Now, through this presentation of a special edition of our publication "Social Thought," which is dedicated to your social teachings, Catholic Charities expresses its appreciation of your teachings in this area. It is our hope that through the work of these scholars and writers we may continue, in the Spirit, to dialogue with you long after you leave our shores. Your words have inspired our minds and bodies to continue to seek the kingdom of the Father through the works of mercy and justice.

We ask your blessing upon our endeavors with and for all those in need.

Pope John Paul II:

Dear brothers and sisters,

I am grateful for your presentation of the vast network of Christian love and human solidarity in which you are engaged. May the Lord sustain you in your zeal. "May mercy, peace and love be yours in ever greater measure" (Jude 1).

1. Catholic Charities is a title that speaks wonderfully well of the generous commitment of the Catholic people of the United States to the cause of human solidarity and Christian love. It gives me great joy to be among you, members of Catholic Charities USA, your associated agencies and your colleague organizations in social ministry. Through your efforts you help to make the loving compassion of our Lord and Savior Jesus Christ present to human needs.

Jesus Christ was born poor, lived poor and died poor. He loved the poor. In his kingdom the poor have a special place. The Church cannot be any different. She must be ever more fully aware of her fundamental duty to reflect in her life and action the very love with which God loves his creatures. For what is at stake is the mystery of God's love as explained in the First Letter of John: "We, for our part, love because he first loved us" (1 Jn 4:19). All service has its first moment in God.

2. You carry on a tradition, and you live out a teaching grounded in Sacred Scripture, proclaimed by the Church and relevant to every age. Service to the needy not only builds up social harmony; it reveals God, our Father, the rescuer of the oppressed. In the Old Testament it was God's love for his people that decreed a special concern for the stranger, the widow and the orphan. As God had treated his people, so were they to treat others. The year of jubilee and the sabbatical year restored economic balance: Slaves were set free, land was returned to its original owners, debts were canceled (cf. Ex 21ff; Lv 25). Justice and mercy alike were served. The prophets repeatedly drew attention to the inner qualities of heart that must animate the exercise of justice and service: "Not as man sees does God see, because man sees the appearance but the Lord looks into the heart" (1 Sm 16:7).

In the New Testament the mystery of God's love is further revealed: "God so loved the world that he gave his only Son" (Jn 3:16). Through the heart of Jesus the fullness of God's infinite mercy appeared in the world. Marveling at the incarnation of God's Son, Mary exclaims that through this child the lowly shall be lifted up, their hunger shall be satisfied and God's mercy shall be extended to all (cf. Lk 1:46-55). Years later, in announcing his own ministry, Jesus sums up his life's program in the words of Isaiah: "to bring glad tidings to the poor, to proclaim liberty to captives, recovery of sight to the blind and release to prisoners, to announce a year of favor from the Lord" (Lk 4:18-19). Jesus identifies himself with the poor and the defenseless: What we do for them is done for him; the service we fail to render them is service denied to him (cf. Mt 25:31-46).

Gross disparities of wealth between nations, classes and persons re-enact the gospel parable of the rich man and the poor man Lazarus. And with the same dire consequences of which the Gospel speaks: "'My child,' replied Abraham, 'remember that you were well off in your lifetime, while Lazarus was in misery. Now he has found consolation here, but you have found torment' " (Lk 16:25). The warning is as valid today as it was 2,000 years ago.

3. From the beginning the Church has worked to carry out this teaching in her ministry. It is not necessary here to trace the extremely varied history of Christian service. The Church has always sought to respond to the stranger, the widow and the orphan; she has founded countless schools, hospitals, hospices, child-care facilities and shelters. In our own times the Second Vatican Council has forcefully reaffirmed the Church's vocation, in fidelity to her Lord, to love all those who are afflicted in any way: to recognize in the poor and the suffering the likeness of her poor and suffering Founder; to do all she can to relieve their needs, striving to serve Christ in them (cf. "Lumen Gentium," 8). Twenty years after the council, the Christian community is more than ever aware that the poor, the hungry, the oppressed, the sick and the handicapped share in a special way in the cross of Christ and therefore need the Church's ministry.

Works of mercy, justice and compassion are basic to the history of the Church in the United States. The two American women who have been numbered among the saints, Frances Xavier Cabrini and Elizabeth Ann Seton, have been thus honored principally because of their work for their poorer brothers and sisters. The initiatives of Catholic charities in the United States go back to before the Declaration of Independence. Countless institutions and structures have been established to assist the orphan, the immigrant, the ethnic groups, all persons in need — of every race and creed. Countless Americans of all extractions have made the compassionate service of their fellow human beings the whole purpose and method of their lives. In particular, generations of Religious, women and men, have consumed themselves in selfless service under the sign of love.

4. The Church has always proclaimed a love of preference for the poor. Perhaps the language is new, but the reality is not. Nor has the Church taken a narrow view of poverty and the poor. Poverty, certainly, is often a matter of material deprivation. But it is also a matter of spiritual impoverishment, the lack of human liberties and the result of any violation of human rights and human dignity. There is a very special and pitiable form of poverty: the poverty of selfishness, the poverty of those who have and will not share, of those who could be rich by giving but choose to be poor by keeping everything they have. These people too need help.

The Christian view is that human beings are to be valued for what they are, not for what they have. In loving the poor and serving those in whatever need, the Church seeks above all to respect and heal their human dignity. The aim of Chris-

tian solidarity and service is to defend and promote, in the name of Jesus Christ, the dignity and fundamental human rights of every person. The Church "bears witness to the fact that this dignity cannot be destroyed, whatever the situation of poverty, scorn, rejection or powerlessness to which a human being has been reduced. She shows her solidarity with those who do not count in a society by which they are rejected spiritually and sometimes even physically. She is particularly drawn with maternal affection toward those children who, through human wickedness, will never be brought forth from the womb to the light of day, as also for the elderly, alone and abandoned. The special option for the poor, far from being a sign of particularism or sectarianism, manifests the universality of the Church's being and mission" (Instruction on Christian Freedom and Liberation, 68).

For "the poor in spirit" the Church has a very special love. She has inherited it from Christ, who called them "blessed" (Mt 5:3). On the one hand the Church knows, from the words of Christ, that despite all human efforts the poor will always be with us (cf. Mt 26:11). On the other hand, in all her efforts to uplift the poor she knows and proclaims the ambivalence of possessions. Indeed, where the pursuit of wealth is treated as the supreme good, human beings become imprisoned in the hardening of their hearts and in the closing of their minds (cf. "Populorum Progressio," 19). For this reason too the Church, in the very act of serving the poor and relieving their sufferings, must also continue to proclaim and serve their higher needs, those of the spirit.

5. Service to those in need must take the form of direct action to relieve their anxieties and to remove their burdens, and at the same time lead them to the dignity of self-reliance. In this respect I wish to express the Church's immense gratitude to the many Americans who are working to help their fellow human beings in all the different forms which relief and development take in today's world. And I solemnly thank the American people for the generous way in which they respond to the appeal for financial support for the many splendid programs of assistance carried out in their name. In the case of the many programs run by the Catholic Church, I wish to invite all who have responsibility for them to ensure that they will always be, and be seen to be, in full accord with Catholic principles of truth and justice.

The organizational and institutional response to needs, whether in the church or in society, is extremely necessary but it is not sufficient in itself. In this regard I would repeat a concern I mentioned in my Apostolic Letter on Human Suffering: "Institutions are very important and indispensable; nevertheless, no institution can by itself replace the human heart, human compassion, human love or human initiative, when it is a question of dealing with the sufferings of another. This refers to physical sufferings, but it is even more true when it is a question of the many kinds of moral suffering and when it is primarily the soul that is suffering" (No. 29).

Furthermore, in the necessary organizational and institutional response to needs, it is essential to avoid reducing human beings to mere units or categories of political or social planning and action. Such a process leads to new and other unjust forms of anonymity and alienation.

6. Service to the poor also involves speaking up for them and trying to reform structures which cause or perpetuate their oppression. As committed Catholics involved in helping to meet people's many concrete needs, you are still called to reflect on another dimension of a worldwide problem: the relationship between rich societies and poor societies, rich nations and poor nations. Your insights must be prayerfully joined

to those of many other people to see what can be done as soon as possible to purify the social structures of all society in this regard.

In the final analysis, however, we must realize that social injustice and unjust social structures exist only because individuals and groups of individuals deliberately maintain or tolerate them. It is these personal choices, operating through structures, that breed and propagate situations of poverty, oppression and misery. For this reason, overcoming "social" sin and reforming the social order itself must begin with the conversion of our hearts. As the American bishops have said: "The Gospel confers on each Christian the vocation to love God and neighbor in ways that bear fruit in the life of society. That vocation consists above all in a change of heart: a conversion expressed in praise of God and in concrete deeds of justice and service" ("Economic Justice for All: Catholic Social Teaching and the U.S. Economy," 327).

To many people, mercy and conversion may seem like poor tools for solving social problems. Some are tempted to accept ideologies that use force to carry out their programs and impose their vision. Such means sometimes produce what appear to be successes. But these successes are not real. Force and manipulation have nothing to do with true human development and the defense of human dignity. Catholic social teaching is totally different not only as regards goals, but also as regards the means to be used. For the Christian, putting right human ills must necessarily take into account the reality of creation and redemption. It means treating every human being as a unique child of God, a brother or sister of Jesus Christ. The path of human solidarity is the path of service; and true service means selfless love, open to the needs of all, without distinction of persons, with the explicit purpose of reinforcing each person's sense of God-given dignity.

7. Solidarity and service are above all a duty of Christian love which must involve the whole community. When we are tempted to congratulate ourselves on what we have done, we must bear soberly in mind the words of Jesus: "When you have done all you have been commanded to do, say, 'We are useless servants. We have done no more than our duty'" (Lk 17:10). When we are faced with the vastness of this duty of love, with the boundless needs of the poor in America and throughout the world, when we are disappointed by slowness and setbacks in the reform of structures and in our own conversion, let us not lose heart, and let us not settle for what has already been accomplished. Love can overcome great obstacles, and God's love can totally transform the world.

As the Church tries to express Christian solidarity in generous service, she also wishes to draw attention to the importance of worship and prayer and their relationship to service. In looking to the example of Christ, the Church can never forget that all Christ's actions were accompanied by prayer. It is in prayer that the church develops and evaluates her social consciousness and unceasingly discovers anew her vocation to serve the needy of the world, as Jesus did. Addressing a group of American bishops during their last "ad limina" visit, I spoke of this specifically Christian and ecclesial dimension of all social and charitable action:

"Only a worshiping and praying Church can show herself sufficiently sensitive to the needs of the sick, the suffering, the lonely — especially in the great urban centers — and the poor everywhere. The Church as a community of service has first to feel the weight of the burden carried by so many individuals and families, and then strive to help alleviate these burdens. The discipleship that the Church discovers in prayer she expresses in deep interest for Christ's brethren in the modern world and for their many different needs. Her concern, manifested in various ways, embraces — among others — the areas of housing, education, health care, unemployment, the administration of justice, the special needs of the aged and the handicapped. In prayer, the Church is confirmed in her solidarity with the weak who are oppressed, the vulnerable who are manipulated, the children who are exploited, and everyone who is in any way discriminated against" (Address of Dec. 3, 1983, No. 6).

8. Catholic Charities and related organizations exist essentially to spread Christian love. It is especially through charitable activities at the parish level that the entire church in the United States joins in the tasks of mercy, justice and love. We have seen today how Catholic Charities and all its colleague associations have lent God their own flesh — their hands and feet and hearts — so that his work may be done in our world. For your long and persevering service — creative and courageous, and blind to distinctions of race or religion — you will certainly hear Jesus' words of gratitude: "You did it for me" (Mt 25:40).

Gather, transform and serve! When done in the name of Jesus Christ, this is the spirit of Catholic Charities and of all who work in this cause, because it is the faithful following of the One who did "not come to be served but to serve" (Mk 10:45). By working for a society which fosters the dignity of every human person, not only are you serving the poor, but you are renewing the founding vision of this nation under God! And may God reward you abundantly!

Address to Hispanics San Antonio, Sept. 13

Pope John Paul II:

Dear brothers and sisters in Christ,

1. This is a moment of great joy for me. I have looked forward to this meeting with you, members of the Hispanic community of San Antonio, present here as representatives of all your Hispanic brothers and sisters in the United States. You are here too as a parish community, and through you, therefore, my words are addressed to every parish community throughout the United States.

I greet each one of you with love in our Lord and Redeemer Jesus Christ. I am particularly happy to speak to you in the beautiful Spanish language in this square named in honor of Our Lady of Guadalupe. Our gathering here is a vivid reminder in the current Marian year of the special place of the mother of the Redeemer in the mystery of Christ and of the Church. It speaks to us of how dear our Blessed Mother has always been to you people of Hispanic culture and how important she continues to be today in your lives of faith and devotion. Marian shrines and places of pilgrimage are a kind of "geography" of faith by which we seek to meet the mother of God in order to find a strengthening of our Christian life (cf. "Redemptoris Mater," 28). Popular devotion to the Blessed Virgin Mary is rooted in sound doctrine, and authentic religious experience is appropriate and important in the lives of all Christ's followers.

2. The Hispanic heritage of San Antonio and the Southwest is very important for the Church. Spanish was the language of the first evangelizers of this continent, precisely in this region.

The missions here in San Antonio and throughout the Southwest are visible signs of the many years of evangelization and service carried out by the first missionaries. Their preaching of salvation in Jesus Christ was authenticated by their own integrity of life and by the spiritual and corporal works of mercy and love which they performed. Following their example, thousands of dedicated priests, Religious and lay people have labored to build up the Church here. Today it is your turn, in fidelity to the Gospel of Jesus Christ, to build your lives on the rock of your Christian faith. It is your turn to be evangelizers of each other and of all those whose faith is weak or who have not yet given themselves to the Lord. May you be no less zealous in evangelization and in Christian service than your forebears!

3. Today I wish to speak to you about your parish, which is the place and community in which you nourish and express your Christian life. I wish to speak of the parish as the family of families, for parish life is especially related to the strengths and weaknesses and needs of the families that make it up. There are, of course, many things that could be said about parish life; today it is only possible for me to emphasize certain aspects.

It is useful to begin with a well-known passage from the New Testament which helps us to keep in mind just why the members of a Catholic parish come together in the name of Jesus. In the Acts of the Apostles we read about the early Christians: "They devoted themselves to the apostles' instruction and the communal life, to the breaking of bread and prayers" (2:42). Instruction in the faith of the apostles, the building up of a living community, the Eucharist and the other sacraments, and the life of prayer — these are essential factors of the life of every parish.

4. First, instruction or catechesis. Everyone needs to be instructed in the faith. St. Paul summarizes it this way: "Everyone who calls on the name of the Lord will be saved. But how shall they call on him in whom they have not believed? And how can they believe unless they have heard of him? And how can they hear unless there is someone to preach?" (Rom 10:13-14). In a parish the faith is proclaimed and transmitted in many ways: through the liturgy and especially the Eucharist with its appropriate homilies; through religious instruction in schools and catechetical programs; through adult religious education; through prayer groups and associations for pastoral activity; through the Catholic press.

There are two things that I wish to emphasize about transmitting the faith. Catechesis has an objective content. We cannot invent the faith as we go along. We must receive it in and from the universal community of faith, the Church to whom Christ himself has entrusted a teaching office under the guidance of the Spirit of truth. Every catechist must sincerely and reverently be able to apply to himself or herself the words of Jesus: "My doctrine is not my own, it comes from him who sent me" (Jn 7:16; cf. "Catechesi Tradendae," 6). Likewise, every baptized person, precisely by reason of being baptized has the right to receive the authentic teaching of the church regarding doctrinal and moral aspects of Christian life (cf. Canon 229; "Catechesi Tradendae," 14).

The other point I wish to make about instruction in the faith is that family catechesis precedes, accompanies and enriches all other forms of catechesis (cf. "Catechesi Tradendae," 68). This means that the parish, in considering its catechetical programs, should give particular attention to its families. But above all it means that the family itself is the first and most appropriate place for teaching the truths of the faith, the practice of Christian virtues and the essential values of human life.

5. The second aspect of parish life that is contained in the text from the Acts of the Apostles concerns the parish's task of building up a living community. I have already said that every parish is a family of families. The vitality of a parish greatly depends on the spiritual vigor, commitment and involvement of its families. The family in fact is the basic unit of society and of the Church. It is "the domestic church." Families are those living cells which come together to form the very substance of parish life. Some are healthy and filled with the love of God, which is poured forth into our hearts through the Holy Spirit who has been given to us (cf. Rom 5:5). In some there is little energy for the life of the Spirit. Some have broken down altogether. The priests and their collaborators in a parish must try to be very close to all families in their need for pastoral care and to provide the support and spiritual nourishment they require.

The pastoral care of families is a vast and complex field of the Church's ministry, but it is a most urgent and pressing service. Each parish must be fully committed to it, especially in the face of so much breakdown and undermining of family life in society. I appeal to all priests, — pastors, associates and all concerned — to the permanent deacons and to the Religious and lay leaders to do everything possible, working together, to serve the family as effectively as possible. This involves proclaiming the whole truth about marriage and family life: the exclusive nature of conjugal love, the indissolubility of marriage, the Church's full teaching on the transmission of life and the respect due to human life from the moment of conception until natural death, the rights and duties of parents with regard to the education of their children, especially their religious and moral education, including proper sex education. Parents and family members must, moreover, be helped and sustained in their struggle to live by the sacred truths of faith. The Church must furnish families with the spiritual means of persevering in their sublime vocation and of growing in the special holiness to which Christ calls them.

6. Just as the parish is responsible for the family, so the family must be aware of its obligations to the parish, which is the larger family. Today Catholic couples and families must think especially of the service which they have a duty to render to other couples and families, especially those who experience problems. This apostolate of couple to couple and family to family can be carried out in many ways: prayer, good example, formal or informal instruction or counseling and material assistance of many sorts (cf. "Familiaris Consortio," 71). I appeal to you, the Catholic families of the United States: Be true families, united, reconciled and loving; and be true Catholic families — prayerful communities living the Catholic faith, open to the needs of others, taking part fully in the life of the parish and of the Church at large.

7. Another fundamental aspect of parish life is the worthy celebration of the sacraments, including sacramental marriage. This sacrament forms the stable basis of the whole Christian community. Without it, Christ's design for human love is not fulfilled, his plan for the family is not followed. It is precisely because Christ established marriage as a sacrament and willed it to be a sign of his own permanent and faithful love for the Church that the parish must explain to the faithful why all trial marriages, merely civil marriages, free unions and divorces do not correspond to Christ's plan.

The sacramental life of the Church is centered above all upon the Eucharist, which celebrates and brings about the unity of the Christian community — unity with God and unity with one another. In the Mass, the sacrifice of the cross is perpetuated throughout the centuries until Christ comes again. The body and blood of the Lord are given to us as our spiritual food. The parish community has no greater task or privilege than to gather, like Christ's first disciples, for "the breaking of the bread" (Acts 2:42).

I now repeat especially to all parishes the invitation already addressed to the whole Church: to promote and foster public and private devotion to the Holy Eucharist also outside of Mass (cf. "Inaestimabile Donum," 20ff). For, in the words of the Second Vatican Council: "The most blessed Eucharist contains the Church's entire spiritual wealth, that is, Christ himself" ("Presbyterorum Ordinis," 5).

The sacramental life of a parish extends also to the other sacraments which mark the important moments of the life of individuals and families, and of the entire parochial community. I wish to mention in particular the sacrament of penance and the important need for Catholics to confess their sins regularly. In recent years many have grown neglectful of this wonderful gift by which we obtain Christ's forgiveness of our sins. The state of the sacrament of penance in each parish and in each local church is a good indicator of the authentic maturity of the faith of the priests and people. It is necessary that Catholic families instill in their members a deep love of this beautiful means of reconciliation with our heavenly Father, with the Church and with our neighbor. Parents, more by example than by words, should encourage their children to go to confession regularly. Parishes need to encourage families to do this; they need to support them through proper catechesis. Needless to say, priests, who are the ministers of God's grace in this sacrament, should make certain that the sacrament is conveniently available in its authorized forms.

8. Finally, I refer briefly to the life of prayer as it manifests itself within the Christian community. This is an area in which the interaction between the family and the parish is especially clear and profound. Prayer begins in the home. The prayers that serve us well in life are often those learned at home when we were children. But prayer in the home also serves to introduce the children to the liturgical prayer of the whole Church, it helps all to apply the Church's prayer to everyday events and to the special moments of a family's experience (cf. "Familiaris Consortio," 61).

Everyone involved in parish life should be concerned to encourage and support family prayer by every means available; and families themselves should be making efforts to engage in family prayer and to integrate that prayer into the prayer life of the wider ecclesial community.

I am happy to know that the number of Hispanic priests and men and women Religious is growing. But many more are needed. Young Hispanics: Is Christ calling you? Hispanic families: Are you willing to give your sons and daughters to the Church's service? Do you ask the Lord to send laborers into his harvest? Christ needs Hispanic laborers for the great harvest of the Hispanic community and the whole Church.

9. And finally I wish to encourage all families and parishes not to be inward looking, not to dwell on themselves. Jesus commands us to serve our neighbor, to reach out to those in need. And I ask you especially to reach out to those brothers and sisters in the faith who have drifted away because of indifference or who have been hurt in some way. I invite all you who are unsure about the Church or who doubt that you will be welcome to come home to the family of families, to come home to your parish. You belong there! It is your family in the Church, and the Church is the household of God in which there are no strangers or aliens (cf. Eph 2:19).

We are gathered in front of a parish which is dedicated to

Our Lady of Guadalupe, mother of Jesus, mother of the Church, mother of the Americas, and in particular of Mexico. When Jesus died on the cross, he entrusted his mother to his beloved disciple, John. The Gospel tells us that from that moment the disciple took her into his home (cf. Jn 19:27). What better way is there for you to celebrate this Marian year than by taking Mary, the mother of the Redeemer, into your homes! This means imitating her faith and discipleship; it means keeping her present in your family prayers, especially the family rosary; turning to her, asking her intercession for the grace of conversion and renewal; entrusting yourselves and your families to her maternal care.

May God bless each and every one of you.

May he bless every family and parish.

May the Blessed Virgin of Guadalupe love and protect the Hispanic people of the land.

"Viva la Virgen de Guadalupe!"

Health Workers
Phoenix, Sept. 14

Mr. John E. Curley Jr.:

Your Holiness, we celebrate with you today the feast of the Triumph of the Cross. Christ's triumph is our hope and our salvation, even though our own pilgrimages remain to be completed and our own journeys sometimes seem marked more by burdens than by triumph.

Like Christ, we in the Catholic health care ministry wish to make God's healing presence available to all. By our ministry, we wish all to experience God's love. And yet there are important challenges shaping our capacity to bring God's healing presence to people in the United States.

Our ministry is undergoing extraordinary change. In truth, the Catholic health care ministry in the United States is today a ministry in transition. Four signs of this transition and of the challenges confronting our ministry can be briefly cited.

1. Our ministry has been shaped by the initiative and sacrifice of all those who have preceded us, primarily by institutes of women and men Religious. Indeed, it is a unique characteristic of the Church in the United States that our ministry has been animated by dedicated and gifted women who have persisted in bringing God's healing presence to every corner of our nation.

Paradoxically, even though there are fewer Religious today and, indeed, some religious institutes are assessing their future capacity to maintain their health care apostolates, their ministerial responsibilities are expanding to address new challenges. Religious are accepting the call to new levels of insight and commitment, to new forms of governance and structure. Through their sponsorship activities, Religious are essential to the implementation of Vatican II's theology of shared ministry with the laity. As a consequence, lay persons are participating more fully in our ministry and new forms of ownership and operation are emerging as religious institutes, dioceses and laity explore together alternatives to more traditional forms of sponsorship.

Our challenge is clear. Regardless of what specific collaborations may form our future, we must transform the uncertainties and discomforts of the present by our continued fidelity to the stewardship of this essential Church ministry.

171

2. In the past our ministry was characterized by its service within each local community. Today's Catholic health care ministry, however, must necessarily look beyond traditional local settings to reinforce its continuing capacity to care.

Nationally our ministry is a major undertaking. It encompasses more than 1,000 institutions, and cares for nearly 40 million persons each year. Representing an economic force in excess of $22 billion annually, it is the largest system of health care services in the United States under a single form of ownership. Intricate and multileveled governance, management, organizational and clinical structures are an essential response to the immensity of our undertaking and to the competitiveness and complexities of the various environments in which we serve.

Our challenge is clear. We must carefully integrate true ministry with structural realities to ensure not only the liveliness of our Catholic identity, but that the personhood of our patients is not lost in an impersonal medical and management maze.

3. Always perceived as a wealthy nation, the United States is today struggling with the dilemma of allocating limited resources. Important contributions to this public policy debate have included the U.S. bishops' pastoral letter titled "Economic Justice for All: Catholic Social Teaching and the U.S. Economy" and the report of the Catholic Health Association Task Force on Health Care of the Poor, titled "No Room in the Marketplace."

The health care needs of our nation's poor, the infirm elderly and others with special problems are today competing with other interests for a so-called fair share of economic resources. Sadly, few are competing to care for these special people.

Among the few are those who are gathered in this room. Our ministry is struggling to retain its capacity to grow in the service of all people, particularly those least able to care for themselves. Our struggle is intensified by increasing populations with special needs and decreasing public and private-sector willingness to make expenditures for such care. Our institutions and services are increasingly caught in a tension between our call to care and the need to survive in a potentially ruinous economic climate.

Our challenge is clear. We must remain financially viable if our ministry and our witness are to continue.

4. Secular values, in attempting to control new technology, are conspiring to shape a health care environment in which the sanctity of life and human dignity are at risk. Abortion is but one of the resulting tragedies.

Throughout the spectrum of life, the vast majority of these moral dilemmas occur within health care and health-related settings. Thus, our ministry is often the forum within which the Church is called upon to respond to contemporary moral dilemmas. Relative to these moral dilemmas, Holy Father, we have particular concerns. Our nation's health care environment increasingly poses ethical dilemmas that defy simple answers. Our ministry may well be placed in jeopardy if it cannot come to terms with issues such as:

— Genetics and genetic engineering.
— Technologically assisted human reproduction.
— Organ procurement and transplantation.
— Forgoing life-sustaining medical treatment.
— Human experimentation, and so on.

The list of ethical issues facing the Church and its health care ministry seems endless. We do not raise these issues for discussion during your brief pastoral visit. Rather, we raise them to underscore the serious problems confronting our ministry as we approach the 21st century.

Our challenge is clear. Rather than merely paralleling our society, we must continue to penetrate society. Within our pluralistic society, we represent a countersign to strictly secular values. These witness and ministry opportunities would be lost if we were not present as validly and as vigorously as we are today.

In short, the Catholic health care ministry in the United States is in the midst of transition. These are but four examples of the changes we are experiencing. Change is a constant; it can be either good or bad. We trust that the challenges of change represent opportunities for our ministry to grow in the service of all people. We are determined to move forward and to grow.

In a very human way, the triumph of the cross was foreshadowed when Mary expressed her "fiat" to God's invitation to become the mother of Jesus. Mary pronounced her yes in love, in faith and with a certain trepidation about the future. In this Marian year we in the Catholic health care ministry look especially to Mary for guidance and support. Like her, we must respond to God's call at this time and in this place of service in the ministry. We do so in love, in faith and with a certain trepidation about the future. We recognize that our response, unlike Mary's response, is imperfect and incomplete.

Nevertheless, it is our best response — made meaningful by the women and men who are gathered here today representing the leadership of the Catholic health care ministry in the United States. Whether clergy, religious or laity, whether Catholic or not, we — your sisters and brothers — are joined with you today as the sacrament of Christ present: loving, healing, reconciling, weeping, praying, working, hoping. Through our witness and ministry, we are evidence to all of the triumph of the cross.

Your Holiness, we celebrate who we are, what we are and where we are. And it is with special joy that we welcome you, Holy Father, to our family of the Catholic health care ministry in the United States.

Pope John Paul II:

Dear brothers and sisters, leaders in Catholic health care,

1. In the joy and peace of our Lord Jesus Christ I greet you and thank you for your warm welcome. This meeting gives us the opportunity to honor and give thanks to God for one of the most extensive and fundamental works of the Catholic Church in the United States — all that is embraced in the term "Catholic health care." I am pleased to be able to express to you who represent so many of your country's health care organizations the esteem, support and solidarity of the whole Church. In you, Jesus Christ continues his healing ministry, "curing the people of every disease and illness" (cf. Mt 4:23).

This is the high dignity to which you and your colleagues are called. This is your vocation, your commitment and the path of your specific witness to the presence of God's kingdom in the world. Your health care ministry, pioneered and developed by congregations of women Religious and by congregations of Brothers, is one of the most vital apostolates of the ecclesial community and one of the most significant services which the Catholic Church offers to society in the name of Jesus Christ. I have been told that membership in the Catholic Health Association extends to 620 hospitals and 300 long-term care facilities; that Catholic hospital beds

172

number 11 percent of the total number in the country; that Catholic institutions administer approximately 17 percent of the health care throughout the nation and that they cared for nearly 46 million people last year. I am grateful to Sister Mary Eileen Wilhelm and to your president, Mr. Curley, for illustrating to us this immense network of Christian service.

2. Because of your dedication to caring for the sick and the poor, the aged and the dying, you know from your own daily experience how much illness and suffering are basic problems of human existence. When the sick flocked to Jesus during his earthly life, they recognized in him a friend whose deeply compassionate and loving heart responded to their needs. He restored physical and mental health to many. These cures, however, involved more than just healing sickness. They were also prophetic signs of his own identity and of the coming of the kingdom of God, and they very often caused a new spiritual awakening in the one who had been healed.

The power that went out from Jesus and cured people of his own time (cf. Lk 6:19) has not lost its effect in the 2,000-year history of the Church. This power remains, in the life and prayer of the Church, a source of healing and reconciliation. Ever active, this power confirms the identity of the Church today, authenticates her proclamation of the kingdom of God and stands as a sign of triumph over evil.

With all Catholic health care, the immediate aim is to provide for the well-being of the body and mind of the human person, especially in sickness or old age. By his example, Christ teaches the Christian "to do good by his or her suffering and to do good to those who suffer" ("Salvifici Doloris," 30). This latter aspect naturally absorbs the greater part of the energy and attention of health care ministry. Today in the United States, Catholic health care extends the mission of the Church in every state of the union, in major cities, small towns, rural areas, on the campuses of academic institutions, in remote outposts and in inner-city neighborhoods. By providing health care in all these places, especially to the poor, the neglected, the needy, the newcomer, your apostolate penetrates and transforms the very fabric of American society. And sometimes you yourselves, like those you serve, are called to bow in humble and loving resignation to the experience of sickness — or to other forms of pain and suffering.

3. All concern for the sick and suffering is part of the Church's life and mission. The Church has always understood herself to be charged by Christ with the care of the poor, the weak, the defenseless, the suffering and those who mourn. This means that as you alleviate suffering and seek to heal you also bear witness to the Christian view of suffering and to the meaning of life and death as taught by your Christian faith.

In the complex world of modern health care in industrialized society, this witness must be given in a variety of ways. First, it requires continual efforts to ensure that everyone has access to health care. I know that you have already examined this question in the report of your task force on health care of the poor. In seeking to treat patients equally, regardless of social and economic status, you proclaim to your fellow citizens and to the world Christ's special love for the neglected and powerless. This particular challenge is a consequence of your Christian dedication and conviction, and it calls for great courage on the part of Catholic bodies and institutions operating in the field of health care. It is a great credit to your zeal and efficiency when, despite formidable costs, you still succeed in preventing the economic factor from being the determinant factor in human and Christian service.

Similarly, the love with which Catholic health care is per-formed and its professional excellence have the value of a sign testifying to the Christian view of the human person. The inalienable dignity of every human being is, of course, fundamental to all Catholic health care. All who come to you for help are worthy of respect and love, for all have been created in the image and likeness of God. All have been redeemed by Christ and, in their sufferings, bear his cross. It is fitting that our meeting is taking place on the feast of the Triumph of the Cross. Christ took upon himself the whole of human suffering and radically transformed it through the paschal mystery of his passion, death and resurrection. The triumph of the cross gives human suffering a new dimension, a redemptive value (cf. "Salvifici Doloris," 24). It is your privilege to bear constant witness to this profound truth in so many ways.

The structural changes which have been taking place within Catholic health care in recent years have increased the challenge of preserving and even strengthening the Catholic identity of the institutions and the spiritual quality of the services given. The presence of dedicated women and men Religious in hospitals and nursing homes has ensured in the past, and continues to ensure in the present, that spiritual dimension so characteristic of Catholic health care centers. The reduced number of Religious and new forms of ownership and management should not lead to a loss of a spiritual atmosphere or to a loss of a sense of vocation in caring for the sick. This is an area in which the Catholic laity, at all levels of health care, have an opportunity to manifest the depth of their faith and to play their own specific part in the Church's mission of evangelization and service.

4. As I have said, Catholic health care must always be carried out within the framework of the Church's saving mission. This mission she has received from her divine founder, and she has accomplished it down through the ages with the help of the Holy Spirit, who guides her into the fullness of truth (cf. Jn 16:13; "Lumen Gentium," 4). Your ministry therefore must also reflect the mission of the Church as the teacher of moral truth, especially in regard to the new frontiers of scientific research and technological achievement. Here too you face great challenges and opportunities.

Many times in recent years the Church has addressed issues related to the advances of biomedical technology. She does so not in order to discourage scientific progress or to judge harshly those who seek to extend the frontiers of human knowledge and skill, but in order to affirm the moral truths which must guide the application of this knowledge and skill. Ultimately, the purpose of the Church's teaching in this field is to defend the innate dignity and fundamental rights of the human person. In this regard the Church cannot fail to emphasize the need to safeguard the life and integrity of the human embryo and fetus.

5. The human person is a unique composite — a unity of spirit and matter, soul and body, fashioned in the image of God and destined to live forever. Every human life is sacred, because every human person is sacred. It is in the light of this fundamental truth that the Church constantly proclaims and defends the dignity of human life from the moment of conception to the moment of natural death. It is also in the light of this fundamental truth that we see the great evil of abortion and euthanasia.

Not long ago, in its "Instruction on Respect for Human Life in Its Origin and on the Dignity of Procreation," the Congregation for the Doctrine of the Faith once more dealt with certain vital questions concerning the human person. Once more it defended the sanctity of innocent human life from the moment of conception onward. Once again it affirmed the sacred and inviolable character of the transmission of human life by the procreative act within marriage. It explained that new technologies may afford new means of procreation, but "what is technically possible is not for that very reason morally admissible" (Introduction, 4). To place new human knowledge at the service of the integral well-being of human persons does not inhibit true scientific progress but liberates it. The Church encourages all genuine advances in knowledge, but she also insists on the sacredness of human life at every stage and in every condition. The cause she serves is the cause of human life and human dignity.

6. In the exercise of your professional activities you have a magnificent opportunity, by your constant witness to moral truth, to contribute to the formation of society's moral vision. As you give the best of yourselves in fulfilling your Christian responsibilities, you will also be aware of the important contribution you must make to building a society based on truth and justice. Your service to the sick enables you with great credibility to proclaim to the world the demands and values of the Gospel of Jesus Christ, and to foster hope and renewal of heart. In this respect, your concern with the Catholic identity of your work and of your institutions is not only timely and commendable, it is essential for the success of your ecclesial mission.

You must always see yourselves and your work as part of the Church's life and mission. You are indeed a very special part of the people of God. You and your institutions have precise responsibilities toward the ecclesial community, just as that community has responsibilities toward you. It is important at every level — national, state and local — that there be close and harmonious links between you and the bishops, who "preside in place of God over the flock whose shepherds they are, as teachers of doctrine, priests of sacred worship and officers of good order" ("Lumen Gentium," 20). They, for their part, wish to support you in your witness and service.

7. I have come here today to encourage you in your splendid work and to confirm you in your vital apostolate. Dear brothers and sisters: For your dedication to meeting the health care needs of all people, especially the poor, I heartily congratulate you. You embody the legacy of those pioneering women and men Religious who selflessly responded to the health care needs of a young and rapidly expanding country by developing an extensive network of clinics, hospitals and nursing homes.

Today you are faced with new challenges, new needs. One of these is the present crisis of immense proportions which is that of AIDS and AIDS-related complex. Besides your professional contribution and your human sensitivities toward all affected by this disease, you are called to show the love and compassion of Christ and his Church. As you courageously affirm and implement your moral obligation and social responsibility to help those who suffer, you are individually and collectively living out the parable of the good Samaritan (cf. Lk 10:30-32).

The good Samaritan of the parable showed compassion to the injured man. By taking him to the inn and giving of his own material means, he truly gave of himself. This action, a universal symbol of human concern, has become one of the essential elements of moral culture and civilization. How beautifully the Lord speaks of the Samaritan! He "was neighbor to the man who fell in with the robbers" (Lk 10:36). To be "neighbor" is to express love, solidarity and service, and to exclude selfishness, discrimination and neglect. The message of the parable of the good Samaritan echoes a reality connected with today's feast of the Triumph of the Cross: "The kindness and love of God our Savior appeared ... that we might be

justified by his grace and become heirs, in hope, of eternal life" (Ti 3:4-7). In the changing world of health care, it is up to you to ensure that this "kindness and love of God our Savior" remains the heart and soul of Catholic health services.

Through prayer and with God's help, may you persevere in your commitment, providing professional assistance and selfless personal care to those who need your services. I pray that your activities and your whole lives will inspire and help all the people of America, working together, to make this society a place of full and absolute respect for the dignity of every person from the moment of conception to the moment of natural death. And may God, in whom we live and move and have our being" (Acts 17:28), sustain you by his grace. God bless you and your families and your contribution to America!

Native Americans Phoenix, Sept. 14

Mrs. Alfretta M. Antone:

Your Holiness, Pope John Paul II, we welcome you and thank you for this sacred time together. We are affirmed and encouraged by your support of native peoples throughout the world. We respect you as a great spiritual leader and pray that you can help us on our road of life today.

As we approach 500 years of Catholic Christianity in the Americas, we pray that all who come to this land will respect our grandparents, who have lived on this land for over 50,000 years. Upon initial contact with Europeans, we shared the land given us by our Creator and taught others how to survive here. History, however, stands as a witness to the use and abuse we have experienced in our homelands.

Today little remains of the gifts and richness which our Creator has shared with us, the original peoples of these lands. We ask you to intervene with all people of good will to preserve our homelands for our families, our children and the generations to follow us.

We choose not only to survive, but to live fully. We want to live in harmony with all people and all of creation. We choose to keep alive for all generations the ways of living carved in the stones and bones of our ancestors. We are open to share and receive whatever is good for the life of the human family with all people of good will. Our traditions, our languages, our cultures with their rich teachings and values, our songs and dances, our stories and paintings, our art and ways of living, celebrate who we are as people of many tribes.

We pray that our governments and all our rights as distinct peoples be honored and respected. We ask Your Holiness to do all in your prayer, power and influence to help us secure for our present and future generations the following:

First, that our people be recognized, respected and treated as equals.

Second, that our people determine our own destiny, develop our own lands and resources, plan and make our own decisions in all matters that are properly our own.

Third, that our sacred ways and prayers be respected.

Fourth, that we all learn to live in harmony as brothers and sisters on our Mother Earth.

Fifth, that racism, bigotry and a sense of superiority be laid to rest in our times.

Sixth, that the United States and other governments honor the solemn agreements and treaties they have made with us which safeguard our lands, waters and other natural resources.

Seventh, that just compensation be given for our lands which were taken illegally through theft or violation of treaties with our ancestors.

Eighth, that governments, churches and all people of good will share the goods and resources of Mother Earth so that our people can walk tall, side by side with all people.

Ninth, that the native American people be given the opportunity for a fair share in the resources of the world to provide the necessary housing, health care and general well-being.

Tenth, that our people share equally in the educational, health and social benefits of the Americas.

Eleventh, that our youth be given the necessary support and encouragement to work for a just present and future of our people.

Twelfth, that our people be strengthened in our resolve to overcome the alcohol and drug dependencies which have brought us such great suffering.

We recognize that our native brothers and sisters come from many distinct tribes. We pray that we can work together in unity and mutual respect for both our individual and common good.

We also recognize that many of our native brothers and sisters have exercised their freedom of religion by following either their own traditional sacred ways, another world religion or other Christian traditions. Many of us have chosen the Roman Catholic way of walking with Jesus, speaking his truth and living his life of grace.

As Roman Catholics, we native peoples ask Your Holiness to strengthen and affirm us. Until recent times, many of our people have turned away from the Church. Holy Father, we have always respected the one God, who made all and who is without beginning. The Creator has given us a way of life on Mother Earth. As Catholic natives, we have come to know Jesus as the Son of God who loves us and lives with us. The Holy Spirit works in many ways through our people. We are encouraged by the support the Roman Catholic Church gives us in affirming the beauty and value of our traditional prayers and ceremonies.

Our people are sharing their own cultural gifts in living and celebrating the mysteries of our Catholic faith. Our languages, which we treasure, are now even spoken by some of the missionaries. Yet we still need your help and guidance in certain areas:

First, as native peoples, we seek to follow Jesus Christ in the languages and cultures which God has given us.

Second, we seek a fuller participation in the life of the universal church as bishops, priests, deacons, religious, catechists and in all lay ministries.

Third, we seek a fuller inclusion of our cultural gifts and languages in the sacramental life of the Church.

Fourth, we seek the canonization of Blessed Kateri Tekakwitha. This young Mohawk woman has given our people a beautiful example of a native person living out the Christian Gospel. Through her help, our people are being gathered to the Church.

Your Holiness, as native peoples we are affirmed in our journey and encouraged in our work through your love and support of us. We pray that God will continue to bless you and your ministry.

In the name of all native Americans, we ask Your Holiness for your blessing and guidance as we walk together with God as we live here on Mother Earth and for all time to come.

Pope John Paul II:

Dear brothers and sisters,

1. I have greatly looked forward to this visit with you, the original peoples of this vast country. I greet you with love and respect. I thank you for inviting me to be with you and for sharing with me some aspects of your rich and ancient culture.

I have listened to your concerns and hopes. As your representatives spoke, I traced in my heart the history of your tribes and nations. I was able to see you as the noble descendants of countless generations of inhabitants of this land, whose ways were marked by great respect for the natural resources of land and river, of forest and plain and desert. Here your forefathers cherished and sought to pass on to each new generation their customs and traditions, their history and way of life. Here they worshiped the Creator and thanked him for his gifts. In contact with the forces of nature, they learned the value of prayer, of silence and fasting, of patience and courage in the face of pain and disappointment.

2. The early encounter between your traditional cultures and the European way of life was an event of such significance and change that it profoundly influences your collective life even today. That encounter was a harsh and painful reality for your peoples. The cultural oppression, the injustices, the disruption of your life and of your traditional societies must be acknowledged.

At the same time, in order to be objective, history must record the deeply positive aspects of your peoples' encounter with the culture that came from Europe. Among these positive aspects I wish to recall the work of the many missionaries who strenuously defended the rights of the original inhabitants of this land. They established missions throughout this southwestern part of the United States. They worked to improve living conditions and set up educational systems, learning your languages in order to do so. Above all, they proclaimed the good news of salvation in our Lord Jesus Christ, an essential part of which is that all men and women are equally children of God and must be respected and loved as such. This Gospel of Jesus Christ is today, and will remain forever, the greatest pride and possession of your people.

3. One priest who deserves special mention among the missionaries is the beloved Fray Junipero Serra, who traveled throughout Lower and Upper California. He had frequent clashes with the civil authorities over the treatment of Indians. In 1773 he presented to the viceroy in Mexico City a "representacion," which is sometimes termed a "bill of rights" for Indians. The Church had long been convinced of the need to protect them from exploitation. Already in 1537, my predecessor Pope Paul III proclaimed the dignity and rights of the native peoples of the Americas by insisting that they not be deprived of their freedom or the possession of their property ("Pastorale Officium," May 29, 1537: Denzinger-Schonmetzer 1495). In Spain the Dominican priest Francisco de Vitoria became the staunch advocate of the rights of the Indians and formulated the basis for international law regarding the rights of peoples.

Unfortunately, not all the members of the Church lived up to their Christian responsibilities. But let us not dwell excessively on mistakes and wrongs, even as we commit ourselves to overcoming their present effects. Let us also be grateful to those who came to this land, faithful to the teachings of Jesus, witnesses of his new commandment of love. These men and women, with good hearts and good minds, shared knowledge and skills from their own cultures and shared their most precious heritage, the faith, as well. Now we are called to learn from the mistakes of the past, and we must work together for reconciliation and healing as brothers and sisters in Christ.

4. It is time to think of the present and of the future. Today people are realizing more and more clearly that we all belong to the one human family and are meant to walk and work together in mutual respect, understanding, trust and love. Within this family each people preserves and expresses its own identity and enriches others with its gifts of culture, tradition, customs, stories, song, dance, art and skills.

From the very beginning, the Creator bestowed his gifts on each people. It is clear that stereotyping, prejudice, bigotry and racism demean the human dignity which comes from the hand of the Creator and which is seen in variety and diversity. I encourage you, as native people belonging to the different tribes and nations in the East, South, West and North, to preserve and keep alive your cultures, your languages, the values and customs which have served you well in the past and which provide a solid foundation for the future. Your customs that mark the various stages of life, your love for the extended family, your respect for the dignity and worth of every human being, from the unborn to the aged, and your stewardship and care of the earth: These things benefit not only yourselves but the entire human family.

Your gifts can also be expressed even more fully in the Christian way of life. The Gospel of Jesus Christ is at home in every people. It enriches, uplifts and purifies every culture. All of us together make up the people of God, the body of Christ, the Church. We should all be grateful for the growing unity, presence, voice and leadership of Catholic native Americans in the Church today.

Jesus speaks of the word of God as the seed which falls on good ground and produces abundant fruit (cf. Mt 13:4ff). The seed has long since been planted in the hearts of many of you. And it has already produced the fruits which show its transforming power — the fruits of holiness. The best-known witness of Christian holiness among the native peoples of North America is Kateri Tekakwitha, whom I had the privilege seven years ago of declaring "blessed" and of holding up to the whole Church and the world as an outstanding example of Christian life. Even when she dedicated herself fully to Jesus Christ, to the point of taking the prophetic step of making a vow of perpetual virginity, she always remained what she was, a true daughter of her people, following her tribe in the hunting seasons and continuing her devotions in the environment most suited to her way of life, before a rough cross carved by herself in the forest. The Gospel of Jesus Christ, which is the great gift of God's love, is never in contrast with what is noble and pure in the life of any tribe or nation, since all good things are his gifts.

5. I would like to repeat what I said at my meeting with native peoples at the Shrine of St. Anne de Beaupre during my visit to Canada in 1984:

"Your encounter with the Gospel has not only enriched you; it has enriched the Church. We are well aware that this has not taken place without its difficulties and, occasionally, its blunders. However, you are experiencing this today, the Gospel does not destroy what is best in you. On the contrary, it enriches, as it were, from within the spiritual qualities and gifts that are distinctive of your cultures" (No. 3).

The American bishops' statement on native Americans rightly attests that our Catholic faith is capable of thriving "within each culture, within each nation, within each race, while remaining the prisoner of none" (Statement of May 4, 1977).

Here too I wish to urge the local churches to be truly "catholic" in their outreach to native peoples and to show respect and honor for their culture and all their worthy traditions. From your ranks have come a bishop, a number of priests, many permanent deacons, men and women Religious and lay leaders. To all of you who have an active part in the Church's ministry I wish to express my gratitude and support. But the Church has some special needs at this time. And for this reason I directly appeal to you, especially to you young native Americans, to discover if Jesus is calling you to the priesthood or to the religious life. Hear him and follow him! He will never let you down! He will lead you in the Church to serve your own peoples and others in the best way possible, in love and apostolic generosity.

At the same time I call upon your native Catholic communities to work together to share their faith and their gifts, to work together on behalf of all your peoples. There is much to be done in solving common problems of unemployment, inadequate health care, alcoholism and chemical dependency. You have endured much over hundreds of years, and your difficulties are not yet at an end. Continue taking steps toward true human progress and toward reconciliation within your families and your communities, and among your tribes and nations.

6. One day Jesus said: "The thief comes only to steal and slaughter and destroy. I came that they might have life and have it to the full" (Jn 10:10).

Surely the time has come for the native peoples of America to have a new life in Jesus Christ — the new life of adopted children of God, with all its consequences:

A life in justice and full human dignity!

A life of pride in their own good traditions and of fraternal solidarity among themselves and with all their brothers and sisters in America!

A deeper life in charity and grace, leading to the fullness of eternal life in heaven!

All consciences must be challenged. There are real injustices to be addressed and biased attitudes to be changed. But the greatest challenge is to you yourselves as native Americans. You must continue to grow in respect for your own inalienable human dignity, for the gifts of creation and redemption as they touch your lives and the lives of your peoples. You must unyieldingly pursue your spiritual and moral goals. You must trust in your own future.

As Catholic native Americans, you are called to become instruments of the healing power of Christ's love, instruments of his peace. May the Church in your midst — your own community of faith and fellowship — truly bear witness to the new life that comes from the cross and resurrection of our Lord and Savior Jesus Christ!

Cathedral Address Los Angeles, Sept. 15

Pope John Paul II:

Dear Archbishop Mahony, dear Cardinal Manning, dear brothers and sisters,

1. I greet you today in the name of our Lord Jesus Christ. Through his love and mercy we are gathered together in the

Church to offer praise and thanksgiving to our heavenly Father. Grace and peace be to all of you — the clergy, Religious and laity of this city named in honor of Our Lady of the Angels. May she continue to assist you in praising God both now and forever with the angels, the patroness of this cathedral — St. Vibiana — and all the saints.

I wish to join my voice to the chorus of praise offered to God in the name of Jesus in so many languages and by people of different races and ethnic origins in this great metropolis. It is his name above all that unites us in one household of faith, hope and love. It is the name of Jesus that transcends every division and heals every antagonism within the human family.

As the successor of Peter, I come to you today in the name of Jesus. It cannot be otherwise, since every true minister of the Gospel preaches not himself or any message of human origin, but he preaches Jesus Christ as Lord (cf. 2 Cor 4:5). To the fears, doubts and struggles of individuals and nations, the Church seeks to apply the healing power of that name which belongs to him who alone is the Word of God (cf. Rv 19:13).

2. In a world filled with competing ideologies and so many false and empty promises, the name of Jesus Christ brings salvation and life. The Hebrew word "Jesus" means Savior, as the Angel said to Joseph in his dream: "You are to name him Jesus because he will save his people from their sins" (Mt 1:21). At the very beginning of the Church's mission, St. Peter proclaims that "there is no salvation in anyone else, for there is no other name in the whole world given to men by which they are to be saved" (Acts 4:12). This name is a source of life for those who believe (cf. Jn 20:31); it delivers us from evil and leads us to the truth that alone can set us free (cf. Jn 8:32).

The name of Jesus is therefore a cry of deliverance for all humanity. It has the power to comfort and heal the sick (cf. Acts 3:6; Jas 5:14-15), to cast out demons (cf. Mk 16:17; Lk 10:17; Acts 16:18), and to work every kind of miracle (cf. Mt 7:22; Acts 4:30). Most important, it is in the name of Jesus and through his power that our sins are forgiven (cf. 1 Jn 2:12).

The name of Jesus is at the heart of Christian worship in this cathedral and in every church throughout the world: "Where two or three are gathered in my name, there am I in their midst" (Mt 18:20). The name of Jesus is at the heart of all Christian prayer: "All you ask the Father in my name he will give you" (Jn 15:16). It is a motivation for charity because as Jesus himself explained, "whoever gives you a cup of water to drink because you bear the name of Christ will by no means lose his reward" (Mk 9:41). It calls forth the gift of the Holy Spirit, "the Paraclete, whom the Father will send in my name" (Jn 14:26).

3. My dear brothers and sisters: We are called Christians, and therefore the name of Jesus Christ is also our name. At the baptismal font we received a "Christian name" which symbolizes our communion with Christ and his saints. Our identification with him is reflected in the rule of life which St. Paul proposes in the Letter to the Colossians: "Whatever you do, whether in speech or in action, do it in the name of the Lord Jesus. Give thanks to God the Father through him" (Col 3:17). We are obliged not only to give thanks, but also to speak and act in the name of Jesus even at the risk of being ill-treated, persecuted and hated "for the sake of the name" as Jesus foretold (Acts 5:41; cf. also Mk 13:13; Lk 21:12).

As citizens of the United States, you must give thanks to God for the religious liberty which you enjoy under your Constitution, now in its 200th year. However, freedom to follow your Catholic faith does not automatically mean that it will be easy to "speak and act" in the name of the Lord Jesus with a conscience formed by the word of God authentically interpreted by the Church's teaching (cf. "Dei Verbum," 9f). In a secularized world, to speak and act in the name of Jesus can bring opposition and even ridicule. It often means being out of step with majority opinion. Yet if we look at the New Testament, we find encouragement everywhere for perseverance in this testing of our faith. As the First Letter of St. Peter tells us: "If anyone suffers for being a Christian ... he ought not to be ashamed. He should rather glorify God in virtue of that name" (1 Pt 4:6). And Jesus himself says, "In the world you will have trouble, but take courage, I have conquered the world" (Jn 16:33).

Is not this message extremely important for young people who are trying to live a responsible moral life in the face of a tide of popular culture and peer pressure that is indifferent, if not hostile, to Christian morality? And for their parents, who face daily pressures in the conduct of both their private and public life? And for the clergy and Religious, who may sometimes find it difficult to speak the full truth of the Church's teaching because it is a "hard saying" that many will not readily accept?

4. Dear brothers and sisters: The name of Jesus, like the word of God that he is, is a two-edged sword (cf. Heb 4:12). It is a name that means salvation and life; it is a name that means a struggle and a cross, just as it did for him. But it is also the name in which we find strength to proclaim and live the truth of the Gospel: not with arrogance, but with confident joy; not with self-righteousness, but with humble repentance before God; never with enmity and always with charity.

Dear people of this great Archdiocese of Los Angeles, with its many problems, its enormous challenges and its immense possibilities for good: The name of Jesus is your life and your salvation. It is your pride and joy, and the pride and joy of your families and your parishes. In this name you find strength for your weaknesses and energy for daily Christian living. In your struggle against evil and the Evil One, and in your striving for holiness, the name of Jesus is the source of your hope, because in the name of Jesus you are invincible!

Continue, then, dear Catholic people of Los Angeles to invoke this holy name of Jesus in your joys and your sorrows; continue to teach this name to your children so that they in turn can teach it to their children until the Lord Jesus himself comes in glory to judge the living and the dead!

Youth Teleconference Los Angeles, Sept. 15

Pope John Paul II:

Dear young friends,

1. I think that you already know without my saying it how happy I am to be with you today. Wherever I travel around the world, I always make it a point to meet with young people. A few days ago I was with them in New Orleans, and today I enjoy being with you. From my early days as a young

priest I have spent many hours talking with students on university campuses or while hiking along lakes or in the mountains and hills. I have spent many evenings singing with young men and women like yourselves. Even now as pope, during the summer months various groups of young people come to Castel Gandolfo for an evening, and we sing and talk together.

As you probably know, I often say that you who are young bring hope to the world. The future of the world shines in your eyes. Even now you are helping to shape the future of society. Since I have always placed high hopes in young people, I would like to speak to you today precisely about hope.

2. We cannot live without hope. We have to have some purpose in life, some meaning to our existence. We have to aspire to something. Without hope, we begin to die.

Why does it sometimes happen that a seemingly healthy person, successful in the eyes of the world, takes an overdose of sleeping pills and commits suicide? Why, on the other hand, do we see a seriously disabled person filled with great zest for life? Is it not because of hope? The one has lost all hope; in the other, hope is alive and overflowing. Clearly, then, hope does not stem from talents and gifts or from physical health and success! It comes from something else. To be more precise, hope comes from someone else, someone beyond ourselves.

Hope comes from God, from our belief in God. People of hope are those who believe God created them for a purpose and that he will provide for their needs. They believe that God loves them as a faithful Father. Do you remember the advice that Jesus gave his disciples when they seemed to be fearful of the future? He said: "Do not be concerned for your life, what you are to eat, or for your body, what you are to wear. Life is more important than food and the body more than clothing. Consider the ravens: They do not sow, they do not reap, they have neither cellar nor barn — yet God feeds them. How much more important you are than the birds!" (Lk 12:22-24). Yes, God knows all our needs. He is the foundation for our hope.

3. But what about people who do not believe in God? This is indeed a serious problem, one of the greatest problems of our time — atheism, the fact that many of our contemporaries have no faith in God. When I visited Australia last year, I told a group of children:

"The hardest thing about being pope is to see that many people do not accept the love of Jesus, do not know who he really is and how much he loves them.... (Jesus) does not force people to accept his love. He offers it to them and leaves them free to say yes or no. It fills me with joy to see how many people know and love our Lord, how many say yes to him. But it saddens me to see that some people say no" (Nov. 29, 1986).

Without faith in God, there can be no hope, no lasting, authentic hope. To stop believing in God is to start down a path that can lead only to emptiness and despair.

But those who have the gift of faith live with confidence about things to come. They look to the future with anticipation and joy, even in the face of suffering and pain; and the future that they are ultimately looking toward is everlasting life with the Lord. This kind of hope was very prominent in the life of St. Paul, who once wrote:

"We are afflicted in every way possible, but we are not crushed; full of doubts, we never despair. We are persecuted but never abandoned; we are struck down but never destroyed.... We do not lose heart, because our inner being is renewed each day" (2 Cor 4:8-9, 16).

Only God can renew our inner self each day. Only God can give meaning to life, God who has drawn near to each of us in "Christ Jesus our hope" (1 Tm 1:1).

In the New Testament there are two letters ascribed to St. Peter. In the first of these, he said: "Venerate the Lord, that is, Christ, in your hearts. Should anyone ask you the reason for this hope of yours, be ever ready to reply" (1 Pt 3:15).

Dear young friends: I pray that your faith in Christ will always be lively and strong. In this way you will always be ready to tell others the reason for your hope; you will be messengers of hope for the world.

4. I am often asked, especially by young people, why I became a priest. Maybe some of you would like to ask the same question. Let me try briefly to reply.

I must begin by saying that it is impossible to explain entirely. For it remains a mystery even to myself. How does one explain the ways of God? Yet I know that at a certain point in my life I became convinced that Christ was saying to me what he had said to thousands before me: "Come, follow me!" There was a clear sense that what I heard in my heart was no human voice nor was it just an idea of my own. Christ was calling me to serve him as a priest.

And you can probably tell I am deeply grateful to God for my vocation to the priesthood. Nothing means more to me or gives me greater joy than to celebrate Mass each day and to serve God's people in the Church. That has been true ever since the day of my ordination as a priest. Nothing has ever changed it, not even becoming pope.

Confiding this to you, I would like to invite each of you to listen carefully to God's voice in your heart. Every human person is called to communion with God. That is why the Lord made us, to know him and love him and serve him, and — in doing this — to find the secret to lasting joy.

In the past the Church in the United States has been rich in vocations to the priesthood and religious life. And it could be especially true today. At the same time, the Church needs the gospel witness of holy lay people, in married life and in the single state. Be assured that the Lord knows each of you by name and wishes to speak to your heart in a dialogue of love and salvation. God continues to speak to young people on the banks of the Mississippi River and on the slopes of the Rocky Mountains. God continues to speak in the cities on the West Coast of America and across the rolling hills and plains. God continues to speak to every human person.

Dear young people of America, listen to his voice. Do not be afraid. Open up your hearts to Christ. The deepest joy there is in life is the joy that comes from God and is found in Jesus Christ, the Son of God. He is the hope of the world. Jesus Christ is your hope and mine!

Address to Media
Los Angeles, Sept. 15

Pope John Paul II:

Ladies and gentlemen of the communications industry, dear friends,

1. I am very pleased to be here with you. I would like to be able to greet each one of you personally and to express my regard for you individually. Although this is not possible, I wish to express my sincere respect for all the categories of

the media that you represent — the film industry, the music and recording industry, radio, electronic news, television and all those who inform the world through the written word — and for the diverse functions that you perform as workers, writers, editors, managers and executives. I greet you in the full range of your activities, from the very visible to the relatively hidden.

My visit to Los Angeles, and indeed to the United States, would seem incomplete without this meeting, since you represent one of the most important American influences on the world today. You do this in every area of social communications and contribute thereby to the development of a mass popular culture. Humanity is profoundly influenced by what you do. Your activities affect communication itself: supplying information, influencing public opinion, offering entertainment. The consequences of these activities are numerous and diverse. You help your fellow citizens to enjoy leisure, to appreciate art and to profit from culture. You often provide the stories they tell and the songs they sing. You give them news of current events, a vision of humanity and motives for hope. Yours is indeed a profound influence on society. Hundreds of millions of people see your films and television programs, listen to your voices, sing your songs and reflect your opinions. It is a fact that your smallest decisions can have global impact.

2. Your work can be a force for great good or great evil. You yourselves know the dangers as well as the splendid opportunities open to you. Communication products can be works of great beauty, revealing what is noble and uplifting in humanity and promoting what is just and fair and true. On the other hand, communications can appeal to and promote what is debased in people: dehumanized sex through pornography or through a casual attitude toward sex and human life; greed through materialism and consumerism or irresponsible individualism; anger and vengefulness through violence or self-righteousness. All the media of popular culture which you represent can build or destroy, uplift or cast down. You have untold possibilities for good, ominous possibilities for destruction. It is the difference between death and life — the death or life of the spirit. And it is a matter of choice. The challenge of Moses to the people of Israel is applicable to all of us today: "I set before you life and death.... Choose life" (Dt 30:19).

3. There is something of great interest for all of us in the Constitution of the United States. The same amendment that guarantees freedom of speech and freedom of the press also guarantees freedom of religious practice. The link between the art of human expression and the exercise of religion is profound. Social communications in fact provide an important first step in uniting human beings in mutual love, and this first step is also a step to God, "for God is love" (1 Jn 4:8). Religious practice for its part fosters communication with God. But it also fosters human communication, since human communication is part of that relationship of love for neighbor that is mandated in both the Old and New Testaments.

It is easy to see why the Church has recognized and taught that people have a right to communicate. Linked to this right is the right to information, about which the Second Vatican Council speaks in these words:

"Because of the progress of modern society and the increasing interdependence of its members, it is clear that information has become very useful and generally necessary.... There exists therefore in human society a right to information on the subjects that are of concern to people" ("Inter Mirifica," 5).

In this way, then, the Church recognizes the need for freedom of speech and freedom of the press, just as does your Constitution. But she goes further. Rights imply corresponding duties. The proper exercise of the right to information demands that the content of what is communicated be true and — within the limits set by justice and charity — complete (cf. ibid.). Your very profession invites you to reflect on this obligation to truth and its completeness. Included here is the obligation to avoid any manipulation of truth for any reason. This manipulation, in fact, takes place when certain issues are deliberately passed over in silence in order that others may be unduly emphasized. It also occurs when information is altered or withheld so that society will be less able to resist the imposition of a given ideology.

The obligation to truth and its completeness applies not only to the coverage of news, but to all your work. Truth and completeness should characterize the content of artistic expression and entertainment. You find a real meaning in your work when you exercise your role as collaborators of truth — collaborators of truth in the service of justice, fairness and love.

4. Your industry not only speaks to people and for people; it makes communication possible among them. In this we see how your activities transcend the categories of both rights and duties and confer upon you inestimable privileges. Just before joining you this afternoon, I met with young people in several cities by using satellite links. For me this is just one example of how your industry can help foster communication and unite people in fraternal love. It is within your power to use technology to promote what is deeply human and to direct it to the work of peace. You have marvelous tools which others lack. They must be employed in the service of people's right to communicate.

In today's modern world there is always the danger of communication becoming exclusively one way, depriving audiences of the opportunity to participate in the communication process. Should that happen with you, you would no longer be communicators in the full, human sense. The people themselves, the general public whom you serve, should not be excluded from having the opportunity for public dialogue.

In order to foster such a dialogue you yourselves, as communicators, must listen as well as speak. You must seek to communicate with people and not just speak to them. This involves learning about people's needs, being aware of their struggles and presenting all forms of communications with the sensitivity that human dignity requires — your human dignity and theirs. This applies especially to all audio-visual programs.

5. At the basis of all human rights is the dignity of the human person created in the image and likeness of God (Gn 1:27). A recognition of this human dignity is also a part of your civil tradition in the United States and is expressed in the declaration of your nation's independence: All people are created equal in their human dignity and are endowed by their Creator with inalienable rights to life, liberty and the pursuit of happiness. All other rights too are rooted in human dignity, including the right to maintain one's privacy and not to be exploited in the intimacy of one's family.

The fundamental dignity of the human person is still more strongly proclaimed by the Church. She raises her voice on behalf of people everywhere, declaring the dignity of every human being, every man, woman and child. None is excluded because all bear the image of God. Physical and mental handicaps, spiritual weaknesses and human aberrations cannot obliterate the dignity of man. You will understand why the Church attaches such importance to this principle found on the first page of the Bible; it will later become the basis of the teaching of Jesus Christ as he says: "Always treat others as you would like them to treat you" (Mt 7:12).

In particular, social communications must support human dignity because the world is constantly tempted to forget it. Whether in news or in drama, whether in song or in story, you are challenged to respect what is human and to recognize what is good. Human beings must never be despised because of limitations, flaws, disorders or even sins.

Twenty years ago, my predecessor Pope Paul VI, speaking to a gathering much like this one, told that creative community in Rome: "It is a fact that when, as writers and artists, you are able to reveal in the human condition, however lowly or sad it may be, a spark of goodness, at that very instant a glow of beauty pervades your whole work. We are not asking that you should play the part of moralists, but we are expressing confidence in your mysterious power of opening up the glorious regions of light that lie behind the mystery of human life" (Allocution of May 6, 1967).

As you do precisely this — open up the glorious regions of light that lie behind the mystery of human life — you must ask yourselves if what you communicate is consistent with the full measure of human dignity. How do the weakest and the most defenseless in society appear in your words and images: the most severely handicapped, the very old, foreigners and the undocumented, the unattractive and the lonely, the sick and the infirm? Whom do you depict as having — or not having — human worth?

6. Certainly your profession subjects you to a great measure of accountability — accountability to God, to the community and before the witness of history. And yet at times it seems that everything is left in your hands. Precisely because your responsibility is so great and your accountability to the community is not easily rendered juridically, society relies so much on your good will. In a sense the world is at your mercy. Errors in judgment, mistakes in evaluating the propriety and justice of what is transmitted, and wrong criteria in art can offend and wound consciences and human dignity. They can encroach on sacred fundamental rights. The confidence that the community has in you honors you deeply and challenges you mightily.

7. I would encourage you in yet another way: to respect also your own dignity. All that I have said about the dignity of human beings applies to you.

Daily cares oppress you in ways different from those arising in other kinds of work. Your industry reflects the fast pace of the news and changing tastes. It deals with vast amounts of money that bring with them their own problems. It places you under extreme pressure to be successful, without telling you what "success" really is. Working constantly with images, you face the temptation of seeing them as reality. Seeking to satisfy the dreams of millions, you can become lost in a world of fantasy.

At this point, you must cultivate the integrity consonant with your own human dignity. You are more important than success, more valuable than any budget. Do not let your work drive you blindly; for if work enslaves you, you will soon enslave your art. Who you are and what you do are too important for that to happen. Do not let money be your sole concern, for it too is capable of enslaving art as well as souls. In your life there must also be room for your families and for leisure. You need time to rest and be re-created, for only in quiet can you absorb the peace of God.

You yourselves are called to what is noble and lofty in human living, and you must study the highest expressions of the human spirit. You have a great part in shaping the culture of this nation and other nations. To you is entrusted an important portion of the vast heritage of the human race. In fulfilling your mission you must always be aware of how your activities affect the world community, how they serve the cause of universal solidarity.

8. The Church wishes you to know that she is on your side. For a long time she has been a patron and defender of the arts; she has promoted the media and been in the forefront of the use of new technology. The first book for the printing press of Johannes Gutenberg, the inventor of movable type, was the inspired word of God, the Bible. Vatican Radio was established under the direction of the inventor of radio, Guglielmo Marconi.

Today too the Church stands ready to help you by her encouragement and to support you in all your worthy aims. She offers you her challenge and her praise. I pray that you will welcome that help and never be afraid to accept it.

Ladies and gentlemen of the communications industry: I have set before you the broad outlines of a choice for good within the framework of your profession. I ask you to choose the common good. It means honoring the dignity of every human being.

I am convinced that to a great extent we can share a common hope, rooted in a vision of the human race harmoniously united through communication. I am sure too that all of you, whether Christian or not, will permit me to allude to the great fascination that surrounds the mystery of the communicating word. For Christians, the communicating word is the explanation of all reality as expressed by St. John: "In the beginning was the Word; the Word was in God's presence, and the Word was God" (Jn 1:1). And for all those who hold the Judeo-Christian tradition, the nobility of communication is linked to the wisdom of God and expressed in his loving revelation. Thus the Book of Deuteronomy records God's communication to Israel: "You shall love the Lord your God with all your heart, and with all your soul, and with all your strength. Take to heart these words which I enjoin on you today" (Dt 6:6).

Ladies and gentlemen: As communicators of the human word, you are the stewards and administrators of an immense spiritual power that belongs to the patrimony of mankind and is meant to enrich the whole of the human community. The challenge that opens up before you truly requires generosity, service and love. I am sure that you will strive to meet it. And, as you do, I pray that you will experience in your own lives a deep satisfaction and joy. And may the peace of God dwell in your hearts.

Meeting with Bishops Los Angeles, Sept. 16

Archbishop John L. May:

Most Holy Father, we your brother bishops of the United States welcome you today with all our hearts. With the psalmist we sing in our hearts, "O how good and how pleasant it is for brothers to be together as one."

We are grateful for your coming this second time to our land and to our people. We are amazed and edified by your ongoing care for all the churches in these worldwide pastoral visits of yours. It is difficult enough, we know, to make faithful pastoral visits to the parishes of one diocese. Your pastoral zeal is a beautiful encouragement to us, and we are grateful.

Especially today we thank you, Holy Father, for the generous period of time you are giving to this visit with us bishops. Your hospitality during our "ad limina" visits has been beautiful, and we want to reciprocate.

Very graciously you have acceded to our request for a discussion with us. It is my privilege and joy to present our spokesmen to you: His Eminence Cardinal Joseph Bernardin of Chicago, Archbishop Daniel Pilarczyk of Cincinnati, Archbishop John Quinn of San Francisco and Archbishop Rembert Weakland of Milwaukee. We look forward to their presentations and the response of Your Holiness and our fraternal discussion together. With Peter, your predecessor and patron, we can truly say, "Lord, it is good for us to be here!"

Cardinal Joseph L. Bernardin:

Your presence among us today, Holy Father, brings into clear focus the nature of the Church as a "communio": a communion of particular churches in which and from which exists the one and unique Catholic Church; a communion which is not fully the Church unless united with the bishop of Rome. This communion over which you preside as Peter's successor brings together the strength of our unity in faith and the richness of our diversity as a world Church rooted in every region and culture of the earth.

Just as there is but one faith, one Lord, one baptism, so there can be but one loyalty — to the word of God perennially proclaimed in the Church entrusted to the episcopal college with you, our Holy Father, as its visible head and perpetual source of unity. Today in your presence we celebrate our unity, and we reaffirm our fidelity to and affection for you. Each day when we pray at Mass with our priests and people for John Paul, our pope, and for ourselves as shepherds of our particular churches, we acknowledge this wonderful mystery, the Church, which is always one in its diverse manifestations.

In the name of my brother bishops, I assure you that the Church in the United States has always been and will always be one, holy, catholic and apostolic. Our realization of the mystery of the Church, of course, is situated in the context of our American culture. We live in an open society where everyone prizes the freedom to speak his or her mind. Many tend to question things, especially those matters which are important to them, as religion is. They want to know the reasons why certain decisions are made, and they feel free to criticize if they do not agree or are not satisfied with the explanations. They see this as an integral part of the call to live their lives as responsible, educated adults. It is also important to know that many Americans, given the freedom they have enjoyed for more than two centuries, almost instinctively react negatively when they are told that they must do something, even though in their hearts they may know they should do it. As a result, the impression is sometimes given that there is a certain rebelliousness in many American Catholics, that they want to "go it alone."

I will readily admit that these cultural phenomena, which are not unique to our country, can have problematic ecclesial implications. We must address this reality. However, the majority of the Catholics in the United States have a deep faith and accept the Church as described in the conciliar documents. They contribute to the life of their parish and

diocese as well as the broader Church. In a special way, they support you and want to be united with you as pastor of the universal Church.

As with any living organism which values both its unity and diversity, there are bound to be misunderstandings and tensions at times. Tension in itself need not be debilitating or destructive. Often it is a sign of growth. We know that in the apostolic Church reflected in the New Testament and in the young Church described by the fathers there were disagreements and conflicting points of view.

It was largely for this reason that the Lord gave the Church the ministry of the "episkopoi," or overseers, to provide for the unity of the particular churches and the Petrine ministry to promote and protect the unity of the universal Church. Thus, the Church was provided with those who would have authority to make the decisions necessary for the Church to remain one. The Holy Spirit, present in the Church and working in a particular way through the college of bishops in union with Peter and his successors, have successfully guided the Church through 20 centuries marked by both harmony and strife.

The practical question that must be addressed today, as before (and it was openly discussed at the 1985 extraordinary synod), is how to maintain our unity while affirming the diversity in the local realizations of the Church; how to discern a proper balance between freedom and order. The Second Vatican Council invited us to engage in a discernment which identifies and confirms the elements of truth and grace found in our respective cultures, purifying them of what is evil and elevating them by restoring them to Christ. Faithful to this invitation, we have confronted the realities of our modern age: instant worldwide communication, the desire of people to exercise more control over their lives and destiny, the rising expectations of both men and women, and the insistence that their rights be respected, a heightened national consciousness among peoples even as the world becomes more of a global village. Here in the United States particularly we tend at times to overemphasize our own experience, not always giving adequate recognition to the insights and experiences of others.

In this context we can appreciate two unfortunate tendencies which affect the relationship between the universal Church and the particular churches of our country. When the Holy See reaffirms a teaching which has been part of our heritage for centuries or applies it to today's new realities, it is sometimes accused of retrogression or making new and unreasonable impositions on people. In like manner, when someone questions how a truth might be better articulated or lived today, he or she is sometimes accused of rejecting the truth itself or portrayed as being in conflict with the Church's teaching authority. As a result, both sides are sometimes locked into what seem to be adversarial positions. Genuine dialogue becomes almost impossible.

I know that this is a great concern of yours. You have been given the grace of the Petrine office, and we know that it is your duty to confirm and support the brethren in their understanding and acceptance of the legacy given to us by the Lord himself. And this you do in an extraordinarily generous and effective way. But at times you are misunderstood; some allege that you do not understand the actual situation in which the Church finds herself in the different parts of the world today.

It is also painful for us, as the shepherds of our particular churches, when we are cast in an adversarial position with the Holy See or with certain groups within our own dioceses. Sometimes this is done by persons who do not understand

181

us; sometimes, however, by people at either extreme who simply oppose some of the teaching of the Second Vatican Council.

Thus far, Holy Father, I have spoken of our "communio," of the distinct but complementary responsibilities of the pope and the bishops in a Church that is one but diverse, of some unique aspects of our experience in the United States and of some of the tensions we face.

But how will we resolve some of the problems I have noted so that the universal Church and the particular churches can share the full benefit of their "communio" which acknowledges the hierarchical structures and responsibilities of the Church but is also enriched by a fruitful exchange between the two? The Church in the United States has much to contribute to the universal Church. I am thinking, for example, of our role in the development of the documents on religious freedom and ecumenism of the Second Vatican Council. But how much we have to learn from the universal Church, whose experience touches every corner of the world and reaches back for 20 centuries!

I do not presume to have a complete answer to this question. But perhaps some brief reflections might help us.

First, there has to be in the whole body of the Church a much greater trust in the promise of the risen Christ to be present with his Church and in the living action of the Holy Spirit. We are part of a mystery, a unique convergence of the divine and human. For this reason, we cannot rely only on secular models — although we can surely learn from them.

Second, we must be able to speak with one another in complete candor, without fear. This applies to our exchanges with the Holy See as well as among ourselves as bishops. Even if our exchange is characterized by some as confrontational, we must remain calm and not become the captives of those who would use us to accomplish their own ends.

Third, in such a mutual exchange — conducted with objectivity, honesty and openness — we can discern what will truly enhance the Church's unity and what will weaken or destroy it. Sometimes the outcome of our endeavors will not be immediately evident, but this in itself should not deter us because we must allow for growth and development in certain areas of the Church's life and ministry.

Fourth, we must affirm and continue to grow in our appreciation of the conciliar vision of collegiality as both a principle and a style of leadership in the Church. Here in the United States our national conference has been a visible expression of that collegiality. It has served to enhance the pastoral role of each bishop precisely because it provides a framework and a forum for us to share ideas, to teach and elucidate sound Catholic doctrine, set pastoral directions and develop policy positions on contemporary social issues. I believe that we are learning how to balance this dimension of collegiality with the collegiality of the bishops of the universal Church in union with you as head of the episcopal college.

Finally, we must constantly reaffirm, as we do today, that we are "the Roman Catholic Church. The papacy belongs to the binding content of our faith itself, in its proper place within the hierarchy of truths and in our own Christian life" (Karl Rahner, S.J., "The Shape of the Church to Come," Part 2, c. 2).

Holy Father, on behalf of my brother bishops, I wish to express gratitude for the opportunity to share with you some thoughts which are so central to our ministry as pastors of the Church. In my name and theirs, I reaffirm our affection and fidelity. May the grace of the Lord Jesus Christ, and the love of God, and the fellowship of the Holy Spirit be with us all!

Pope John Paul II:

Dear brothers in our Lord Jesus Christ,

1. Before beginning to respond in the context of our fraternal exchanges, I wish to express to you my deep gratitude: gratitude for your many invitations to make this pastoral visit, gratitude for your presence here today and gratitude for the immense amount of preparation which this visit required. Over and above all this, I thank you for your daily toil and your partnership with me in the Gospel. In a word, I thank you for "your work of faith and labor of love and steadfastness of hope in our Lord Jesus Christ" (1 Thes 1:3).

Cardinal Bernardin has given us an introduction to the extremely important reality of "communio," which is the best framework for our conversation. As bishops, we can never tire of prayerfully reflecting on this subject. Since, as the extraordinary session of the Synod of Bishops in 1985 indicated, "the ecclesiology of communion is the central and fundamental idea of the council's documents" ("Relatio Finalis," C, 1), it follows that we must return time and again to those same documents in order to be imbued with the profound theological vision of the Church which the Holy Spirit has placed before us and which constitutes the basis of all pastoral ministry in the Church's pilgrimage through human history.

The program of our collegial ministry cannot be other than to release into the life stream of ecclesial life all the richness of the Church's self-understanding, which was given by the Holy Spirit to the community of faith in the celebration of the Second Vatican Council. The renewal of Catholic life which the council called for is to be measured not primarily in terms of external structures, but in deeper understanding and more effective implementation of the core vision of her true nature and mission which the council offered to the Church at the close of the second millennium of the Christian era. That renewal depends on the way the council's fundamental insights are authentically received in each particular church and in the universal Church.

At the heart of the Church's self-understanding is the notion of "communio": primarily a sharing through grace in the life of the Father given us through Christ and in the Holy Spirit. "God chose us in him" — in Christ — "before the world began, to be holy and blameless in his sight, to be full of love" (Eph 1:4). This communion has its origin in a divine call, the eternal decree which predestined us to share the image of the Son (cf. Rom 8:28-30). It is realized through sacramental union with Christ and through organic participation in all that constitutes the divine and human reality of the Church, the body of Christ, which spans the centuries and is sent into the world to embrace all people without distinction.

2. It is clear that in the decades since the council this "vertical dimension" of ecclesial communion has been less deeply experienced by many who, on the other hand, have a vivid sense of its "horizontal dimension." Unless, however, the entire Christian community has a keen awareness of the marvelous and utterly gratuitous outpouring of "the kindness and love of God, our Savior" which saved us "not because of any righteous deeds we had done, but because of his mercy" (Ti 3:4-5), the whole ordering of the Church's life and the exercise of her mission of service to the human family will be radically weakened and never reach the level intended by the council.

The ecclesial body is healthy in the measure in which Christ's grace, poured out through the Holy Spirit, is accepted by the members. Our pastoral efforts are fruitful, in the last analysis, when the people of God — we bishops with the clergy,

Religious and laity — are led to Christ, grow in faith, hope and charity, and become authentic witnesses of God's love in a world in need of transfiguration.

Cardinal Bernardin has stated very well that just as there is but one faith, one Lord, one baptism, so there can be but one loyalty — to the word of God perennially proclaimed in the Church entrusted to the episcopal college, with the Roman pontiff as its visible head and perpetual source of unity. The word of God, which is the power of God leading all who believe to salvation (cf. Rom 1:16; "Dei Verbum," 17), is fully revealed in the paschal mystery of the death and resurrection of Jesus Christ. This paschal mystery brings about a salvation that is transcendent and eternal: "He died for us, that all of us ... together might live with him" (1 Thes 5:10). It is the Church's task therefore, while she seeks in every way possible to increase her service to the human family in all its needs, to preach Christ's call to conversion and to proclaim redemption in his blood.

3. The "vertical dimension" of ecclesial communion is of profound significance in understanding the relationship of the particular churches to the universal Church. It is important to avoid a merely sociological view of this relationship. "In and from such individual churches there comes into being the one and only Catholic Church" ("Lumen Gentium," 23), but this universal Church cannot be conceived as the sum of the particular churches or as a federation of particular churches.

In the celebration of the Eucharist these principles come fully to the fore. For, as the council document on the liturgy specifies: "The principal manifestation of the Church consists in the full, active participation of all God's holy people in the same liturgical celebrations, especially in the same Eucharist, in one prayer, at one altar, at which the bishop presides, surrounded by his presbyterate and by his ministers" ("Sacrosanctum Concilium," 41). Wherever a community gathers around the altar under the ministry of a bishop, there Christ is present and there, because of Christ, the one, holy, catholic and apostolic Church gathers together (cf. "Lumen Gentium," 26).

The Catholic Church herself subsists in each particular church, which can be truly complete only through effective communion in faith, sacraments and unity with the whole body of Christ. Last November, in my letter to you during your meeting in Washington, I dealt at some length with this aspect of communion. At that time I wrote:

"The very mystery of the Church impels us to recognize that the one, holy, catholic and apostolic Church is present in each particular church throughout the world. And since the successor of Peter has been constituted for the whole Church as pastor and as vicar of Christ (cf. "Lumen Gentium," 22), all the particular churches — precisely because they are Catholic, precisely because they embody in themselves the mystery of the universal Church — are called to live in communion with him.

"Our own relationship of ecclesial communion — 'collegialitas effectiva et affectiva' — is discovered in the same mystery of the Church. It is precisely because you are pastors of particular churches in which there subsists the fullness of the universal Church that you are, and must always be, in full communion with the successor of Peter. To recognize your ministry as 'vicars and delegates of Christ' for your particular churches (cf. ibid., 27) is to understand all the more clearly the ministry of the Chair of Peter, which 'presides over the whole assembly of charity, protects legitimate variety and at the same time sees to it that differences do not hinder unity but rather contribute to it' (ibid., 13)"(Letter of Nov. 4, 1986).

4. In this perspective too we must see the ministry of the successor of Peter not only as a "global" service reaching each particular church from "outside" as it were, but as belonging already to the essence of each particular church from "within." Precisely because this relationship of ecclesial communion — our "collegialitas effectiva et affectiva" — is such an intimate part of the structure of the Church's life, its exercise calls for each and every one of us to be completely one in mind and heart with the will of Christ regarding our different roles in the college of bishops. The council took pains not only to formulate these roles but also to place the exercise of authority in the Church in its proper perspective, which is precisely the perspective of "communio." In this respect also the council was — in the words of the extraordinary synod — "a legitimate and valid expression and interpretation of the deposit of faith as it is found in Sacred Scripture and in the living tradition of the Church" ("Relatio Finalis," I, 2).

As I also wrote to you last year, I have endeavored to fulfill my role as successor of Peter in a spirit of fraternal solidarity with you. I wish only to be of service to all the bishops of the world, and — in obedience to my specific responsibility at the service of the Church's unity and universality — to confirm them in their own collegial ministry. I have always been greatly encouraged in this task by your fraternal support and your partnership in the Gospel, for which I express to you again my profound gratitude. It is of great importance to the Church that in the full power of the Church's communion we continue to proclaim together Jesus Christ and his Gospel. In this way we ourselves live fully, as successors of the apostles, the mystery of ecclesial communion. At the same time, through our ministry we enable the faithful to enter ever more deeply into the Church's life of communion with the Most Holy Trinity.

Archbishop John R. Quinn:

I. Moral Teaching and the New Realities

Most Holy Father, recognizing the privilege which has been given to me in addressing Your Holiness on the moral teaching of the Church, I would begin by stating my belief that moral theology is an example of human wisdom struggling to understand God's revelation about how we live. Notwithstanding the promised presence and guidance of the Holy Spirit in the Church, this struggle, so dramatically portrayed in the opening sections of "Gaudium et Spes" (cf. Nos. 4-10), is unavoidable for several reasons:

1. We are limited human creatures wrestling with a word the infinite God has spoken.

2. We are affected by the reality of sin.

3. We are profoundly affected by rapid and pervasive change.

The distinguished American theologian, Father John Courtney Murray, S.J., who made such a signal contribution to the council, captures this struggle between human wisdom and God's revelation in the following words:

"(H)istory...does change...the human reality. It evokes situations that never happened before. It calls into being relationships that had not existed. It involves human life in an increasing multitude of institutions of all kinds, which proliferate in response to new human needs and desires as well as in consequence of the creative possibilities that are inexhaustibly resident in human freedom.... 'The nature of man is susceptible of change,' St. Thomas repeatedly states. History continually changes the community of mankind and alters the modes of communication between man and man as these take

form 'through external acts.' In this sense, the nature of man changes in history, for better or for worse, at the same time that the fundamental structure and human nature, and the essential destinies of the human person, remain untouched and intact.

"As all this happens, continually new problems are being put to the wisdom of the wise at the same times that the same old problems are being put to every man, wise or not. The issue is always the same: What is man or society to do, here and now, in order that personal or social action may fulfill the human inclination to act according to reason?" (John Courtney Murray, S.J., "Natural Law and the Public Consensus" in "Natural Law and Modern Society," John Cogley, ed., Cleveland: World Publishing Co., 1962, pp. 66-67).

Father Murray, then, anticipating the thought of "Gaudium et Spes" (Nos. 4-10), here describes one of the fundamental challenges for moral theology: There are "new human needs and desires," new realities, which confront both believers and the Church as a community of moral discourse.

The Church, of course, meets these new human realities with a critical posture. "Gaudium et Spes" itself teaches: "Faith throws new light on everything, manifests God's design for man's total vocation and thus directs the mind to solutions which are fully human" (No. 11).

This perspective of faith in the midst of earthly contingencies continually affirms the supernatural dignity of the human person. The Church is called to be the sign and safeguard of the transcendence of the human person (ibid., 46) and must therefore scrutinize the signs of the times and interpret them in the light of the Gospel. "Thus, in language intelligible to each generation, she can respond to the perennial questions which men ask about this present life and the life to come, and about the relationship of one to the other. We must, therefore, recognize and understand the world in which we live, its expectations, its longings and its often dramatic characteristics" (ibid. 4).

This need to scrutinize the signs of the times and to struggle, in light of the word of God, with the great human questions led the council to call for moral theology to "be renewed by livelier contact with the mystery of Christ and the history of salvation…. It should show the nobility of the Christian vocation of the faithful" ("Optatum Totius," 16).

The council thus calls moral theology to a more evident grounding in the mystery of Christ and a more effective relationship to authentic Christian discipleship. As the Church encounters new and changing realities, moral theology confronts the dual task of the conversion of the mind and the conversion of the heart. In the United States, the first challenge — the conversion of the mind — is to convey to American Catholics that the revolutionary changes which have occurred in personal and societal life in the 20th century are not grounds for dismissing Church teaching as outmoded, but rather that these changes point all the more strongly to the value of the Church's tradition in interpreting new human realities. The second challenge of moral theology — the conversion of the heart — is to convey to American Catholics the reality that the Christian moral life is challenging, but not onerous; that it is a call to holiness by a God who understands our weaknesses and walks with us in our struggle to live out the values of the Gospel; that it is not a set of abstract rules designed to constrict our lives, but a call to pilgrimage and conversion that can enrich our lives. The Christian moral life thus conceived can be summed up in the beautiful words of St. Thomas' hymn: "Per tuas semitas, duc nos quo tendimus ad lucem quam inhabitas" (Office of Corpus Christi, "Sacris Solemniis").

II. The New Realities Facing the Church in the United States
Most Holy Father, turning now to more practical aspects of the matter, I would like in a brief and summary fashion to touch on some of these critical new realities as the Church faces them in the United States:

1. The fact that the United States is a major military power in the world.

2. Pervasive divorce and family instability, which so greatly harm the ability of the family to be the basic transmission belt of civilization and religion.

3. The immensely high standard of living enjoyed by a great part of American society and the responsibilities as well as the human problems this standard of living creates.

4. The development of new medical technologies which aid both in the generation and prolongation of life, and the shocking paradox that the noble profession of medicine, the servant of human life and well-being, has also become a destroyer of human life through widespread abortion.

5. The constantly developing insights of the psychological and sociological sciences into the nature of human sexuality and of the human emotional life.

6. The sexual revolution, which has created a permissive climate in which sexual activity is declared to have a value independent of other human responsibilities and moral exigencies.

7. The dramatically altered and changing social status of women, with its concomitant impact on personal meaning and social identity.

8. The increased, widespread high level of education among American Catholics and its impact on their understanding of and expectations about their role in the Church.

Our constant effort as pastors to focus the moral tradition of the Church faithfully on these complex and rapidly changing issues is a source of tremendous difficulties. We accept the great transcendent moral imperatives of the Gospel and the Church's perennial teaching. We recognize our grave obligation to teach courageously and bear witness to the whole, and not just part, of the Gospel, even in the face of ridicule and opposition. At the same time, we also recognize that we cannot fulfill our task simply by an uncritical application of solutions designed in past ages for problems which have qualitatively changed or which did not exist in the past.

Rooted in the mystery of Christ, guided by the teaching of the Church and calling to a life of authentic discipleship, moral theology must respond to these new human realities in a manner which at once reflects what newness there is in these issues, the legitimate development of the human sciences, the enduring nature of the human person, the tradition of moral wisdom in the Church and the absolute claims of the Gospel.

The Church has indeed met this challenge in some remarkable ways. For instance, the 1987 "Instruction on Respect for Human Life in Its Origin and on the Dignity of Procreation" of the Congregation for the Doctrine of the Faith speaks to the moral seriousness of certain technological aspects of modern reproductive medicine stating forthrightly: "The human being is to be respected and treated as a human person from the moment of conception; and therefore from that same moment his rights as a person must be recognized, among which in the first place is the inviolable right of every innocent human being to life" (No. I:1).

In the area of sexual morality, both "Gaudium et Spes" and

"Humanae Vitae" underlined the meaning of the "special sacrament" that is marriage witnessing to the intrinsic relationship between the procreative and unitive meanings of the marital union.

The Congregation for the Doctrine of the Faith's 1986 "Letter to Bishops of the Catholic Church on the Pastoral Care of Homosexual Persons," while affirming the consistent moral teaching of the Church against homosexual acts, at the same time affirmed the fundamental dignity and freedom of homosexual persons by making clear their "transcendent nature" and "supernatural vocation," which invests homosexual persons with an "intrinsic dignity ... (which) must always be respected in word, in action and in law" (Nos. 7 and 10).

The 1983 pastoral letter of the American bishops, "The Challenge of Peace: God's Promise and Our Response," confronts the moral dimensions of the nuclear arms race as a "new urgency" underlining the uniquely "destructive nature of the modern war" (No. 231).

The 1986 document of the American bishops, "Economic Justice for All: Catholic Social Teaching and the U.S. Economy," faces the moral implications of what it means to be "among the most economically powerful nations on earth" (No. 6).

These examples from the social, medical and sexual moral teaching of the Holy See and of the American bishops indicate the Church's dialogue with the new human realities and the Church's careful effort to lay new foundations for a critical mediation of the moral tradition in a transformed cultural and social context.

III. Moral and Pastoral Reflections

Most Holy Father, these examples of the Church's wisdom struggling with God's revelation suggest some important moral and pastoral reflections.

First: The recent pastoral letters of the American bishops just referred to employ a moral pedagogy which distinguishes "universally binding moral principles found in the teaching of the Church" from "specific applications, observations and recommendations which allow for diversity of opinion on the part of those who assess the factual data of situations differently" (Summary, 9). It is a pedagogy which distinguishes between principles and prescriptions in moral teaching, but does not thereby deny the value of prescriptions. Nor does it mean to imply that there are not or cannot be binding prescriptions in the Church. As Karl Rahner has noted, "The only defense of the inheritance of the past is the conquest of the future. But, for that we need ... practical prescriptions, not only abstract principles" (Karl Rahner, S.J., "The Practice of Faith," Crossroad, 1984, No. 48, "Principles and Prescriptions," pp. 225-228).

Second: We as pastors are greatly concerned that some particular areas of the Church's teaching in both sexual and social morality are at times subjected to negative criticism in our country and sometimes even by Catholics of good will. This can, in some instances, be ascribed to the permissive, narcissistic and consumer qualities of our society. Indeed, in such a setting, people's sensitivity to these kinds of difficult and challenging moral teachings can be dulled, their ability to hear and willingness to listen reduced. Nevertheless, we bishops feel that this problem must be mentioned in any presentation of the current situation of the moral teaching of the Church, and we regard it as a continuing incentive to search more carefully for more effective ways of translating the Church's teaching into more attractive language — even when presenting the difficult or corrective teachings of the Gospel — so that "in language intelligible to each generation, (the Church) can respond to the perennial questions which men ask" ("Gaudium et Spes," 4).

Third: We firmly believe that an authoritative teaching office has been entrusted to us in our communion with you as bishop of Rome and successor of Peter. In fulfillment of this sacred responsibility, we have experienced the value of dialogue, as elaborated by Paul VI in "Ecclesiam Suam." We have found it an effective mode of coming to understand more fully the nature of the moral questions posed by our times, to formulate various responses, to deepen insight into the "sensus fidelium" and to fulfill in an efficacious manner our teaching office. Dialogue and discussion, of course, are never a substitute for the decisions of the magisterium. But they are, and have been, as Cardinal Newman has so effectively shown, its indispensable prolegomenon.

Fourth: The Church's magisterium needs to encourage moral theologians in their difficult task, as Your Holiness has done, for example, in speaking to scholars at The Catholic University of America in 1979, in "Laborem Exercens" and in your commentaries on Genesis. We are grateful for the unselfish assistance we bishops continually receive from them in carrying out the public and pastoral work of the Church.

IV. Conclusion

Most Holy Father, as moral theology continues its struggle to understand God's revelation, new human problems and realities are constantly developing. But we do not forget that the revelation of God par excellence is found in the cross of Christ, which makes God's folly wiser than human wisdom. Often human wisdom in a given age appears to have the last word. But the cross brings a perspective that changes judgments radically. And the Church's moral teaching is there to see to it that the cross is allowed to be the hermeneutic it is intended to be in moral theology, which otherwise is in danger of becoming a discipline "which tells me what God has no right to expect of me." The Gospel, we can never forget, is always a call to "more." "I tell you, unless your holiness surpasses that of the scribes and the Pharisees, you shall not enter the kingdom of God," Jesus said (Mt 5:20).

Moral theology then, like the Church itself, should bring "to mankind light kindled from the Gospel and put at its disposal those saving resources which the Church, herself, under the guidance of the Holy Spirit, receives from her Founder.... (It should) offer to mankind the honest assistance of the Church to foster that brotherhood of all men which corresponds to their destiny ... (and) seek but a solitary goal: to carry forward the work of Christ himself under the lead of the befriending Spirit. And Christ entered this world to give witness to the truth, to rescue and not to sit in judgment, to serve and not to be served" ("Gaudium et Spes," 3).

Pope John Paul II:

5. Archbishop Quinn has spoken of the Church as a community that wishes to remain faithful to the moral teaching of our Lord Jesus Christ. To proclaim a body of moral teaching is in fact an inseparable part of the Church's mission in the world. From the beginning, the Church under the guidance of the Holy Spirit has striven to apply God's revelation in Christ to all the many aspects of our living in this world, knowing that we are called to "lead a life worthy of the Lord and pleasing to him in every way" (Col 1:10).

It is sometimes reported that a large number of Catholics today do not adhere to the teaching of the Church on a number of questions, notably sexual and conjugal morality, divorce and remarriage. Some are reported as not accepting the Church's clear position on abortion. It has also been noted that there is a tendency on the part of some Catholics to be selective in their adherence to the Church's moral teachings. It is sometimes claimed that dissent from the magisterium is totally compatible with being a "good Catholic" and poses no obstacle to the reception of the sacraments. This is a grave error that challenges the teaching office of the bishops of the United States and elsewhere. I wish to encourage you in the love of Christ to address this situation courageously in your pastoral ministry, relying on the power of God's truth to attract assent and on the grace of the Holy Spirit, which is given both to those who proclaim the message and to those to whom it is addressed.

We must also constantly recall that the teaching of Christ's Church — like Christ himself — is a "sign of contradiction." It has never been easy to accept the gospel teaching in its entirety, and it never will be. The Church is committed, both in faith and morals, to make her teaching as clear and understandable as possible, presenting it in all the attractiveness of divine truth. And yet the challenge of the Gospel remains inherent in the Christian message transmitted to each generation. Archbishop Quinn has made reference to a principle with extremely important consequences for every area of the Church's life: "(T)he revelation of God par excellence is found in the cross of Christ, which makes God's folly wiser than human wisdom. Often human wisdom in a given age appears to have the last word. But the cross brings a perspective that changes judgments radically." Yes, dear brothers, the cross — in the very act of revealing mercy, compassion and love — changes judgments radically.

6. A number of other general points may be made. First, the Church is a community of faith. To accept faith is to give assent to the word of God as transmitted by the Church's authentic magisterium. Such assent constitutes the basic attitude of the believer and is an act of the will as well as of the mind. It would be altogether out of place to try to model this act of religion on attitudes drawn from secular culture.

Within the ecclesial community, theological discussion takes place within the framework of faith. Dissent from Church doctrine remains what it is, dissent; as such it may not be proposed or received on an equal footing with the Church's authentic teaching.

Moreover, as bishops we must be especially responsive to our role as authentic teachers of the faith when opinions at variance with the Church's teaching are proposed as a basis for pastoral practice.

I wish to support you as you continue to engage in fruitful dialogue with theologians regarding the legitimate freedom of inquiry, which is their right. You rightly give them sincere encouragement in their difficult task and assure them how much the Church needs and deeply appreciates their dedicated and constructive work. They, on their part, will recognize that the title "Catholic" theologian expresses a vocation and a responsibility at the service of the community of faith and subject to the authority of the pastors of the Church. In particular, your dialogue will seek to show the inacceptability of dissent and confrontation as a policy and method in the area of Church teaching.

7. Speaking on your behalf, Archbishop Quinn has shown full awareness of the seriousness of the challenge facing your teaching ministry. He has spoken of the dual task of the con-

version of the mind and the conversion of the heart. The way to the heart very often passes through the mind, and throughout the length and breadth of the Church there is need today for a new effort of evangelization and catechesis directed to the mind. Elsewhere I have mentioned the relationship between the Gospel and culture. Here I wish to underline the importance of the formation of the mind at every level of Catholic life.

Catholic children and young people need to be given an effective opportunity to learn the truths of the faith in such a way that they become capable of formulating their Catholic identity in terms of doctrine and thought. Here the Catholic press can make a magnificent contribution to raising the general level of Catholic thought and culture. Seminaries, especially, have the responsibility of ensuring that future priests should acquire a high level of intellectual preparation and competence. Continuing education programs for priests, religious and laity play an important part in stimulating a necessary and serious intellectual approach to the multitude of questions confronting faith in our contemporary world.

A crucial aspect of this "apostolate of the mind" concerns the duty and right of bishops to be present in an effective way in Catholic colleges and universities and institutes of higher studies in order to safeguard and promote their Catholic character, especially in what affects the transmission of Catholic doctrine. It is a task which requires personal attention on the part of bishops, since it is a specific responsibility stemming from their teaching office. It implies frequent contacts with teaching and administrative personnel and calls for providing serious programs of pastoral care for students and others within the academic community. Much is already being done, and I take the opportunity to encourage you to seek ways of intensifying these apostolates.

One of the greatest services we bishops can render to the Church is to consolidate present and future generations of Catholics in a sound and complete understanding of their faith. The ecclesial community will thus be wonderfully strengthened for all aspects of Christian moral living and for generous service. The intellectual approach that is needed, however, is one intimately linked to faith and prayer. Our people must be aware of their dependence on Christ's grace and on the great need to open themselves ever more to its action. Jesus himself wants us all to be convinced of his words: "Apart from me you can do nothing" (Jn 15:5).

Archbishop Rembert G. Weakland:

Perhaps the first question that should be asked is: Who are the Catholic laity in the United States of America today? They form 28 percent of the total population of the nation (up 8 percent from 1947) and are moving rapidly into the upper echelons of society, business and politics. Products of the fine Catholic educational tradition of the Church in the United States of America, they continue to place weight on further education; Catholics represent a higher percentage of students in the nation's colleges than their percentage in the general population. Thus, it can be assumed they will continue to take a prominent role in U.S. society and culture in the future. This picture stands in striking contrast to their position before the Second World War when they were mostly working-class immigrants, considering themselves second-class citizens at best. Now the Church in the United States of America can boast of having the largest number of educated faithful in the world.

186

Most sociologists analyzing the rise of Catholics in U.S. society note that they remain very much attached to their Church. It is true that since the Second World War Mass attendance on a weekly basis declined perceptibly. In 1958, 74 percent said they had attended Mass in the past seven days; while in 1985, 53 percent answered the question positively, 71 percent saying they went to Mass at least once a month. This figure has been stable for the last 10 years. The defection rate today is not much different than in the 1950s. More admit to increased reading of the Bible, more attendance at other Church functions and surveys show a remarkable increase in confession in the last 10 years (up from 18 percent in 1977 who said they had been to confession in the past eight weeks to 23 percent in 1986 who said they had gone to confession in the last 30 days). There exists a high rate of contentment with the changes of Vatican Council II, especially among the intellectuals. It should also be noted that the rise in social status among Catholics did not alter perceptibly their concern for social problems and their more open stance in that regard.

"Today American Catholics no longer worry about being accepted — they worry about how to lead" ("The American Catholic People: Their Beliefs, Practices and Values," George Gallup Jr. and Jim Castelli, New York, 1987, p. 2).

Yet these trends pose new challenges to episcopal leadership. Five areas will be mentioned.

1. The faithful are more inclined to look at the intrinsic worth of an argument proposed by the teachers in the Church than to accept it on the basis of the authority itself. Since so often that teaching touches areas where many of the faithful have professional competency (from medical-moral issues to complex economic ones, for example), they wish to be able to contribute through their own professional skills to solving the issues. This demands a new kind of collaboration and a wider range of consultation on the part of the teaching office of the Church. Before their peers, Catholic intellectuals are also more sensitive to the credibility of the Church if such competency is not maintained.

2. Moreover, in the area of political issues Catholics in the United States of America are jealous of their tradition of freedom and deeply resent being told how to vote on an issue or for which candidate to vote. In fact, any interference might have just an opposite effect on them. This poses the delicate balance to the bishops of teaching correct doctrine, but of avoiding what could look like taking sides in partisan disputes or using their religious authority in a way that might seem to interfere in the political process.

In all of these cases an authoritarian style is counterproductive, and such authority for the most part then becomes ignored.

3. The faithful are demanding more help from the teaching authority of the Church on how to bring the Gospel to their professional or work world, their societal and political involvement. They sense the dualism between their private life and morality and their other commitments. They realize the complexity of these issues, are not looking for facile solutions but only to be prodded, encouraged and sustained in their search. More than anything, they are looking for a spirituality that integrates their life, that does not condemn the technological world in which they live and work, that helps them sift the good from the bad, that permits them to reinforce the good. They sense the tensions between their work concerns and their family responsibilities and seek help from their faith to unify all these demands with the gospel imperatives.

4. The faithful want to contribute their skills and knowledge to the life and growth of the Church. They often feel there are not sufficient opportunities for them to use their professional skills within the Church, that they are held back by a fear that can look like clericalism or clerical control on the part of Church leadership.

5. Women, in particular, seek to be equal partners in sharing the mission of the Church. The Church in the United States of America owes a tremendous debt to the religious women who built the educational and health systems that have been among the strengths of our Church. There are no words to explain so much pain on the part of so many competent women today who feel they are second-class citizens in a Church they love. That pain turns easily to anger and is often shared and transmitted to the younger generation of men and women. Women do not want to be treated as stereotypes of sexual inferiority, but want to be seen as necessary to the full life of a Church that teaches and shows by example the co-discipleship of the sexes as instruments of God's kingdom. They seek a Church where the gifts of women are equally accepted and appreciated. Many of them do not yet see the Church imaging such a co-discipleship, but fear that it is still one of male superiority and dominance.

Catholic women repudiate those forms of feminism that undermine the importance of family or that go contrary to their nature; but many do not see the Church as yet striving for a structure where women are considered as equal partners, where the feminine is no longer subordinate but seen in a holistic mutuality with the masculine as forming the full image of the divine.

In your Angelus talk at Castel Gandolfo on Aug. 16, you rightly pointed out, Holy Father, that the Gospel is "rich in the presence of women" and that, "even if women are not called to the typical mission which the Lord entrusted to the apostles as their own" (namely, as you have clearly stated often, that involving ordination to the priesthood), "nevertheless women are given roles of great importance in relationship to the spreading of the good news of the kingdom." You rightly point out the role of Mary herself as exemplar. Women today want to reclaim that scriptural sense of co-discipleship.

For a complete picture of the pastoral tasks facing the bishops of the United States of America, one would have to say something of the charismatic renewal and its impact; on the discovery of the Bible in the personal life of the faithful; on the fundamentalist trends in the United States of America; on the many social concerns movements (e.g., the Catholic Worker) and spiritual renewal movements in general (e.g., Renew). Negatively, one would also have to say something of the large number of divorces and the breakup of so many families. The influence of affluence on societal values and the possible evils of consumerism and waste would also have to be mentioned as pastoral concerns.

But no picture would be complete without speaking of other groups which add so much to the vitality and spiritual richness of the Church in the United States of America: the Hispanic, black and Asian communities. All of these in recent decades have provided a new dimension to Church life. For example, the Hispanic and black Catholics have evolved a pastoral plan that meets their special needs as they take their place in American society and contribute to the life of the whole Church. All of these groups can be special targets of fundamentalist sects that seek to offer them a sense of community, material help and uncomplicated assurance of salvation. (It should be noted in honesty that such fundamentalist temptations are also found at all levels of U.S. Catholic society.)

187

These groups, however, are facing the challenges of U.S. culture realistically under good leadership and are a young and rejuvenating element in the Church in the United States of America.

The Catholic Church has a clear duty to fight racism as it opens its doors to these newer cultural expressions of the faith; it is evident that good will does not seem to be enough here. The Church must also fight for the rights of so many of these populations who live in poverty and are without work; the Church must also continue its educational thrust among them.

One of the pastoral problems the Catholic Church faces in the United States of America is to remain very conscious of the needs of the less fortunate. As the majority of Catholics rise to positions of power and prestige, they must be challenged to use their influence to create a more equal society and to assume a larger international leadership role as well. We bishops have attempted to do this with our recent pastoral letters. They reflect this new situation of our faithful and challenge them to bring the Gospel, not just into consonance with their personal lives, but also to the world situation in which we all live and where lay Catholics in the United States of America can and should assume a more positive role of moral leadership.

Pope John Paul II:

8. The synod to be held this coming month in Rome will undoubtedly deal in further detail with the many important points raised by Archbishop Weakland in his presentation on the role of the laity. These remarks, like my own, particularly concern the Catholic laity in the United States.

It has been stated that "the Church in the United States of America can boast of having the largest number of educated faithful in the world." This statement has many implications. The situation which it describes is cause for humble rejoicing and gratitude because it represents a major achievement: the sustained educational effort by the Church in this country for many, many decades. At the same time the education of the faithful offers great promise and potential in the years ahead. For "it can be assumed they will continue to take a prominent role in U.S. society and culture in the future."

Primarily through her laity, the Church is in a position to exercise great influence upon American culture. This culture is a human creation. It is created through shared insight and communication. It is built by an exchange among the people of a particular society. And culture, while having a certain dynamic endurance, is always changing and developing as a way of life. Thus the American culture of today stands in continuity with your culture of 50 years ago. Yet it has changed; it has been greatly influenced by attitudes and currents of thought.

But how is the American culture evolving today? Is this evolution being influenced by the Gospel? Does it clearly reflect Christian inspiration? Your music, your poetry and art, your drama, your painting and sculpture, the literature that you are producing — are all those things which reflect the soul of a nation being influenced by the spirit of Christ for the perfection of humanity?

I realize these are difficult questions to answer, given the complexity and diversity of your culture. But they are relevant to any consideration of the role of the Catholic laity, "the largest number of educated faithful in the world." And it is above all the laity, once they have themselves been inspired by the Gospel, who bring the Gospel's uplifting and purifying influence to the world of culture, to the whole realm of thought and artistic creativity, to the various professions and places of work, to family life and to society in general. As bishops, with the task of leading the laity and of encouraging them to fulfill their ecclesial mission in the world, we must continue to support them as they endeavor to make their specific contribution to the evolution and development of culture and to its impact on society.

9. With reference to this question, and in such areas as politics, economics, mass media and international life, the service we bring is primarily a priestly service: the service of preaching and teaching the word of God with fidelity to the truth, and of drawing the laity ever more into the dialogue of salvation. We are charged to lead our people to holiness, especially through the grace of the Eucharist and the whole sacramental life. The service of our pastoral leadership, purified in personal prayer and penance, far from bearing an authoritarian style in any way, must listen and encourage, challenge and at times correct. Certainly, there is no question of condemning the technological world, but rather of urging the laity to transform it from within so that it may receive the imprint of the Gospel.

10. We serve our laity best when we make every effort to provide for them, and in collaboration with them, a comprehensive and solid program of catechesis with the aim of "maturing the initial faith and of educating the true disciple of Christ by means of a deeper and more systematic knowledge of the person and the message of our Lord Jesus Christ" ("Catechesi Tradendae," 19). Such a program will also assist them in developing that habit of discernment which can distinguish the spirit of the world from the Spirit of God and which can distinguish authentic culture from elements that degrade human dignity. It can provide them a solid basis for growing in their knowledge and love of Jesus Christ through continual conversion and personal commitment to the demands of the Gospel.

11. In speaking of the laity, I feel a particular desire to support you in all you are doing on behalf of family life. Archbishop Weakland has mentioned "the large number of divorces and the breakup of so many families" as a special pastoral problem. I know that all of us feel great sadness and deep pastoral concern for all those whose lives are affected in this way.

As you will recall, on the occasion of your "ad limina" visits four years ago I spoke at some length on the topic of marriage. Without repeating all that I said on that occasion, I wish to encourage you to continue in your many zealous and generous efforts to provide pastoral care to families. I also urge you in the face of all the trends which threaten the stability of marriage, the dignity of human love and the dignity of human life as well as its transmission, never to lose confidence and courage. Through the grace given us as pastors we must endeavor to present as effectively as possible the whole teaching of the Church, including the prophetic message contained in "Humanae Vitae" and in "Familiaris Consortio."

The faithful teaching of the intrinsic relationship between the unitive and procreative dimensions of the marriage act is, of course, only a part of our pastoral responsibility. With pastoral solicitude for couples "Familiaris Consortio" pointed out that "the ecclesial community at the present time must take on the task of instilling conviction and offering practical help to those who wish to live out their parenthood in a truly responsible way.... This implies a broader, more decisive and more systematic effort to make the natural methods of regulating fertility known, respected and applied" (No. 35).

On the occasion of the last "ad limina" visits I stated:

"Those couples who choose the natural methods perceive the profound difference — both anthropological and moral — between contraception and natural family planning. Yet they may experience difficulties; indeed they often go through a certain conversion in becoming committed to the use of the natural methods, and they stand in need of competent instruction, encouragement and pastoral counseling and support. We must be sensitive to their struggles and have a feeling for the needs that they experience. We must encourage them to continue their efforts with generosity, confidence and hope. As bishops we have the charism and the pastoral responsibility to make our people aware of the unique influence that the grace of the sacrament of marriage has on every aspect of married life, including sexuality (cf. "Familiaris Consortio," 33). The teaching of Christ's Church is not only light and strength for God's people, but it uplifts their hearts in gladness and hope.

"Your episcopal conference has established a special program to expand and coordinate efforts in the various dioceses. But the success of such an effort requires the abiding pastoral interest and support of each bishop in his own diocese, and I am deeply grateful to you for what you do in this most important apostolate" (Address of Sept. 24, 1983).

12. My profound gratitude to you extends to the many other areas in which, with generous dedication, you have worked for and with the laity. These include your persevering efforts at promoting peace, fostering justice and supporting the missions. In the area of the defense of human life, you have worked with exceptional commitment and constancy. Already during the "ad limina" visits of 1978, Paul VI drew attention to this activity of yours, assuring you of the appreciation of the Holy See. Because of their exceptional importance, I wish to quote at some length his words of strong support for you and make them my own:

"In the name of Jesus Christ, we thank you for your ministry at the service of life. We know that you have labored precisely in order that the words of the Good Shepherd would be fulfilled: 'that they may have life and have it to the full.' Under your leadership, so many of the Catholic people — priests, deacons, Religious and laity — have joined in numerous initiatives aimed at defending, healing and promoting human life.

"With the enlightenment of faith, the incentive of love and an awareness of your pastoral accountability, you have worked to oppose whatever wounds, weakens or dishonors human life. Your pastoral charity has found a consistent expression in so many ways — all related to the question of life, all aimed at protecting life in its multiple facets. You have endeavored to proclaim in practice that all aspects of human life are sacred.

"In this regard, your efforts have been directed to the eradication of hunger, the elimination of subhuman living conditions and the promotion of programs on behalf of the poor, the elderly and minorities. You have worked for the improvement of the social order itself. At the same time, we know that you have held up to your people the goal to which God calls them: the life above, in Christ Jesus (cf. Phil 3:14).

"Among your many activities at the service of life there is one which, especially at this juncture of history, deserves our strongest commendation and our firmest support: It is the continuing struggle against what the Second Vatican Council calls the 'abominable crime' of abortion ("Gaudium et Spes," 51). Disregard for the sacred character of life in the womb weakens the very fabric of civilization: It prepares a mentality

and even a public attitude that can lead to the acceptance of other practices that are against the fundamental rights of the individual. This mentality can, for example, completely undermine concern for those in want, manifesting itself in insensitivity to social needs; it can produce contempt for the elderly to the point of advocating euthanasia; it can prepare the way for those forms of genetic engineering that go against life, the dangers of which are not yet fully known to the general public.

"It is therefore very encouraging to see the great service you render to humanity by constantly holding up to your people the value of human life. We are confident that, relying on the words of the Good Shepherd, who inspires your activity, you will continue to exercise leadership in this regard, sustaining the entire ecclesial community in their own vocation at the service of life.

"It is also a source of worldwide honor that in your country so many upright men and women of differing religious convictions are united in a profound respect for the laws of the Creator and Lord of life, and that by every just means at their disposal they are endeavoring, before the witness of history, to take a definitive stand for human life" (Address of May 26, 1978).

Nine years have passed since these words were spoken and yet they are still relevant today — relevant in their prophetic vision, relevant in the needs they express, relevant in the defense of life.

13. In his encyclical "Pacem in Terris," Pope John XXIII placed the question of the advancement of women in the context of the characteristics of the present day, "the signs of the times." He made it clear that the cause in question was one of human dignity. This is indeed the aim of all the Church's efforts on behalf of women: to promote their human dignity. The Church proclaims the personal dignity of women as women — a dignity equal to that of men's dignity. This dignity must be affirmed in its ontological character even before consideration is given to any of the special and exalted roles fulfilled by women as wives, mothers or consecrated women.

There are many other aspects involved in the question of women's equal dignity and responsibility, which will undoubtedly be properly dealt with in the forthcoming Synod of Bishops. At the basis of all considerations are two firm principles: the equal human dignity of women and their true feminine humanity. On the basis of these two principles "Familiaris Consortio" has already enunciated much of the Church's attitude toward women, which reflects the "sensitive respect of Jesus toward the women that he called to his following and his friendship" (No. 22). As I have stated and as Archbishop Weakland has pointed out, women are not called to the priesthood. Although the teaching of the Church on this point is quite clear, it in no way alters the fact that women are indeed an essential part of the gospel plan to spread the good news of the kingdom. And the Church is irrevocably committed to this truth.

Archbishop Daniel E. Pilarczyk:

Most Holy Father, I have been asked to speak about certain implications of lay, religious and clerical vocations in the United States. With your permission, I would like to address these issues by positing a single question and treating it in a format that is familiar to us all.

"Quaeritur": Whether the ministry of the Church in the

United States is in a state of turmoil and crisis.

"Et videtur quod sit."

"Primo." The number of vocations to religious life has declined considerably. In 1962, there were 173,000 women Religious in the United States and 12,000 religious brothers. In 1986, there were 114,000 sisters and 7,000 brothers.

"Secundo." The number of diocesan and religious priests has increased since 1962 from 56,000 to 57,000, but this latter number also includes many thousand priests who are retired because of infirmity and age. Moreover, during this same period, the number of Catholics in our country has increased by nearly 10 million, changing the ratio of priests to Catholics from 771 to 920.

"Tertio." The number of seminarians and candidates for religious life has declined to the point where it seems clear that there will be far fewer priests and Religious to minister to the faithful of our country in the years ahead.

"Quarto." The rise of lay ministry within the Church has led some to voice serious concern about the clericalization of the laity and the laicizing of the clergy.

"Quinto." Questions continue to be voiced about the wisdom of the Church's discipline of priestly celibacy and about the Church's teaching on the ordination of women, as well as about certain other Church teachings.

"Sexto." Our society is becoming increasingly secular and therefore increasingly inhospitable to Christian belief, with the result that ministry to believers and unbelievers alike is more demanding than it was in the past.

"Sed contra."

"Primo." We have witnessed the development of an intense and lively participation of lay persons and non-clerical Religious in the ministry of the Church, a participation which includes lay teachers in our Catholic schools and, in our parishes, full-time catechetical directors (directors of religious education), youth ministers, home visitors, business managers and general pastoral ministers.

"Secundo." We have been blessed with some 8,000 permanent deacons in our country since the Second Vatican Council.

"Tertio." There is an increased understanding of and appreciation for religious life on the part of bishops and priests thanks, in large part, to the pontifical commission which you yourself established, Holy Father.

"Quarto." Various kinds of spiritual renewal programs have grown up within the Church over the past two decades which have led hundreds of thousands of our people to a deeper knowledge and a greater assimilation of their Catholic faith.

"Quinto." There is an increasingly urgent awareness on the part of almost every segment of the Church in our country of the need to undertake greater efforts of evangelization.

"Sexto." Thanks to the collaboration of other persons in the Church's ministry, priests no longer have to attend personally to every single task in their parishes and are freer to focus their energies on specifically priestly activities such as preaching, liturgical celebration and leadership of the Christian community.

"Respondeo dicendum," first of all, Holy Father, that no brief overview of the ministerial realities of the Church in our country can do justice to the breadth and variety of the Church's life here. I suspect that every bishop in this room could and would add several other items of concern and of encouragement to the list which I have presented.

Next, I would be untrue to my mandate if I did not observe that certain aspects of our present situation are a source of great anxiety for us bishops. Will there be enough priests in the future to do the specifically priestly work that will need doing? How can we better identify and address the real questions of Church order and doctrine which face us? Will there be enough material resources (i.e., money) to offer appropriate wages and suitable health and retirement benefits to the increasing number of lay persons who work in and for the Church? Sometimes we are afraid as we look toward the future, which seems to hold so many unknowns.

At the same time I am convinced, and I believe my brother bishops are also convinced, that what we are experiencing here in our country bears the marks of the work of the Holy Spirit.

What we are experiencing is a broadening of the concept of Church vocation and Church ministry, a concept which formerly included only priests and Religious, but which now includes lay persons in an ever increasing number of capacities and Religious in capacities different from those in which they served previously. Most emphatically, the specific roles and implications of ordained ministry and of vowed religious life have to be carefully maintained, as does the urgency of the need for Christian witness by lay persons in the world. But at the same time, we welcome the developments which are making the Church in our country a Church of ever deepening participation and collaboration instead of a gathering of the active few and the passive many.

Concomitant with this development is an increasing appreciation for spirituality: for prayer, for Sacred Scripture, for preaching, for the liturgy, for spiritual direction. We are by no means a nation of mystics, but we are increasingly a Catholic community which realizes that external conformity to rites and rules, important as that is, is not enough.

Overall, Holy Father, I believe that the Holy Spirit is hard at work among the dioceses and parishes of our country. One of the implications of the theme that I was asked to develop (lay, religious and clerical vocations in the United States) is, I believe, that Catholic people in our country have available to them a depth and variety of ministry in the Church far greater than ever before. And for that, we bishops are profoundly grateful to all our collaborators in the Church's ministry and grateful for the opportunity to express our thanks to them in the presence of the Church's universal pastor.

I hope that my presentation does not sound like the prayer of the Pharisee in the temple, grateful that he is not like the rest of sinful humankind (cf. Lk 18:9ff). God knows that it is not our intent here today to hold up for universal imitation an "American way" of being church. We don't want a merely "American" church. We want a Catholic Church to flourish in our country. God also knows that we have plenty of problems and plenty of loose ends to deal with. At the same time, though, we felt that it was important for us bishops to take the opportunity of being with Your Holiness to speak of some of the very positive implications of lay, religious and clerical vocations in our country.

And now I am in a position to respond to the original "quaestio" around which I have constructed these remarks. "Quaerebatur" whether the ministry of the Church in the United States is in a state of turmoil and crisis. "Et respondeo affirmative," but it is not the turmoil and crisis of death and decay, but of development and of life.

"Dixi, Beatissime Pater."

Pope John Paul II:

14. My interest in the question of vocations is well known to all of you. It is a recurring theme in my conversations with

bishops around the world. It is one of the subjects I frequently speak about in my meetings with young people. It is a crucial factor for the future of the Church as we draw near to the beginning of the third millennium. Therefore, I am very pleased that you have chosen this topic as one of those to be emphasized today.

Archbishop Pilarczyk has presented an "overview of the ministerial realities of the Church in this country," mentioning aspects that offer much consolation to you as bishops and aspects which are cause for pastoral concern. He mentioned that it was important "to speak of some of the very positive implications of lay, religious and clerical vocations in America." In doing this, he rightly drew attention to the way that the Holy Spirit is at work in your midst, something that we must indeed be ever attentive to and grateful for. As "Lumen Gentium" reminds us:

"The Spirit guides the Church into the fullness of truth (cf. Jn 16:13) and gives her unity of fellowship and service.... By the power of the Gospel the Spirit makes the Church grow, perpetually renews her and leads her to perfect union with her Spouse" (No. 4).

It is indeed encouraging to note how lay people in ever-increasing numbers have become involved in the life of the Church and how this has led to "a depth and variety of ministry far greater than ever before." Certainly, the more active participation of the laity in the mission of the Church is an eloquent sign of the fruitfulness of the Second Vatican Council, one for which we all give thanks. And I am confident that the forthcoming Synod of Bishops will give fresh impetus to this participation and solid direction for its continued growth and consolidation.

It is important for our people to see clearly that the ministry of the ordained priest and the involvement of the laity in the Church's mission are not at all opposed to one another. On the contrary, the one complements the other. Just as the priestly ministry is not an end in and of itself, but serves to awaken and unify the various charisms within the Church, so too the involvement of the laity does not replace the priesthood, but supports it, promotes it and offers it space for its own specific service.

At this time, I would like to make a few remarks about vocations to the priesthood and to the religious life.

The insufficient number of seminarians and candidates for religious life is indeed a cause of pastoral concern for all of us, for we know that their public witness to the Gospel and their specific roles in the Church are irreplaceable. In many parts of the world the Church is experiencing, as Archbishop Pilarczyk observed, that "society is becoming increasingly secular and therefore increasingly inhospitable to Christian belief." It is especially difficult today for young people to make the generous sacrifices entailed in accepting God's call. Yet it is possible for them to do so through grace and with the support of the community. And it is precisely in this situation that we are called to bear witness to the hope of the Church.

In our pastoral mission we must often evaluate a situation and decide on a course of action. We must do this with prudence and pastoral realism. At the same time we know that today, as always, there are "prophets of doom." We must resist them in their pessimism and continue in our efforts to promote vocations to the priesthood and the religious life.

Prayer for vocations remains the primary way to success, since Jesus himself left us the commandment: "Beg the harvest master to send out laborers to gather his harvest" (Mt 9:38). I ask you therefore to encourage prayer for vocations among all the people, particularly among priests and Religious themselves but also in families, where the first seeds of vocations are usually planted, and in schools and religious education programs. The prayers of the elderly and the sick have an efficacy that must not be forgotten.

In addition to prayer, young people must be invited. It was Andrew who brought his brother Peter to the Lord. It was Philip who brought Nathanael. And how many of us and of our priests and Religious came to hear the Lord's call through the invitation of someone else? Your own presence among the youth is a blessing and an opportune time to extend this invitation to them and to ask young people themselves to pray for vocations.

Just last Thursday, speaking in Miami about vocations to the priesthood, I emphasized the basis of our hope:

"There is still one more factor to be considered in evaluating the future of vocations, and it is the power of Christ's paschal mystery. As the Church of Christ, we are all called to profess his power before the world; to proclaim that he is able, in virtue of his death and resurrection, to draw young people to himself in this generation as in the past; to declare that he is strong enough to attract young men even today to a life of self-sacrifice, pure love and total dedication to the priesthood. As we profess this truth, as we proclaim with faith the power of the Lord of the harvest, we have a right to expect that he will grant the prayers that he himself has commanded to be offered. The present hour calls for great trust in him who has overcome the world."

15. I would like to thank you for all you are doing to ensure a solid formation for the priesthood in the United States. The apostolic visitation to the seminaries has been carried out with generous collaboration. And I am grateful for the letters many of you have sent me expressing your appreciation for this initiative and telling me of the many positive effects which have resulted from it.

At the same time, your pastoral interest and personal involvement in seminary training are something that can never end. It is too central a task and too important a priority in the life of the Church. The Church of tomorrow passes through the seminaries of today. With the passing of time, the pastoral responsibility will no longer be ours. But at present the responsibility is ours, and it is heavy. Its zealous fulfillment is a great act of love for the flock.

In particular, I ask you to be vigilant that the dogmatic and moral teaching of the Church is faithfully and clearly presented to the seminarians, and fully accepted and understood by them. On the opening day of the Second Vatican Council, Oct. 11, 1962, John XXIII told his brother bishops: "The greatest concern of the ecumenical council is this: that the sacred deposit of Christian doctrine should be more effectively guarded and taught." What Pope John expected of the council is also a primary concern for priestly formation. We must ensure that our future priests have a solid grasp of the entirety of the Catholic faith; and then we must prepare them to present it in turn to others in ways that are intelligible and pastorally sound.

16. I cannot let this opportunity pass without expressing once again my gratitude for the great interest you have taken in the religious life. I am pleased to note, as Archbishop Pilarczyk has said, that there is "an increased understanding of and appreciation for religious life on the part of bishops and priests, thanks, in large part, to the pontifical commission" established in 1983.

In asking the commission to study the problem of vocations, I did so "with a view to encouraging a new growth and fresh move forward in this most important sector of the Church's life." The response which you have all made to this request has been most gratifying. And I know you will continue with this important effort. The religious life is a precious gift from the Lord, and we must continue to assure Religious of the love and esteem of the Church.

17. There are many other issues, dear brother bishops, which come to mind as we reflect together in this extraordinary hour of ecclesial communion. All of them touch us in our role as pastors and challenge our apostolic love and zeal.

Because of its importance in the life of the Church, I spoke to the priests in Miami about confession and our own need to receive the sacrament regularly. I also expressed my gratitude for their generous ministry in making confession available to the faithful. In this regard I would ask you as bishops to make every effort to ensure that the important norms of the universal Church with regard to the use of general absolution are understood and observed in a spirit of faith. In this regard I would ask that the post-synodal apostolic exhortation "Reconciliatio et Paenitentia" continue to be the object of prayerful reflection.

18. I wish to encourage you also in the pastoral care that you give to homosexual persons. This includes a clear explanation of the Church's teaching, which by its nature is unpopular. Nevertheless, your own pastoral experience confirms the fact that the truth, howsoever difficult to accept, brings grace and often leads to a deep inner conversion. No matter what problem individual Christians have, and no matter what degree of response to grace they make, they are always worthy of the Church's love and Christ's truth. All homosexual and other persons striving to fulfill the Gospel precept of chastity are worthy of special encouragement and esteem.

19. From time to time the question of sex education, especially as regards programs being used in schools, becomes a matter of concern to Catholic parents. The principles governing this area have been succinctly but clearly enunciated in "Familiaris Consortio." First among these principles is the need to recognize that sex education is a basic right and duty of parents themselves. They have to be helped to become increasingly more effective in fulfilling this task. Other educational agencies have an important role, but always in a subsidiary manner, with due subordination to the rights of parents.

Many parents will undoubtedly be heartened by the reference in the pastoral letter of the bishops of California, "A Call to Compassion," to an absolutely essential aspect of this whole question: "The recovery of the virtue of chastity," they wrote, "may be one of the most urgent needs of contemporary society." We cannot doubt that the Catholic Church in the United States, as elsewhere, is called to make great efforts to assist parents in teaching their children the sublime value of self-giving love; young people need great support in living this fundamental aspect of their human and Christian vocation.

20. Among your many pastoral obligations is the need to provide for the spiritual care of the military and their dependents. This you do through the Military Ordinariate. The functioning of this extended archdiocese requires the fraternal and sensitive collaboration of all the bishops in permitting and encouraging priests to commit themselves to this worthy ministry. The Church is grateful to all the chaplains who generously serve God's people in this particular situation, with its special needs.

21. I wish at this time to offer you my encouragement as you seek to guide the Church of God in so many areas: as you seek to lead your people in fulfilling their mission within the United States and well beyond her boundaries. Everything

you do to help your people to look outside themselves to Christ in need is a great ecclesial and apostolic service.

My final word is about our pastoral identity as bishops of Jesus Christ and his Church. Because of this identity we are called to holiness and to daily conversion. In speaking to you eight years ago in Chicago I stated: "The holiness of personal conversion is indeed the condition for our fruitful ministry as bishops of the Church. It is our union with Jesus Christ that determines the credibility of our witness to the Gospel and the supernatural effectiveness of our activity" (Discourse of Oct. 5, 1979). May God give us all this great gift of union with Jesus and allow us to live it together in strength and joy, in the communion of the Church of God.

Dodger Stadium Mass Los Angeles, Sept. 16

Pope John Paul II:

"The Lord has made his salvation known in the sight of the nations"(Ps 98:2).

Dear brother bishops, dear brothers and sisters in Christ, people of this city of our Lady of the Angels, once known as "El Pueblo de Nuestra Señora de los Angeles," citizens of this state of California,

1. Today, from this city of Los Angeles on the Pacific Coast in which are gathered all the bishops of the United States, we return together to the Upper Room in Jerusalem. We hear words from the prayer which Christ pronounced there. Surrounded by his apostles, Jesus prays for the Church of every time and place. He says to the Father: "I do not pray for them alone. I pray also for those who will believe in me through their word" (Jn 17:20). Christ, the one eternal priest of the new and everlasting covenant, prays for us, for all of us gathered here, for everyone who lives here in Los Angeles on the west coast of the United States of America, for everyone in the world. Yes, every one of us is included in this priestly prayer of the Redeemer.

2. Jesus says to the Father: "I pray also for those who will believe in me through their word" (Jn 17:20). This is the Church of all ages that he is praying for. How many generations of disciples have already heard these words of Christ! How many bishops, priests, men and women Religious, and how many parents and teachers in the course of the centuries have passed on this word of salvation! In how many places of the world, among how many peoples and nations, has this mystery of the redemption continued to unfold and bear fruit! It is the word of salvation from which the Church has grown and continues to grow. This is true for the universal Church and for each local church. It is true for the church in Los Angeles, which is visited today by the bishop of Rome, the successor of Peter.

In 1769 Father Junipero Serra and his Franciscan companions brought the word of God to California. Leaving behind all that was familiar and dear to them, they freely chose to come to this area to preach the good news of our Lord Jesus Christ. This initial effort of evangelization very quickly showed impressive results as thousands of native Americans accepted the Gospel and were baptized. Soon, a whole series of missions was established all along "El Camino Real," each of them bearing the name of a saint or a mystery of the Christian faith: San Diego, San Bernardino, San Gabriel, San Buenaventura, Santa Barbara, San Fernando and all the rest.

Within years of this first missionary effort, immigrants began to settle in California. Coming mostly from Mexico and Spain, these early settlers had already been evangelized and thus they brought as part of their heritage the Catholic and apostolic faith. Little did they know at the time that, in God's providence, they were initiating a pattern which would characterize California for years to come.

Subsequently California has become a haven for immigrants, a new home for refugees and migrants, a place where people from every continent have come together to fashion a society of the most varied ethnic diversity. Many of these, like their earliest predecessors, have brought not only their specific cultural traditions but also the Christian faith. As a result, the church in California, and particularly the church in Los Angeles, is truly catholic in the fullest sense, embracing peoples and cultures of the widest and richest variety.

Today in the church in Los Angeles, Christ is Anglo and Hispanic, Christ is Chinese and black, Christ is Vietnamese and Irish, Christ is Korean and Italian, Christ is Japanese and Filipino, Christ is native American, Croatian, Samoan and many other ethnic groups. In this local church the one risen Christ, the one Lord and Savior, is living in each person who has accepted the word of God and been washed clean in the saving waters of baptism. And the Church, with all her different members, remains the one body of Christ, professing the same faith, united in hope and in love.

3. What does Jesus pray for in the Upper Room the night before his passion and death? "That all may be one as you, Father, are in me, and I in you; I pray that they may be one in us, that the world may believe that you sent me" (Jn 17:21). "One in us" — the mystery of the inscrutable divine Being, the mystery of the intimate life of God: the divine unity and at the same time the Trinity. It is the divine "we" of the Father, and the Son and the Holy Spirit. And even though it is not attainable in its absolute fullness, this most perfect unity is the real model for the Church. According to the teaching of the Second Vatican Council, "the Church shines forth as a people made one by the unity of the Father, the Son and the Holy Spirit" ("Lumen Gentium," 4).

It is for this type of unity for the Church of all times that Christ prays in the Upper Room: "that they may be one, as we are one — I living in them, you living in me — that their unity may be complete. So shall the world know that you sent me, and that you loved them as you loved me" (Jn 17:22-23). This is the unity of the Church's communion, which is born from the communion of three persons in the Most Holy Trinity.

4. People of all times and places are called to this communion. This truth of revelation is first presented to us in today's liturgy through the image of the holy city of Jerusalem found in the reading from the prophet Isaiah, who writes: "Nations shall walk by your light, and kings by your shining radiance. Raise your eyes and look about; they all gather and come to you: your sons come from afar, and your daughters in the arms of their nurses" (Is 60:3-5). Isaiah spoke these words in Jerusalem as he foresaw a great light which would descend upon the city: This light is Christ. The awesome movement toward Christ of people from all over the world begins as a result of the Gospel. Animated by the Holy Spirit, in the power of the cross and resurrection of Christ, this movement of people culminates in a new unity of humanity. Thus, the words of Jesus come to pass: "And I — once I am lifted up from the earth — will draw all men to myself" (Jn 12:32).

The Second Vatican Council gave prominence to this dimension of the unity of the Church, above all in the teaching on the people of God. "This people, while remaining one and unique, is to be spread throughout the whole world and must exist in all ages, so that the purpose of God's will may be fulfilled" ("Lumen Gentium," 13).

5. However, that people is at the same time the body of Christ. The body is yet another image, and in a certain sense another dimension, of the same truth of the unity that we all constitute in Christ under the action of the Holy Spirit. Accordingly, St. Paul exhorts us: "Make every effort to preserve the unity which has the Spirit as its origin and peace as its binding force. There is but one body and one Spirit, just as there is but one hope given all of you by your call. There is one Lord, one faith, one baptism; one God and Father of all, who is over all, and works through all, and is in all" (Eph 4:3-6). The unity for which Christ prayed in the Upper Room is realized in this way. It does not come from us, but from God: from the Father, through the Son, in the Holy Spirit.

6. This unity does not at all erase diversity. On the contrary, it develops it. There is constantly "unity in diversity." Through the work of the one Lord, by means of the one faith and the one baptism, this diversity — a diversity of human persons, of individuals — tends toward unity, a unity which is communion in the likeness of God the Trinity.

The unity of the body of Christ gives life; at the same time it serves diversity and develops it. This is the diversity of "everyone" and at the same time of "each one." It is the truth that we find in the letter to the Ephesians where Paul writes: "Each of us has received God's favor in the measure in which Christ bestows it.... It is he who gave apostles, prophets, evangelists, pastors and teachers in roles of service for the faithful to build up the body of Christ" (Eph 4:7, 11-12). As such then it is the Holy Spirit who is the source of both the unity and the diversity in the Church: the unity because it finds its origin solely in the Spirit; the diversity since the Spirit bestows the variety of gifts, the variety of vocations and ministries found in the Church, which is the body of Christ and at the same time the people of God.

7. The saints whom we honor in today's liturgy, Cornelius and Cyprian, remind us of one concrete example of unity in diversity: the unity of the universal Church, which is served by the successor of St. Peter, and the diversity of the particular churches, which help to build up the whole body through the leadership of the local bishops.

Pope St. Cornelius was called to shepherd the universal Church in the middle of the third century, a time of religious persecution from without and a time of painful dissension within. His efforts to strengthen the Church's communion were greatly aided by the persuasive talents of the bishop of Carthage, St. Cyprian, who while caring for his own flock also promoted unity throughout North Africa. These two men of different backgrounds and temperaments were united by a mutual love for the Church and by their zeal for the unity of the faith. How appropriate that we should observe their feast on the day when the present successor of Peter is meeting with the bishops of the United States.

The feast focuses our attention on a basic truth, namely that the unity of the members of the Church is deeply affected by the unity of the bishops among themselves and by their communion with the successor of Peter. The Second Vatican Council put it this way: "The Roman pontiff, as the successor of Peter, is the perpetual and visible source and foundation of the unity of the bishops and of the multitude of the faithful. The individual bishop, however, is the visible principle and foundation of unity in his particular church, fashioned after the model of the universal Church. In and from such individual churches there comes into being the one and only Catholic Church" ("Lumen Gentium," 23).

8. The Church's concrete methods of evangelization and her efforts to promote peace and justice are shaped to a large extent by the fact that the Church is one and yet diverse. The good news of Jesus must be proclaimed in the language that particular people understand, in artistic symbols that give meaning to their experience, in ways that correspond as far as possible to their own aspirations and needs, their manner of looking at life and the way in which they speak to God. At the same time there must be no betrayal of the essential truth while the Gospel is being translated and the Church's teaching is being passed down.

The ethnic universality of the Church demands a keen sensitivity to authentic cultures and a real sense of what is required by the process of inculturation. In this regard, Pope Paul VI stated very accurately the task to be done:

"The question is undoubtedly a delicate one. Evangelization loses much of its force and effectiveness if it does not take into consideration the actual people to whom it is addressed, if it does not use their language, their signs and symbols, if it does not answer the questions they ask and if it does not have an impact on their concrete life. But on the other hand, evangelization risks losing its power and disappearing altogether if one empties or adulterates its content under the pretext of translating it; if, in other words, one sacrifices this reality and destroys the unity without which there is no universality" ("Evangelii Nuntiandi," 63).

Closely aligned with the Church's evangelization is her action on behalf of peace and justice, and this too is deeply influenced by her pastoral concern for particular peoples, especially for refugees, immigrants and the poor. For over 200 years, the Church has welcomed the waves of new immigrants to the shores of your country. It was the love and compassion of the Church that so many new arrivals first felt when they stepped onto the soil of this young nation. While that continuous pastoral care of the immigrant was focused primarily on the East Coast in the early decades, that pastoral outreach now extends to virtually every major city in the country. Los Angeles — where this evening we celebrate the diversity of peoples who make up your country — has now become the new major point of entry for the latest waves of immigrants.

I commend you, my brother bishops and all of those working closely with you, for your active collaboration in helping several million undocumented immigrants to become legal residents. This pastoral care of the immigrant in our own day reflects the love of Christ in the Gospels and the legitimate work of the Church in carrying on the challenge of the Lord, "I was a stranger and you welcomed me" (Mt 25:35).

9. The Church faces a particularly difficult task in her efforts to preach the word of God in all cultures in which the faithful are constantly challenged by consumerism and a pleasure-seeking mentality, where utility, productivity and hedonism are exalted while God and his law are forgotten. In these situations where ideas and behavior directly contradict the truth about God and about humanity itself, the Church's witness must be unpopular. She must take a clear stand on the word of God and proclaim the whole gospel message with great confidence in the Holy Spirit. In this effort, just as in all others, the Church shows herself to be the sacrament of salvation for the whole human race, the people God has chosen to be his channel of peace and reconciliation in a world torn by division and sin.

While the Church's unity is not her own achievement but a precious gift from the Lord, it is nonetheless her serious responsibility to be an instrument for guarding and restoring unity in the human family. She does this by being faithful to the truth and by directly opposing the devil, who is "the father of lies." She does this by efforts to break down prejudice and ignorance as she fosters new understanding and trust. She also promotes unity by being a faithful channel of Christ's mercy and love.

10. Today, with the very prayer for unity said by Christ in the Upper Room, we celebrate the liturgy of the Eucharist here on the rim of the Pacific, in the city that takes its name from the angels. And with the psalmist, we say: "Sing to the Lord a new song, for he has done wondrous deeds" (Ps 98:1).

Yes, God has done so many wondrous deeds that confirm his salvific action in our world — the "God and Father of all, who is over all, and works through all, and is in all" (Eph 4:6). The Lord has made his salvation known: "He has revealed his justice." He constantly remembers "his kindness and his faithfulness" (Ps 98:2-3). This is the way God is, the God of our faith, the Father of our Lord Jesus Christ.

The angels in heaven see "the face of God" in the beatific vision of glory. All of us, people of this planet, walk in faith toward that same vision. And we walk in hope. We draw the strength of this hope from the same prayer of Christ in the Upper Room. Did not Christ say in the words addressed to the Father: "I have given them the glory you gave me that they may be one, as we are one — I living in them, you living in me" (Jn 17:22-23)?

"The glory ... I gave to them." We are called in Christ to share in the glory that is part of the beatific vision of God.

Truly "all the ends of the earth have seen the salvation by our God." For this reason: "Sing to the Lord a new song!" (Ps 98:3, 1). Amen.

Consecration to Mary Los Angeles, Sept. 16

Pope John Paul II:

1. I wish at this time to turn my thoughts once more to the woman of faith and of all salvation history: Mary, the mother of Jesus and mother of his Church; Mary, the patroness of the United States under the title of her Immaculate Conception.

I entrust to you, Virgin Mother of God, all the faithful of this land. I entrust them to you not only as individual men and women in the nobility of their personhood, but as the Christian community, living corporately the life of your divine Son.

I entrust to you my brother bishops in their great mission as servant pastors of God's people, in communion with the successor of Peter. I entrust to you all the priests, who minister generously in the name of the Good Shepherd; all the deacons bearing witness to Christ's servanthood; all women and men Religious proclaiming by their lives the holiness of God; all the laity working in virtue of their baptism and confirmation to order all temporal affairs according to the plan of God.

I entrust to you all the holy people of God — the pilgrim people of God — called to be mindful of their Christian dignity, called to conversion, called to eternal life.

In particular I entrust to you the families of America, in their quest for holiness, in their struggle against sin, in their vocation to be vital cells in the body of Christ. I ask you to bless all husbands and wives, all fathers and mothers, and to confirm them in their high vocation of human love and openness to life. I entrust to you the children of this generation, asking you to preserve them in innocence, to protect them from all harm and abuse, and to let them grow up in a world of peace and justice and fraternal love.

I entrust to you all the women of the Church and the cause of their true human advancement in the world and their ever fuller participation in the life of the Church, according to the authentic plan of God. May they discover in you, O Mary, and in the freedom that was yours — from that moment of supreme liberation in your immaculate conception — the secret of living totally their femininity in fulfillment, progress and love.

I commend to your protection the young people that make up the future of the United States. I pray that in your Son Jesus Christ they may grasp the meaning of life and come to understand deeply their call to serve their fellow human beings; that they may discover the profound fulfillment of chaste love, and the joy and strength that come from Christian hope.

I offer to your loving care the elderly people with all their sufferings and joys, and with their yet unfinished mission of service in your Church. I ask you to console and assist the dying, and to renew within the whole community a sense of the importance of human life at every stage, even when it is weak and defenseless.

I ask you to assist the single people with their special needs and special mission. Give them strength to live according to the Beatitudes and to serve with generosity and gladness.

2. I entrust to you all those engaged in the great Christian struggle of life: all those who, despite human weaknesses and repeated falls, are striving to live according to the word of God; all those who are confused about the truth and are tempted to call evil good and darkness light; all those who are yearning for truth and grasping for hope.

I ask you to show yourself once again as a mother with that deep human concern which was yours at Cana of Galilee. Help all those weighed down by the problems of life. Console the suffering. Comfort the sad and dejected, those tormented in spirit, those without families, loved ones or friends.

Assist the poor and those in need, and those subjected to discrimination or other forms of injustice. Come to the help of the unemployed. Heal the sick. Aid the handicapped and disabled so that they may live in a manner befitting their dignity as children of God. Stir up the consciences of us all to respond to the needs of others with justice, mercy and love.

3. Through your intercession I ask that sinners may be reconciled, and that the whole church in America may become ever more attentive to Christ's call to conversion and to holiness of life.

I pray that all those baptized in Christ your Son will be strengthened in the great cause of Christian unity, according to his will.

I ask your prayers so that citizens may work together to conquer evil with good, oppose violence, reject war and its weapons, satisfy hunger, overcome hatred and remedy all forms of personal, social, national and international injustice.

I ask you to strengthen the Catholic people in truth and love, in their obedience to the commandments of God and in their fidelity to the sacraments.

Virgin Mother of God, Our Lady of the Angels: I entrust to you the whole church in America. Help her to excel in sacrifice and service. Purify her love, renew her life and con-

vert her constantly to the Gospel of your Son. Lead her children with all their Christian and non-Christian brethren to eternal life, for the glory of your Son Jesus Christ, who lives and reigns with the Father in the unity of the Holy Spirit, forever and ever. Amen.

Laguna Seca Mass Monterey, Sept. 17

Pope John Paul II:

"Be careful not to forget the Lord, your God" (Dt 8:11).

Dear brothers and sisters of the Monterey Peninsula, brothers and sisters of California and other areas of the United States,

1. Originally these words were addressed by Moses to the Israelite people as they were on the point of entering the Promised Land — land with streams of water, with springs and fountains welling up in the hills and valleys, a land producing an abundance of every fruit and food, a land where the people would lack nothing (cf. Dt 8:7-9). Today these words are addressed to the people of God here in Monterey, in the state of California, against the background of an extraordinary beauty of land and sea, of snowcapped mountains and deep lakes, oak groves and forests of fir and pine and mighty redwoods, a land among the richest and most fruitful of the Earth. Yes, today, these words are addressed to all of us gathered here: "Be careful not to forget the Lord, your God."

2. These words, pronounced thousands of years ago, have still today a special meaning and relevance. Moses, the great teacher of his people, was concerned that in their future prosperity they might abandon God — the God who brought them out of the land of slavery and guided them through the desert with its parched ground, feeding them with manna along the way (cf. Dt 8:15-16). Moses knew the tendency of the human heart to cry out to the Lord in time of need, but easily "to neglect his commandments and decrees and statutes" (cf. Dt 8:11) in the time of well-being and prosperity. He knew that God is easily forgotten.

In our own day are we not perhaps witnesses of the fact that often in rich societies, where there is an abundance of material well-being, permissiveness and moral relativism find easy acceptance? And where the moral order is undermined, God is forgotten and questions of ultimate responsibility are set aside. In such situations a practical atheism pervades private and public living.

From the moment of original sin, man has been inclined to see himself in the place of God. He often thinks, just as Moses warned he might: "It is my own power and the strength of my own hand that has obtained for me this wealth" (Dt 8:17). He acts as if the One who is the source of all life and goodness were just not there. He ignores a fundamental truth about himself: the fact that he is a creature; that he has been created and owes everything to his Creator, who is also his Redeemer.

In these closing years of the 20th century, on the eve of the third millennium of the Christian era, a part of the human family — the most economically and technically developed part — is being specially tempted, perhaps as never before, to imitate the ancient model of all sin — the original rebellion that expressed itself saying: "I will not serve." The temptation today is to try to build a world for oneself, forgetting the

195

Creator and his design and loving providence. But sooner or later we must come to grips with this: that to forget God, to feign the death of God, is to promote the death of man and of all civilization. It is to threaten the existence of individuals, communities and all society.

3. Today's readings from the New Testament are in contrast to such a position. They speak of God's presence which permeates the human heart and the whole of created reality. Jesus teaches that the reign of God is like the growth of the seed that a man scatters on the ground (cf. Mk 4:26-29). Certainly human activity is essential. Man "goes to bed and gets up every day...." He plants. And "when the crop is ready he wields the sickle." Even the rich valleys of California would produce nothing without human ingenuity and toil. But the word of God says that "the soil produces of itself first the blade, then the ear, finally the ripe wheat in the ear" (v. 28). As if to say: The growth of the wheat and its maturing, which greatly depends on the fertility of the soil, comes from the nature and vitality of creation itself. Consequently there is another source of growth: the One who is above nature and above the man who cultivates the earth.

In a sense, the Creator "hides himself" in this life-giving process of nature. It is the human person, with the help of intellect and faith, who is called to "discover" and "unveil" the presence of God and his action in all of creation: "So may your way be known upon earth; among all nations, your salvation" (Ps 67:3).

If the parable of the seed indicates the growth of the kingdom of God in the world, the words of St. Paul in the second reading speak of how God's generous giving aims at drawing "good works" from the human heart: "God can multiply his favors among you ... for good works." The whole of human activity must be finalized in works of justice, peace and love. All human work — including, in a very direct way, the noble work of agriculture in which many of you are engaged — is to be carried out at the service of man and for the glory of God.

4. The land is God's gift. From the beginning, God has entrusted it to the whole human race as a means of sustaining the life of all those whom he creates in his own image and likeness. We must use the land to sustain every human being in life and dignity. Against the background of the immense beauty of this region and the fertility of its soil, let us proclaim together our gratitude for this gift, with the words of the responsorial psalm: "The earth has yielded its fruit, the Lord our God has blessed us" (Ps 67:7).

As we read in Genesis, human beings earn their bread by the sweat of their brows (Gn 3:17). We toil long hours and grow weary at our tasks. Yet work is good for us. "Through work man not only transforms nature, adapting it to his own needs, but he also achieves fulfillment as a human being and indeed in a sense becomes 'more a human being'" ("Laborem Exercens," 9).

The value of work does not end with the individual. The full meaning of work can only be understood in relation to the family and society as well. Work supports and gives stability to the family. Within the family, moreover, children first learn the human and positive meaning of work and responsibility. In each community and in the nation as a whole, work has a fundamental social meaning. It can, moreover, either join people in the solidarity of a shared commitment or set them at odds through exaggerated competition, exploitation and social conflict. Work is a key to the whole social question, when that "question" is understood to be concerned with making life more human (cf. "Laborem Exercens," 3).

5. Agricultural work exemplifies all these principles — the potential of work for the fulfillment of the human person, the "family" dimension of work and social solidarity. Agricultural work is — as Pope John XXIII described it — a vocation, a God-given mission, a noble task and a contribution to civilization (cf. "Mater et Magistra," 149). God has blessed the United States with some of the richest farm land in the world. The productivity of American agriculture is a major success story. Clearly, it is a history of hard and wearying work, of courage and enterprise, and it involves the interaction of many people: growers, workers, processors, distributors and finally consumers.

I know too that recently thousands of American farmers have been introduced to poverty and indebtedness. Many have lost their homes and their way of life. Your bishops and the whole Church in your country are deeply concerned; and they are listening to the voices of so many farmers and farm workers as they express their anxieties over the costs and the risks of farming, the difficult working conditions, the need for a just wage and decent housing, and the question of a fair price for products. On an even wider scale is heard the voice of the poor, who are bewildered in a land of plenty and still experience the pangs of hunger.

6. All agree that the situation of the farming community in the United States and in other parts of the world is highly complex and that simple remedies are not at hand. The Church, on her part, while she can offer no specific technical solutions, does present a social teaching based on the primacy of the human person in every economic and social activity. At every level of the agricultural process, the dignity, rights and well-being of people must be the central issue. No one person in this process — grower, worker, packer, shipper, retailer or consumer — is greater than the other in the eyes of God.

Giving voice therefore to the sufferings of many, I appeal to all involved to work together to find appropriate solutions to all farm questions. This can only be done in a community marked by a sincere and effective solidarity — and, where still necessary, reconciliation — among all parties to the agricultural productive process.

And what of our responsibility to future generations? The earth will not continue to offer its harvest, except with faithful stewardship. We cannot say we love the land and then take steps to destroy it for use by future generations. I urge you to be sensitive to the many issues affecting the land and the whole environment, and to unite with each other to seek the best solutions to these pressing problems.

7. Each one of us is called to fulfill his or her respective duties before God and before society. Since the Church is constrained by her very nature to focus her attention most strongly on those least able to defend their own legitimate interests, I appeal to landowners, growers and others in positions of power to respect the just claims of their brothers and sisters who work the land. These claims include the right to share in decisions concerning their services and the right to free association with a view to social, cultural and economic advancement (cf. "Laborem Exercens," 21). I also appeal to all workers to be mindful of their own obligations of justice and to make every effort to fulfill a worthy service to mankind.

New legislation in your country has made it possible for many people, especially migrant farm workers, to become citizens rather than remain strangers among you. Many of these people have worked here with the same dream that your ancestors had when they first came. I ask you to welcome these new citizens into your society and to respect the human dignity of every man, woman and child.

Two hundred years after the Constitution confirmed the United States as a land of opportunity and freedom, it is right to hope that there may be a general and renewed commitment to those policies needed to ensure that within these borders equity and justice will be preserved and fostered. This is an ever present requirement of America's historical destiny.

It is also important for America at this time to look beyond herself and all her own needs to see the even greater needs of the poorer nations of the world. Even as local communities mobilize to work ever more effectively for the integral human advancement of their own members, they must not forget their brothers and sisters elsewhere. We must be careful not to forget the Lord, but we must be careful also not to forget those whom he loves.

8. The hidden attributes of the Creator are reflected in the beauty of his creation. The beauty of the Monterey Peninsula attracts a great number of visitors; as a result so many of you are involved in the tourist industry. I greet you and encourage you to see your specific work as a form of service and of solidarity with your fellow human beings.

Work — as we have seen — is an essential aspect of our human existence, but so also is the necessary rest and recreation which permit us to recover our energies and strengthen our spirit for the tasks of life. Many worthwhile values are involved in tourism: relaxation, the widening of one's culture and the possibility of using leisure time for spiritual pursuits. These include prayer and contemplation and pilgrimages, which have always been a part of our Catholic heritage; they also include fostering human relationships within the family and among friends. Like other human activities, tourism can be a source of good or evil, a place of grace or sin. I invite all of you who are involved in tourism to uphold the dignity of your work and to be always willing to bear joyful witness to your Christian faith.

9. Dear brothers and sisters: It is in the Eucharist that the fruits of our work — and all that is noble in human affairs — become an offering of the greatest value in union with the sacrifice of Jesus Christ, our Lord and Savior. In fostering what is authentically human through our work and through deeds of justice and love, we set upon the altar of the Lord those elements which will be transformed into Christ: "Blessed are you Lord, God of all creation. Through your goodness we have this bread to offer, which earth has given and human hands have made. It will become for us the bread of life."

I ask you to join with me in praising the Most Holy Trinity for the abundance of life and goodness with which you have been gifted: "The earth has yielded its fruit. God, our God, has blessed us" (Ps 67:7). But may your abundance never lead you to forget the Lord or cease to acknowledge him as the source of your peace and well-being. Your prayer for yourselves and for all your brothers and sisters must always be an echo of the psalm: "May God have pity on us and bless us; may he let his face shine on us" (Ps 67:2).

For years to come may the Lord's face shine on this land, on the church in Monterey and on all America: "From sea to shining sea." Amen.

Carmel Mission Visit Monterey, Sept. 17

Pope John Paul II:

Dear Bishop Shubsda, dear brothers and sisters,
1. I come today as a pilgrim to this Mission of San Carlos, which so powerfully evokes the heroic spirit and heroic deeds of Fray Junipero Serra and which enshrines his mortal remains. This serene and beautiful place is truly the historical and spiritual heart of California. All the missions of "El Camino Real" bear witness to the challenges and heroism of an earlier time, but not a time forgotten or without significance for the California of today and the Church of today.

These buildings and the men who gave them life, especially their spiritual father, Junipero Serra, are reminders of an age of discovery and exploration. The missions are the result of a conscious moral decision made by people of faith in a situation that presented many human possibilities, both good and bad, with respect to the future of this land and its native peoples. It was a decision rooted in a love of God and neighbor. It was a decision to proclaim the Gospel of Jesus Christ at the dawn of a new age, which was extremely important for both the European settlers and the native Americans.

2. Very often at crucial moments in human affairs God raises up men and women whom he thrusts into roles of decisive importance for the future development of both society and the Church. Although their story unfolds within the ordinary circumstances of daily life, they become larger than life within the perspective of history. We rejoice all the more when their achievement is coupled with a holiness of life that can truly be called heroic. So it is with Junipero Serra, who in the providence of God was destined to be the apostle of California and to have a permanent influence over the spiritual patrimony of this land and its people, whatever their religion might be. This apostolic awareness is captured in the words ascribed to him: "In California is my life and there, God willing, I hope to die." Through Christ's paschal mystery, that death has become a seed in the soil of this state that continues to bear fruit "thirty- or sixty- or a hundredfold" (Mt 13:9).

Father Serra was a man convinced of the Church's mission, conferred upon her by Christ himself, to evangelize the world, to "make disciples of all the nations, baptizing them in the name of the Father and of the Son and of the Holy Spirit" (Mt 28:19). The way in which he fulfilled that mission corresponds faithfully to the Church's vision today of what evangelization means: "(T)he Church evangelizes when she seeks to convert, solely through the divine power of the message she proclaims, both the personal and collective consciences of people, the activities in which they engage, and the lives and concrete milieux which are theirs" ("Evangelii Nuntiandi," 18).

He not only brought the Gospel to the native Americans, but as one who lived the Gospel he also became their defender and champion. At the age of 60 he journeyed from Carmel to Mexico City to intervene with the viceroy on their behalf — a journey which twice brought him close to death — and presented his now famous "Representacion" with its "bill of rights," which had as their aim the betterment of every phase of missionary activity in California, particularly the spiritual and physical well-being of its native Americans.

3. Father Serra and his fellow missionaries shared the conviction found everywhere in the New Testament that the Gospel is a matter of life and salvation. They believed that in offering to people Jesus Christ, they were doing something of immense value, importance and dignity. What other explanation can there be for the hardships that they freely and gladly endured like St. Paul and all the other great missionaries before them: difficult and dangerous travel, illness and isolation, an ascetical lifestyle, arduous labor, and also like St. Paul,

that "concern for all the churches" (2 Cor 11:28) which Junipero Serra, in particular, experienced as "presidente" of the California missions in the face of every vicissitude, disappointment and opposition.

Dear brothers and sisters: Like Father Serra and his Franciscan brethren, we too are called to be evangelizers, to share actively in the Church's mission of making disciples of all people. The way in which we fulfill that mission will be different from theirs. But their lives speak to us still because of their sure faith that the Gospel is true and because of their passionate belief in the value of bringing that saving truth to others at great personal cost. Much to be envied are those who can give their lives for something greater than themselves in loving service to others. This, more than words or deeds alone, is what draws people to Christ.

This single-mindedness is not reserved for great missionaries in exotic places. It must be at the heart of each priest's ministry and the evangelical witness of every Religious. It is the key to their personal sense of well-being, happiness and fulfillment in what they are and what they do. This single-mindedness is also essential to the Christian witness of the Catholic laity. The covenant of love between two people in marriage and the successful sharing of faith with children require the effort of a lifetime. If couples cease believing in their marriage as a sacrament before God or treat religion as anything less than a matter of salvation, then the Christian witness they might have given to the world is lost. Those who are unmarried must also be steadfast in fulfilling their duties in life if they are to bring Christ to the world in which they live.

"In him who is the source of my strength I have strength for everything" (Phil 4:13). These words of the great missionary, St. Paul, remind us that our strength is not our own. Even in the martyrs and saints, as the liturgy reminds us, it is "(God's) power shining through our human weakness" (Preface of Martyrs). It is the strength that inspired Father Serra's motto: "Always forward, never back." It is the strength that one senses in this place of prayer so filled with his presence. It is the strength that can make each one of us, dear brothers and sisters, missionaries of Jesus Christ, witnesses of his message, doers of his word.

Mission Dolores Address San Francisco, Sept. 17

Pope John Paul II:

Dear Archbishop Quinn, dear brothers and sisters in Christ,
1. Thank you for your very kind welcome to San Francisco. It is a joy to be here with all of you. As I begin my pastoral visit to your historic city, I extend fraternal greetings to all the citizens of this metropolitan area. In the love of Christ I greet my brothers and sisters of the Catholic community. And in a special way I welcome this opportunity to be with you who are present in this basilica dedicated to Our Lady of Sorrows. May the grace and peace of God our Father and our Lord Jesus Christ be with you all.

San Francisco! Both in name and by history you are linked to the spirit of St. Francis of Assisi. And thus, as I come to your city on this pastoral visit, I think of all that St. Francis means not only to yourselves but to people all around the world. There is something about this man who was born over 800 years ago in a little Italian town that continues in our day to inspire people of vastly different cultures and religions.

St. Francis was a man of peace and gentleness, a poet and lover of beauty. He was a man of poverty and simplicity, a man in tune with the birds and animals, enchanted by all of God's creation. Above all, Francis was a man of prayer whose whole life was shaped by the love of Jesus Christ. And he wished to live in a way that spoke in the clearest terms of the everlasting love of God.

As I come today then to the city of San Francisco, I come in the spirit of this saint, whose whole life proclaims the goodness and mercy of God.

2. Accordingly, I wish to speak to you about the all-embracing love of God. St. John says: "Love, then, consists in this: not that we have loved God but that he has loved us and has sent his Son as an offering for our sins" (1 Jn 4:10). God's love for us is freely given and unearned, surpassing all we could ever hope for or imagine. He does not love us because we have merited it or are worthy of it. God loves us, rather, because he is true to his own nature. As St. John puts it, "God is love, and he who abides in love abides in God, and God in him" (1 Jn 4:16).

The greatest proof of God's love is shown in the fact that he loves us in our human condition, with our weaknesses and our needs. Nothing else can explain the mystery of the cross. The apostle Paul once wrote: "You can depend on this as worthy of full acceptance: that Christ Jesus came into the world to save sinners. Of these, I myself am the worst. But on that very account I was dealt with mercifully, so that in me, as an extreme case, Jesus Christ might display all his patience, and that I might become an example to those who would later have faith in him and gain everlasting life" (1 Tm 1:15-16).

The love of Christ is more powerful than sin and death. St. Paul explains that Christ came to forgive sin and that his love is greater than any sin, stronger than all my personal sins or those of anyone else. This is the faith of the Church. This is the good news of God's love that the Church proclaims throughout history and that I proclaim to you today: God loves you with an everlasting love. He loves you in Christ Jesus, his Son.

3. God's love has many aspects. In particular, God loves us as our Father. The parable of the prodigal son expresses this truth most vividly. You recall that moment in the parable when the son came to his senses, decided to return home and set off for his father's house. "While he was still a long way off, his father caught sight of him and was deeply moved. He ran out to meet him, threw his arms around his neck and kissed him" (Lk 15:20). This is the fatherly love of God, a love always ready to forgive, eager to welcome us back.

God's love for us as our Father is a strong and faithful love, a love which is full of mercy, a love which enables us to hope for the grace of conversion when we have sinned. As I said in my encyclical on the mercy of God: "The parable of the prodigal son expresses in a simple but profound way the reality of conversion. Conversion is the most concrete expression of the working of love and of the presence of mercy in the human world.... Mercy is manifested in its true and proper aspect when it restores to value, promotes and draws good from all the forms of evil existing in the world" ("Dives in Misericordia," 6).

It is the reality of God's love for us as our father that explains why Jesus told us when we pray to address God as "Abba, Father" (cf. Lk 11:2; Mt 6:9).

4. It is also true to say that God loves us as a mother. In this regard God asks us, through the prophet Isaiah: "Can a mother forget her infant, be without tenderness for the child of her womb? Even should she forget, I will never forget you" (Is 49:15). God's love is tender and merciful, patient and full of understanding. In the Scriptures and also in the living memory of the Church, the love of God is indeed depicted and has been experienced as the compassionate love of a mother.

Jesus himself expressed a compassionate love when he wept over Jerusalem, and when he said: "O Jerusalem, Jerusalem.... How often would I have gathered your children together as a hen gathers her brood under her wings" (Lk 13:34).

5. Dear friends in Christ: the love of God is so great that it goes beyond the limits of human language, beyond the grasp of artistic expression, beyond human understanding. And yet it is concretely embodied in God's Son, Jesus Christ, and in his body, the Church. Once again this evening, here in Mission Dolores Basilica, I repeat to all of you the ageless proclamation of the Gospel: God loves you!

God loves you all, without distinction, without limit. He loves those of you who are elderly, who feel the burden of the years. He loves those of you who are sick, those who are suffering from AIDS and from AIDS-related complex. He loves the relatives and friends of the sick and those who care for them. He loves us all with an unconditional and everlasting love.

In the spirit of St. Francis, then, I urge you all to open your hearts to God's love, to respond by your prayers and by the deeds of your lives. Let go of your doubts and fears, and let the mercy of God draw you to his Heart. Open the doors of your hearts to our God who is rich in mercy.

"See what love the Father has bestowed on us in letting us be called children of God! Yet that is what we are" (1 Jn 3:1).

Yes, that is what we are today and forever: children of a loving God!

Meeting with Religious
San Francisco, Sept. 17

Sister Helen Garvey:

It is a privilege, Pope John Paul II, to address you on behalf of the 130,000 women Religious of the United States of America. May the Spirit of God be in my heart and on my lips at this special moment in the history of the Church and in the history of women Religious.

The life of women Religious in this country is a life rich in ministerial service to God's people. It is a life whose very meaning is rooted in spirituality, in an attentive, active response to God's loving presence within us and among us. It is a life grounded in the life and mission of Jesus Christ. The story of the mission of Jesus takes us back almost 2,000 years to a synagogue in Nazareth.

"Jesus came to Nazareth where he had been reared, and entering the synagogue on the Sabbath as he was in the habit of doing, he stood up to do the reading and found the passage where it was written: 'The Spirit of the Lord is upon me;

therefore God has anointed me, sending me to bring glad tidings to the poor, to proclaim liberty to captives, recovery of sight to the blind and release to prisoners, to announce a year of favor from our God.' Rolling up the scroll he gave it back to the assistant and sat down. All in the synagogue had their eyes fixed on him. Then he began by saying to them, 'Today this scripture passage is fulfilled in your hearing'" (Lk 4:16-21).

In imitation of Jesus, women Religious seek to fulfill this passage to the extent that our very real limitations allow. In a world of expanding technology, in a world of unequal distribution of resources, in a world of increasing numbers of persons condemned to live in poverty, we open ourselves to the spirit of Jesus. We open ourselves to the power of the word of God. Let us unfurl the scroll again; let us contemplate the scroll and read therein the experience of women Religious of the United States.

—In an inner-city school in Chicago, Ill., a woman Religious works tirelessly developing the reading skills of third-graders. While teaching these children, she evokes abilities of critical thinking; she fosters human dignity; she represents the distinguished tradition of the women Religious of the United States, who built the Catholic school system, the pride of the Catholic Church in the United States.

—In southern Mississippi, in a cramped dingy space a woman Religious participates with women prisoners as they produce beautiful, multicolored quilts. Through her relationship with these women, she learns about vulnerability, oppression and redemption. Her mission is not only to bring the Gospel to these women but, more important, to learn the Gospel from them.

—In Los Angeles, Calif., a professionally prepared woman Religious administers a large Catholic hospital. Her ministry effectively facilitates the care of the sick, a ministry central to the service of women Religious throughout the world for hundreds of years, a ministry sorely in need of the ethical values brought to it by a woman Religious. Her service to the sick concretizes the essential value of human dignity.

—In rural Iowa, darkness surrounds a chapel where women Religious chant the office at 3:00 a.m.. This prayer, celebrated morning after morning, testifies to the presence of God in our world. It testifies to the power, beauty and transcendence of the contemplative life.

—In Minneapolis, Minn., a woman Religious cooperates with other health care personnel in developing programs for AIDS victims. In this ministry she reflects the Church's traditional concern for the most abandoned.

—In a small town in Idaho, a woman Religious, who is a pastoral administrator, works with a lay committee as together they plan a parish renewal program. Their common efforts are a realization of the imperative of the Vatican document "Lumen Gentium," which insisted that all Christians are called to "the fullness of Christian life and to the perfection of charity" (cf. Chapter 5).

—In Washington, D.C., a woman Religious testifies at a Senate hearing about legislation affecting the poor. In her well-researched and relentless efforts, she promotes the systemic change essential to enhancing human dignity.

—In a poor neighborhood in New Mexico, a woman Religious welcomes an abused woman into a shelter for battered women. Her ministry reaches out to those persons concretely affected by the impoverishment of women.

—In a classroom at a Catholic college in Boston, Mass., a woman Religious, a full professor of English, explores the interpretation of a Shakespearean play with a small group of

English majors. This woman Religious exemplifies the extraordinary leadership of religious congregations in the field of college/university education. Her ministry, like that of her predecessors, probes the deepest meaning of the human spirit in its quest for knowledge, truth and beauty.

—In a barrio in Recife, Brazil, a woman Religious from the United States reflects on the Gospel as a member of a base community. Her presence in Latin America symbolizes the ministry of U.S. missionary congregations throughout the world; the response of U.S. Catholics to Pope John XXIII's call to service in Latin America; the interdependence of all persons on this planet.

The ministries described here are merely illustrative of the complete picture of the ministries of women Religious in the United States. These ministries are exercised in a context of faith and in a context of lack of faith. They are exercised in a world thirsting for holiness, thirsting for God. These ministries, sustained and nourished by the prayer and suffering of retired sisters, are a priceless gift to the Church, the nation and the world.

We women who minister in these diverse ways are women who prize our identity as women of God and as women of the Church. We responded eagerly to the call for renewal issued by the Second Vatican Council when the council directed us to renew the life of our congregations in the light of the Gospel, the founding spirit and the signs of the times.

This renewal, as well as the universal call to holiness emphasized by the council, opened religious life to a rebirth of the spirit. This rebirth of the spirit is a continuing action, an action which invites us to ongoing, faithful, loving response. Through this response women Religious:

—Experience a revitalized prayer life based on the Gospel.

—Create a community life characterized by profound respect for persons.

—Develop different governmental structures which foster participation in decision making.

—Initiate new ministries addressing unmet needs.

—Expand our awareness of global relationships and responsibilities; and

—Work for peace and justice through systemic change.

In our work for peace and justice, we answer the plea of Pope Paul VI, who insisted "Religious must hear the cry of the poor, rising up more pressing than ever" ("Evangelica Testificatio," 17). In working for peace and justice, we reflect your own call, Pope John Paul II, that the Church consecrate herself to "the poor, the suffering, those without influence, resources and assistance" with a "love that is neither exclusive nor excluding, but rather preferential" (Letter to Bishops of Brazil, April 1986, No. 3).

Our response to the needs of the poor, as well as our response to the fundamental call of the Spirit for ongoing conversion, is characterized by struggle. We women Religious struggle with our own personal sinfulness, our tendency to selfishness, to isolation. We struggle with our congregational sinfulness, our preoccupation with internal issues at the expense of mission.

At the same time we recognize that our experience is a place where God speaks and where God reveals God's self. We desire for ourselves, and for all believing women, complete incorporation in the Church. In its critical decision-making responsibility, the Church needs the fullness of women's gifts and the strength of women's commitments.

Women, in the company of all God's people who experience the blessings of our Church, nation and world, also contend with sinfulness in our Church, nation and world.

Acknowledging the essential holiness of the Church, nevertheless we contend with the reality of sin in the Church when we encounter the inability to dialogue with an openness born of love. We contend with national sinfulness, materialism, militarism and the stockpiling of nuclear weapons, which threatens the very future of creation. We contend with international sinfulness, the disregard for the value and dignity of human life evidenced in widespread abuse of human rights, disinterest in the plight of the poor, the abuse of women, racism and abortion. We confront what is not of God in ourselves and in our congregation, in the nation, in the Church and in the world.

In the midst of this struggle we experience a profound sense of thanksgiving, thanksgiving for the loving kindness and fidelity of our God, who brings new life to our religious congregations; thanksgiving for the "greatest grace of our century, the Second Vatican Council" (1985 Synod of Bishops, Final Report, II, D, 7); thanksgiving for the leadership of the U.S. bishops in proclaiming the historic pastorals on peace and the economy; thanksgiving for this great country, the United States of America, for its blessings of freedom, of due process, of respect for individual rights; thanksgiving for your own great love for the poor and oppressed, Pope John Paul II, your challenge to give of our substance; thanksgiving for the prophets among us urging us to a deeper commitment to peace and justice; thanksgiving to the people of God, who share with us the mystery of the death and resurrection of Jesus; thanksgiving for the believers of other faiths who work with us for the advancement of human dignity everywhere. Ultimately, we experience a profound sense of thanksgiving for the spirit of God, whose love is poured out in our hearts through the Holy Spirit, who has been given to us.

The Spirit calls us to deeper communion, to the intimate communion of the people of God in Jesus Christ which is the Church. We yearn for this intimate communion within the Church and with all of our brothers and sisters on this planet. We yearn for the complete communion given us in Jesus. We yearn for this communion while experiencing divisions among us. These divisions reflect some of the critical questions of our time.

—How can the nations of the world develop a genuine global community of peace?

—How can the resources of the earth be put at the service of the entire human family?

—How can the full rich fabric of human life be reverenced and brought to plenitude?

—How can the wonders of science and technology be directed by the force of moral values?

—How can each person in the Church realize the fullness of baptismal grace?

—How can women participate completely in the life of the Church and in the life of society? How can their rich, generous, loving spirit influence the great issues of our time, the great mission of our Church?

These questions require genuine dialogue, the dialogue which Pope Paul VI eloquently described as clear, meek, trusting and prudent (cf. "Ecclesiam Suam," 83). Such a dialogue finds its source, its strength and its meaning in the word of God named Jesus, Jesus who announced his mission in Nazareth over 2,000 years ago. May his Spirit be present with us today, opening us to dialogue, to communion, to mission. May his Spirit be upon us bringing good tidings to the poor, proclaiming liberty, announcing the favor of God.

Father Stephen Tutas:

Introduction

In the name of the men Religious — 8,500 brothers and 22,000 priest Religious — I want to thank you for scheduling this time to speak to Religious in the United States as well as to the American Religious serving the Church in other lands.

In meeting with us, you also honor those who have gone before us. Religious women and men, most of them missionaries from Europe, were instrumental in founding the dioceses and parishes, seminaries and schools, colleges and hospitals, movements and ministries, which have developed so abundantly in the history of our country. And with new members from the United States, our religious communities were enabled not only to help build up the Church here, but also to reach out in service to the building up of God's reign around the world.

At this moment in our history as religious communities and as the Church in the United States, we find ourselves in the midst of a profound transition. In this transition many of us have found direction for our life and action in the words of Pope Paul VI who said that the work of the Second Vatican Council can be summed up in a single objective: *"to make the Church of the 20th century ever better fitted for proclaiming the Gospel to the people of the 20th century."* We are trying to realize this objective in our own religious communities and to cooperate with others in the building of a Church that calls forth the gifts entrusted to each and every member of the body of Christ.

As our participation in the living out of the theme of your visit, *"Unity in the Work of Service: Building up the Body of Christ,"* the men Religious selected "collaboration" as the theme for our 1987 national assembly, held last month in Duquesne. Collaboration with women Religious, the diocesan clergy and the laity has been intensified in recent years as a result of the ongoing dialogue between bishops and Religious in this country. The Pontifical Commission on Religious Life chaired by Archbishop John Quinn has helped us come to a better appreciation of the ecclesial dimension of our vocation. As a consequence of the better mutual relations between bishops and Religious in the United States, it is our hope that we can develop structures for even better collaboration in the future.

Our concern for collaboration is not limited to the local scene. By written communications and regular meetings, we have experienced an ever greater mutual understanding between ourselves and the Congregation for Religious and Secular Institutes. We are grateful for the efforts that the congregation is making to understand our hopes and concerns in giving us an opportunity to discuss an issue that affects us before a decision is made. It is important to us that the regular channels of communication are used, namely the unions of superiors general and the national conferences of Religious.

As Religious we are committed to the renewal of our own communities and to collaborating with others for the renewal of the Church.

Renewal of Our Communities

Within our own communities, our attempt to become ever better fitted for proclaiming the Gospel to the people of the 20th century is effecting a profound renewal. In examining our founding charisms in the light of the needs of the world today, we have formulated a new vision of religious life that finds expression in our revised constitutions and rules of life approved by the Holy See. But the process of renewing our

lives individually and as communities has just begun.

Our renewal as Religious begins with our appreciation of the value of religious life in itself. For that reason, your address to the plenaria of the Congregation for Religious and Secular Institutes on the role of the brother in the Church was especially encouraging for us men Religious. It is our conviction that the vocation of the brother expresses in a particularly evident way the authentic nature of religious life as such. And in our U.S. context, which highlights equality of rights, opportunities and duties for all, we believe that effective promotion of the vocation of the brother is best realized when brothers have the possibility of equal access to positions of governance. We believe that in a religious community all members, whether priest or lay, should be accorded participation in the internal life of each institute to the fullest extent compatible with its charism. Your words to the plenaria have helped to give full recognition to the brothers and have reminded the priest Religious of their specific identity as members of religious communities. Among the elements of renewal, one of the most challenging is the communitarian dimension of our lives. Those who feel called by God to religious life in the United States today invariably tell us about their hopes for community. In striving to renew our religious communities, we want to make them places where all love and are loved, where all strive to bring out the best in others, where we call forth the gifts God has given each of us, where we recognize Christ as the central person in our lives. And we want our communities to be open to the larger community around us so that we can participate effectively in the renewal of the Church open to the world.

Renewal of the Church

In our commitment to evangelization in the modern world, the agenda of the Church is our agenda as Religious. We want to collaborate with others in working for the radical transformation of the world according to the principles of the Gospel. We want to do our part to help make human life more fully human.

We are energized when you and the bishops of the Church in the United States call all Christians to be prophetic as you have done through your repeated insistence on the importance of evangelizing culture and as the American bishops have done in the pastoral letters *"The Challenge of Peace"* and *"Economic Justice for All."* As members of a democratic society in union with others who share the same ideals, we realize the great opportunity and responsibility we have to help fashion the economic and political structures of life in the United States of America.

While we feel called to oppose many currents in our culture, we also recognize values and gifts in American culture which we find especially rich for the Church today. We see the need to help build the church in the United States in a way that responds to the needs of the American people and in a style that is appropriate to our culture, which values equality, freedom, openness and participation in decision making that affects our lives. We esteem initiative and creativity, imagination and the pioneering spirit; we believe in dialogue, collaboration, participation and communication. Through prayerful reflection and community discussion, province assemblies and general chapters, we Religious try to discern what God is calling us to be and to do at this time in history. We believe that our best experience of community discernment is one of the gifts we can offer the local churches where we are engaged. We want to join with others in a common discernment to see how we can help make the church in the United States *ever better fitted for proclaiming the Gospel to the American people.*

As members of international communities, we are heartened by the developing global awareness in the church in the United States. We have close bonds with our fellow Religious in Canada and in Latin America. Through our missionaries we experience the vitality of the Church in other cultures. All of us have much to learn from each other.

Here in the United States we are excited about the developing role of the laity in the Church. Many of our communities have programs to support the laity in their response to the call of the Church in our time. We are confident that the coming synod will help us move forward toward a realization of the vision of Church stated in the Second Vatican Council documents, especially in terms of shared responsibility. Likewise, we are especially hopeful about recognizing the rightful role of women — Religious or lay, married or single — in the church in the United States.

Our experience is that the church in the United States is enriched by an atmosphere which enables everyone — bishops; diocesan clergy; Religious women and men; lay people, married and single — to participate fully in making the Church ever better fitted for proclaiming the Gospel to the American people.

Conclusion

In summary, as we Religious strive to help each other in this period of transition, listening together to the ways God speaks to us, we recognize our mission not only to renew our communities, but also to collaborate with others in the Church in responding to the call to profound change given us by the Second Vatican Council. Through our own experience of renewal, we see our mission as Religious to be messengers of hope in a time of transition.

In the months preceding this historic meeting with you, we have been united with you in thought and prayer in the hope that our time together here in San Francisco would mark a significantly new moment not only for ourselves as Religious, but also for the entire church in the United States.

Now in this solemn time of prayer and reflection with you, we know we are not alone. Many here in the United States and throughout the world are united with us in prayer for the success of this meeting. And we are confident this is a moment of great grace. For when men and women, open to the Spirit, are gathered together, great things happen. And when the community of faith is united in person with the vicar of Christ, the power of the Spirit is tangibly present. It is with this faith that we are gathered here this evening.

Pope John Paul II:

Dear sisters and brothers in Christ, dear Religious of the United States of America,

1. In their deepest spiritual significance, the Vespers that we are praying together are the voice of the bride addressing the bridegroom (cf. "Sacrosanctum Concilium," 84). They are also the voice of the bridegroom, "the very prayer which Christ himself, together with his body, addresses to the Father" (ibid.). With one and the same voice the bride and the bridegroom praise the Father in the unity of the Holy Spirit.

In this liturgical song of praise we give expression to "the real nature of the true Church" — "both human and divine, visible and yet invisibly endowed, eager to act and yet devoted

to contemplation, present in the world and yet not at home in it" (ibid., 2). It is precisely the presence of God in human life and human affairs that you proclaim through your religious consecration and the practice of the evangelical counsels. It is to the reality of God's love in the world that you bear witness by means of the many forms of your loving service to God's people.

2. Dear religious sisters and religious priests and brothers: For me, this is one of the most important moments of my visit. Here, with all of you, men and women Religious of the United States, and in the spiritual presence of all the members of your congregations spread throughout this land or serving in other countries, I give heartfelt thanks to God for each and every one of you. He who is mighty has done great things for you, holy is his name! (cf. Lk 1:49).

I greet each one of you with love and gratitude. I thank you for the warm welcome you have given me, and I thank Sister Helen Garvey and Father Stephen Tutas, who have presented a picture of your dedicated lives. I rejoice because of your deep love of the Church and your generous service to God's people. Every place I have visited in this vast country bears the marks of the diligent labor and immense spiritual energies of Religious of both contemplative and active congregations in the Church. The extensive Catholic educational and health care systems, the highly developed network of social services in the Church — none of this would exist today were it not for your highly motivated dedication and the dedication of those who have gone before you. The spiritual vigor of so many Catholic people testifies to the efforts of generations of Religious in this land. The history of the church in this country is in large measure your history at the service of God's people.

As we remember your glorious past, let us be filled with hope that your future will be no less beneficial for the church in the United States and no less a prophetic witness of God's kingdom to each new generation of Americans.

3. The single most extraordinary event that has affected the Church in every aspect of her life and mission during the second half of the 20th century has been the Second Vatican Council. The council called the whole Church to conversion, to "newness of life," to renewal — to a renewal that consists essentially in an ever increasing fidelity to Jesus Christ, her divine founder. As "men and women who more closely follow and more clearly demonstrate the Savior's self-giving" ("Lumen Gentium," 42), it is only natural that Religious should have experienced the call to renewal in a radical way. Thousands of Religious in the United States have generously responded to this call and continue to live it with profound commitment. The results, the good fruits of this response, are evident in the Church: We see a Gospel-inspired spirituality, which has led to a deepening of personal and liturgical prayer; a clearer sense of the Church as a communion of faith and love in which the grace and responsibility entrusted to each member are to be respected and encouraged; a new appreciation of the legacy of your founders and foundresses so that the specific charism of each congregation stands out more clearly; a heightened awareness of the urgent needs of the modern world where Religious, in close union with the bishops and in close collaboration with the whole Church, seek to carry on the work of the good Shepherd, the good Samaritan and the good Teacher.

It would be unrealistic to think that such a deep and overall process of renewal could take place without risks and errors, without undue impatience on the part of some and undue fears on the part of others. Whatever the tension and polarization occasioned by change, whatever the mistakes made in the past, I am sure that all of you are convinced that the time has come to reach out once again to one another in a spirit of love and reconciliation, both within and beyond your congregations.

During the past two decades there have also been profound insights into the meaning and value of religious life. Many of these insights, conceived in the experience of prayer and penance and authenticated by the teaching charism of the Church, have contributed greatly to ecclesial life. These insights have borne witness to the enduring identity of religious consecration and mission in the life of the Church. At the same time they have testified to the need for Religious to adapt their activity to the needs of the people of our times.

4. Fundamental to the council's teaching on religious life is an emphasis on the ecclesial nature of the vocation to observe the evangelical counsels. Religious consecration "belongs inseparably to the life and holiness of the Church" ("Lumen Gentium," 44). "The counsels are a divine gift, which the Church has received from her Lord and which she ever preserves with the help of his grace" (ibid., 43). It was precisely within this ecclesial context that in 1983 I asked the bishops of the United States to render a pastoral service by offering to those of you whose institutes are engaged in apostolic works special encouragement and support in living your ecclesial vocation to the full. I now wish to thank the bishops and all of you for your very generous collaboration in this important endeavor. In particular I thank the pontifical commission headed by Archbishop John Quinn. By God's grace there now exists a fresh cooperative spirit between your religious institutes and the local churches.

Your continuing participation in the mission of the Church at the diocesan and parish levels is of inestimable value to the well-being of the local churches. Your communion with the local bishops and collaboration with the pastoral ministry of the diocesan clergy contributes to a strong and effective spiritual growth among the faithful. Your creative initiatives in favor of the poor and all marginalized persons and groups, whose needs might otherwise be neglected, are deeply appreciated. Your evangelizing and missionary work both at home and in other parts of the world is one of the great strengths of the church in the United States. Alongside your traditional apostolates — which are as important now as ever before and which I encourage you to appreciate in their full significance — you are engaged in almost every area of defending human rights and of building a more just and equitable society. This is a record of unselfish response to the Gospel of Jesus Christ. Yes, the entire church in the United States benefits from the dedication of American Religious to their ecclesial mission.

5. At the same time you are concerned about certain weaknesses affecting the structure of your institutes. The decline in vocations and the aging of your membership are serious challenges for each one of your institutes and for the corporate reality of religious life, and yet these are not new phenomena in the long experience of the Church. History teaches us that in ways generally unpredictable the radical "newness" of the Gospel message is always able to inspire successive generations to do what you have done, to renounce all for the sake of the kingdom of God, in order to possess the pearl of great price (cf. Mt 13:44-45).

You are called at this hour to fresh courage and trust. Your joyful witness to consecrated love — in chastity, poverty and obedience — will be the greatest human attraction for young people to religious life in the future. When they sense the authenticity of renewal in you and your communities, they too will be disposed to come and see! The invitation is directly from Christ, but they will want to hear it from you too. Your own essential contribution to vocations will come through fidelity, penance and prayer, and through confidence in the power of Christ's paschal mystery to make all things new.

In the best traditions of Christian love, you will know how to show your special appreciation for the aged and infirm members of your communities, whose contribution of prayer and penance, suffering and faithful love is of immense value to your apostolates. May they always be comforted in knowing that they are respected and loved within their own religious families.

6. Your vocation is of its very nature a radical response to the call which Jesus extends to all believers in their baptismal consecration: "Seek first his kingship over you, his way of holiness" (Mt 6:33). Your response is expressed by your vowed commitment to embrace and live in community the evangelical counsels. Through chastity, poverty and obedience you live in expectation of an eschatological kingdom where "they neither marry nor are given in marriage" (Mt 22:30). And so, even now, "where your treasure is there your heart is also" (Mt 6:21).

Through your religious profession, the consecration which the Holy Spirit worked in you at baptism is powerfully directed anew to the perfection of charity. By practicing the vows, you constantly die with Christ in order to rise to new life with him (cf. Rom 6:8). In fidelity to your vow of chastity, you are empowered to love with the love of Christ and to know that deep encounter with his love which inspires and sustains your apostolic love for your neighbor. Treading the path of poverty, you find yourselves truly open to God and aligned with the poor and suffering, in whom you see the image of the poor and suffering Christ (cf. Mt 25:31ff). And through obedience, you are intimately united with Jesus in seeking always to fulfill the Father's will. Through such obedience there is unlocked in you the full measure of Christian freedom which enables you to serve God's people with selfless and unfailing devotion. The Catholic people, and indeed the vast majority of your fellow citizens, have the highest respect for your religious consecration, and they look to you for the "proof" of the transcendent Christian hope that is in you (cf. 1 Pt 3:15).

7. The disciple, though, is not above the Master. It is only right for you to expect, as has always been the Church's understanding, that if you follow the laws of Christ's kingdom — in essence, the new commandment of love and the new values proclaimed in the Beatitudes — you will be in conflict with the "wisdom of this age" (cf. 1 Cor 2:6). In a particularly personal and courageous way, Religious have always been in the front line of this never-ending struggle.

Today the encounter between the saving message of the Gospel and the forces that shape our human culture calls for a profound and prayerful discernment of Christ's will for his Church at this moment of her life. In this regard the Second Vatican Council remains the necessary point of reference and the guiding light. This discernment is the work of the whole Church. No person or group of people can claim to possess sufficient insights so as to monopolize it. All members of the Church, according to the ministry received for the good of the whole body, must be humbly attuned to the Holy Spirit, who guides the Church into the fullness of truth (cf. Jn 16:13; "Lumen Gentium," 4), and produces in her the fruits of his action, which St. Paul lists as "love, joy, peace, patient endurance, kindness, generosity, faith, mildness and chastity" (Gal 5:22-23). And since the Holy Spirit has placed in the

Church the special pastoral charism of the magisterium, we know that adherence to the magisterium is an indispensable condition for a correct reading of "the signs of the times" and hence a condition for the supernatural fruitfulness of all ministries in the Church.

You indeed have an important role in the Church's dialogue with the complex and varied cultural environment of the United States. The first law of this dialogue is fidelity to Christ and to his Church. And in this fundamental act of faith and trust you already show the world the basis of your special position within the community of God's people. Also required for this dialogue is a true understanding of the values involved in America's historical experience. At the same time the Christian concepts of the common good, of virtue and conscience, of liberty and justice, must be distinguished from what is sometimes inadequately presented as the expression of these realities. As Religious, you are especially sensitive to the implications of this dialogue with the world in which you are called to live and work. As men and women consecrated to God, you are aware of having a special responsibility to be a sign — an authentic prophetic sign — that will speak to the Church and to the world, not in terms of easy condemnation, but humbly showing forth the power of God's word to heal and uplift, to unite and bind with love.

At this important moment of the history of the human family it is essential for the Church to proclaim the full truth about God — Father, Son and Holy Spirit — and the full truth about our human condition and destiny as revealed in Christ and authentically transmitted through the teaching of the Church. The faithful have the right to receive the true teaching of the Church in its purity and integrity, with all its demands and power. When people are looking for a sure point of reference for their own values and their ethical choices, they turn to the special witnesses of the Church's holiness and justice — to you Religious. They expect and want to be convinced by the example of your acceptance of God's word.

8. Dear sisters and brothers: The life we now live is not our own; Christ is living in us. We still live our human life, but it is a life of faith in the Son of God, who loved us and gave himself for us (cf. Gal 2:20). In these words St. Paul sums up the core of our Christian experience and even more so the heart of religious life. The validity and fruitfulness of religious life depend upon union with Jesus Christ.

Union with Christ demands a true interior life of prayer, a life of closeness to him. At the same time it enables you to be effective witnesses before the world of the healing and liberating power of the paschal mystery. It means that above all in your own lives and in your own communities the paschal mystery is first being celebrated and experienced through the Eucharist and the sacrament of penance. In this way your works of charity and justice, of mercy and compassion will be true signs of Christ's presence in the world.

9. The challenges which you faced yesterday you will face again tomorrow. The thousand tasks that now draw upon your courage and your energies will hardly disappear next week, next month, next year. What then is the meaning of our meeting? What "word of the Lord" is addressed to us here? As the one who for the time being has been given the place of the fisherman from Galilee, as the one who occupies the Chair of Peter for this fleeting hour in the Church's life, allow me to make my own the sentiments of the reading from our Evening Prayer: "Be examples to the flock" (1 Pt 5:3) — examples of faith and charity, of hope and joy, of obedience, sacrifice and humble service. And "when the Chief Shepherd appears, you will win for yourselves the unfading crown of glory" (v. 4).

To the contemplative Religious of the United States, whose lives are hidden with Christ in God, I wish to say a word of profound thanks for reminding us that "here we have no lasting city" (Heb 13:14), and that all life must be lived in the heart of the living God. May the whole Church in this land recognize the primacy and efficacy of the spiritual values which you represent. The Second Vatican Council deliberately chose to call you "the glory of the Church" ("Perfectae Caritatis," 7).

Brothers and sisters, men and women Religious of the United States: Your country needs the witness of your deep spirituality and your commitment to the life-giving power of the Gospel. America needs to see all the power of love in your hearts expressed in evangelizing zeal. The whole world needs to discover in you "the kindness and love of God our Savior" (Ti 3:4). Go forward, therefore, in the mystery of the dying and rising of Jesus. Go forward in faith, hope and charity, expending yourselves in the Church's mission of evangelization and service. Always be examples to the flock. And know that "when the Chief Shepherd appears, you will win for yourselves the unfading crown of glory" (1 Pt 5:4).

In this Marian year of grace may you find joy and strength in an ever greater devotion to Mary, the Virgin Mother of the Redeemer. As "the model and protectress of all consecrated life" (Canon 663.4), may she lead each one of you to perfect union with her Son, our Lord Jesus Christ, and to ever closer collaboration in his redemptive mission. And may the example of Mary's discipleship confirm you all in generosity and love.

Meeting with Laity
San Francisco, Sept. 18

Mrs. Donna Hanson:

We, the American Catholic laity, 98 percent of the Catholic church in the United States, welcome you to our land of rich diversity. I speak to you this morning from my own perspective: woman, wife, mother of two sons, social minister in Catholic Charities and volunteer chairperson of the National Advisory Council of the National Conference of Catholic Bishops. In preparation for today I have spent much time in consultation with my lay sisters and brothers. They were pleased to be asked their opinions; it is now my hope to give voice to their dreams and desires.

The microcosm of Church represented here today gives you some perspective of my difficult challenge. In this assembly of 3,000 are people from virtually every profession, culture and ethnic diversity in the United States. To this assembly we bring differing political perspectives and varied experiences of Church. We are young and old, rich and poor; we are unique yet unified in our love of Christ and his Church. Although our loyalty to the Church is deep, we are committed to call her to even deeper gospel faithfulness. Unity, not division, is our goal; service, not power, is our mission.

The native Americans, the original inhabitants of our land, provide me with a central theme for today. Their wise counsel is, "Never judge another's life until you have walked in their shoes for a day." It is my hope that today we may walk together.

On our journey I would like to tell you about our unique American culture. I would like for you to know how our experience and tradition have helped to form us in our faith and continue to impact us in our families and in our parishes.

Your Holiness, the U.S. Declaration of Independence expresses the country's founding belief that all men, women and children are created equal. The reason that my great-grandparents immigrated to this country was to escape the famine in Ireland and persecution in Germany. Yet as I grew up in the southern United States, I watched my father and his compatriots build a church so that the black Catholics in our community could have a separate place of worship. In 1960 I saw billboards that proclaimed: "Why Bible-reading Christians could not in conscience vote for John F. Kennedy for president."

From these early life experiences I, like so many others, learned to question immigration practices, civil injustices, religious persecution. Today my culture compels me to continue questioning those in leadership positions. I question them about public policies related to abortion, development of nuclear arms, the exploitation of our environment. Not to question, not to challenge, not to seek understanding is to be less than a mature, educated and committed citizen.

When I come to my Church, I cannot discard my cultural experiences. Though I know the Church is not a democracy ruled by popular vote, I expect to be treated as a mature, educated and responsible adult. Not to question, not to challenge, not to have authorities involve me in a process of understanding is to deny my dignity as a person and the rights granted to me both by Church and society.

Your Holiness, within my circle of friends there are those who are ranchers and those who are city dwellers, those who are politically conservative and avant-garde liberals, some who are traditional and some who are progressive Catholics. I rejoice that within my culture there is room for this incredible diversity. The challenge before the church in the United States is to be welcoming of these same diversities. Can we be as inclusive as Christ, who reached out to the woman at the well, who invited a tax collector to be his apostle, who brought the centurion's daughter back to life? Can we reach out and be more inclusive of women, our inactive clergy, homosexuals, the divorced and all people of color?

Your Holiness, the diversity in our culture is mirrored in our families. We are traditional families, extended families, single parents, widowed and divorced. In our families we often struggle with the tensions between gospel values and the excesses of our society. For many newly formed families there is the challenge of being a loving spouse while at the same time making responsible decisions about parenthood. In our young families we often juggle the demands of homemaking with the need for employment. In our growing families there is the challenge of helping our young adult children understand their sexuality as well as appreciate the dangers of drugs and alcohol. In our maturing families there is the balance of nurturing our grandchildren while caring for our frail, elderly parents.

Your Holiness, in our parish communities we are also experiencing significant change. The lay members of our Church are now among the best educated and the most highly theologically trained in the world. Yet we hunger for spiritual education and formation. We long for structures in which to truly share responsibility. As the pastors in our immigrant churches worked alongside us to build labor unions and the most comprehensive Catholic school network in the world, we were building both Church and society from the bottom up.

Today our parishes are in transition. Many parishes do not have a resident pastor. Eucharistic celebrations are limited, and our people cannot regularly receive the sacrament of reconciliation. Lay ministers are involved as never before, but full acceptance by both clergy and the people of God has not been fully realized.

At the same time, in other parishes the pastors, deacons, men and women Religious, and professional and volunteer lay ministers work side by side. They experience the needs of the people, and together they respond: with housing for the elderly, with shelters for the homeless, with immigration counseling for the undocumented. They reach out in love: in peer ministry to the engaged, married, widowed, divorced. They reach out in hope: in bringing the eucharistic Christ to the homebound. They reach out in faith: in study and reflection on the word of God. They create small communities of faith; they take Christ into the marketplace; they are the Church in the world.

But how does all of this come together for those of us here today? I began by suggesting a walk. My request now is that you permit me to walk with you.

Let me walk with you so that I can understand the challenge of being Peter's successor. Let me share the burdens you carry as you reflect on the pain of your people: persecution in your beloved Poland, starvation in Ethiopia, consumerism in the United States.

Let me walk with you as you seek to preserve orthodox teachings and challenge the world with gospel values. Let me also be at your side as you plead for peace on every continent.

Let me walk with you as you prepare for the synod on the laity. I know that we in the United States are not representative of the majority of people in the world. At the same time, I know that our concerns are universal: family; spirituality; and collaboration.

Your Holiness, please let me know that you are also willing to walk with me. Accustomed as I am to dialogue, consultation and collaboration, I do not always feel that I am heard. In my cultural experience, questioning is neither rebellion nor dissent. Rather, it is a desire to participate and is a sign of both love and maturity.

Walk with me. My family experiences continually remind me that examples speak louder than words. To become the family of God it is imperative that both we parents and the Church witness the Gospel we preach. Above all, we must be just, compassionate and forgiving.

Your Holiness, please walk with each one of us. Like you, we gladly give our lives in service to the Church. Like you, we seek forgiveness seventy times seven. Yet we know that we are a pilgrim people, that we are individually gifted and that the Holy Spirit speaks uniquely to each one of us. We are all children of God: May we continue to walk and talk together?

Dr. Patrick S. Hughes:

Your Holiness, I speak to you as a lay person who shares the vision, commitment and competence that are characteristic of so many American lay Catholics today. As a professional who works for the church of the Archdiocese of San Francisco, I also represent the tens of thousands of men and women who have dedicated their lives to serve the people of God throughout the United States as professional lay ministers.

Lay Professionals Increasing

Our numbers are increasing. In the Archdiocese of San Francisco, for example, two of the four members of the archbishop's immediate staff are lay persons. Half of our archdiocesan agencies are headed by lay persons, and two-thirds of our departments and divisions have lay persons in the top administrative positions. Statistics from our parishes, schools and other institutions mirror the same reality. The Archdiocese of San Francisco is a microcosm of what is happening in the United States and the world. Because of their commitment to the Gospel and the discernment of their own vocation, more lay people are working within ecclesial structures. Their ministry contributes tremendous time, energy and talent to the Church. The entire Church benefits greatly because of this contribution.

Identity of Lay Professionals

This increase of lay professionals in ecclesial settings often causes some misunderstanding of who we are. There are those who too readily divide life and ministry into two distinct realities: "the world" for lay people and "the Church" for priests and vowed Religious. Because our work does not readily fit into these categories, we are at times perceived with some ambiguity. This lack of clarity is in many ways a result of the present transitional state of our Church. Sometimes, too, we must clarify our own identities. Often the first ones hired for a new ministry, we must create job descriptions which have no precedent. If we are the first lay person to occupy a role traditionally held by a priest or vowed Religious, we struggle with the communities we serve to find new understandings and expectations for that role. Enthusiastic about our work, we often find ourselves striving to balance our commitments to both our families and our ministries.

Our certainty of vocation, however, comes from the personal discernment of our baptismal call and of our particular gifts. The declining numbers of priests and members of religious communities are not the cause of our response to the Church's needs. For many of us the Second Vatican Council was a significant personal turning point. We began to see ourselves as active adult participants in the life of the Church. This new awareness came to some of us through an adult conversion experience. For many of us this new consciousness of ourselves as Church came as a gradual awakening to the reality of our being called and being sent.[1] However it occurred, as a result of that "rebirth of Christ," [2] we wanted to give our lives more explicitly to serve within the Church.

Our Solidarity with All People

We firmly believe that the joy and hope, the grief and anguish of all people, "especially of those who are poor or afflicted in any way," [3] are ours as well. Our ministries bring us a great deal of personal satisfaction. We experience the joy promised by Christ to all who identify themselves with their brothers and sisters. We are grateful for the opportunities to serve and to respond, to be present with others on their sacred journeys through time.

Special Concerns

Now Your Holiness, however, we wish to address five areas of special concern. While these concerns are related specifically to lay professionals, they are shared by many others with whom we collaborate in ministry as well as by many lay people in the Church.

Vocational Awareness

Our first area of concern is in regard to vocational aware-ness. More laity are becoming aware, as you have said, that their Christian vocation corresponds to the evangelical call.[4] In many ways the responsibility for deciding how to live out our baptismal commitment is personal. It is rooted in our individual lives of prayer and our participation in the sacramental life of the Church. This discernment is aided by our prayerful dialogue with others, ordained and lay.

Lay persons working with the Church and those considering this vocational option need the help of the Church.

We would benefit greatly if more dioceses would provide educational and employment information for lay people. It is important that diocesan vocation offices promote the universal call to ministry, including the call to full-time lay ministry as a vocation and value to the Church. It is important that we publicly and ceremonially celebrate the ministry provided by lay persons. The ongoing spiritual life of lay ministers must also be respected and supported. Let us witness the unity of service we proclaim.

Ministerial Formation

A second area of concern has to do with the ministerial formation of lay people. There are now over 200 programs in 120 dioceses which prepare laity for Church ministry.[5] The laity in these programs bring a new perspective to the study of theology and the vital work of ministry. We believe that these formation programs must take seriously the diversity of lay experiences. Lay persons need to be involved in the formation, administration and evaluation of these programs. We also believe that greater cooperative efforts in the formation of Church professionals — clerical, religious and lay — would have advantages for all.

Theological and ministerial formation transforms those involved in it and is a source of the ongoing transformation of both the Church and society. The Church's mission demands that formation be available for all members. Financial assistance should be provided by the Church to those laity who are unable to participate because of cost.[6]

Women in Ministry

A third area of concern has to do specifically with women in ministry. We acknowledge the great diversity of opinions among women themselves regarding their participation in Church life. We also acknowledge that there has been some progress in the Church as more women have moved into significant ministerial positions. Still, "sexism" remains a major issue among those who work for the Church.[7] "We believe that sexism must be rejected because it is sinful, as stated in several recent world synods. Furthermore, promotion of the role of women in the Church is not simply for the sake of women. The Church needs the feminine dimension if it is to bring the full power of God's creative energy to bear on the needs of our world."

Bishop James Malone stated his own concern when he addressed his fellow bishops last November: "Increasingly voices are raised insisting that more needs to be done to effect this equality (of women).... The years given to remedy it are not limitless." [8] We agree.

Personnel Issues

As lay professionals, we are also concerned about personnel issues associated with our work. We believe that our work helps us achieve fulfillment as human beings and that, as you have said, it "constitutes a foundation for the formation of family life." [9] Many of us serve the Church with lower salaries than we would enjoy if we were employed at commensurate positions within other institutions. This is not a statement of complaint, but a simple recognition of our special commitment to serve the Church in an explicit way. We hope, however, that the Church will continue to commit itself to the establishment of equal and just salaries for men and women in Church jobs. Established procedures of accountability for hiring, promotion or firing, as well as clear grievance procedures and methods of due process,[10] need to continue to be developed.

Availability of the Eucharist

Finally, we too are concerned about the declining numbers of the ordained. As laity, we cannot overlook the closing of parishes and the declining availability of full participation in the Eucharist, the heart of our Christian faith and community. Again, as Bishop Malone cautioned us: "If trends continue, by the year 2000 we will have half the number of active priests serving the Church in this country."[11] We are concerned not only about this decrease, but also about its effects upon the ordained, many of whom are already confronted with unrealistic role expectations. We affirm the dignity and worth of all ministries and encourage the ongoing discernment of what is the nature of ordained ministry and who should be called to it. We are convinced that ordained ministry is intimately related to the ministries of all, and when one form of ministry is impoverished, all suffer.

Commitment to Collaboration

In the name of the thousands of lay professionals who are working within the Church, I want to thank you, Your Holiness, for listening to these concerns. While we are a new phenomenon in the Church, we also believe that we are heirs before we are pioneers. We bring not only competence and enthusiasm to our ministries, but also a commitment to collaboration: to cooperate in whatever ways we can for the building up of the kingdom of God. We affirm the lay vocation and the growth of lay ministries wherever they may occur for they truly are a sign of hope in today's Church.

Thank you.

Footnotes

[1] See Edward C. Sellner, "Discernment of Vocation for Pastoral Ministry," Spirituality Today, Spring 1985: 47-58. Emilie Griffin, "Turning: Reflections on the Experience of Conversion" (Garden City, N.Y.: Doubleday 1980), describes a pattern in many people's experience of adult conversion.

[2] Dogmatic Constitution on the Church, 32.

[3] Pastoral Constitution on the Church in the Modern World, 1.

[4] See John Paul II, "To the Youth of the World," (Washington: U.S. Catholic Conference 1985), pp. 32-33.

[5] See Suzanne Elsesser and Rev. Eugene Hemrick, "Preparing Laity for Ministry: A Report on Programs in Catholic Dioceses Throughout the United States," unpublished paper, 1986, which explains and explores the data from Elsesser, ed., "Preparing Laity for Ministry: A Directory of Programs in Catholic Dioceses throughout the United States" (Washington: USCC 1986). The data is a result of a recent survey developed by the National Conference of Catholic Bishops Committee on the Laity in conjunction with the National Association for Lay Ministry. The programs in this study do not include the thousands of lay women and men presently enrolled in Stephen Ministries, Befrienders and other forms of volunteer ministry formation.

[6] See especially "Ministries," Segundo Encuentro Pastoral (Washington: NCCB Committee on Evangelization) pp. 357-59.

[7] See Marian Schwab, "Career Lay Ministers: Who Are They and What Do They Care About?" unpublished paper summarizing research conducted by the National Association for Lay Ministry on the concerns of lay professionals in the United States.

[8] Bishop James Malone, "Presidential Address to the General Meeting of the NCCB-USCC," Nov. 10, 1986, p. 5.

[9] Pope John Paul II, "On Human Work" (Washington: USCC 1981), pp. 20ff.

[10] See National Association of Church Personnel Administrators, "Just Treatment for Those Who Work for the Church" (Cincinnati: NACPA National Office 1986), for recommendations regarding personnel issues.

[11] Bishop Malone, pp. 5-6.

Pope John Paul II:

"To him whose power now at work in us can do immeasurably more than we ask or imagine — to him be glory in the Church and in Christ Jesus through all generations" (Eph 3:20-21).

Dear brothers and sisters, dear Catholic lay people of America,

1. I am grateful to you for your kind welcome and pleased to be with you this morning in glorifying the Father, "in the Church and in Christ Jesus," through the working of the Holy Spirit. I also wish to thank you for the informative presentations which have been made in the name of the Catholic laity of the United States.

The reading from the Letter of St. Paul to the Ephesians which we heard a few moments ago has a deep meaning for the life of each one of us. The text movingly describes our relationship with God as he reveals himself to us in the mystery of the Most Holy Trinity. St. Paul reminds us of two fundamental truths: first, that our ultimate vocation is to glorify the God who created and redeemed us; and second, that our eternal and highest good is to "attain to the fullness of God himself" — to participate in the loving communion of the Father and the Son and the Holy Spirit for all eternity. God's glory and our good are perfectly attained in the kingdom of heaven.

The apostle Paul also reminds us that salvation, which comes as a free gift of divine love in Christ, is not offered to us on a purely individual basis. It comes to us through and in the Church. Through our communion with Christ and with one another on earth, we are given a foretaste of that perfect communion reserved for heaven. Our communion is also meant to be a sign or sacrament which draws other people to Christ, so that all might be saved.

This gift of the redemption, which originates with the Father and is accomplished by the Son, is brought to fruition in our individual lives and in the life of the world by the Holy Spirit. Thus we speak of the gifts of the Spirit at work within the Church — gifts which include the hierarchical office of shepherding the flock and gifts given to the laity so that they may live the Gospel and make their specific contribution to the Church's mission.

The council tells us that "everyone in the Church does not proceed by the same path, nevertheless all are called to sanctity and have received an equal privilege of faith through the justice of God (cf. 2 Pt 1:1). And if by the will of Christ some are made teachers, dispensers of mysteries and shepherds on behalf of others, yet all share a true equality with regard to the dignity and activity common to all the faithful for the building up of the body of Christ" ("Lumen Gentium," 32). Through a great diversity of graces and works, the children of God bear witness to that wonderful unity which is the work of one and the same Spirit.

2. Dear brothers and sisters: It is in the context of these

mysteries of faith that I wish to reflect with you on your role as laity in the Church today. What is most fundamental in your lives is that by your baptism and confirmation you have been commissioned by our Lord Jesus Christ himself to share in the saving mission of his Church (cf. "Lumen Gentium," 33). To speak of the laity is to speak of hundreds of millions of people like yourselves of every race, nation and walk of life who each day seek, with the help of God, to live a good Christian life. To speak of the laity is to speak of the many of you who draw from your parish the strength and inspiration to live your vocation in the world. It is to speak also of those of you who have become part of national and international ecclesial associations and movements that support you in your vocation and mission.

Your struggles and temptations may differ according to your various situations, but all of you cherish the same basic hope to be faithful to Christ and to put his message into practice. You all cherish the same basic hope for a decent life for yourselves and an even better life for your children. All of you must toil and work and bear the sufferings and disappointments common to humanity, but as believers you are endowed with faith, hope and charity. And often your charity reaches heroic dimensions within your families or among your neighbors and co-workers. To the extent that your resources and duties in life permit, you are called to support and actively to participate in Church activities.

It is within the everyday world that you the laity must bear witness to God's kingdom; through you the Church's mission is fulfilled by the power of the Holy Spirit. The council taught that the specific task of the laity is precisely this: to "seek the kingdom of God by engaging in temporal affairs and by ordering them according to the plan of God" ("Lumen Gentium," 31). You are called to live in the world, to engage in secular professions and occupations, to live in those ordinary circumstances of family life and life in society from which is woven the very web of your existence. You are called by God himself to exercise your proper functions according to the spirit of the Gospel and to work for the sanctification of the world from within, in the manner of leaven. In this way you can make Christ known to others, especially by the witness of your lives. It is for you as lay people to direct all temporal affairs to the praise of the Creator and Redeemer (cf. ibid.).

The temporal order of which the council speaks is vast. It encompasses the social, cultural, intellectual, political and economic life in which all of you rightly participate. As lay men and women actively engaged in this temporal order, you are being called by Christ to sanctify the world and to transform it. This is true of all work, however exalted or humble, but it is especially urgent for those whom circumstances and special talent have placed in positions of leadership or influence: men and women in public service, education, business, science, social communications and the arts. As Catholic lay people you have an important moral and cultural contribution of service to make to the life of your country. "Much will be required of the person entrusted with much" (Lk 12:48). These words of Christ apply not only to the sharing of material wealth or personal talents, but also to the sharing of one's faith.

3. Of supreme importance in the mission of the Church is the role that the laity fulfill in the Christian family. This role is above all a service of love and a service of life.

The love of husband and wife, which is blessed and sealed in the sacrament of marriage, constitutes the first way that couples exercise their mission. They serve by being true to themselves, to their vocation of married love. This love, which embraces all the members of the family, is aimed at forming a community of persons united in heart and soul, an indissoluble communion where the love of spouses for each other is a sign of Christ's love for the Church.

The service of life rests on the fact that husband and wife cooperate with God in transmitting the gift of human life in the procreation of children. In this most sacred responsibility, the service of life is intimately united to the service of love in the one conjugal act, which must always be open to bringing forth new life. In his encyclical "Humanae Vitae," Pope Paul VI explained that in the task of transmitting life, husband and wife are called to "conform their activity to the creative intention of God, expressed in the very nature of marriage and of its acts, and manifested by the constant teaching of the Church" (No. 10).

While "love and life constitute the nucleus of the saving mission of the Christian family in the Church and for the Church" ("Familiaris Consortio," 50), the family also performs a service of education, particularly within the home, where the parents have the original and primary role of educating their children. The family is likewise an evangelizing community where the Gospel is received and put into practice, where prayer is learned and shared, where all the members, by word and deed and by the love they have for one another, bear witness to the good news of salvation.

At the same time we must recognize the difficult situation of so many people with regard to family living. There are many with special burdens of one kind or another. There are the single-parent families and those who have no natural family; there are the elderly and the widowed. And there are those separated and divorced Catholics who, despite their loneliness and pain, are striving to preserve their fidelity and to face their responsibilities with loving generosity. All of these people share deeply in the Church's mission by faith, hope and charity, and by all their many efforts to be faithful to God's will. The Church assures them not only of her prayers and spiritual nourishment, but also of her love, pastoral concern and practical help.

Although, in fidelity to Christ and to his teaching on Christian marriage, the Church reaffirms her practice of not admitting to eucharistic Communion those divorced persons who have remarried outside the Church, nevertheless, she assures these Catholics too of her deep love. She prays for them and encourages them to persevere in prayer, to listen to the word of God and to attend the eucharistic sacrifice, hoping that they will "undertake a way of life that is no longer in contradiction to the indissolubility of marriage" ("Familiaris Consortio," 84). At the same time the Church remains their mother, and they are part of her life.

4. I wish to express the deep gratitude of the Church for all the contributions made by women over the centuries to the life of the Church and of society. In speaking of the role of women, special mention must of course be made of their contribution, in partnership with their husbands, in begetting life and in educating their children. "The true advancement of women requires that clear recognition be given to the value of their maternal and family role, by comparison with all other public roles and all other professions" ("Familiaris Consortio," 23). The Church is convinced, however, that all the special gifts of women are needed in an ever-increasing measure in her life, and for this reason hopes for their fuller participation in her activities. Precisely because of their equal dignity and responsibility, the access of women to public functions must be ensured. Regardless of the role they perform, the Church proclaims the dignity of women as women — a dignity equal to men's dignity and revealed as such in the account of creation contained in the word of God.

5. The renewal of the Church since the council has also been an occasion for increasing lay participation in all areas of ecclesial life. More and more, people are joining with their pastors in collaboration and consultation for the good of their diocese and parish. An increasing number of lay men and women are devoting their professional skills on a full-time basis to the Church's efforts in education, social services and other areas, or to the exercise of administrative responsibilities. Still others build up the body of Christ by direct collaboration with the Church's pastoral ministry, especially in bringing Christ's love to those in the parish or community who have special needs. I rejoice with you at this great flowering of gifts in the service of the Church's mission.

At the same time we must ensure both in theory and in practice that these positive developments are always rooted in the sound Catholic ecclesiology taught by the council. Otherwise we run the risk of "clericalizing" the laity or "laicizing" the clergy, and thus robbing both the clerical and lay states of their specific meaning and their complementarity. Both are indispensable to the "perfection of love," which is the common goal of all the faithful. We must therefore recognize and respect in these states of life a diversity that builds up the body of Christ in unity.

6. As lay men and women you can fulfill this great mission authentically and effectively only to the extent that you hold fast to your faith in communion with the body of Christ. You must therefore live in the conviction that there can be no separation between your faith and your life, and that apart from Christ you can do nothing (cf. Jn 15:5). Since union with God in Christ is the goal of all Christian living, the laity are called to prayer: personal prayer, family prayer, liturgical prayer. Generations of devout lay people have found great strength and joy in invoking the Blessed Virgin Mary, especially through her rosary, and in invoking the saints.

In particular, the laity must realize that they are a people of worship called to service. In the past I had occasion to emphasize this aspect of the life of the laity in the United States: "All the striving of the laity to consecrate the secular field of activity to God finds inspiration and magnificent confirmation in the eucharistic sacrifice. Participating in the Eucharist is only a small portion of the laity's week, but the total effectiveness of their lives and all Christian renewal depends on it: the primary and indispensable source of the true Christian spirit!" ("Ad Limina Discourse," July 9, 1983).

7. Every age poses new challenges and new temptations for the people of God on their pilgrimage, and our own is no exception. We face a growing secularism that tries to exclude God and religious truth from human affairs. We face an insidious relativism that undermines the absolute truth of Christ and the truths of faith, and tempts believers to think of them as merely one set of beliefs or opinions among others. We face a materialistic consumerism that offers superficially attractive but empty promises conferring material comfort at the price of inner emptiness. We face an alluring hedonism that offers a whole series of pleasures that will never satisfy the human heart. All these attitudes can influence our sense of good and evil at the very moment when social and scientific progress requires strong ethical guidance. Once alienated from Christian faith and practice by these and other deceptions, people often commit themselves to passing fads or to bizarre beliefs that are either shallow or fanatical.

We have all seen how these attitudes have a profound influence on the way people think and act. It is precisely in this society that lay men and women like yourselves, all the Catholic laity, are called to live the Beatitudes, to become leaven, salt and light for the world, and sometimes a "sign of contradiction" that challenges and transforms that world according to the mind of Christ. No one is called to impose religious beliefs on others, but to give the strong example of a life of justice and service, resplendent with the virtues of faith, hope and charity.

On moral issues of fundamental importance, however, it is at times necessary to challenge publicly the conscience of society. Through her moral teaching the Church seeks to defend — for the benefit of all people — those basic human values that uphold the good which humanity seeks for itself and that protect the most fundamental human rights and spiritual aspirations of every person.

The greatest challenge to the conscience of society comes from your fidelity to your own Christian vocation. It is up to you, the Catholic laity, to incarnate without ceasing the Gospel in society — in American society. You are in the forefront of the struggle to protect authentic Christian values from the onslaught of secularization. Your great contribution to the evangelization of your own society is made through your lives. Christ's message must live in you and in the way you live and in the way you refuse to live. At the same time, because your nation plays a role in the world far beyond its borders, you must be conscious of the impact of your Christian lives on others. Your lives must spread the fragrance of Christ's Gospel throughout the world.

St. Paul launched a great challenge to the Christians of his time, and today I repeat it to all the laity of America: "Conduct yourselves, then, in a way worthy of the Gospel of Christ, so that, whether I come and see you or am absent, I may hear news of you, that you are standing firm in one spirit, with one mind, struggling together for the faith of the Gospel, not intimidated in any way" (Phil 1:27-28).

8. Dear brothers and sisters, representatives of the millions of faithful and dedicated Catholic laity of the United States: In bringing my reflections to a conclusion I cannot fail to mention the Blessed Virgin Mary, who reveals the Church's mission in an unparalleled manner. She, more than any other creature, shows us that the perfection of love is the only goal that matters, that it alone is the measure of holiness and the way to perfect communion with the Father, the Son and the Holy Spirit. Her state in life was that of a lay woman, and she is at the same time the mother of God, the mother of the Church and our mother in the order of grace.

The council concluded the Dogmatic Constitution on the Church with an exhortation on the Blessed Virgin. In doing so, the council expressed the Church's ancient sentiments of love and devotion for Mary. Let us especially during this Marian year make our own these sentiments, imploring her to intercede for us with her Son, for the glory of the Most Holy and Undivided Trinity (cf. No. 69).

Candlestick Park Mass San Francisco, Sept. 18

Pope John Paul II:

"Go ... and make disciples of all nations" (Mt 28:19). "It was in Antioch that the disciples were called Christians for the first time" (Acts 11:26).

Dear fellow Christians, dear brothers and sisters,

1. Today, here on the west coast of America, in San Francisco, we hear once again the words with which Jesus sends the apostles into the world after his resurrection. He hands on to them a mission. He sends them forth as he himself had been sent by the Father.

These words of Christ come at the end of his earthly messianic mission. In his cross and resurrection are found the basis for his "authority both in heaven and on earth" (Mt 28:18). This is the authority of the Redeemer, who through the blood of his cross has ransomed the nations. In them he has established the beginning of a new creation, a new life in the Holy Spirit; in them he has planted the seed of the kingdom of God. In the power of his authority, as he is leaving the earth and going to the Father, Christ says to his apostles: "Go … and make disciples of all nations. Baptize them in the name of the Father, and of the Son, and of the Holy Spirit. Teach them to carry out everything I have commanded you. And know that I am with you always, until the end of time" (Mt 28:19-20).

2. The Acts of the Apostles describe the beginning of this mission. The point of departure was the Upper Room in Jerusalem. From Jerusalem the travels of the apostles and of their first collaborators led them first to the neighboring countries and to the people who lived there. In today's second reading we hear that the witnesses of the crucified and risen Christ reached Phoenicia, Cyprus and Antioch (cf. Acts 11:19).

This occurred also as a result of the dispersion which began with the death of the deacon Stephen and with the persecution of the disciples of Jesus. We know that, at the stoning of Stephen, Saul of Tarsus was present as a persecutor. But the Acts of the Apostles later present him as Paul, after his conversion on the road to Damascus. Together with Barnabas, Paul worked for a whole year in Antioch, and there "they instructed many people." And it was precisely "in Antioch that the disciples were called Christians for the first time" (Acts 11:26).

3. What does it mean to be a Christian?

It means accepting the testimony of the apostles concerning the crucified and risen Christ. Indeed, it means accepting Christ himself, who works in the power of the Holy Spirit. This acceptance is expressed in baptism, the sacrament in which we are born again of water and the Holy Spirit (cf. Jn 3:5). In this sacrament Christ comes to meet us spiritually. As St. Paul teaches, we are baptized into Christ's death. Together with him we die to sin in order to rise with him, to pass from the death of sin to life in God, to the life of sanctifying grace. To new life!

Christians then are those who have been baptized. We are those to whom Christ has come with the salvific power of his paschal mystery, those whose lives have been totally shaped by this salvific power. Indeed, baptism gives us an indelible sign — called a character — with which we are marked throughout all our earthly life and beyond. This sign is with us when we die and when we find ourselves before the judgment of God. Even if in practice our lives are not Christian, this indelible sacramental sign of baptism remains with us for all eternity.

4. The readings of today's liturgy permit us to respond still more fully to the question: What does it mean to be a Christian?

In the book of the prophet Isaiah we read about "the mountain of the Lord's house" (Is 2:2), raised above all things. The prophet says: "All nations shall stream toward it; many peoples shall come and say: 'Come, let us climb the Lord's mountain, to the house of the God of Jacob, that he may instruct us in his ways, and we may walk in his paths.' For from Zion shall go forth instruction, and the word of the Lord from Jerusalem" (Is 2:2-3). Yes, the word of the Lord did go forth from Jerusalem. This word is the word of the Gospel. The word of the cross and resurrection. Christ charged his apostles to go forth with this word to all the nations — to proclaim it and to baptize.

Through baptism Christ comes to every person with the power of his paschal mystery. To accept Christ through baptism, to receive new life in the Holy Spirit — this is what it means to become a Christian. In this way, through the centuries, individuals and entire nations have become Christian.

To be a Christian means to go up to the mountain to which Christ leads us. To enter into the temple of the living God that is formed in us and in our midst by the Holy Spirit. To be Christian means to continue to become Christian, learning from Christ the ways of the Lord so as to be able "to walk in his paths" (cf. Is 2:3). To be a Christian means to become one every day, ascending spiritually toward Christ and following him. In fact, as we recall, when Christ first called those who were to become his disciples, he said to them: "Follow me."

5. "It was in Antioch that the disciples were called Christians for the first time." And it was more than 200 years ago that people in the San Francisco area were called Christians for the first time. Since the arrival of the first settlers and the missionary efforts of Father Palou and his companions, there have always been Christians in San Francisco — people of the most varied cultural backgrounds who have believed God's word, been baptized and followed in the footsteps of the Lord.

Here is a city built on hopes: the hopes of Father Serra's Franciscan missionaries who came to preach the good news, the hopes of pioneers who came to make their fortunes, the hopes of people who came here to seek peace, the hopes of those who still come to find refuge from violence, persecution or dire poverty. It is the city in which some 40 years ago statesmen met to establish the United Nations, an expression of our common hopes for a world without war, a world committed to justice and governed by fair laws.

But this city was built also with hard work and effort. Here the Church advanced from the little Mission Dolores to the establishment of the Archdiocese of San Francisco in 1853. It took effort and determination for the city and the church to recover from the devastating effects of the severe earthquake and terrible fire in the spring of 1906. Yes, it takes great effort to move from initial enthusiasm to something that will really last. "There are in the end," St. Paul tells us, "three things that last: faith, hope and love, and the greatest of these is love" (1 Cor 13:13). It is precisely these virtues — faith and hope and love — that have directed and sustained all the efforts of the church in San Francisco in the past and that will sustain her well into the future.

6. "It was in Antioch that the disciples were called Christians for the first time." Here in San Francisco and in every city and place it is necessary for the followers of Jesus to deepen their communion with him so that they are not just Christians in name. The primary means the Church has always employed for this task is a systematic catechesis.

When Jesus sent his disciples forth on mission, he told them to baptize and to teach. Baptism alone is not sufficient. The initial faith and the new life in the Holy Spirit, which are received in baptism, need to advance to fullness. After having begun to experience the mystery of Christ, his followers must develop their understanding of it. They must come to know better Jesus himself and the kingdom which he proclaimed; they must discover God's promises in the Scriptures and learn the requirements and demands of the Gospel.

In the Acts of the Apostles we are told that the members of the first Christian community in Jerusalem "devoted themselves to the apostles' instruction and the communal life, to the breaking of bread and the prayers" (Acts 2:42). Here we have a model of the Church that can serve as a goal of all catechesis. For the Church needs continually to feed on God's word, which comes to us from the apostles, and she needs to celebrate the Eucharist, to be faithful to regular prayer and bear witness to Christ in the ordinary life of the community.

The experience of history has proved the importance of a carefully programmed study of the whole of the Christian mystery. "Teach them to carry out everything I have commanded you," Jesus tells the apostles (cf. Mt 28:20). There is no substitute for a systematic presentation of all the essentials of our Catholic faith, a presentation which can provide the basis for sound judgments about the problems of life and society, and which can prepare people to stand up for what they believe with both humility and courage. As I stated in my Apostolic Exhortation on Catechesis: "Firm and well-thought-out convictions lead to courageous and upright action.... Authentic catechesis is always an orderly and systematic initiation into the revelation that God has given of himself to humanity in Christ Jesus, a revelation stored in the depths of the Church's memory and in Sacred Scripture, and constantly communicated from one generation to the next by a living, active 'traditio'" (No. 22).

7. What is the purpose of catechesis? What does it mean not only to be called Christians, but truly to be Christians? It means being identified with Christ not only at Mass on Sunday — which is extremely important — but also in all the other activities of life. In speaking about our relationship to him, Jesus himself said: "Remember what I told you: No slave is greater than his master. If they persecuted me, they will also persecute you. If they kept my word, they will also keep yours" (Jn 15:20).

To be identified with Christ means that we must live according to God's word. As the Lord told his first disciples: "You will live in my love if you keep my commandments, even as I have kept my Father's commandments and live in his love" (Jn 15:10). For this reason the Church never ceases to proclaim the whole of the gospel message, whether it is popular or unpopular, convenient or inconvenient. And the Church is ever mindful of her great task to call people to conversion of mind and heart, just as Jesus did. The first words spoken by Jesus in the Gospel are these: "This is the time of fulfillment. The reign of God is at hand! Reform your lives and believe in the Gospel" (Mk 1:15).

8. Those who accept the grace of conversion and who live according to God's word find that, with God's grace, they begin to put on the mind and heart of Christ. They become increasingly identified with Christ, who is a sign of contradiction. It was Simeon who first foretold that the newborn son of Mary would be for his own people a sign of contradiction. He tells the Virgin Mother: "This child is destined to be the downfall and the rise of many in Israel, a sign that will be opposed" (Lk 2:34). And so it happened. Jesus met with opposition in the message that he preached and in the all-embracing love that he offered to everyone. Almost from the beginning of his public ministry, he was in fact "a sign that people opposed."

Simeon's words hold true for every generation. Christ re-mains today a sign of contradiction — a sign of contradiction in his body, the Church. Therefore, it should not surprise us if in our efforts to be faithful to Christ's teachings we meet with criticism, ridicule or rejection. "If you find that the world hates you," the Lord told the Twelve, "know that it has hated me before you. If you belonged to the world, it would love you as its own; the reason it hates you is that you do not belong to the world. But I chose you out of the world" (Jn 15:18-19).

These words of our loving Savior are true for us not only as individuals but also as a community. In fact, the witness to Christ of the entire Christian community has a greater impact than that of a single individual. How important, then, is the gospel witness of every Christian community, but especially the most fundamental of them all, the Christian family. In the face of many common evils, the Christian family that truly lives the truth of the Gospel in love is most certainly a sign of contradiction; and at the same time it is a source of great hope for those who are eager to do good. Parishes, too, and dioceses and all other Christian communities which "do not belong to the world" find themselves meeting opposition precisely because they are faithful to Christ. The mystery of the cross of Christ is renewed in every generation of Christians.

9. When Jesus Christ sent his apostles throughout all the world, he ordered them to "teach all the nations" (cf. Mt 28:19-20).

The Gospel, and together with it the salvific power of Christ's redemption, is addressed to every person in every nation. It is also addressed to entire nations and peoples. In his vision, the prophet Isaiah sees the peoples who go up to the mountain of the house of the Lord, asking to be instructed in his ways and to walk in his paths (cf. Is 2:2-3). We too ask to walk in the paths of the living God, the Creator and Redeemer, the one God who lives in inscrutable unity as Father, Son and Holy Spirit.

Continuing to describe his vision, Isaiah says: "He shall judge between the nations, and impose terms on many peoples. They shall beat their swords into plowshares and their spears into pruning hooks; one nation shall not raise the sword against another, nor shall they train for war again" (Is 2:4).

How greatly we desire to see the future of humanity in the light of these prophetic words! How greatly we desire a world in which justice and peace prevail! Can the Church, which has come forth from such a prophecy — the Church of the Gospel — ever cease to proclaim the message of peace on earth? Can she ever cease to work for the true progress of peoples? Can she ever cease to work for the true dignity of every human person?

To be Christian also means to proclaim this message untiringly in every generation, in our generation, at the end of the second millennium and at the threshold of the third!

"O house of Jacob, come, let us walk in the light of the Lord!" Amen.

To Polish-Americans Hamtramck, Sept. 19

Pope John Paul II:

"You are to be my witnesses ... to the ends of the earth" (Acts 1:8).

Dear Polish brothers and sisters of America.

1. In the course of my lengthy pilgrimage to the Church in the United States, God has led me to Detroit, the largest community of people of Polish origin after Chicago.

Right from the beginning I wish to tell you two things: First, as St. Paul would say, I have longed to come to you. I have greatly desired to be with you in this important moment, to give prominence to the solicitude of the Church and my own personal apostolic solicitude for you, and to manifest publicly the natural bonds, the bonds of blood, origin, faith, culture and, to a certain extent also, of language and of love for our common mother, the homeland: your homeland or that of your parents or forebears.

And I wish also to extend our meeting today, which is necessarily limited by time and place, to all the United States and in a certain sense to all of America. I see it as a meeting with the entire American Polonia, with every American man and woman whose origin is drawn from the old country on the Vistula, with every Pole whose destiny it is to live in this land.

I wish then to meet both those whose roots have been deeply set here for generations and those who, while their hearts are still filled with the scenery of the land of their birth, are seeking a new beginning, certainly not without difficulty. In saying this, I am well aware that I find myself before the largest part of the Polish emigration in the world, which constitutes a large part of the church in the United States. Even today there are more than 800 Polish parishes.

"You are to be my witnesses ... to the ends of the earth."

How can we not thank God then for this meeting and for our prayer together? How can we not thank those who have made it possible and those who have prepared this encounter? The American authorities and those of the American Polonia, the bishops, priests, sisters, lay people, the various organizations.

Together with the host of this encounter, Archbishop Edmund Szoka, I wish to greet most cordially and to welcome all of you who are gathered here and all the guests who honor us with their presence. I cordially greet all those who are spiritually united with us.

I extend a word of cordial greetings to all our brothers and sisters from other Slavic nations and in particular from the kindred Ukrainian community, who are present here in large number.

I cordially greet the entire Ukrainian community of Detroit. You are close to my heart. As you solemnly celebrate the millennium of Christianity in the Rus of Kiev and in the Ukraine, from the depths of my Slavic heart I bless all the sons and daughters of St. Vladimir and St. Olga, as well as all the faithful of the church in the Ukraine and in the diaspora.

2. Meanwhile, today we wish to be closely united with the sons and daughters of Poland who live on this continent, with all who share or should share in the historical heritage of the same homeland and the same Church. In this way we find ourselves together before the homeland and the whole nation, before its history, its heritage, before its "yesterday" and its "today." And at the same time we find ourselves before all the heritage of Polonia in this vast and rich country which has received and continues to receive so many people from all continents, nations, races and languages; the country that became the homeland for your forebears is also yours.

If we recall the past, if we look attentively at our "today," we do so above all with thought and concern for the future. For, as it has been said: "The nation which lets itself be cut off from its tradition descends to the level of a tribe" (A. Slominski).

We recall briefly the first Poles who, according to the chronicles, came to North America in 1608 and settled in Jamestown, Va. And then those who in the second half of the 18th century gave the beginning to Polonia in Michigan.

The greatest wave of emigration took place, as is known, at the end of the last century and at the beginning of the present century. It was an economic emigration. There were enterprising, hard-working people, worthy people who in the homeland were unable to find food. They left a Poland which had been torn apart by partitions and, as the latest arrivals, they were viewed in different ways. Most often they were uneducated. They brought with them no material riches, but they possessed two great values: an innate love of the faith and of the Polish spirit. Besides, many of them had left with the thought of returning after a time. They did not think that their descendants would put down stable roots in a new country and would collaborate fruitfully in its construction at the end of the second and beginning of the third millennium after Christ.

Their tears, suffering, difficulties, humiliations, wanderings and nostalgia are known and described. Yet it was they who built all that is until now, and will remain in the future, the glory and the patrimony of Polonia in North America.

First of all, they created a whole network of parishes with monumental churches, schools, hospitals, houses of assistance, organizational structures, the press, publications. We recall here Father Leopold Moczygemba and his nearly hundred parishioners who on Christmas Eve 1854 founded the first Polish parish and gave rise to the village of Panna Maria (the Virgin Mary) in Texas. And also those who in 1872 founded the first Polish parish in Detroit, dedicated to St. Albertus. With great emotion I journey spiritually as a pilgrim to these two places.

Moreover, these immigrants have produced a great number of priestly and religious vocations, and thousands of vocations of women Religious, both to Polish congregations and to others. There arose also the various new Polish congregations of women. All this served to make the contribution of the immigrants to the development of religious life and to ecclesiastical structures a great and irreplaceable treasure for the church in America.

The same spirit was deepened and developed by the different Catholic organizations — both by the older ones which have been more than 100 years in existence as well as by those which were established more recently. It is not possible to mention all of them here. However, I came to know of them in the course of earlier visits to the United States as archbishop of Krakow and through their letters to me in Rome on different occasions.

This faithful dedication to the Church is closely tied to a love for Poland and everything associated with it. One has only to think of the volunteers for General Haller's army during World War I; the financial support for independence activities before the year 1918 and in particular for the support of the Polish Committee in Paris; the enormous gifts and loans to Poland after it regained its independence and began to rise from destruction and ruin. Nor may we forget that this same generation of immigrants, by hard work and sacrifice, also secured a better life for their children and grandchildren.

Another page in the history of Polonia was written by Sts. Cyril and Methodius Seminary, established in Detroit and later transferred to Orchard Lake, which not long ago celebrated its centenary. This seminary grew out of a true love of the

Church and out of an attachment to the Polish spirit. Using the language of the Second Vatican Council, we may say that it sought to read "the signs of the times" and to meet the needs of Polish immigration. It developed into a complete scientific and educational complex, from which more than 3,000 priests for the service of Polish immigrants and approximately 15,000 immigrant leaders have come forth. It disseminates Polish culture and the liturgy in the Polish language, and contributes to the preservation of awareness concerning the Polish origins of so many Americans. To the representatives of Orchard Lake who are here today I express gratitude for all that has been accomplished in the past; my hope is for a constant fidelity and a new responsiveness to the needs of today's Church and of Polonia as it exists in the world today.

Later history witnessed new events, new trials and a new wave of emigrants.

As a result of World War II and its aftermath, many more Poles came to the United States. These emigrants were different than the first group in that they came with a higher level of culture and with a different national and political consciousness that retained a strong solidarity with the homeland and the nation. A word of acknowledgment is due to the Polish American Congress for its many activities on behalf of the nation and also to the Catholic League, which provided great material aid to the church in Poland after the war and continues to provide that aid today. For this I wish to express the heartfelt gratitude of the church in Poland as well as my own personal gratitude.

The most recent great undertaking of Polonia throughout the world, but especially of Polonia in the United States and of some American friends, is the foundation in the Vatican and the pilgrim house, the Center for Polish Christian Culture and the documentation center in Rome which that foundation operates.

I know that efforts continue; for example, the establishment of associations of friends of the foundation to ensure the continued activity and development of these institutions. God will surely reward them.

And so, having touched only briefly on past history, we arrive at the present and the tasks the present creates for Polonia and the Church.

The last wave of emigration, like those that preceded it, also becomes a "sign of the times" for today and a challenge. It calls us to reflection and action. Each emigration has brought with it a new richness as well as new problems. There have been and there continue to be cases of harmful divisions, even splits, which have impeded Polonia in the United States from playing the full role of which it is capable in both the religious and spiritual spheres and the social and political spheres.

3. Thus there remains, always alive and very real, a process of integration that is twofold. It is integration in the sense of a growth in awareness and maturity in Polonia itself and integration within the country which is now your home.

Dear brothers and sisters: The more you are aware of your identity, your spirituality, your history and the Christian culture out of which your ancestors and parents grew and you yourselves have grown, the more you will be able to serve your country, the more capable will you be of contributing to the common good of the United States.

Precisely out of concern for the common good, this country — in the face of a diversity of peoples, races and cultures unknown elsewhere — has sought integration in various ways. Theories include "nativism," the "melting pot" and others that proved incapable of giving results. Today there is talk of the ethnic principle, of "roots," since from these roots the full personality of the individual, the community and the nation arises.

The Church wishes to be at the service of such personal and social integration. I have spoken of this on numerous occasions and many documents of the Church address this issue. It is necessary to study them and put them into practice.

Today I wish to repeat once again the words of the poet: "There are so many strengths in the nation," and I wish to pray with him: "Make us feel the strength" (S. Wyspianski, "Liberation").

Our strength comes from faith, from God himself and from our millenary heritage in which there resounds in such a vibrant way the paschal mystery of Christ: his passion and resurrection. This richness has been manifested and continues to be manifested in the love of ideals, of truth, of freedom — "ours and yours," in the love of peace and in respect for the dignity of individuals and of nations.

In our own day there have been moments when these values have shone before the whole world with special brightness. Who among us, and not only us, can forget first the beatification and then the canonization of that son of Polish soil and spiritual son of St. Francis, the humble priest St. Maximilian Mary Kolbe, who in the midst of atrocities and the inhumanity of the concentration camp exhibited once again before all of contemporary humanity that love unto the end!

These values, this richness, this inheritance were also manifested in a fuller way and acquired a new light during my three pilgrimages to the homeland. I dwell only on the saints and the blessed because they express most fully that which is partially in each of us individually and in all of us together. At the same time they are the most perfect models on our pilgrimage toward our final destiny in Christ.

There is Blessed Brother Albert Chmielowski, a patriot and artist, who wished to be all kindness in the face of Polish poverty and toward the needy; Blessed Raphael Kalinowski; Blessed Ursula Ledochowska; Blessed Caroline Kozka, a simple country girl who gave her life in defense of her dignity; finally, the last in order of time, Blessed Michael Koza, bishop and martyr of Dachau.

But this inheritance, as a testimony of the Polish soul, has also been manifested in recent years in another form when the millennial Christian nation reclaimed its own dignity and legitimate rights.

Among other things, I spoke of this on the Polish sea coast, and much of what I said refers to the whole world, including the United States. There, on the Baltic, "the word 'solidarity' was spoken … in a new way that at the same time confirms its eternal content.… In the name of man's future and the future of humanity, it was necessary to say that word 'solidarity.' Today it rolls like a wide wave over the face of the world, which realizes that we cannot live according to the principle of 'all against all,' but only according to another principle 'all with all,' 'all for all.' Solidarity must take precedence over conflict. Only then can humanity survive, can each nation survive and develop within the great human family.… Solidarity means a way of existing, for example, of a nation, in its human variety, in unity, with respect for differences, for all the diversity that exists among people, and so, unity in variety, in plurality. All this is contained in the concept 'solidarity'" (Address in Gdynia, June 11, 1987).

4. With justifiable pride and gratitude we may turn to the great authors of our culture: to writers, poets, artists, politicians, to religious and spiritual guides, to all those who also in this land have pointed out new ways to the human spirit.

Tadeusz Kosciuszko, Kazimierz Pulaski, Wlodzimierz Krzyzanowski, Ignacy Paderewski, Helena Modrzejewska, Artur Rubinstein and the already-mentioned Father Leopold Moczygemba, Father Jozef Dabrowski, founder of the Polish seminary, Father Theodore Gieryk and Jan Barzynski, Father Witold Buhaczewski and so many others, without forgetting the authors and leaders alive today.

But along with them we remember too the unknown multitudes of mothers and fathers of families who, guided by their force of temperament and sense of faith, living an authentic Christian life and in fidelity to God and their human ideals, were able to mold those lofty ideas into the values that model and determine everyday living. In their daily lives they themselves lived those values, forged down through the centuries, and they succeeded in transmitting them in their families to each new generation. How many priests are there today who bear witness that they owe their priestly vocation in the first place to their saintly mothers.

Perhaps the most threatened institution in today's world is precisely the family. For that reason, the Church "wishes to offer guidance and support to those Christians and others who are trying to keep sacred and to foster the natural dignity of the married state and its superlative value" ("Gaudium et Spes," 47).

The fundamental task of the family is to serve life, "transmitting by procreation the divine image from person to person" ("Familiaris Consortio," 28).

Faithfulness to the family extends also to education. The Second Vatican Council teaches that "since parents have conferred life on their children, they have a most solemn obligation to educate their offspring. Hence, parents must be acknowledged as the first and foremost educators of their children" ("Gravissimum Educationis," 3).

Family — the domestic church.

"You are to be my witnesses..."

5. I now wish to address you, "servants of Christ and administrators of the mysteries of God" (1 Cor 4:1); you the priests, the pastors of Polonia. I have spoken at length about the priesthood during this present visit to the United States. In the context of the present meeting I wish to thank you for all the good that the American Polonia has received and continues to receive from your ministry. Remember that the Polish emigration is important for Poland, just as Poland is important for the emigration. From your awareness of and relationship to our common Christian heritage will depend, in great part, the bonds between your faithful and the nation of which they are sons and daughters, bonds of faith, culture and language. Respect for and preservation of this heritage should constitute one of the fundamental principles of your pastoral care. How consoling it is that young people throughout the world are experiencing a growing interest in their past. Young people discover themselves as they search for the foundations of their own identity, its sources and roots, the first strata from which it proceeds.

I know that our young people living here are very much a part of this process and that more and more they are willing to learn the history, the language and all the richness of the homeland from which their forebears came. They gladly say: "I am proud to be American." But they are no less proud of their origins, especially when they know more about them, because then they feel no complex. Help them in this learning and liberation. Then too, meet the spiritual needs of the most recent emigration. Do not lose heart. Do not be enclosed in the golden tower of prejudice, routine, pastoral minimalism and ease.

Do not diminish, do not reduce, do not close whatever serves the true well-being of the faithful, strengthens their

spiritual relationship with the Savior and leads to genuine growth of the spirit.

6. Dear brothers and sisters: "You are to be my witnesses ... to the ends of the earth." This announcement and call was addressed by Christ to the apostles shortly before his ascension. Before that, he said to them: "You will receive power when the Holy Spirit comes down on you" (Acts 1:8). That is, you are to be my witnesses when you receive the power of the Holy Spirit. We are witnesses of Christ in the power of the Holy Spirit.

The Holy Spirit is the beginning, the source, the foundation of Christian life in the new era of the history of salvation, in the time of the Church, in the time of mission, in the time of witness. May his power fill your hearts and minds and wills to enable you to bear witness to Christ with your own witness and that of your forefathers, with the witness of the millenary Christian heritage of that land that has the right and wishes to call you her sons and daughters.

This heritage is marked in a special way by the presence of the Blessed Virgin, the mother of God, Mary blessed by God. She who "defends bright Czestochowa and shines in the morning gate!" Our poet cried out to her: "Carry there my soul full of nostalgia!" Your hearts do not feel nostalgia because you are already sons and daughters of this land and citizens of this country. Still, may Mary carry your souls toward everything that is good, beautiful, great; toward those values that make life worth living. This we ask of her, especially today. This we ask of her in the Marian year.

Now I wish to bless all of you present, your families and dear ones, the children and young people, the sick, the old, those who are alone. I bless the priests, the deacons, the Religious families of men and women, the seminarians, the parishes, the places of work and recreation. I bless the whole of Polonia in North America.

Meeting with Deacons Detroit, Sept. 19

Deacon Samuel E. Taub:

Your Holiness, it is with great joy and a sense of history that we greet you. We praise God for this day and the milestone which it marks in the growth and development of the permanent diaconate in our country.

Gathered here are representatives of the permanent deacons and wives of deacons in the United States, a group which represents a remarkable and unparalleled flowering of ministry in response to the invitation of the fathers of Vatican Council II and the call of the bishops of the United States.

We represent in a unique way the diversity of the local churches in our country: the celibate and married status, family structures, ethnic richness, the whole range of socio-economic backgrounds, the geographic spread of our country, ages, work experience, neighborhood roots, vocations, ministries of sacrament, word and charity.

We are gathered in a city known as a symbol of industrial achievement and the American dream, yet familiar for all the challenges facing life in an era of change, necessary adjustment and, inevitably, by social change with consequent human cost, a city which knows the faces of human needs. This is a city which had an early Catholic presence which has responded to the needs of a pluralistic, multicultured society. It is in such a setting, replicated many times over in our country, that the restoration and the renewal of the permanent diaconate have their origins and development. It is also in this city that the first of four permanent diaconate formation programs was begun in 1969, just a short 18 years ago.

It is in this context that the restoration of the permanent diaconate is an example of the Church reaching into her history and tradition in restoring a ministry which was instituted by the apostles, ordaining men to a lifetime of service, not unto the priesthood but to the ministry of charity.

We are keenly aware that the focal point of the deacon's mission and ministry is the human person, who has been created by God with dignity that is unique, sacred and inviolable. We are coming to appreciate increasingly how the diaconate can be and is a means of strengthening the presence of the Church in the marketplace. We continue to remind ourselves that, as we are a recognized sacramental sign of service, it is expected that we be a catalyst for an expanding notion of Church and ministry and that we see the empowerment of the laity as one of our prime responsibilities.

Permanent deacons are assuming increasingly responsible ministries of service and administration. In this we are beginning to have a new appreciation of the fact that we are deacons 24 hours a day and that no matter where we may be we are "heralds of the Gospel," giving witness within the community of faith, in our neighborhoods and at our workplaces as to who and what we are for the life of the Church.

Assembled with us are wives of deacons who, in a demonstration of mutual sacrificial love, give unstingily in sharing husband and father, their own lives, convenience and needs with the Church as they encourage, heal and sustain the husband's diaconal commitment.

It is in this context, in the love with which faithful sons and daughters greet their Father, that we ask you to address us.

Pope John Paul II:

Dear brothers in the service of our Lord, dear wives and collaborators of these men ordained to the permanent diaconate,

1. I greet you in the love of our Lord Jesus Christ in whom, as St. Paul tells us, God has chosen us, redeemed us and adopted us as his children (cf. Eph 1:3ff). Together with St. Paul and together with you today, I praise our heavenly Father for these wonderful gifts of grace.

It is a special joy for me to meet with you because you represent a great and visible sign of the working of the Holy Spirit in the wake of the Second Vatican Council, which provided for the restoration of the permanent diaconate in the Church. The wisdom of that provision is evident in your presence in such numbers today and in the fruitfulness of your ministries. With the whole Church, I give thanks to God for the call you have received and for your generous response. For the majority of you who are married, this response has been made possible by the love and support and collaboration of your wives. It is a great encouragement to know that in the United States over the past two decades almost 8,000 permanent deacons have been ordained for the service of the Gospel.

It is above all the call to service that I wish to celebrate with you today. In speaking of deacons, the Vatican Council said that "strengthened by sacramental grace, in communion with

the bishop and his presbyterate, they serve the people of God in the service of the liturgy, the word and charity" ("Lumen Gentium," 29). Reflecting further on this description, my predecessor Paul VI was in agreement with the council that "the permanent diaconate should be restored ... as a driving force for the Church's service ("diakonia") toward the local Christian communities and as a sign or sacrament of the Lord Christ himself, who 'came not to be served but to serve'" ("Ad Pascendum," Aug. 15, 1972, Introduction). These words recall the ancient tradition of the Church as expressed by the early Fathers such as Ignatius of Antioch, who says that deacons are "ministers of the mysteries of Jesus Christ ... ministers of the Church of God" ("Ad Trallianos," II, 3). You, dear brothers, belong to the life of the Church that goes back to saintly deacons like Lawrence, and before him to Stephen and his companions, whom the Acts of the Apostles consider "deeply spiritual and prudent" (Acts 6:3).

This is at the very heart of the diaconate to which you have been called: to be a servant of the mysteries of Christ and, at one and the same time, to be a servant of your brothers and sisters. That these two dimensions are inseparably joined together in one reality shows the important nature of the ministry which is yours by ordination.

2. How are we to understand the mysteries of Christ of which you are ministers? A profound description is given to us by St. Paul in the reading we heard a few moments ago. The central mystery is this: God the Father's plan of glory to bring all things in the heavens and on earth into one under the headship of Christ, his beloved Son. It is for this that all the baptized are predestined, chosen, redeemed and sealed with the Holy Spirit. This plan of God is at the center of our lives and the life of the world.

At the same time, if service to this redemptive plan is the mission of all the baptized, what is the specific dimension of your service as deacons? The Second Vatican Council explains that a sacramental grace conferred through the imposition of hands enables you to carry out your service of the word, the altar and charity with a special effectiveness (cf. "Ad Gentes," 16). The service of the deacon is the Church's service sacramentalized. Yours is not just one ministry among others, but it is truly meant to be, as Paul VI described it, a "driving force" for the Church's "diakonia." By your ordination you are configured to Christ in his servant role. You are also meant to be living signs of the servanthood of his Church.

3. If we keep in mind the deep spiritual nature of this "diakonia," then we can better appreciate the interrelation of the three areas of ministry traditionally associated with the diaconate, that is, the ministry of the word, the ministry of the altar and the ministry of charity. Depending on the circumstances, one or another of these may receive particular emphasis in an individual deacon's work, but these three ministries are inseparably joined together as one in the service of God's redemptive plan. This is so because the word of God inevitably leads us to the eucharistic worship of God at the altar; in turn, this worship leads us to a new way of living which expresses itself in acts of charity.

This charity is both love of God and love of neighbor. As the First Letter of John teaches us, "One who has no love for the brother he has seen cannot love the God he has not seen.... Whoever loves God must also love his brother" (1 Jn 4:20-21). By the same token, acts of charity which are not rooted in the word of God and in worship cannot bear lasting fruit. "Apart from me," Jesus says, "you can do nothing" (Jn 15:5). The ministry of charity is confirmed on every page of the Gospel; it demands a constant and radical conversion of heart. We have a forceful example of this in the Gospel of Matthew proclaimed earlier. We are told: "Offer no resistance to injury." We are commanded: "Love your enemies and pray for your persecutors." All of this is an essential part of the ministry of charity.

4. Certainly today's world is not lacking in opportunities for such a ministry, whether in the form of the simplest acts of charity or the most heroic witness to the radical demands of the Gospel. All around us many of our brothers and sisters live in either spiritual or material poverty or both. So many of the world's people are oppressed by injustice and the denial of their fundamental human rights. Still others are troubled or suffer from a loss of faith in God or are tempted to give up hope.

In the midst of the human condition it is a great source of satisfaction to learn that so many permanent deacons in the United States are involved in direct service to the needy: to the ill, the abused and battered, the young and old, the dying and bereaved, the deaf, blind and disabled, those who have known suffering in their marriages, the homeless, victims of substance abuse, prisoners, refugees, street people, the rural poor, the victims of racial and ethnic discrimination and many others. As Christ tells us, "as often as you did it for one of my least brothers, you did it for me" (Mt 25:40).

At the same time, the Second Vatican Council reminds us that the ministry of charity at the service of God's redemptive plan also obliges us to be a positive influence for change in the world in which we live, that is, to be a leaven — to be the soul of human society — so that society may be renewed by Christ and transformed into the family of God (cf. "Gaudium et Spes," 40ff). The "temporal order" includes marriage and the family, the world of culture, economic and social life, the trades and professions, political institutions, the solidarity of peoples and issues of justice and peace (cf. "Apostolicam Actuositatem," 7; "Gaudium et Spes," 46ff). The task is seldom an easy one. The truth about ourselves and the world, revealed in the Gospel, is not always what the world wants to hear. Gospel truth often contradicts commonly accepted thinking, as we see so clearly today with regard to evils such as racism, contraception, abortion and euthanasia — to name just a few.

5. Taking an active part in society belongs to the baptismal mission of every Christian in accordance with his or her state in life, but the permanent deacon has a special witness to give. The sacramental grace of his ordination is meant to strengthen him and to make his efforts fruitful, even as his secular occupation gives him entry into the temporal sphere in a way that is normally not appropriate for other members of the clergy. At the same time, the fact that he is an ordained minister of the Church brings a special dimension to his efforts in the eyes of those with whom he lives and works.

Equally important is the contribution that a married deacon makes to the transformation of family life. He and his wife, having entered into a communion of life, are called to help and serve each other (cf. "Gaudium et Spes," 48). So intimate is their partnership and unity in the sacrament of marriage that the Church fittingly requires the wife's consent before her husband can be ordained a permanent deacon (Canon 1031.2). As the current guidelines for the permanent diaconate in the United States point out, the nurturing and deepening of mutual sacrificial love between husband and wife constitute perhaps the most significant involvement of a deacon's wife in her husband's public ministry in the Church ("Guidelines," National Conference of Catholic Bishops, p. 110). Today especially this is no small service.

In particular, the deacon and his wife must be a living example of fidelity and indissolubility in Christian marriage before a world which is in dire need of such signs. By facing in a spirit of faith the challenges of married life and the demands of daily living, they strengthen the family life not only of the church community but of the whole of society. They also show how the obligations of family, work and ministry can be harmonized in the service of the Church's mission. Deacons and their wives and children can be a great encouragement to all others who are working to promote family life.

Mention must also be made of another kind of family, namely the parish, which is the usual setting in which the vast majority of deacons fulfill the mandate of their ordination "to help the bishop and his presbyterate." The parish provides an ecclesial context for your ministry and serves as a reminder that your labors are not carried out in isolation, but in communion with the bishop, his priests and all those who in varying degrees share in the public ministry of the Church. Permanent deacons have an obligation to respect the office of the priest and to cooperate conscientiously and generously with him and with the parish staff. The deacon also has a right to be accepted and fully recognized by them and by all for what he is: an ordained minister of the word, the altar and charity.

6. Given the dignity and importance of the permanent diaconate, what is expected of you? As Christians we must not be ashamed to speak of the qualities of a servant to which all believers must aspire, and especially deacons, whose ordination rite describes them as "servants of all." A deacon must be known for fidelity, integrity and obedience, and so it is that fidelity to Christ, moral integrity and obedience to the bishop must mark your lives, as the ordination rite makes clear (cf. also "Ad Pascendum," Introduction). In that rite the Church also expresses her hopes and expectations for you when she prays:

"Lord, may they excel in every virtue: in love ... concern ... unassuming authority ... self-discipline and in holiness of life. May their conduct exemplify your commandments and lead your people to imitate their purity of life. May they remain strong and steadfast in Christ, giving to the world the witness of a pure conscience. May they ... imitate your Son, who came, not to be served but to serve."

Dear brothers: This prayer commits you to lifelong spiritual formation so that you may grow and persevere in rendering a service that is truly edifying to the people of God. You who are wives of permanent deacons, being close collaborators in their ministry, are likewise challenged with them to grow in the knowledge and love of Jesus Christ. And this of course means growth in prayer — personal prayer, family prayer, liturgical prayer.

Since deacons are ministers of the word, the Second Vatican Council invites you to constant reading and diligent study of the Sacred Scriptures, lest — if you are a preacher — you become an empty one for failing to hear the word in your own heart (cf. "Dei Verbum," 25). In your lives as deacons you are called to hear and guard and do the word of God in order to be able to proclaim it worthily. To preach to God's people is an honor that entails a serious preparation and a real commitment to holiness of life.

As ministers of the altar you must be steeped in the spirit of the liturgy and be convinced above all that it is "the summit toward which the activity of the Church is directed and at the same time the source from which all her power flows" (cf. "Sacrosanctum Concilium," 10). You are called to discharge your office with the dignity and reverence befitting the liturgy, which the council powerfully describes as being "above all the worship of the divine majesty" (ibid., 33). I join you in thanking all those who devote themselves to your training, both before and after your ordination, through programs of spiritual, theological and liturgical formation.

7. "Sing a new song unto the Lord! Let your song be sung from mountains high!" Sing to him as servants, but also sing as friends of Christ, who has made known to you all that he has heard from the Father. It was not you who chose him, but he who chose you to go forth and bear fruit — fruit that will last. This you do by loving one another (cf. Jn 15:15ff). By the standards of this world, servanthood is despised, but in the wisdom and providence of God it is the mystery through which Christ redeems the world. And you are ministers of that mystery, heralds of that Gospel. You can be sure that one day you will hear the Lord saying to each of you: "Well done, good and faithful servant, enter into the joy of your Lord" (cf. Mt 25:21).

Dear brothers and sisters: As one who strives to be "the servant of the servants of God," I cannot take leave of you until together we turn to Mary as she continues to proclaim: "I am the servant of the Lord" (Lk 1:38). And in the example of her servanthood we see the perfect model of our own call to the discipleship of our Lord Jesus Christ and to the service of his Church.

Hart Plaza Address Detroit, Sept. 19

Pope John Paul II:

Dear friends,

1. I am happy that almost at the end of my second pastoral visit to the United States I am able to address such a large number of people in this well-known industrial city of Detroit. I greet all of you most cordially: Christian leaders and leaders of other religions; civic leaders from the federal, state and municipal governments; people of various races and ethnic backgrounds, fellow Catholics; Christian and non-Christian brothers and sisters; men and women of good will!

I feel that I must thank the Lord our God for this wonderful occasion. Detroit is a place where work, hard daily work — that privilege, duty and vocation of the human person (cf. "Laborem Exercens," 9) — is a truly distinctive characteristic of urban life. This is indeed a city of workers and very many of you here — men and women, younger people and older people, immigrants and native-born Americans — earn your living and that of your families in and around Detroit through the work of your hands, your mind, indeed your whole person. And many of you suffer from the problems that not infrequently characterize the work situation in an industrial urban setting.

This is why I would like to make reference to a subject which, as you are well aware, is close to my heart. This subject is social progress and human development in relation to the requirements of justice and to the building of a lasting peace both in the United States and throughout the world.

Of course, dear friends, dear people of Detroit and this whole area, it is you I have primarily in mind in dealing with such a subject — you who have been created in the image and likeness of God, you who have been redeemed by the blood of the Savior, you who are children of God and brothers and sisters of Christ, you who for all of these reasons possess an incomparable dignity. But in looking at you assembled here in Hart Plaza, I see beyond you all the people of this country and the peoples of the whole world. I see all the men and women who, like you, are confronted every day anew with the obligation and the challenge to provide for their livelihood and for the livelihood of their family through their own work. Work means any activity, whether manual or intellectual, whatever its nature or whatever its circumstances, by which a human being earns his or her daily bread and contributes to science and progress, civilization and culture (cf. "Laborem Exercens," 1). Human work is such a fundamental dimension of human existence that one cannot speak about it without touching upon all its aspects.

2. Social progress and human development are the concern of all. They are of particular concern to the Church. From the very beginning of her existence in time the Church has endeavored to fathom the total richness of the message which Jesus Christ proclaimed both by his words and his actions. Sent by the Father to assume our humanity and bring salvation to all, the Lord Jesus provided us with the key to understanding our humanity. He taught us about our origin and destiny, which are in God. He taught us the transcendent value of all human life and the supreme dignity of the human person, created in the image and likeness of God (cf. Gn 1:27). He taught us that human life is fulfilled in knowing and loving God, and in loving our neighbor according to the measure of God's love for us. He invited us to follow him, to become his disciples. He summoned us to be converted in our hearts by entering into the mystery of his passion, death and resurrection. He revealed that we are God's partners in bringing creation to fulfillment. And he now fashions us into a chosen people, a communion of faith with a commitment to his kingdom.

In fidelity to Christ, the Church has endeavored to bring his message to bear on all aspects of life throughout the changing circumstances in the course of the centuries, bringing out from the heritage of the Gospel "both the new and the old" (Mt 13:52). New challenges affecting the life of every person individually and of society as a whole have presented themselves at every turn on the path of humanity through history. In trying to meet those challenges, the people of God have always turned to the message of Jesus in order to discover the principles and the values that would ensure solutions in consonance with the dignity and destiny of the human person. Throughout her history the Church has listened to the words of Scripture and has sought to put them into practice in the midst of different political, economic and social circumstances. This has been a truly common effort. Individual Christians have struggled to be faithful to the gospel inspiration in their daily lives; centers of learning have contributed their specialized studies; groups and associations have addressed issues of particular concern; communities have developed practical initiatives; individual bishops and episcopal conferences have provided guidance; and the magisterium of the Church has made pronouncements and issued documents. In a continuous interaction, the Church has thus developed a tradition of thought and practical guidelines that are called the social teaching of the Church. This social teaching has recently been expressed in documents of the Second Vatican Council and in writings of the popes, who have systematically addressed the rapid changes in contemporary society.

Also today the various categories of the people of God — according to their respective calling — continue to address the social problems in their various historical and cultural settings.

3. Today, dear friends, on this last day of my second extended visit to the United States of America, I would urge you to continue your personal involvement in that never-ending quest for justice and peace. Under the guidance and inspiration of the Church's magisterium — which is that of the pope and of the bishops in union with him — each one of you is called to make a contribution. Each one of you must be instrumental in promoting a social order that respects the dignity of the human person and serves the common good. Each one of you has an irreplaceable contribution to make to secure a social order of justice in peace. In your country today, participation at different levels of economic, social and political life has greatly intensified the awareness of the unique dignity of every human person and at the same time reinforced your sense of responsibility to yourselves and to others. As Christians you find in your faith a deep motivation for your social responsibility and involvement. Do not let this hour pass without renewing your commitment to action for social justice and peace. Turn to the Gospel of Jesus Christ to strengthen your resolve to become instruments for the common good! Learn from the Gospel that you have been entrusted with the justice and peace of God! We are not merely the builders of justice according to the standards of this world, but we are the bearers of the life of God, who is himself justice and peace! Let your endeavors to achieve justice and peace in all the spheres of your lives be a manifestation of God's love!

In a setting similar to this one some eight years ago in New York's Yankee Stadium, I proclaimed the gospel challenge contained in the parable of the rich man and Lazarus. You are all familiar with this marvelous lesson in social responsibility which Jesus left us. Knowing your faith and your openness to challenge, I now ask you today: What have you done with that parable? How many times in the past eight years have you turned to that parable to find inspiration for your Christian lives? Or have you put it aside thinking that it was no longer relevant to you or to the situation in your country?

4. In any modern society, no matter how advanced, there will always be situations, some old and some new, that summon your Christian sense of justice to action. Our Lord has said: "The poor you will always have with you" (Mt 26:11). You must therefore discover the poor in your midst. There is poverty among you when the old and the weak are neglected and their standard of living constantly declines. There is poverty when illness takes away the wage earner from a family. There is material need and suffering in those areas or groups where unemployment risks becoming endemic. There is poverty in the future of those that cannot enjoy the benefits of basic education.

Some modern technological developments contain the potential for new hardships and injustice and must therefore be part of our concern. The introduction of robotics, the rapid development of communications, the necessary adaptation of industrial plants, the need to introduce new skills in management — these are but some of the factors that, if not analyzed carefully or tested as to their social cost, may produce undue hardship for many, either temporarily or more permanently.

These are just a few areas where our social responsibility is challenged. Others include the situation of marriage and family life and the factors that threaten their underlying values; the respect for the sacredness of unborn human life; the situation of newly arrived immigrants; open or disguised expressions of discrimination based on "race, origin, color, culture,

sex or religion" ("Octogesima Adveniens," 16). To the degree that its social conscience is sensitive, every community will discover where instances of injustice or threats to peace still exist or are potentially present.

But the very attempt to look at some of the challenges in the domestic scene brings us to another important consideration regarding progress and human development. I am referring to the international dimension.

5. Without implying in any way that domestic or national problems do not exist any more — and they most certainly do — it becomes ever more evident that such local or national problems and their solutions are fundamentally linked with realities that transcend the boundaries of countries. Not only do decisions taken by one nation affect other regions of the world, but the solution to many domestic problems can no longer be found except on an international and even a worldwide level. All major problems that concern the life of the human person in society have become world problems. Any decision that is envisaged in the political, economic or social sphere must be considered within the context of its worldwide repercussions. What now most deeply affects any debate on social progress and human development is the fact of worldwide interdependence.

Already 20 years ago, in 1967, Pope Paul VI wrote at the very beginning of his encyclical letter "On the Development of Peoples" ("Populorum Progressio"): "Today the principal fact that we must all recognize is that the social question has become worldwide" (No. 3). In following years this affirmation of Paul VI was further vindicated by a succession of events. There was the emergence on the political scene of peoples who, after centuries of colonial domination and dependence, demanded ever more forcefully their rightful place among the nations and in international decision making. A worldwide economic crisis brought home the fact that there exists an increasingly interdependent economy. The continuing existence of millions of people who suffer hunger or malnutrition and the growing realization that the natural resources are limited make clear that humanity forms a single whole. Pollution of air and water threatens more and more the delicate balance of the biosphere on which present and future generations depend and makes us realize that we all share a common ecological environment. Instant communication has linked finance and trade in worldwide dependence.

The poorer nations of the world are inclined to view this interdependence as a continuing pattern of economic domination by the more developed countries, while the latter sometimes view interdependence as the opening up of new opportunities for commerce and export. Interdependence clearly demands that relations between nations be seen in this new context and that the social question needs an appropriate ethic. Nobody can say anymore: "Let others be concerned with the rest of the world!" The world is each one of us!

6. When I addressed the participants of the 68th session of the International Labor Organization, on June 15, 1982, I was able to state:

"There is a common good which can no longer be confined to a more or less satisfactory compromise between sectional demands or between purely economic requirements. New ethical choices are necessary; a new world conscience must be created; each of us without denying his origin and the roots of his family, his people and his nation or the obligations arising therefrom, must regard himself as a member of this great family, the world community.... This means that the worldwide common good requires a new solidarity without frontiers" (No. 10).

The Church's social teaching sees this new solidarity as a consequence of our faith. It is the attitude, in the international reality, of those who heed the Lord's commandment: "Love one another as I have loved you" (Jn 15:12). It is the consequence of our faith in the mystery of creation: that God has created every human person in his own image and likeness. Every human being is endowed with the same fundamental and inalienable dignity. Every individual is called to acknowledge this fundamental equality within the unity of the human family. Everyone is invited to respect the common destiny of everyone else in God. Everyone is asked to accept that the goods of the earth are given by God to all for the benefit of all.

For the disciple of Christ, solidarity is a moral duty stemming from the spiritual union of all human beings, who share a common origin, a common dignity and a common destiny. In creating us to live in society in a close network of relations with each other, and in calling us through redemption to share the life of the Savior not merely as individuals but as members of a pilgrim people, God himself has created our basic interdependence and called us to solidarity with all. This teaching is formulated in an incomparably effective manner in the parable of the good Samaritan who took care of the man who was left half dead along the road from Jerusalem to Jericho. We all travel that road and are tempted to pass by on the other side. Referring to the Samaritan, who was moved by compassion, Jesus told his listeners: "Go, and do the same." Today, Jesus repeats to all of us when we travel the road of our common humanity: "Go, and do the same" (cf. Lk 10:37).

7. In speaking to you about social progress and human development, I feel impelled to stress the international dimension because of the objective need to promote a new worldwide solidarity.

There is also another reason why I am especially mindful today of the larger international scene. You know well that the bishop of Rome and the Holy See follow closely international activities and therefore have a special interest in the work of the United Nations in New York. I would have liked very much to visit once again its headquarters, as I did in 1979 and as Pope Paul VI did in 1965. I regret that I am not able to accept at this time the kind invitation which the secretary general of the United Nations has extended to me for a new visit. The interest of the Catholic Church in this international organization is linked to the importance of the issues that it treats and to the reasons for which it was founded. To work for the establishment and maintenance of a just and lasting peace is a goal that deserves support and collaboration. This is in fact why the United Nations was created in the first place in that bright daylight which followed the long drawn-out night of World War II. I pray that despite its inevitable shortcomings it will be able to fulfill ever more effectively its unique role of service to the world, a service that the world truly needs.

The United Nations deals with disarmament and arms control — the control of nuclear weapons in the first place, but also biological, chemical and conventional weapons. Its patient, painstaking and sometimes even frustrating dedication to this cause of paramount importance for the world and all its people is recognized and appreciated as being an incentive and support for the bilateral negotiations by the superpowers for arms reduction. Here it is indeed a question that must be addressed with an unfailing commitment, extreme lucidity and a clear sense of the value of human life and the integrity of creation.

The United Nations is also concerned with many of the other conditions for true peace. It is fitting here to reflect on some

of them in relation to the international dimension of the social question.

In the first place, I would like to single out the concern for human rights. You remember, I am sure, that the United Nations adopted more than 40 years ago the Universal Declaration on Human Rights. The basic inspiration of this important document was the recognition that the way toward a peaceful and just world must necessarily pass through the respect for each human being, through the definition and recognition of the basic human rights, and through the respect for the inalienable rights of individuals and of the communities of peoples. The adoption of the universal declaration was followed over the years by many declarations and conventions on extremely important aspects of human rights in favor of women, of children, of handicapped persons, of equality between races and especially the two international covenants on economic, social and cultural rights and on civil and political rights, together with an optional protocol. In 1981 the General Assembly also adopted a solemn declaration against every form of religious intolerance. The United Nations must also be given proper credit for having set up the Commission for Human Rights as a monitoring organ to follow carefully the positive and negative developments in this important field. The commitment of the United Nations to human rights goes hand in hand with its commitment to peace. Experience has taught that disrespect or lack of respect for human rights, oppression of the weak, discrimination because of sex, color, origin, race or religion create conflict and jeopardize peace. Here again, what concerns human beings in any one place affects all human beings everywhere.

Through the different specialized institutions and programs, the United Nations develops its commitment to a more just and equitable international society. This work and commitment include the struggle against diseases and illiteracy; action undertaken for the advancement of women; protecting the rights of children and the handicapped; the development of international law; the peaceful use of atomic energy; the protection and preservation of famous monuments which belong to the cultural patrimony of humanity; the defense of the environment; the struggle against hunger, malnutrition and underdevelopment; and the defense of the homeless.

8. The existence and activities of the United Nations, its achievements and also its failures underline in a dramatic way the need for reinforcing international authority at the service of the global common good. It is already a sign of great progress that the importance of global social issues and the need for effectively promoting peace are becoming more universally recognized. It is also a sign of hope that an international organization, formed by the great majority of states, tries within the limited means at its disposal and notwithstanding internal and external difficulties to increase the awareness of worldwide problems and their appropriate solutions.

It is also a marvelous challenge for all the peoples and nations of the world — now that every day we become more aware of our interdependence — to be called upon by the urgent demands of a new solidarity that knows no frontiers. Now that we move toward the threshold of the third millennium of Christianity, we are given the unique chance for the first time in human history to make a decisive contribution to the building up of a true world community. The awareness that we are linked in common destiny is becoming stronger; the efforts to reach that goal are being multiplied by men and women of good will in a diversity of activities — political as well as economic, cultural as well as social. People in all walks of life and nations and governments alike are being challenged in the name of our common humanity, in the name of the rights of every human being and in the name of the rights of every nation.

In order to succeed and give the correct answer to the many demands that the de facto interdependence of all nations makes upon the sense of solidarity of all, we must create a just balance between the constraints put by interdependence upon the nations and the call for effective solidarity addressed to all the nations. In the life of every nation, social progress and human development are ensured by the respect given to the rights of the human person. The human person's very existence in dignity and his or her rightful participation in the life of the community are safeguarded by the deep respect that every person entertains for the dignity and the rights of every fellow human being. In the same way, respect for the rights of peoples and nations must safeguard the existence in liberty of every nation and thus make possible its rightful and effective participation in all aspects of international life. Without this, it would be impossible to speak about solidarity. In order to be capable of global solidarity nations must first of all respect the human rights of their citizens and in turn be recognized by their people as the expression of their sovereignty; second, nations must respect the full rights of their fellow nations and know that also their rights as a nation will not be disavowed.

9. Dear friends: America is a very powerful country. The amount and quality of your achievements are staggering. By virtue of your unique position as citizens of this nation, you are placed before a choice and you must choose. You may choose to close in on yourselves, to enjoy the fruits of your own form of progress and to try to forget about the rest of the world. Or, as you become more and more aware of your gifts and your capacity to serve, you may choose to live up to the responsibilities that your own history and accomplishments place on your shoulders. By choosing this latter course, you acknowledge interdependence and opt for solidarity. This, dear friends, is truly a human vocation, a Christian vocation, and for you as Americans it is a worthy national vocation.

10. In drawing attention to the need for an ever greater social consciousness in our day, I also wish to draw attention to the need for prayer. Prayer is the deepest inspiration and dynamism of all social consciousness. In speaking to the bishops of America in 1983 I stated:

"It is indeed in prayer that a social consciousness is nurtured and at the same time evaluated. It is in prayer that the bishop, together with his people, ponders the need and exigencies of Christian service…. Through prayer the church realizes the full import of Christ's words: 'This is how all will know you for my disciples: your love for one another' (Jn 13:35). It is in prayer that the Church understands the many implications of the fact that justice and mercy are among 'the weightier matters of the law' (Mt 23:23) Through prayer, the struggle for justice finds its proper motivation and encouragement, and discovers and maintains truly effective means" ("Ad Limina" Address, Dec. 3, 1983).

Finally, to you the Catholic people of Detroit and all this area I repeat the words with which Paul VI concluded his message to the Call to Action Conference that was held 11 years ago in this very city of Detroit:

"In the tradition of the Church, any call to action is first of all a call to prayer. And so you are summoned to prayer and above all to a greater sharing in Christ's eucharistic sacrifice…. It is in the Eucharist that you find the true Christian spirit that will enable you to go out and act in Christ's

name." And for all of you dear friends, people of every religion, race and ethnic group, I ask God's help so that you may be ever more aware of global interdependence and ever more sensitive to human solidarity.

Silverdome Mass Detroit, Sept. 19

Pope John Paul II:

"Conduct yourselves in a way worthy of the Gospel of Christ" (Phil 1:27).

Dear brothers and sisters in Christ,

1. The apostle Paul addresses this appeal to the Christians of Philippi. And today the Church's liturgy repeats this appeal to all who believe in Christ. As my visit to your country comes to an end, it is my special joy this evening to reflect on those words with you, the people of the Church in Detroit as well as visitors from elsewhere in Michigan, from nearby Canada and from other areas.

From the humble beginnings of the foundation of Detroit in the year 1701, the proclamation of God's word in this region has continued unbroken despite hardships and setbacks and has reached a level of maturity and a fruitfulness unimagined by the early missionaries. Many years separate us from the first celebration of the Eucharist by the priests who accompanied Cadillac, the founder of Detroit, and yet we know that our communion this evening in the body and blood of Christ also links us with them and with all who have gone before us in faith.

With you, I give thanks to God for the courage, dedication and perseverance of the many clergy, Religious and laity who worked so hard during all these years, first to share their faith with the native Americans of this area and then to preserve and spread the faith among those of almost every race and nation who settled here. I also give thanks with you for the intrepid Catholic faith of so many of your parents and grandparents who came to Michigan in order to find liberty and in order to build a better life for themselves and especially for you, their children and grandchildren. Whatever may be the path by which you have received the gift of your Catholic faith, it is due in some measure to those who have gone before you here. Their voices are joined to that of St. Paul when he says to us: "Conduct yourselves in a way worthy of the Gospel of Christ."

2. We read this exhortation this evening in the light of the gospel parable of the workers sent by the owner of an estate into his vineyard after he has agreed with them on the daily wage. Our Lord often taught through parables like this one. By using images from daily life, he led his hearers to insights about the kingdom or reign of God. Using parables, he was able to raise their minds and hearts from what is seen to what is unseen. When we remember that the things of this world already bear the imprint of God's kingdom, it is not surprising that the imagery of the parables is so well suited to the gospel message.

On the one hand, the vineyard of which Jesus speaks is an earthly reality, as is the work to be done in it. On the other hand, the vineyard is an image of the kingdom of God. This kingdom is described in the Gospels as "the vineyard of the Lord."

3. Let us reflect for a moment on the first of these realities — the earthly vineyard — as a workplace, as the place where you and I must earn our daily bread. As I said in the encyclical "Laborem Exercens":

"Man must work, both because the Creator has commanded it and because of his own humanity, which requires work in order to be maintained and developed. Man must work out of regard for others, especially his own family, but also for the society he belongs to, the country of which he is a child and the whole human family of which he is a member, since he is the heir to the work of generations and at the same time a sharer in building the future of those who will come after him in the succession of history" (No. 16).

Accordingly, the Church considers it her task to focus attention on the dignity and rights of workers, to condemn violations of that dignity and those rights, and to provide guidance for authentic human progress (cf. "Laborem Exercens," 1). The Church's goal is to uplift ever more the family of mankind in the light of Christ's word and by its power.

Central to the Church's teaching is the conviction that people are more important than things; that work is "for man" and not man "for work"; that the person is both the subject and purpose of all work and cannot be reduced to a mere instrument of production; that the person is to be valued for what he or she is rather than for what he or she owns (cf. "Laborem Exercens," 6, 12; "Gaudium et Spes," 35). This last truth in particular reminds us that the only gift we can offer God that is truly worthy of him is the gift of ourselves, as we discover in the message of today's gospel parable.

4. That message, as I mentioned, has to do with a spiritual reality, the kingdom of God, toward which Jesus seeks to raise the minds and hearts of his listeners. He begins today's parable with the words: "The reign of God is like the case of the owner of an estate who went out at dawn to hire workmen for his vineyard" (Mt 20:1). That our Lord is speaking about more than just human work and wages should be clear from the owner's actions and the ensuing conflict between him and some of the workers. It is not that the owner refuses to honor the agreement about wages. The dispute arises because he gives the same pay to everybody, whether the person worked all day or only part of the day. Each receives the sum which had been agreed upon. Thus the owner of the estate shows generosity to the latecomers, to the indignation of those who had worked all day. To them this generosity seems to be an injustice. And what response does the owner give? "I am free," he says, "to do as I please with my money, am I not? Or are you envious because I am generous?" (Mt 20:15).

In this parable we find one of those seeming contradictions, those paradoxes, that appear in the Gospel. It arises from the fact that the parable is describing two different standards. One is the standard by which justice is measured by things. The other standard belongs to the kingdom of God, in which the way of measuring is not the just distribution of things but the giving of a gift and, ultimately, the greatest gift of all — the gift of self.

5. The owner of the estate pays the workers according to the value of their work, that is, the sum of one denarius. But in the kingdom of God the pay or wages is God himself. This is what Jesus is trying to teach. When it comes to salvation in the kingdom of God, it is not a question of just wages, but of the undeserved generosity of God, who gives himself as the supreme gift to each and every person who shares in divine life through sanctifying grace.

Such a recompense or reward cannot be measured in material terms. When a person gives the gift of self, even in human relations, the gift cannot be measured in quantity. The gift is one and undivided because the giver is one and undivided.

How can we receive such a gift? We look to St. Paul for an answer. His words in the Letter to the Philippians are fascinating: "I firmly trust and anticipate that I shall never be put to shame for my hopes.... Christ will be exalted through me, whether I live or die. For, to me, 'life' means Christ; hence dying is so much gain" (Phil 1:20-21).

With these words of St. Paul we find ourselves at the very heart of that standard of measurement which belongs to the kingdom of heaven. When we receive a gift, we must respond with a gift. We can only respond to the gift of God in Jesus Christ — his cross and resurrection — in the way that Paul responded — with the gift of ourselves. All that Paul is, is contained in this gift of self: both his life and his death. The gift of a person's life cannot be valued merely in terms of the number of hours spent in an earthly vineyard.

St. Paul, and everyone like him, realizes that one can never match or equal the value of God's gift of himself to us. The only measure that applies is the measure of love. And love's measure, as St. Bernard says, is to love without measure ("De Diligendo Deo," I, 1). This makes it possible for the last to be first, and the first last (cf. Mt 20:16).

6. There is another episode, in the Gospel of Luke, when Jesus says to one of the Pharisees who is scandalized at the behavior of a woman known to be a sinner: "Her many sins are forgiven because of her great love" (Lk 7:47). We do well to reflect upon the love in the heart of this woman, who washed the Lord's feet with her tears and wiped them with her hair. We can imagine the bitter sorrow that led her to such an extravagant gesture. Yet by giving herself humbly to God, she discovered the far greater and undeserved gift of which we have spoken, namely, God's gift of himself to her. Through this exchange of gifts, the woman found herself once again, only now she was healed and restored. "Your sins are forgiven," Jesus says to her, "go in peace (v. 48).

For us too, sinners that we are, it is all too easy to squander our love, to use it in the wrong way. And like the Pharisee, we do not easily understand the power of love to transform. Only in the life, death and resurrection of Christ do we come to see that love is the measure of all things in the kingdom of God, because "God is love" (1 Jn 4:8). We can fully experience love in this life only through faith and repentance.

7. "Conduct yourselves in a way worthy of the Gospel of Christ." As Christians we live and work in this world, which is symbolized by the vineyard, but at the same time we are called to work in the vineyard of the Lord. We live this visible earthly life and at the same time the life of the kingdom of God, which is the ultimate destiny and vocation of every person. How then are we to conduct ourselves worthily in regard to these two realities?

In the Credo of the People of God proclaimed by my predecessor Paul VI, we find an answer to that question — an answer that reflects the faith of the Church in the light of the Second Vatican Council, particularly the Pastoral Constitution on the Church in the Modern World:

"We confess that the kingdom of God ... is not of this world ... and that its growth cannot be confused with the progress of civilization, science or technology. The true growth of the kingdom of God consists in an ever deeper knowledge of the unfathomable riches of Christ; in an ever stronger hope in eternal blessings, in an ever more fervent response to the love of God.... But this same love also leads the Church to show constant concern for the true temporal welfare of people.... Although the Church does not cease to remind her children that here they have no lasting city, she also urges them to contribute — according to their vocation and means — to the welfare of this their earthly home ... and to devote themselves to helping the poorest and neediest of their brothers and sisters. This intense solicitude of the Church ... for the needs of people, their joys and hopes, their griefs and labors, is nothing other than her great desire to be present with them in order to illuminate them with the light of Christ and gather them into one in him who alone is their Savior" (Credo of the People of God, June 30, 1968).

Dear brothers and sisters: These words tell us what is meant by conduct worthy of the Gospel of Christ — that Gospel which we have heard and believed, and are called to live every day. And today in this eucharistic sacrifice we offer our work, our activities, our whole lives to the Father through his Son, Jesus Christ. We call upon God to accept the gift of ourselves.

8. "The Lord is just in all his ways and holy in all his works. The Lord is near to all who call upon him, to all who call upon him in truth" (Ps 145:17-18).

In the first reading, the prophet Isaiah speaks in the name of the Lord, who in the gospel parable is symbolized by the owner of the vineyard. The Lord says: "My thoughts are not your thoughts, nor are your ways my ways.... As high as the heavens are above the earth, so high are my ways above your ways and my thoughts above your thoughts" (Is 55:8-9).

And so, my brothers and sisters, "Conduct yourselves in a way worthy of the Gospel of Christ," that is to say, measure the things of this world by the standard of the kingdom of God.

Not the other way around!

Not the other way around!

"Seek the Lord while he may be found, call to him while he is near" (Is 55:6).

He is near! The Lord is near!

The kingdom of God is within us. Amen.

Departure Ceremony Detroit, Sept. 19

Vice President Bush

Your Holiness, when you arrived in Miami nine days ago, you said, "I come to you, America, with sentiments of friendship, reverence and esteem. I come as one who already knows you and loves you, as one who wishes you to fulfill completely your noble destiny of service to the world."

At this, the conclusion of your historic and inspirational trip to our land, I can imagine no more fitting words than your own to say on behalf of America: We say farewell, Your Holiness, with sentiments of friendship, reverence and esteem. We do so as a land that knows you and loves you, that wishes you to fulfill completely your noble destiny of service to the world.

In your nine years as pope, you have traveled to 68 countries on 36 foreign trips covering hundreds of thousands of miles — all "to tell the story of God's love in the world." Now, for the second time, you have brought that message to America, and millions have listened.

From the thunder and lightning of Tamiami Park to the baking heat of San Antonio, from the rousing festivity of New Orleans to the spiritual dialogue with your bishops in Los Angeles, with your speeches and your homilies you have deeply touched the hearts and souls of all Americans — especially those of your fellow Catholics, more than 50 million strong.

You have not only preached but listened — to heartfelt and often painful dissent. Yet you have infused your moral authority with love and your challenging spirit with joy.

Your forceful words lead us to see God's love as tough love — love that demands commitment from us, love that challenges as well as forgives. It is a message for our times, when so many Americans — searching for meaning amid affluence — are turning once again to the religious and ethical values on which this great nation rests.

Our land is built on freedom — but as you have taught, "Freedom develops best if it keeps to the rules of morality." We must teach our children the difference between right and wrong, honesty and dishonesty, liberty and license — in our homes and in our churches and in our schools. And in our own lives, we must not accept politics without principles or commerce without conscience.

Your Holiness, in this land of many peoples you have spoken with special resonance to our millions of Hispanics, who have grown so rapidly in importance both in your church and the American community — and you have used your remarkable gift of language to speak to them directly in their native Spanish.

And now you have used your native tongue to touch a special chord in the sons and daughters of Poland who gathered with you today. Next week I leave for Poland, and it was my privilege today to receive your thoughts about that journey.

To all of us throughout this land — but nowhere more than here in Michigan, with its large and vigorous union movement — the proud and courageous people of Poland have given a new and noble meaning to the word "solidarity."

I go to Poland, to use your words upon arriving in Miami, "as a pilgrim — a pilgrim in the cause of justice and peace and human solidarity, striving to build up the one human family."

Your Holiness, I have traveled widely too, and I have witnessed startling demonstrations of faith in places where I least expected them. As ambassador to China, I met with Mao Tse-Tung shortly before he died, in a secluded villa not far from the Great Hall of the People. He was ill and frail, and he said to me, "I am going to heaven soon." And then he added, "I have already received an invitation from God."

And at the funeral in Moscow of Secretary Brezhnev — a funeral with soldiers and bayonets and ceremony, but without the word of God — I watched as the grieving widow approached the casket to say her last farewell.

There, in the cold gray center of that totalitarian state, Mrs. Brezhnev took one last look at her husband, and then, in an unmistakable gesture, leaned forward to trace the sign of the cross over her husband's chest. It was visible proof that despite official policy and dogma for six decades, God was still very much alive in the Soviet Union.

And in your own homeland of Poland, at a time of difficulty and danger, your Church has provided the people with strength and comfort and inspiration — still more evidence that you cannot wipe out by force of law that which makes its home in the human heart.

Your Holiness, it is with sadness that we see you go.

Although today you leave our soil, you will remain here in our hearts. We pray you will have a rewarding trip to our neighbors in Canada and a safe journey home to the Vatican. And we part with the fervent hope that you will soon return again — to teach us, to challenge us and to raise our eyes to the light of God.

Pope John Paul II:

Mr. Vice President, dear friends, dear people of America,

1. Once again God has given me the joy of making a pastoral visit to your country — the United States of America. I am filled with gratitude to him and to you. I thank the vice president for his presence here today, and I thank all of you from my heart for the kindness and warm hospitality that I have received everywhere.

I cannot leave without expressing my thanks to all those who worked so hard to make this visit possible. In particular I thank my brother bishops and all their collaborators, who for many months have planned and organized all the details of the last 10 days. My gratitude goes to all those who provided security and ensured such excellent public order. I thank all those who have worked to make this visit above all a time of fruitful evangelization and prayerful celebration of our unity in faith and love.

I am also grateful to the people of other churches and creeds and to all Americans of good will who have accompanied me in person or through the media as I traveled from city to city. A particular word of thanks goes to the men and women of the media for their constant and diligent assistance in bringing my message to the people and in helping me to reach millions of those with whom otherwise I would have had no contact. Most important, I am grateful to all those who supported me by their prayers, especially the elderly and the sick, who are so dear to the heart of Jesus Christ.

As I leave, I express my gratitude to God also for what he is accomplishing in your midst. With the words of St. Paul, I too can say with confident assurance "that he who has begun the good work in you will carry it through to completion, right up to the day of Christ Jesus" (Phil 1:6-7). And so I am confident too that America will be ever more conscious of her responsibility for justice and peace in the world. As a nation that has received so much, she is called to continued generosity and service toward others.

2. As I go, I take with me vivid memories of a dynamic nation, a warm and welcoming people, a church abundantly blessed with a rich blend of cultural traditions. I depart with admiration for the ecumenical spirit that breathes strongly throughout this land, for the genuine enthusiasm of your young people and for the hopeful aspirations of your most recent immigrants. I take with me an unforgettable memory of a country that God has richly blessed from the beginning until now.

America the beautiful! So you sing in one of your national songs. Yes, America, you are beautiful indeed and blessed in so many ways:

—In your majestic mountains and fertile plains.

—In the goodness and sacrifice hidden in your teeming cities and expanding suburbs.

—In your genius for invention and for splendid progress.

—In the power that you use for service and in the wealth that you share with others.

—In what you give to your own and in what you do for others beyond your borders.

—In how you serve and in how you keep alive the flame of hope in many hearts.

—In your quest for excellence and in your desire to right all wrongs.

Yes, America, all this belongs to you. But your greatest beauty and your richest blessing is found in the human person: in each man, woman and child, in every immigrant, in every native-born son and daughter.

3. For this reason, America, your deepest identity and truest character as a nation is revealed in the position you take toward the human person. The ultimate test of your greatness is the way you treat every human being, but especially the weakest and most defenseless ones.

The best traditions of your land presume respect for those who cannot defend themselves. If you want equal justice for all and true freedom and lasting peace, then, America, defend life! All the great causes that are yours today will have meaning only to the extent that you guarantee the right to life and protect the human person.

—Feeding the poor and welcoming refugees.

—Reinforcing the social fabric of this nation.

—Promoting the true advancement of women.

—Securing the rights of minorities.

—Pursuing disarmament, while guaranteeing legitimate defense.

All this will succeed only if respect for life and its protection by the law are granted to every human being from conception until natural death.

Every human person — no matter how vulnerable or helpless, no matter how young or how old, no matter how healthy, handicapped or sick, no matter how useful or productive for society — is a being of inestimable worth created in the image and likeness of God. This is the dignity of America, the reason she exists, the condition for her survival — yes, the ultimate test of her greatness: to respect every human person, especially the weakest and most defenseless ones, those as yet unborn.

With these sentiments of love and hope for America, I now say goodbye in words that I spoke once before: "Today, therefore, my final prayer is this: that God will bless America, so that she may increasingly become — and truly be — and long remain — 'one nation, under God, indivisible. With liberty and justice for all'" (Oct. 7, 1979).

May God bless you all.

God bless America!

Photographic Credits

(by number)

Ken Akers, 48, 59

Janna Avalon, 35

James Baca, 68, 69, 74, 75, 76, 84, 98, 99

Melanie Bell, 3, 14, 16, 17

Dwight Cendrowski, 113

Michael Collopy, 101, 102, 103, 104, 105, 107, 109

Bill Frost, 41

Ed Kalsch, 19

Arturo Mari, dust jacket cover photograph

Frank Methe, 28

Mike Okoniewski, 4a, 4b, 5, 9, 11, 21, 24, 29, 30, 32, 33, 34, 46, 47, 52, 56, 78, 80, 81, 87, 97, 100, 110, 112, 117, 119, 120, and the photographs on pp. 8 and 136

Brad Reynolds, S.J., 123, 124, 125

Joe Rimkus, Jr., 1, 2, 6, 7, 8, 10, 20, 22, 23, 25, 26, 31, 36, 37, 38, 39, 40, 42, 43, 44, 45, 49, 50, 53, 54, 55, 57, 60, 62, 63, 64, 65, 66, 67, 70, 71, 72, 73, 77, 79, 82, 83, 85, 86, 88, 89, 90, 91, 92, 93, 94, 95, 96, 106, 108, 111, 114, 116, 118, 122, and photographs on pp. 2 and 138, and on the dust jacket.

Cris Sheridan, 12, 13

Dan Smith, 121

Don Stevenson, 61

Thomas J. Tracy, 18, 51, 58, and the photograph on p. 6

United Press International, 15

Jim West, 115

Mary Wimberly, 27